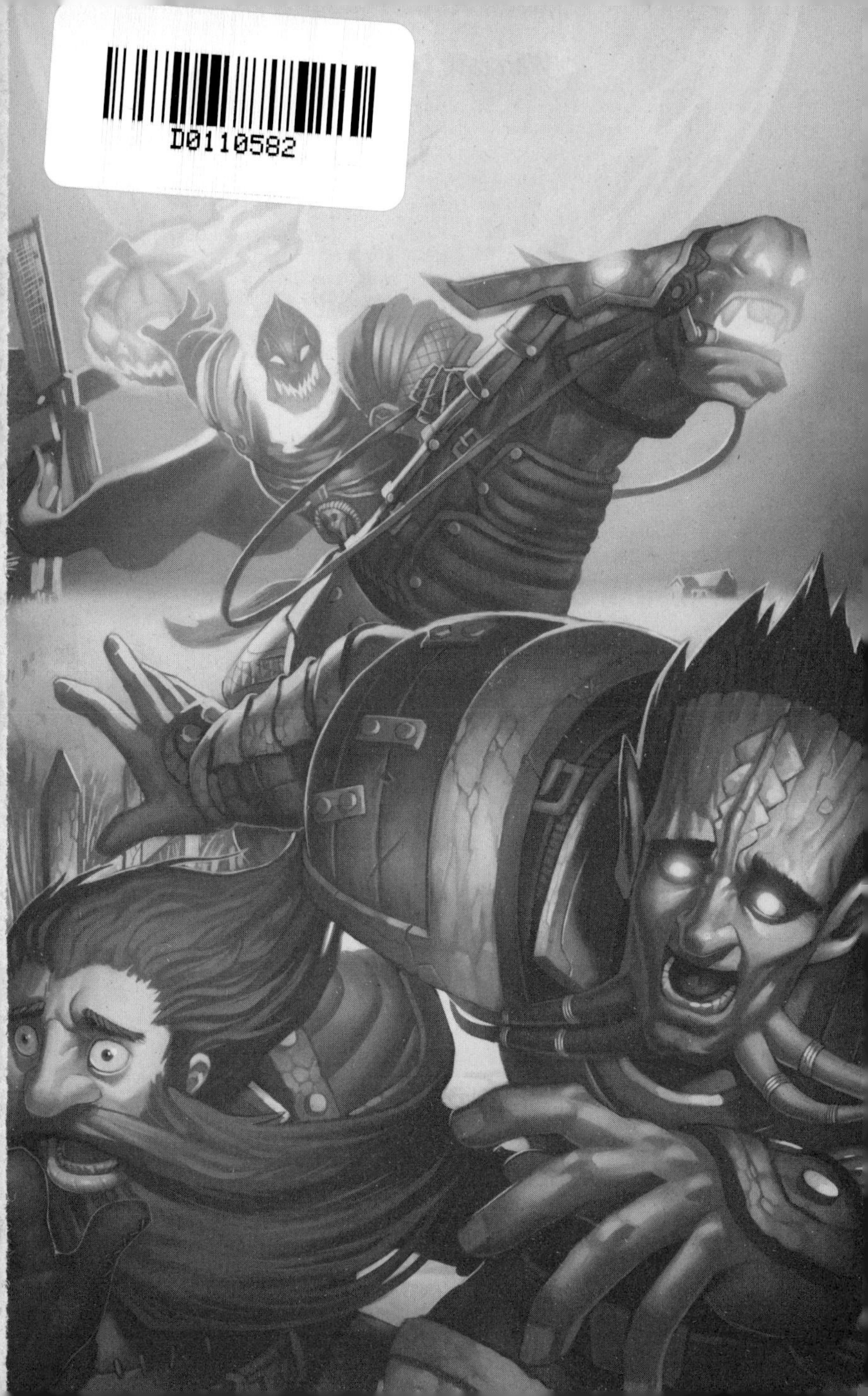

Layout and Lettering - Michael Paolilli
Creative Consultant - Michael Paolilli
Graphic Designer - Louis Csontos
Cover Artist - UDON with Saejin Oh

Editor - Troy Lewter
Print Production Manager - Lucas Rivera
Managing Editor - Vy Nguyen
Senior Designer - Louis Csontos
Director of Sales and Manufacturing - Allyson De Simone
Associate Publisher - Marco F. Pavia
President and C.O.O. - John Parker
C.E.O. and Chief Creative Officer - Stu Levy

BLIZZARD ENTERTAINMENT

Senior Vice President, Creative Development - Chris Metzen
Director, Creative Development - Jeff Donais
Lead Developer, Licensed Products - Mike Hummel
Publishing Lead, Creative Development - Rob Tokar
Senior Story Developer - Micky Neilson
Story Developer - James Waugh
Art Director - Glenn Rane
Director, Global Business
Development and Licensing - Cory Jones
Associate Licensing Manager - Jason Bischoff
Historian - Evelyn Fredericksen
Additional Development - Samwise Didier and Tommy Newcomer

A  Manga

TOKYOPOP and ⬤ are trademarks or registered trademarks of TOKYOPOP Inc.

TOKYOPOP Inc.
5900 Wilshire Blvd. Suite 2000
Los Angeles, CA 90036

E-mail: info@TOKYOPOP.com
Come visit us online at www.TOKYOPOP.com

ISBN: 978-1-4278-1526-2

First TOKYOPOP printing: September 2009
10 9 8 7 6 5 4 3 2 1
Printed in the USA

LEGENDS

VOLUME FIVE

HAMBURG // LONDON // LOS ANGELES // TOKYO

WARCRAFT

LEGENDS

VOLUME FIVE

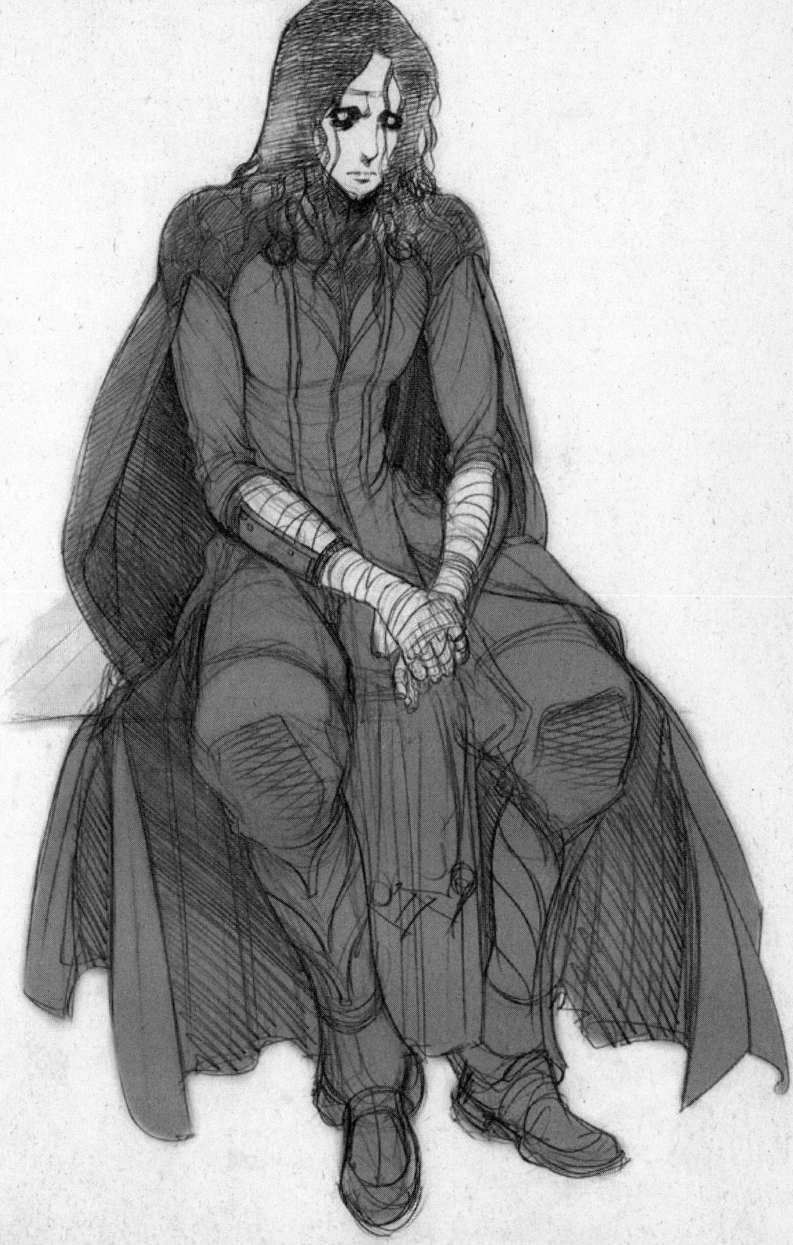

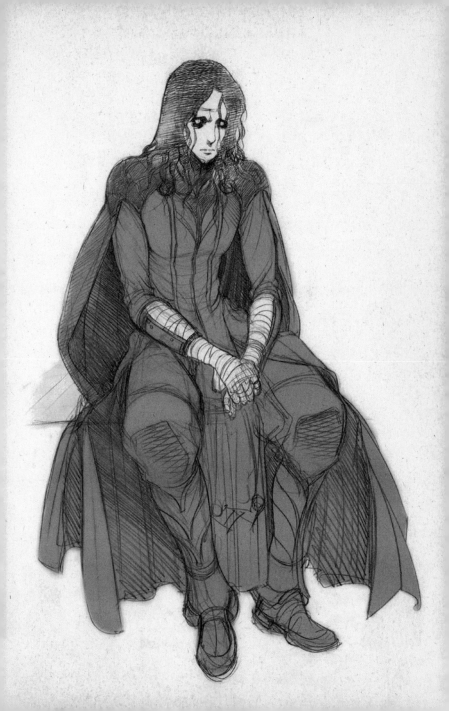

WARCRAFT

LEGENDS
VOLUME FIVE

A WARRIOR
MADE--PART 2

WRITTEN BY CHRISTIE GOLDEN

PENCILS BY IN-BAE KIM
INKS BY IN-BAE KIM & MI-JIN BAE
TONES BY MARA AUM

EDITORIAL TRANSLATION: JANICE KWON
LETTERER: MICHAEL PAOLILLI

STORY SO FAR

Draka was a Frostwolf clan orc born with a frail and weak body.
Though loved unconditionally by her parents, the same can't be
said for her fellow clan members, who viewed Draka's condition
as an embarrassment--so much so that they banished Draka and
her parents to the outskirts of the village.

Years later, when Draka was a young woman, she decided to
take her destiny into her own hands and restore her family's
honor. To do this she sought the council of Mother Kashur, the
kind, elderly village shaman. Draka begged Mother Kashur to
create a potion or spell to make her stronger and rid her of her
shameful, sickly body.

Mother Kashur agreed to help, and requested Draka make an
arduous journey to find the three ingredients she would need
for the spell: for speed and grace she would need the feather
of a windroc, for support of her clan the horn of a talbuk, and
finally, for strength and determination, the fur of a clefthoof.
With renewed hope for redemption, Draka set out on her
dangerous journey.

At first it was difficult even finding shelter and hunting food
for herself, but through perseverance Draka gradually
developed enough skills and confidence to not only survive,
but to face her first challenge--the windroc. Tracking the bird
to its nest in Terokkar forest proved difficult as the terrain was
harsh, but Draka managed to overcome her fears and confront
the bird. Through skills she developed while hunting game for
food, Draka was able to spear and kill the bird--and obtain the
first ingredient of the spell!

And now, with two more ingredients left, her path to honor
has only just begun as the hardest challenges have yet to be
conquered...

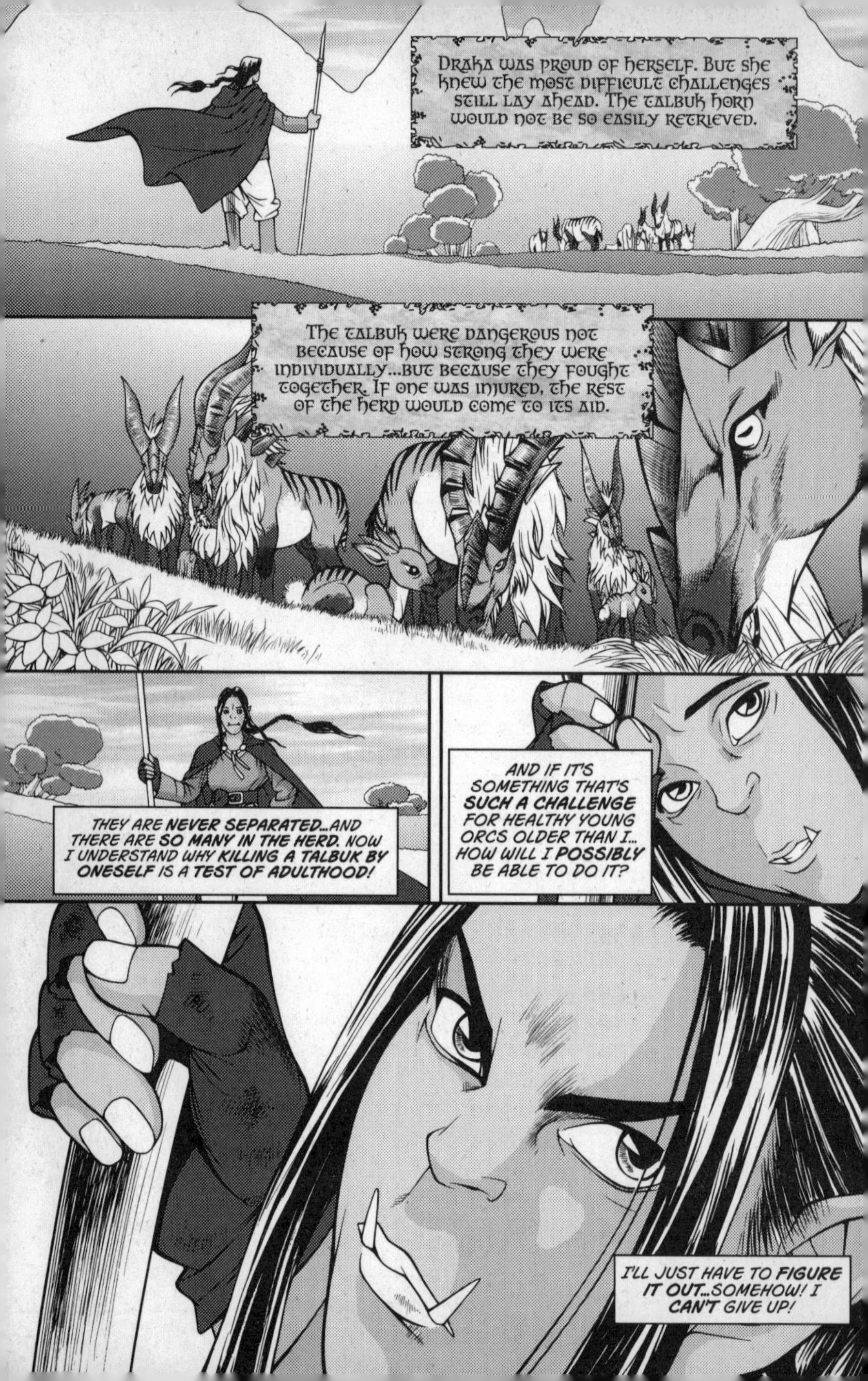
DRAKA WAS PROUD OF HERSELF. BUT SHE KNEW THE MOST DIFFICULT CHALLENGES STILL LAY AHEAD. THE TALBUK HORN WOULD NOT BE SO EASILY RETRIEVED.
THE TALBUK WERE DANGEROUS NOT BECAUSE OF HOW STRONG THEY WERE INDIVIDUALLY...BUT BECAUSE THEY FOUGHT TOGETHER. IF ONE WAS INJURED, THE REST OF THE HERD WOULD COME TO ITS AID.
THEY ARE NEVER SEPARATED...AND THERE ARE SO MANY IN THE HERD. NOW I UNDERSTAND WHY KILLING A TALBUK BY ONESELF IS A TEST OF ADULTHOOD!
AND IF IT'S SOMETHING THAT'S SUCH A CHALLENGE FOR HEALTHY YOUNG ORCS OLDER THAN I... HOW WILL I POSSIBLY BE ABLE TO DO IT?
I'LL JUST HAVE TO FIGURE IT OUT...SOMEHOW! I CAN'T GIVE UP!

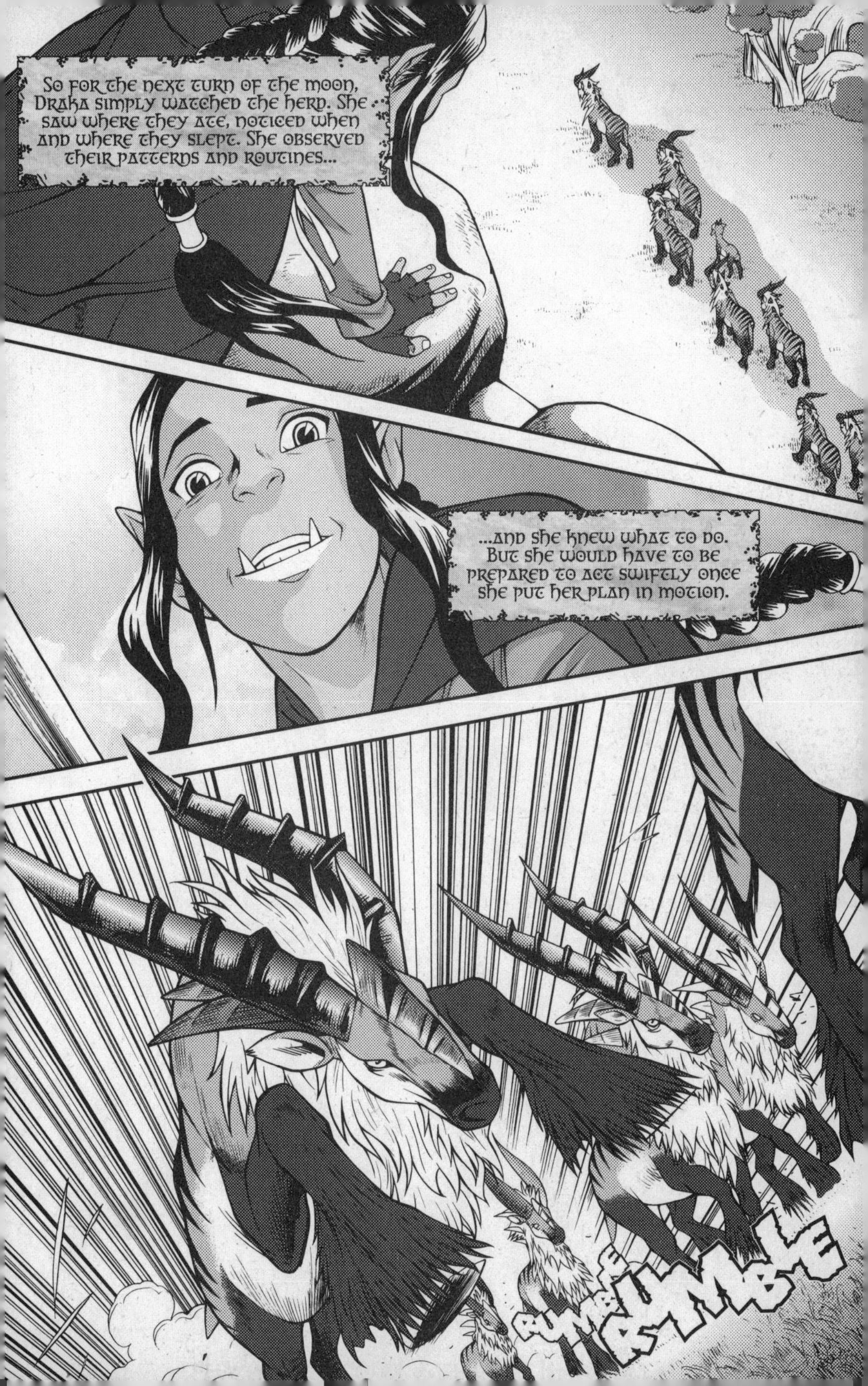
So for the next turn of the moon, Draka simply watched the herd. She saw where they ate, noticed when and where they slept. She observed their patterns and routines...
...and she knew what to do. But she would have to be prepared to act swiftly once she put her plan in motion.
RUMBLE RUMBLE

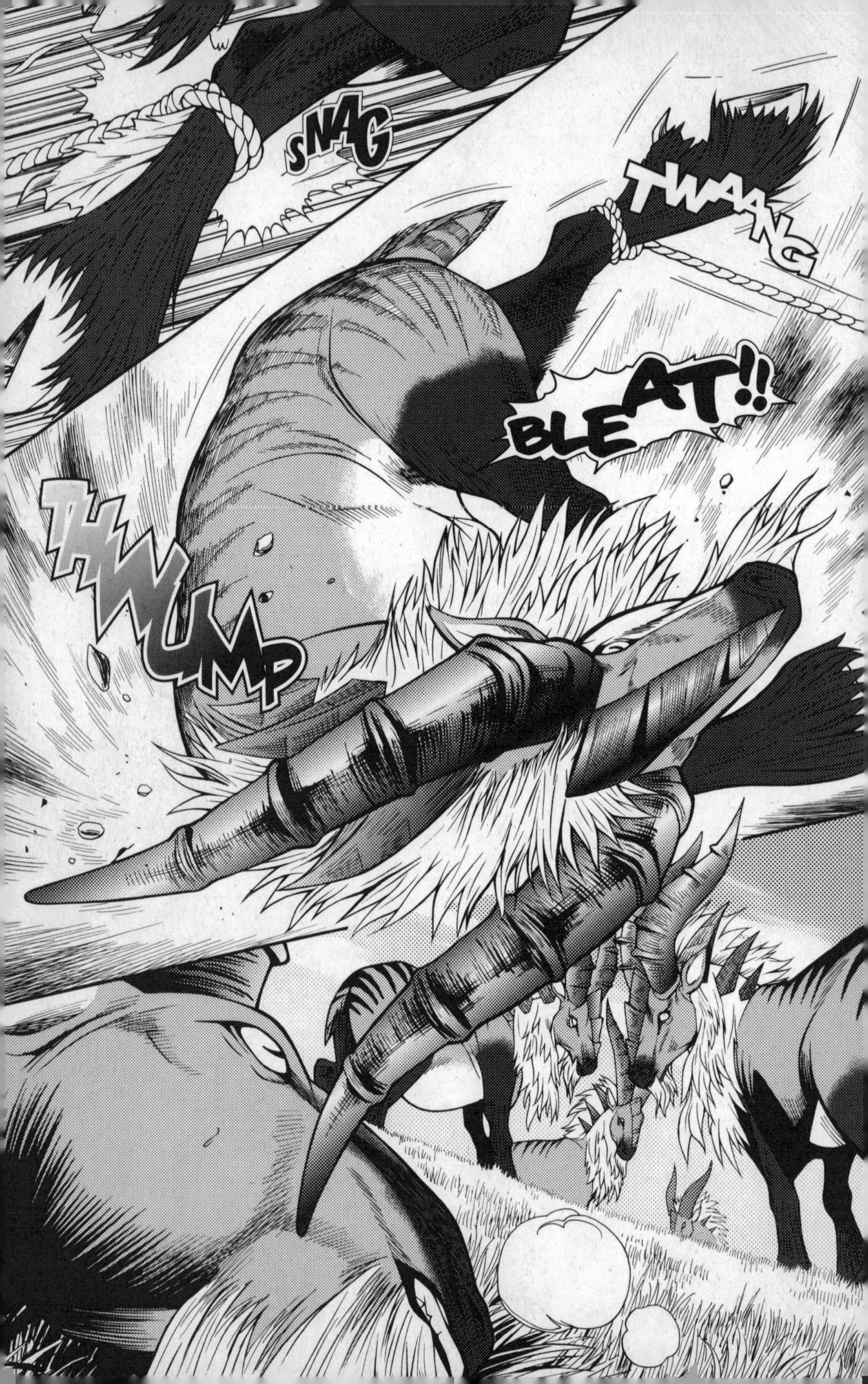
SNAG
TWAANG
BLEAT!!
THWUMP

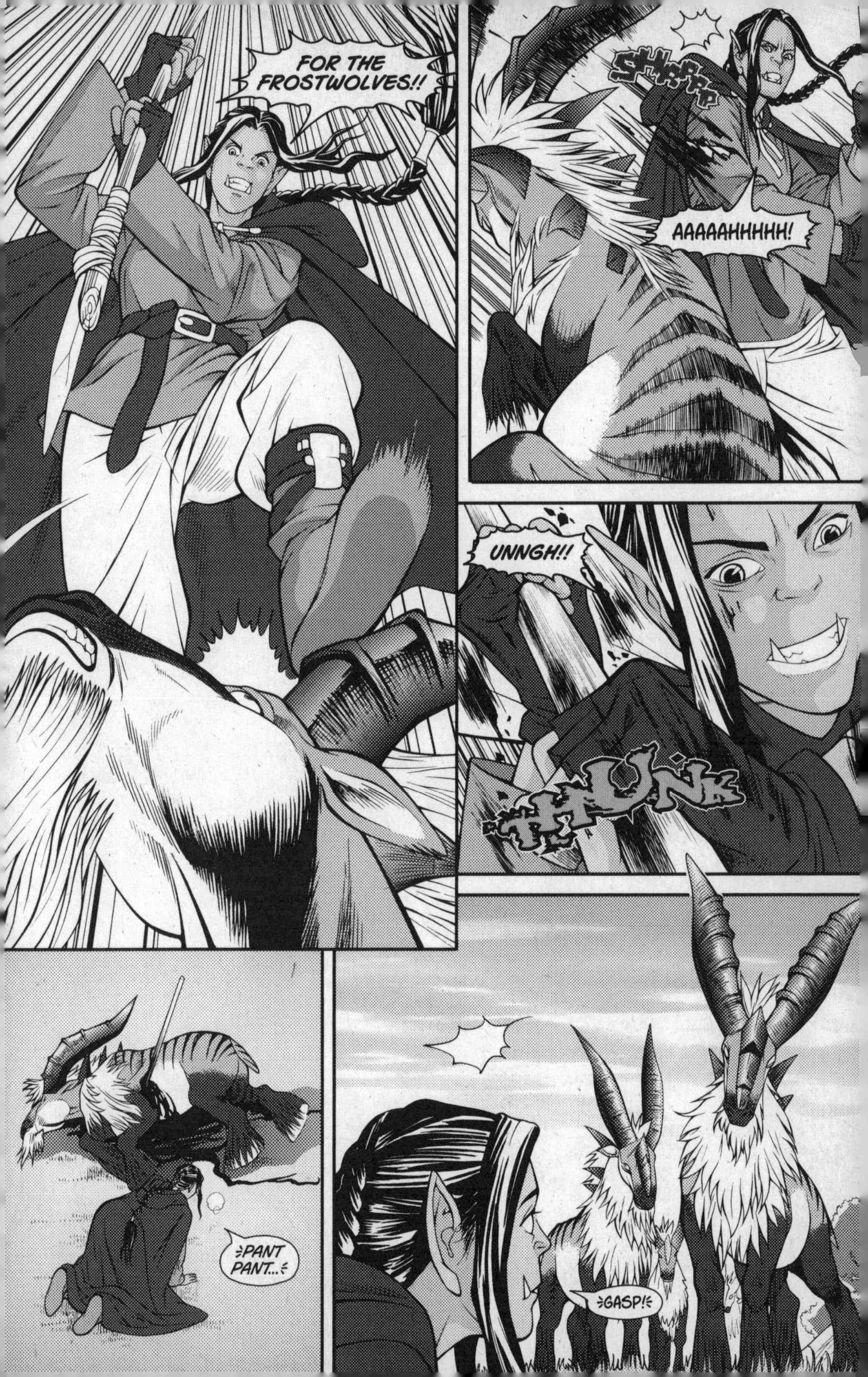
FOR THE FROSTWOLVES!!
SHRRRP
AAAAAHHHHH!
UNNGH!!
THUNK
PANT PANT...
GASP!

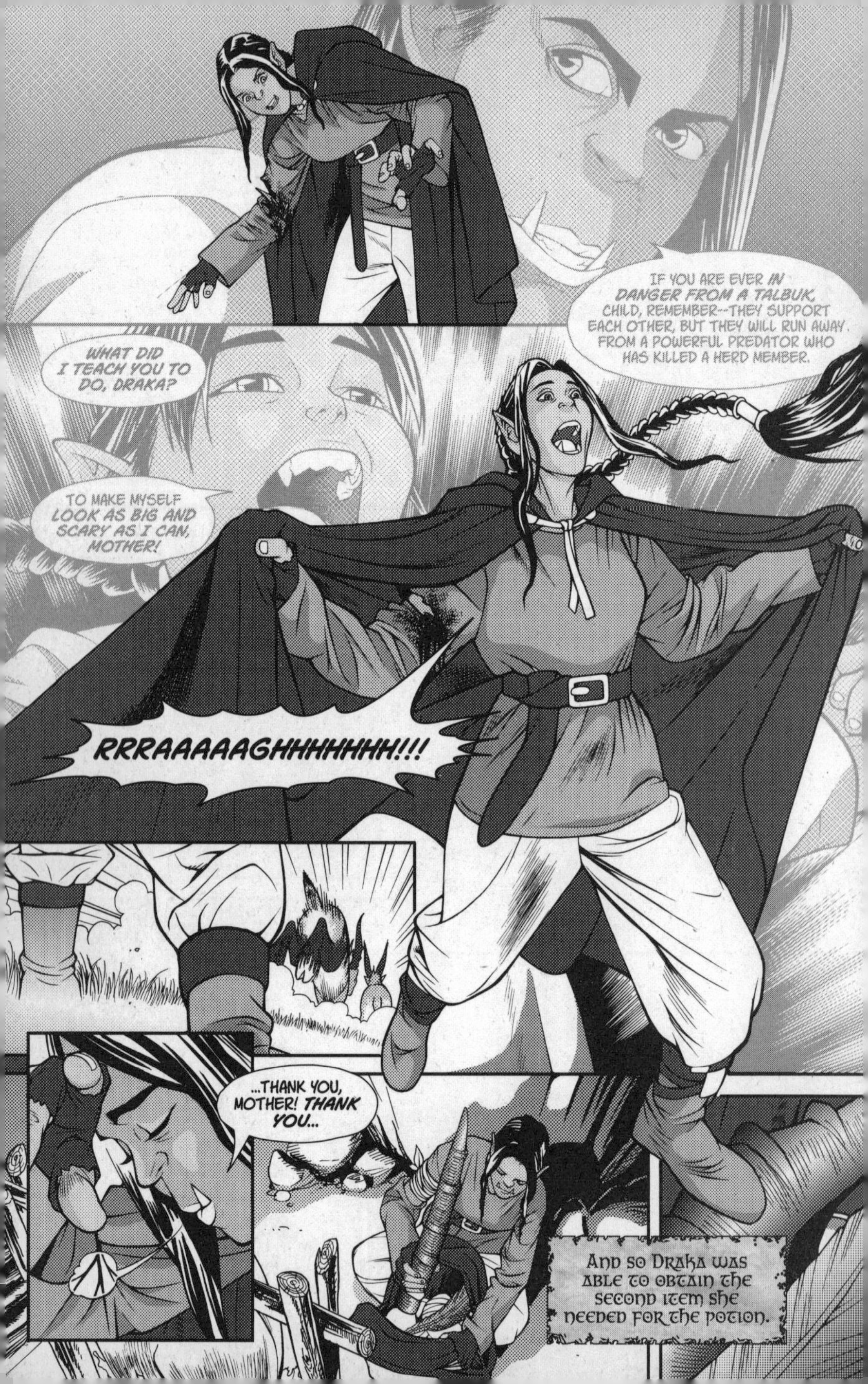

IF YOU ARE EVER *IN DANGER FROM A TALBUK,* CHILD, REMEMBER--THEY SUPPORT EACH OTHER, BUT THEY WILL RUN AWAY FROM A POWERFUL PREDATOR WHO HAS KILLED A HERD MEMBER.
WHAT DID I TEACH YOU TO DO, DRAKA?
TO MAKE MYSELF *LOOK AS BIG AND SCARY AS I CAN, MOTHER!*
RRRAAAAAGHHHHHHH!!!
...THANK YOU, MOTHER! *THANK YOU...*
And so Draka was able to obtain the second item she needed for the potion.

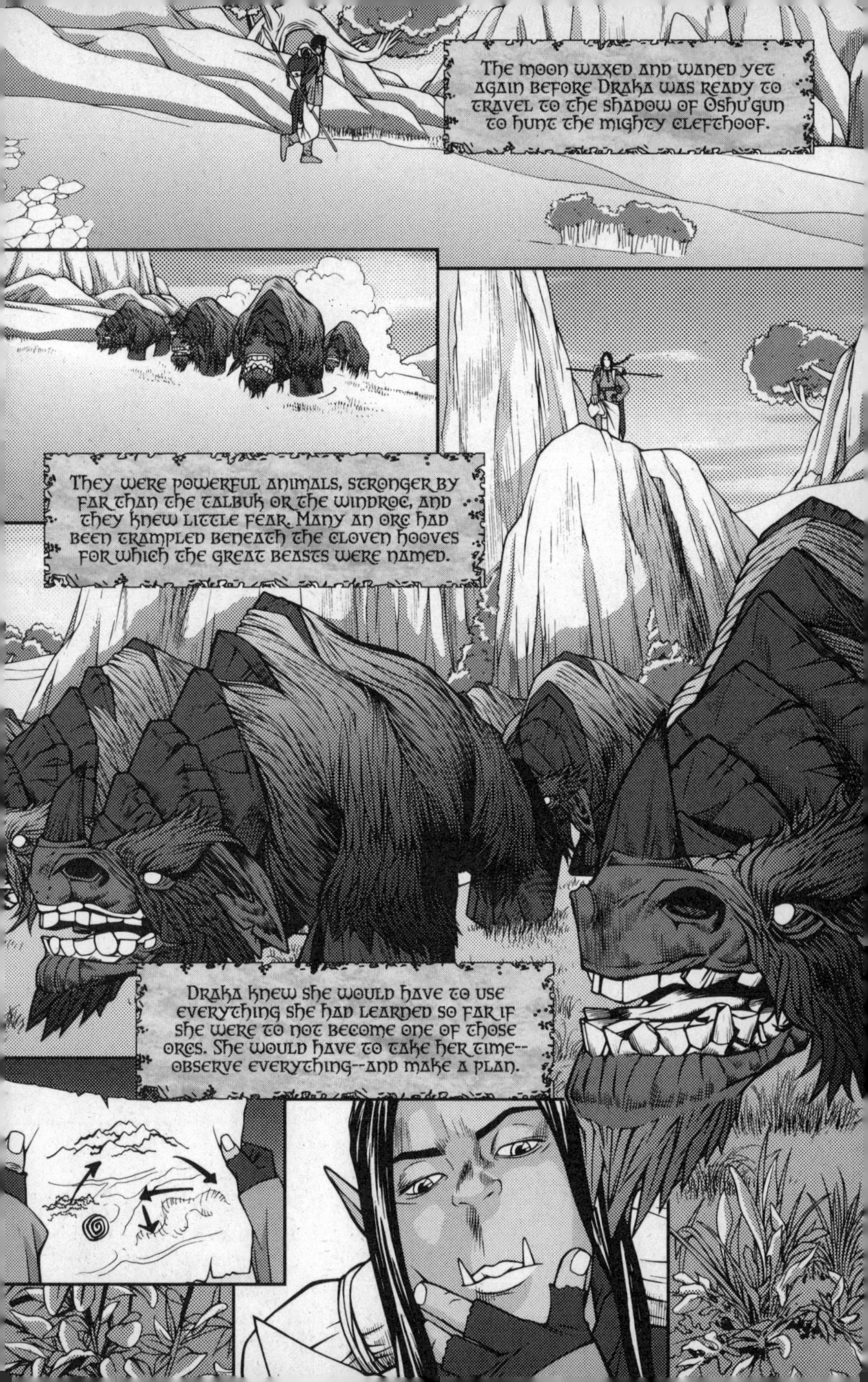
The moon waxed and waned yet again before Draka was ready to travel to the shadow of Oshu'gun to hunt the mighty clefthoof.
They were powerful animals, stronger by far than the talbuk or the windroc, and they knew little fear. Many an orc had been trampled beneath the cloven hooves for which the great beasts were named.
Draka knew she would have to use everything she had learned so far if she were to not become one of those orcs. She would have to take her time--observe everything--and make a plan.

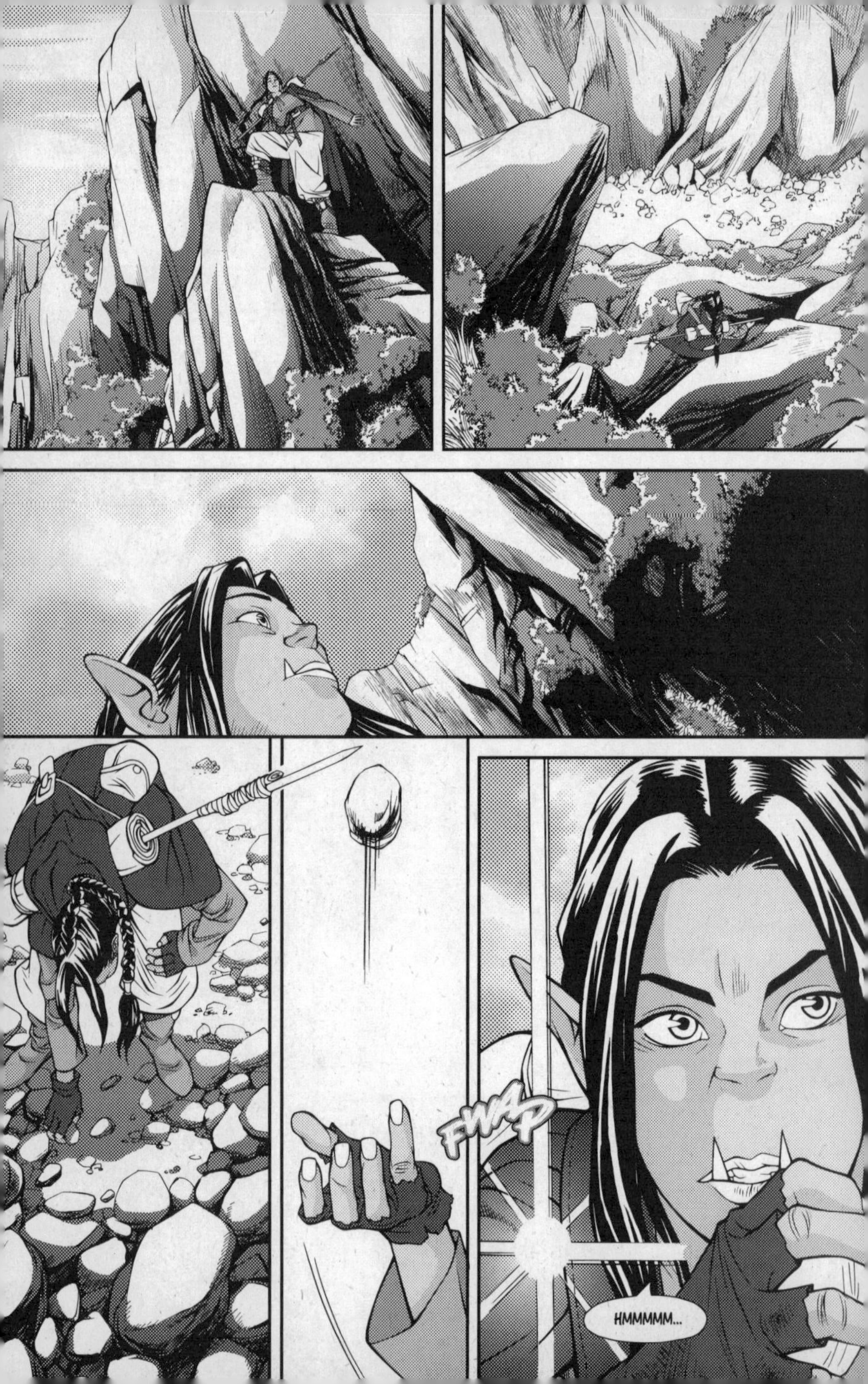
FWAP
HMMMMM...

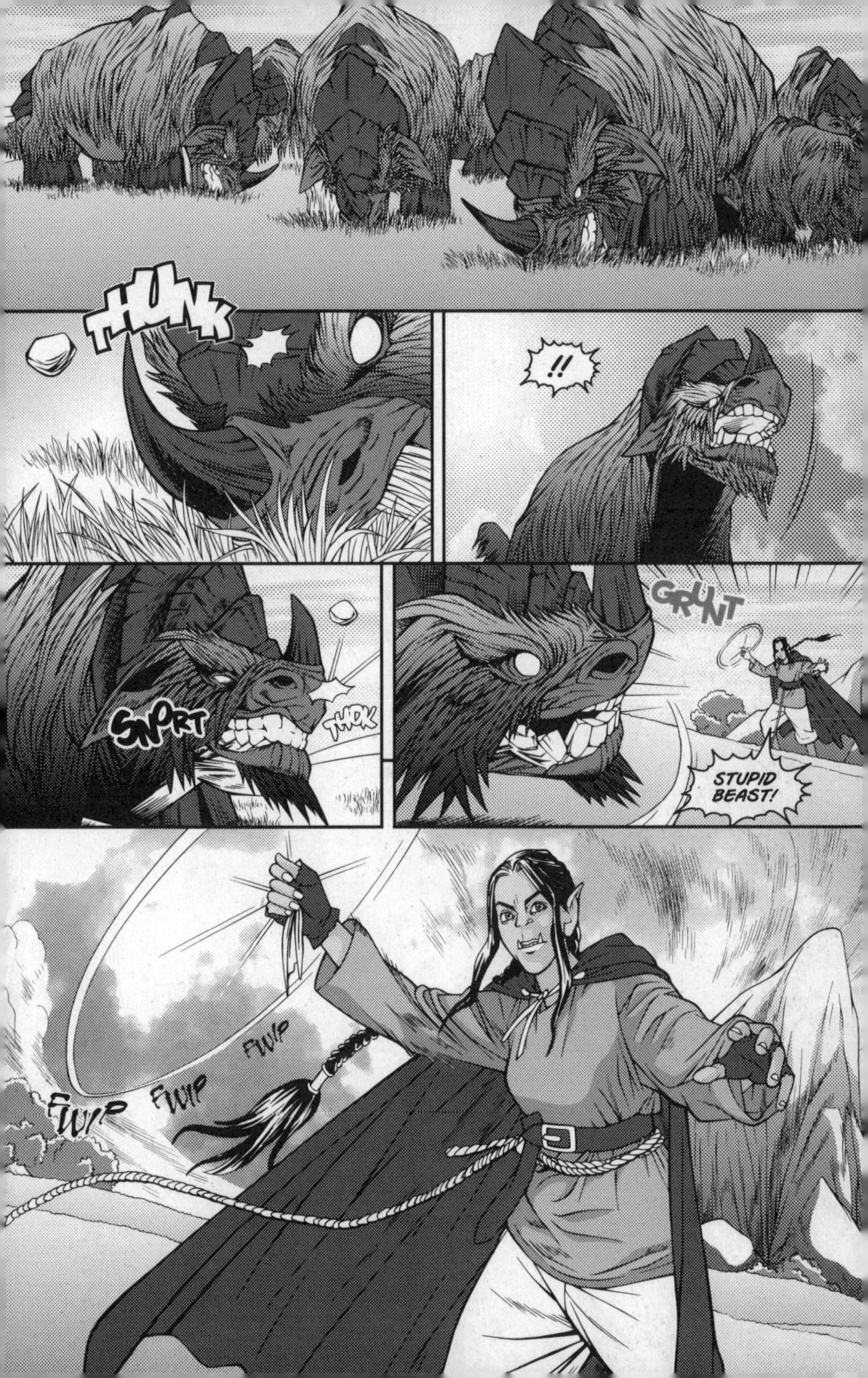
THUNK
!!
SNORT
THDK
GRUNT
STUPID BEAST!
FWIP
FWIP
FWIP

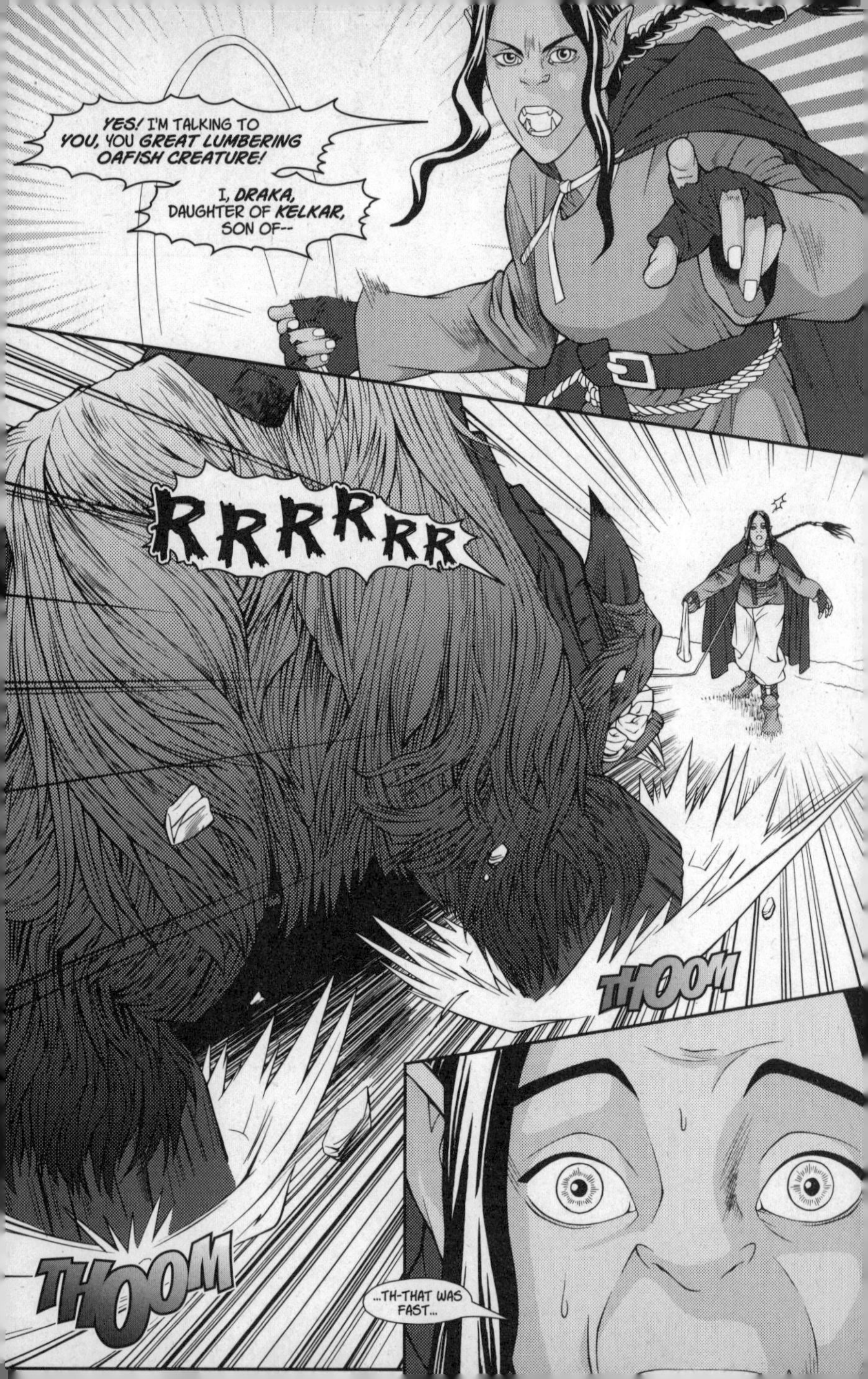
YES! I'M TALKING TO YOU, YOU GREAT LUMBERING OAFISH CREATURE!
I, DRAKA, DAUGHTER OF KELKAR, SON OF--
RRRRRRR
THOOM
THOOM
...TH-THAT WAS FAST...

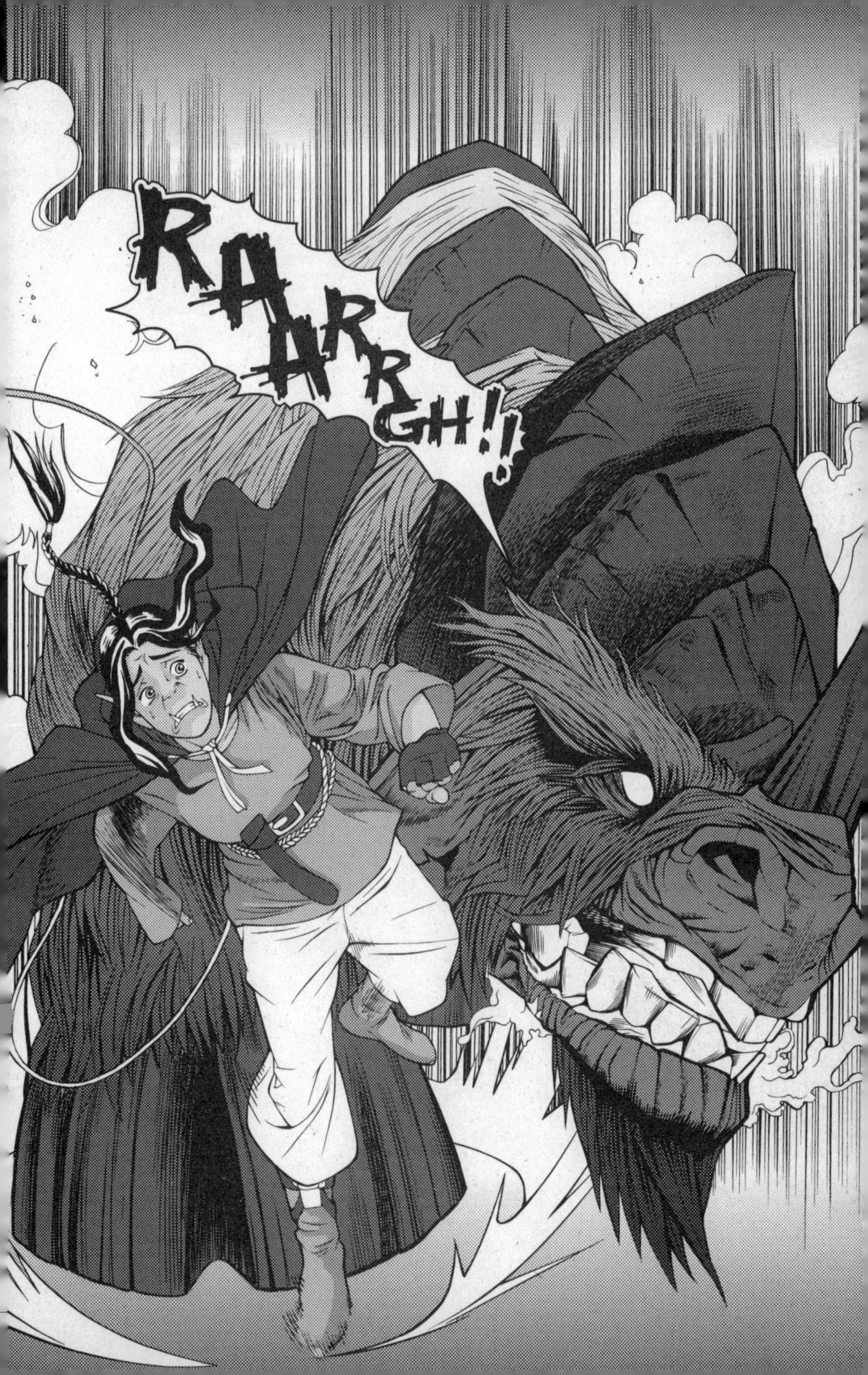
RAARRGH!!

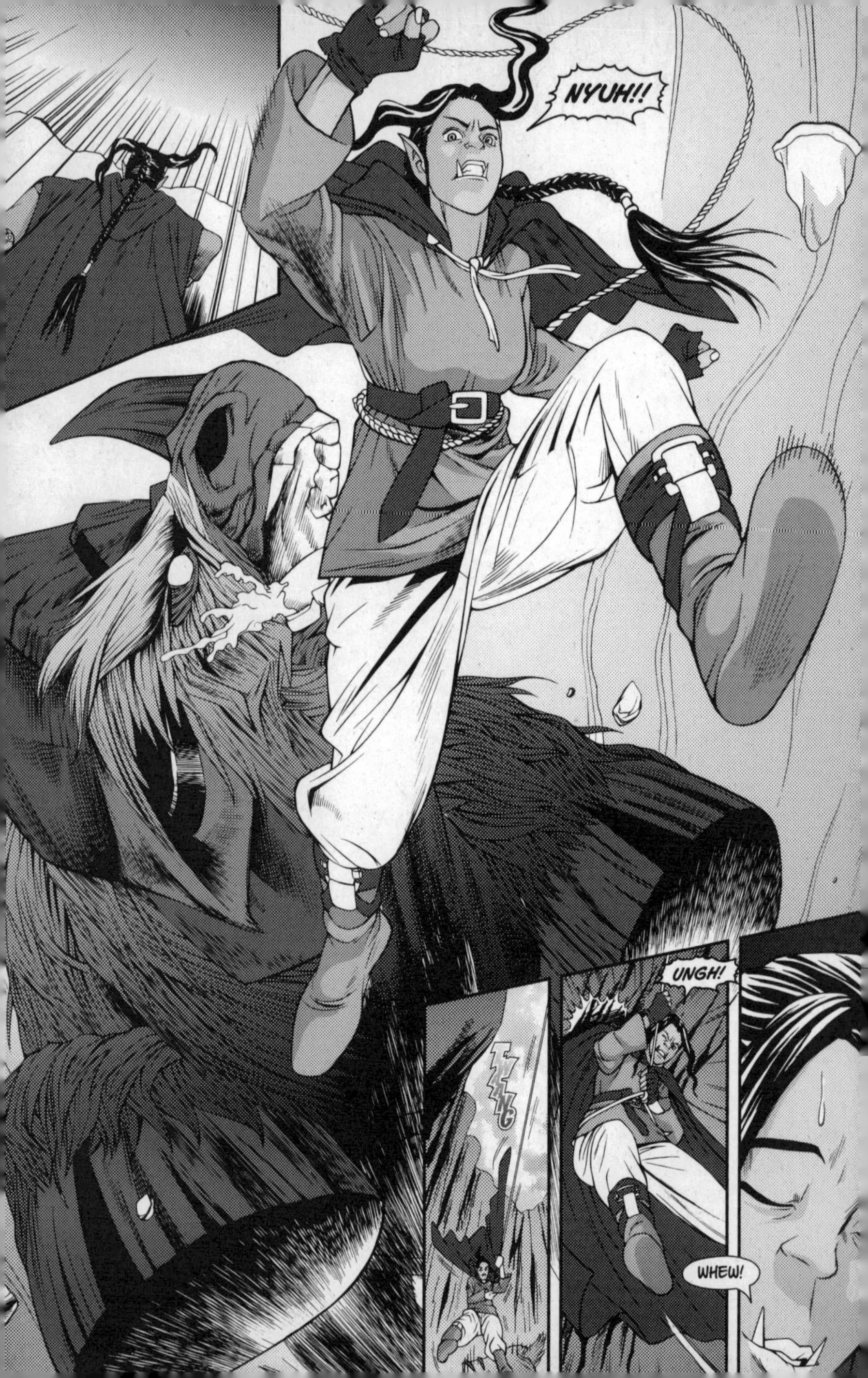
NYUH!!
TZING
UNGH!
WHEW!

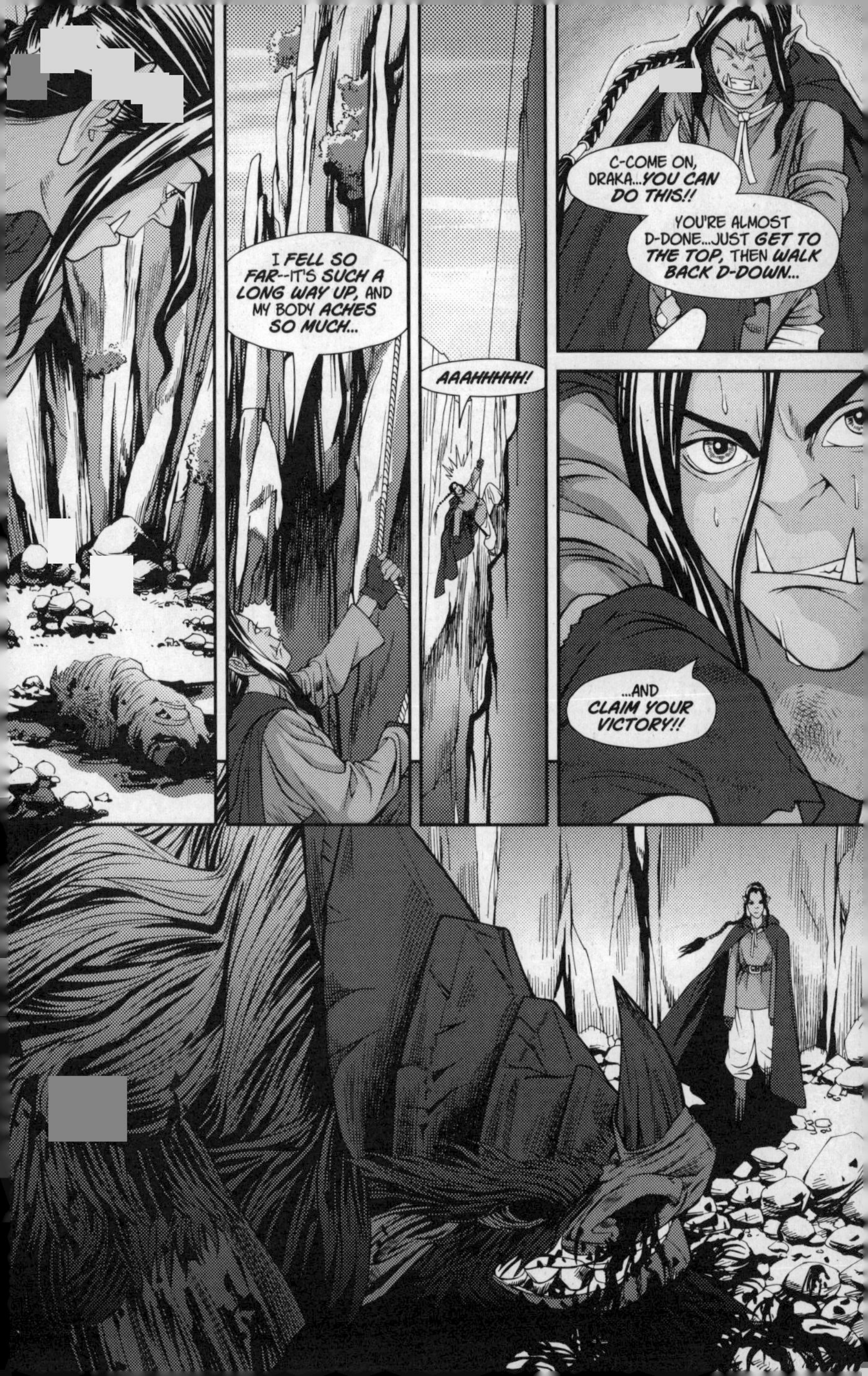
I FELL SO FAR--IT'S SUCH A LONG WAY UP, AND MY BODY ACHES SO MUCH...
AAAHHHHH!
C-COME ON, DRAKA...YOU CAN DO THIS!!
YOU'RE ALMOST D-DONE...JUST GET TO THE TOP, THEN WALK BACK D-DOWN...
...AND CLAIM YOUR VICTORY!!

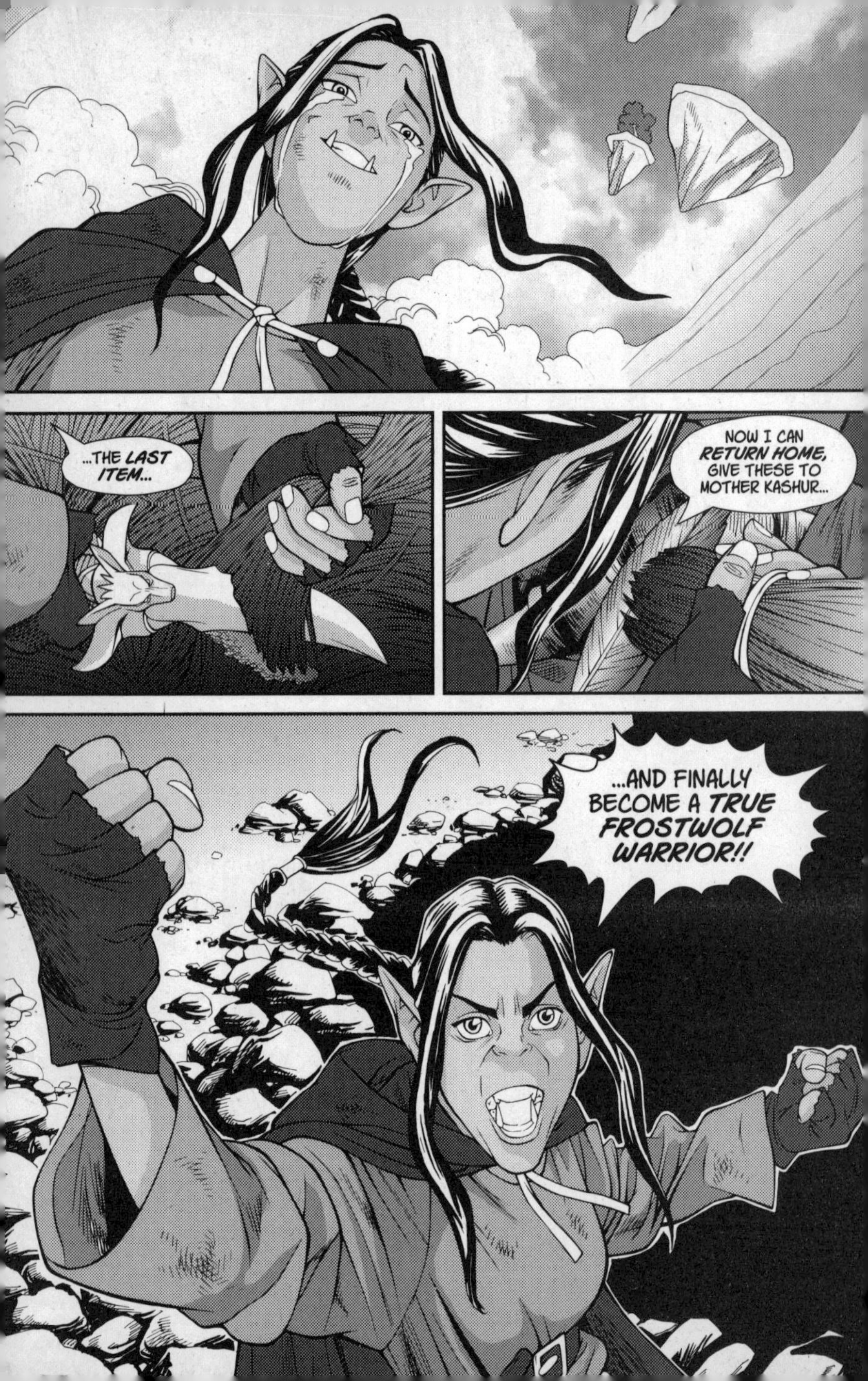
...THE *LAST* *ITEM*...
NOW I CAN *RETURN HOME,* GIVE THESE TO MOTHER KASHUR...
...AND FINALLY BECOME A *TRUE* *FROSTWOLF* *WARRIOR!!*

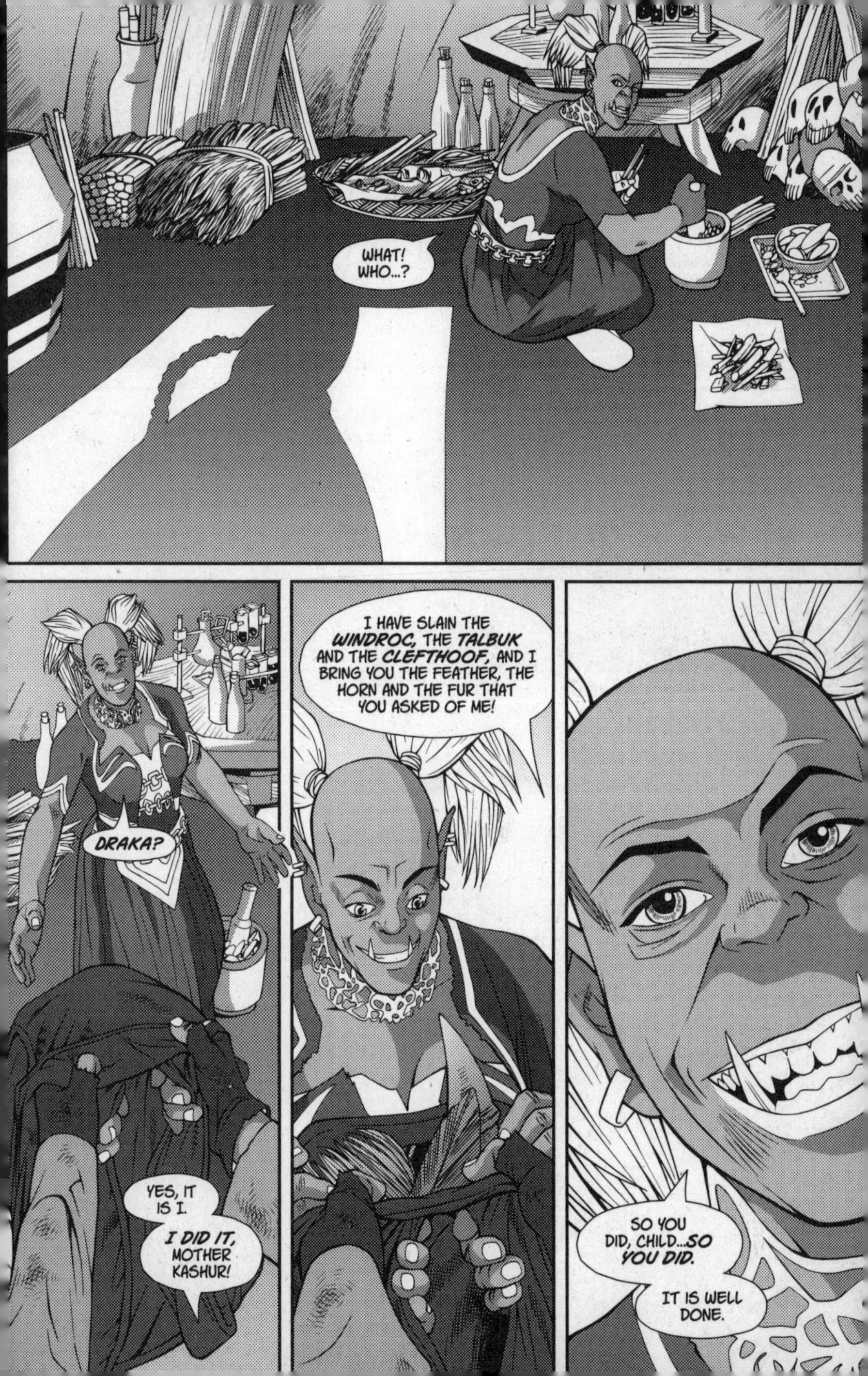
WHAT! WHO...?
DRAKA?
YES, IT IS I.
I DID IT, MOTHER KASHUR!
I HAVE SLAIN THE WINDROC, THE TALBUK AND THE CLEFTHOOF, AND I BRING YOU THE FEATHER, THE HORN AND THE FUR THAT YOU ASKED OF ME!
SO YOU DID, CHILD...SO YOU DID.
IT IS WELL DONE.

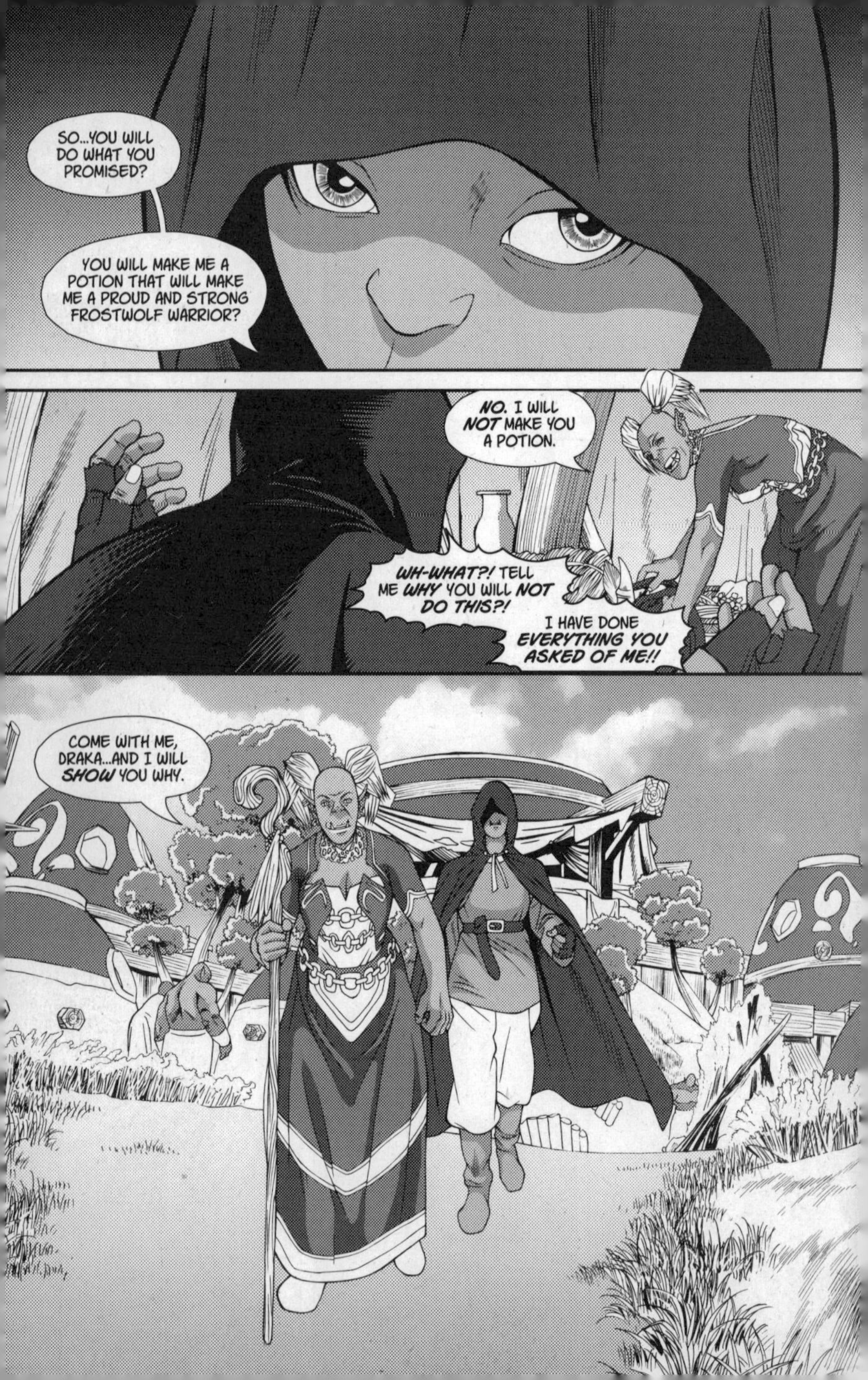

SO...YOU WILL DO WHAT YOU PROMISED?
YOU WILL MAKE ME A POTION THAT WILL MAKE ME A PROUD AND STRONG FROSTWOLF WARRIOR?
NO. I WILL NOT MAKE YOU A POTION.
WH-WHAT?! TELL ME WHY YOU WILL NOT DO THIS?!
I HAVE DONE EVERYTHING YOU ASKED OF ME!!
COME WITH ME, DRAKA...AND I WILL SHOW YOU WHY.

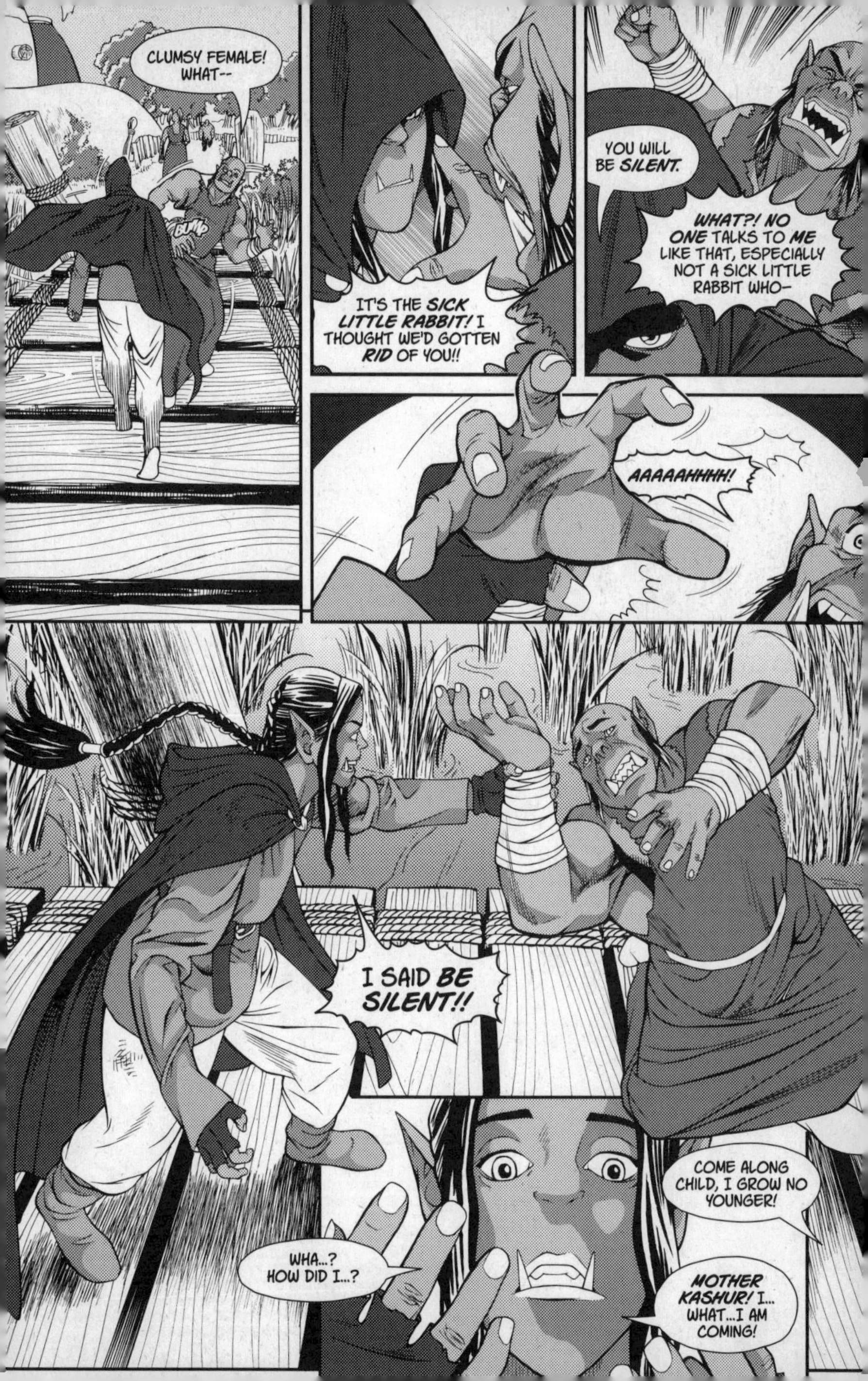
CLUMSY FEMALE! WHAT--
BUMP
IT'S THE SICK LITTLE RABBIT! I THOUGHT WE'D GOTTEN RID OF YOU!!
YOU WILL BE SILENT.
WHAT?! NO ONE TALKS TO ME LIKE THAT, ESPECIALLY NOT A SICK LITTLE RABBIT WHO–
AAAAAHHHH!
I SAID BE SILENT!!
COME ALONG CHILD, I GROW NO YOUNGER!
WHA...? HOW DID I...?
MOTHER KASHUR! I... WHAT...I AM COMING!

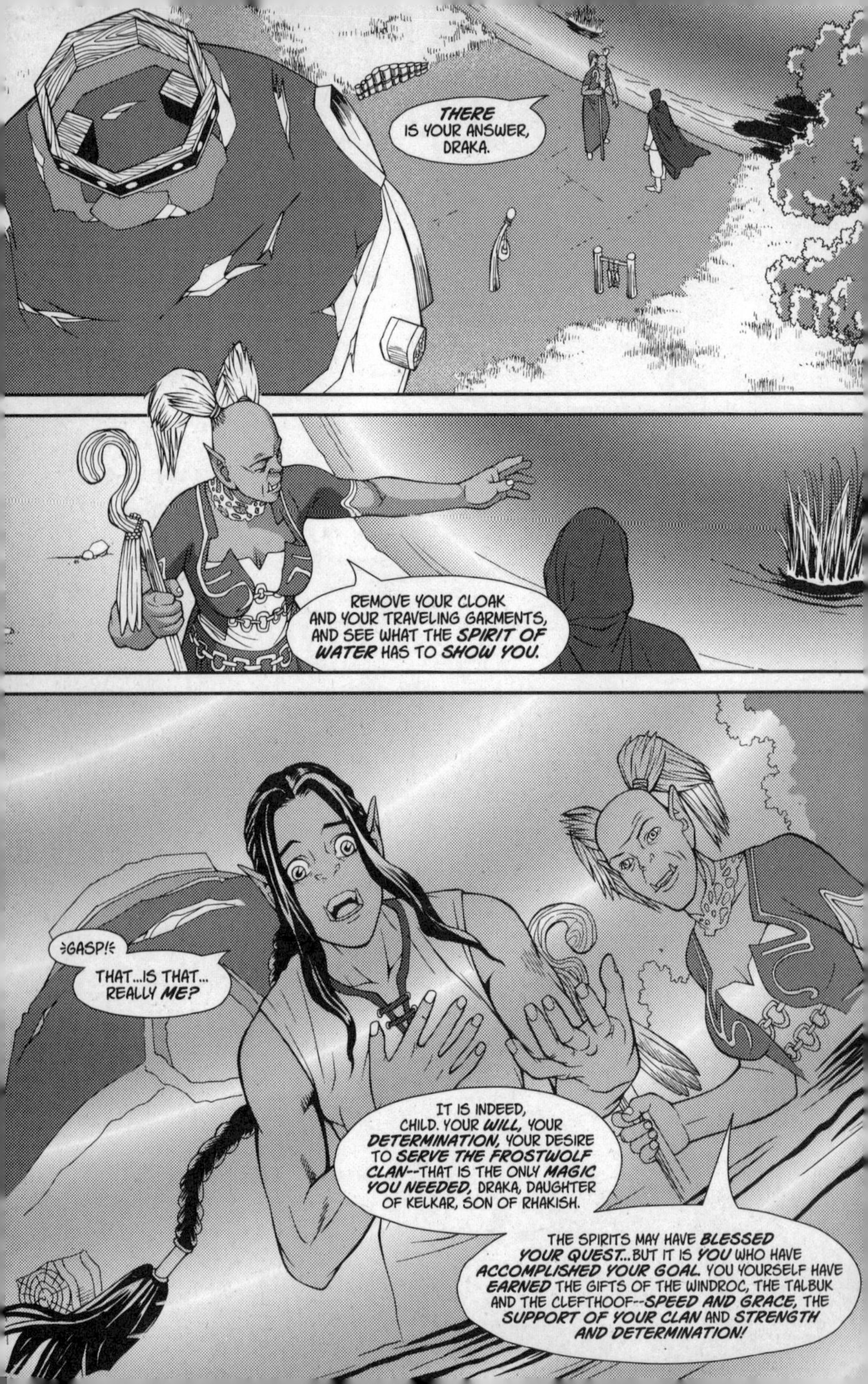
THERE IS YOUR ANSWER, DRAKA.
REMOVE YOUR CLOAK AND YOUR TRAVELING GARMENTS, AND SEE WHAT THE SPIRIT OF WATER HAS TO SHOW YOU.
GASP!
THAT...IS THAT... REALLY ME?
IT IS INDEED, CHILD. YOUR WILL, YOUR DETERMINATION, YOUR DESIRE TO SERVE THE FROSTWOLF CLAN--THAT IS THE ONLY MAGIC YOU NEEDED, DRAKA, DAUGHTER OF KELKAR, SON OF RHAKISH.
THE SPIRITS MAY HAVE BLESSED YOUR QUEST...BUT IT IS YOU WHO HAVE ACCOMPLISHED YOUR GOAL. YOU YOURSELF HAVE EARNED THE GIFTS OF THE WINDROC, THE TALBUK AND THE CLEFTHOOF--SPEED AND GRACE, THE SUPPORT OF YOUR CLAN AND STRENGTH AND DETERMINATION!

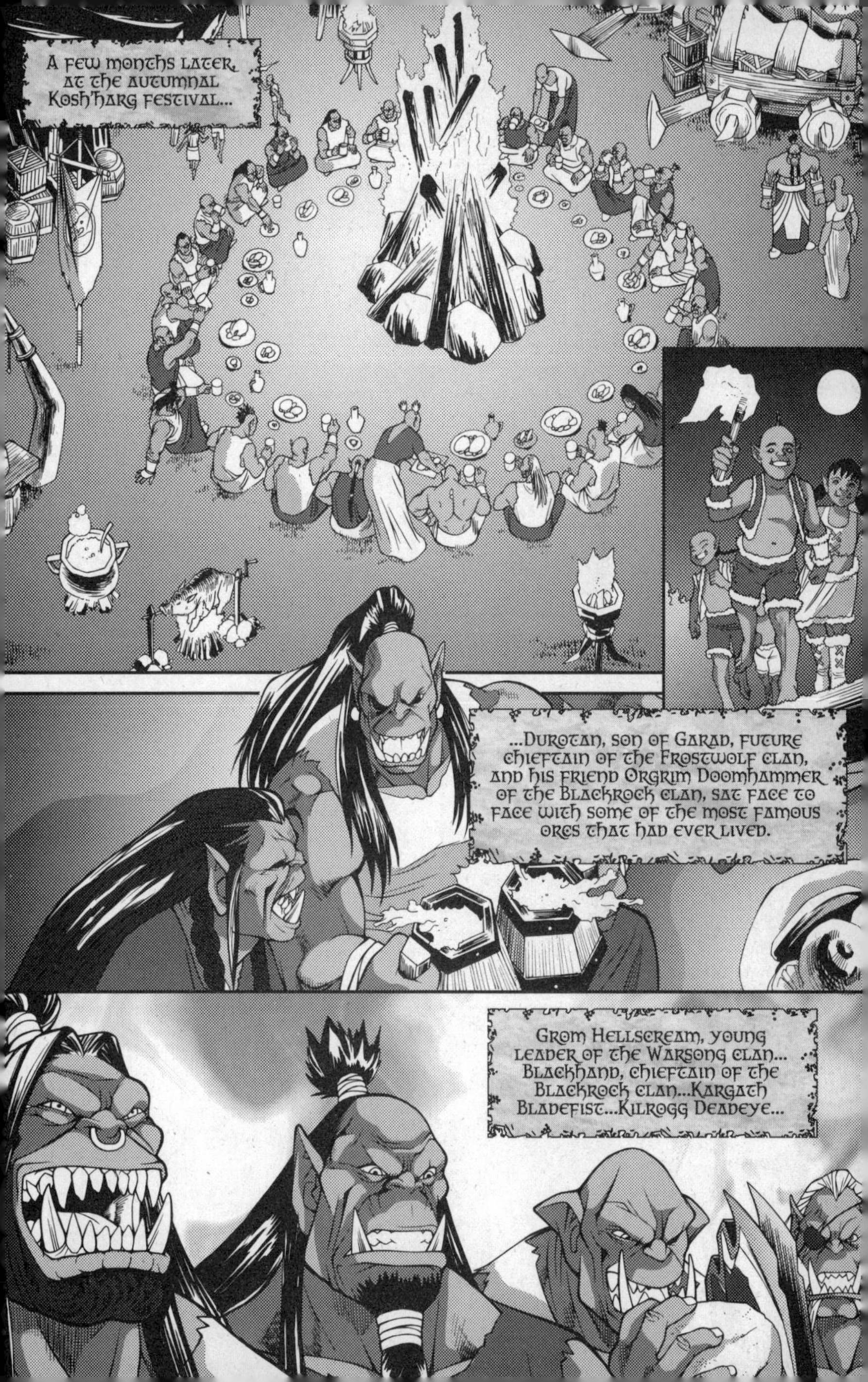
A FEW MONTHS LATER, AT THE AUTUMNAL KOSH'HARG FESTIVAL...
...DUROTAN, SON OF GARAD, FUTURE CHIEFTAIN OF THE FROSTWOLF CLAN, AND HIS FRIEND ORGRIM DOOMHAMMER OF THE BLACKROCK CLAN, SAT FACE TO FACE WITH SOME OF THE MOST FAMOUS ORCS THAT HAD EVER LIVED.
GROM HELLSCREAM, YOUNG LEADER OF THE WARSONG CLAN... BLACKHAND, CHIEFTAIN OF THE BLACKROCK CLAN...KARGATH BLADEFIST...KILROGG DEADEYE...

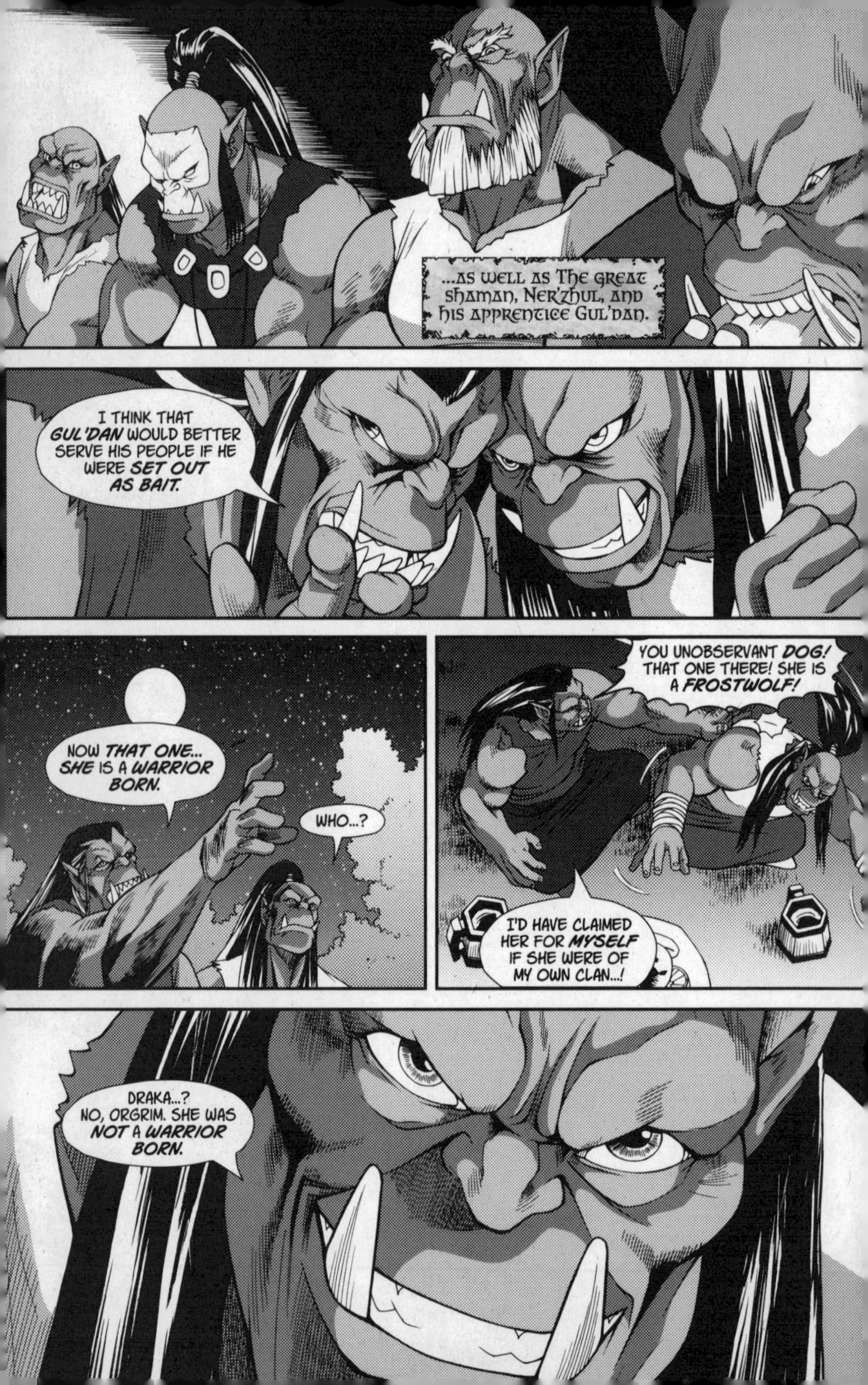
...AS WELL AS THE GREAT SHAMAN, NER'ZHUL, AND HIS APPRENTICE GUL'DAN.
I THINK THAT GUL'DAN WOULD BETTER SERVE HIS PEOPLE IF HE WERE SET OUT AS BAIT.
NOW THAT ONE... SHE IS A WARRIOR BORN.
WHO...?
YOU UNOBSERVANT DOG! THAT ONE THERE! SHE IS A FROSTWOLF!
I'D HAVE CLAIMED HER FOR MYSELF IF SHE WERE OF MY OWN CLAN...!
DRAKA...? NO, ORGRIM. SHE WAS NOT A WARRIOR BORN.

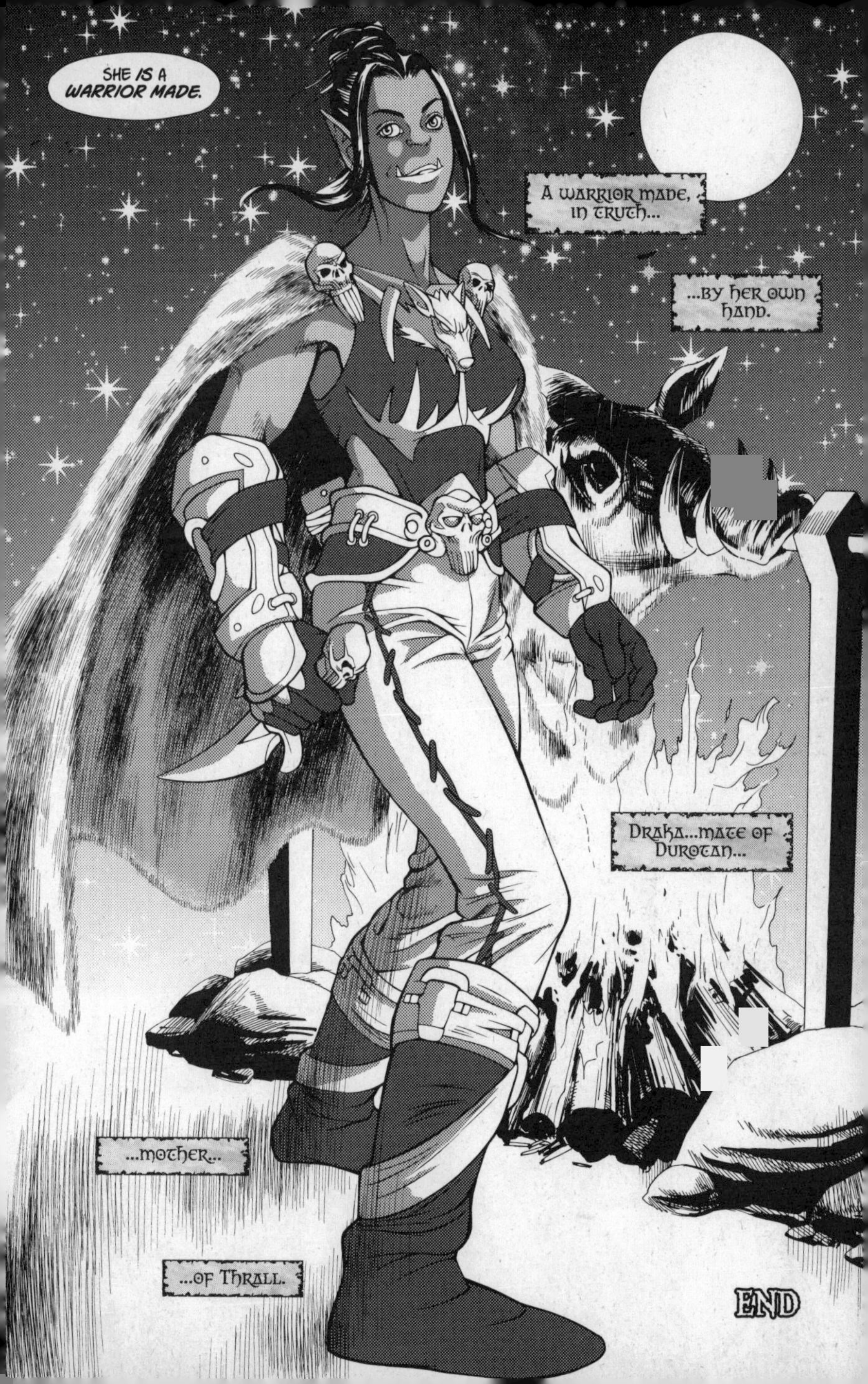
SHE IS A WARRIOR MADE.
A WARRIOR MADE, IN TRUTH...
...BY HER OWN HAND.
DRAKA...MATE OF DUROTAN...
...MOTHER...
...OF THRALL.
END

WARCRAFT®

LEGENDS™

VOLUME FIVE

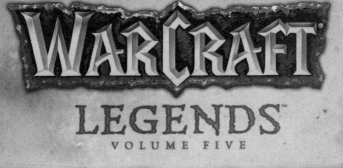

WARRIOR: UNITED

WRITTEN BY GRACE RANDOLPH

PENCILS BY ERICA AWANO
INKS BY TOMAS AIRA & LEANDRO RIZZO
TONES BY GONZALO DUARTE

RETOUCH ARTIST & LETTERER: MICHAEL PAOLILLI

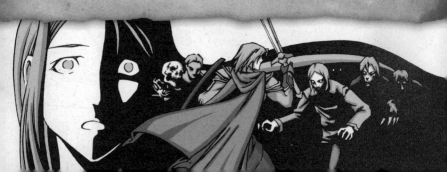

STORY SO FAR

The Wildhammer dwarves are a close-knit clan, yet one of their own, a dwarf named Kardan, was raising a human girl named Lieren. Kardan kept the details surrounding Lieren's past a secret, even to Lieren herself. And though he raised her as any loving father would, Lieren still felt like an outsider, which lead to an obsession with uncovering her past.

One night Lieren secretly followed Kardan to the high elf retreat Quel'Danil, where she made a shocking discovery... she had a twin sister named Loania. Raised by a high elf named Voldana, Loania--just like Lieren--had no knowledge of her past, or that she had a twin sister.

With their ruse revealed, it was with guilty hearts that Kardan and Voldana told the girls how they accompanied their birth father, a human paladin named Dougan, on his mission to rescue villagers from the cursed tower of Karazhan. Unfortunately, brave hearts and noble intentions were not enough to defeat the evil within and they were forced to retreat...but not before Dougan was killed in the process. Kardan and Voldana sadly delivered the news to Dougan's wife but, so immense was her grief her mind snapped, rendering her unfit to raise their twin baby girls. And so Kardan and Voldana decided to honor their fallen colleague by raising the twin daughters as their own.

While Lieren and Loania shared little in common besides their appearance, they both insisted on going to see their mother. However, upon arrival at their old home, the twins learned that their mother had died, only to be reborn as one of the undead. The girls set upon the grisly task of finding and freeing their mother from her rotting prison of flesh...by beheading her.

It was then, with their mother's soul finally laid to rest, Lieren and Loania swore an oath at her grave...

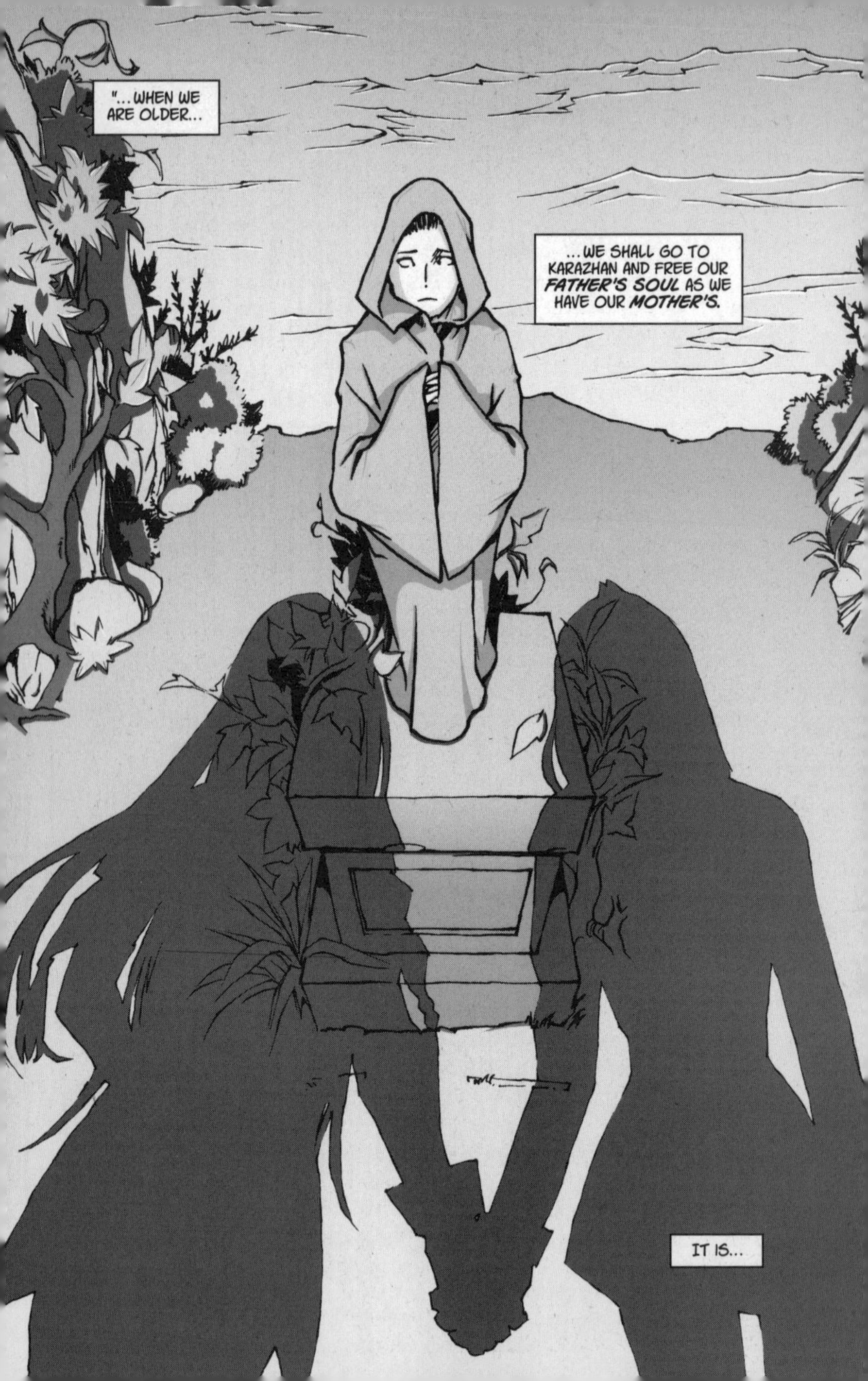
"...WHEN WE ARE OLDER...
...WE SHALL GO TO KARAZHAN AND FREE OUR **FATHER'S SOUL** AS WE HAVE OUR **MOTHER'S.**
IT IS...

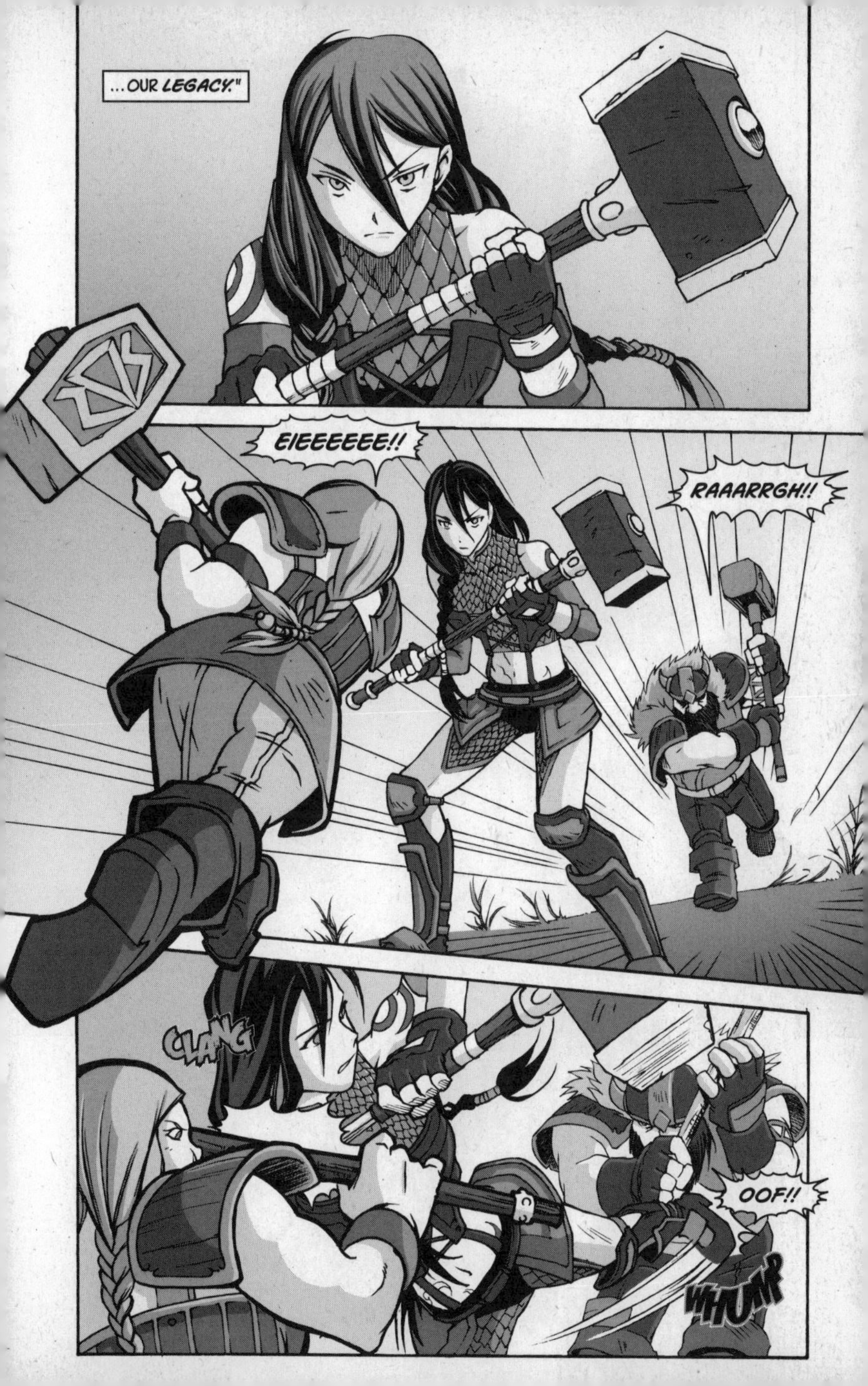
...OUR LEGACY."
EIEEEEEE!!
RAAARRGH!!
CLANG
OOF!!
WHUMP

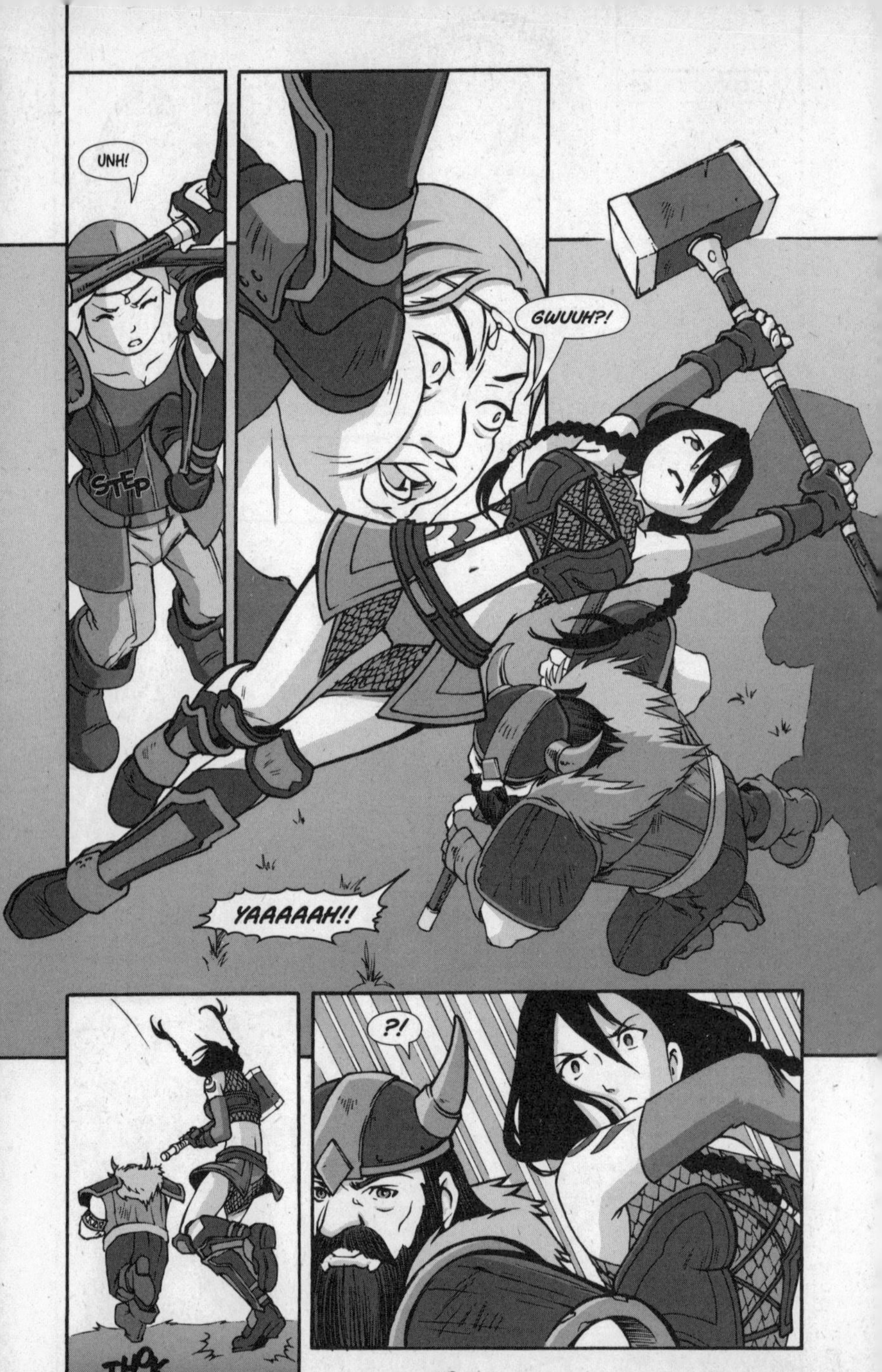
UNH!
STEP
GWUUH?!
YAAAAAH!!
THOK
?!

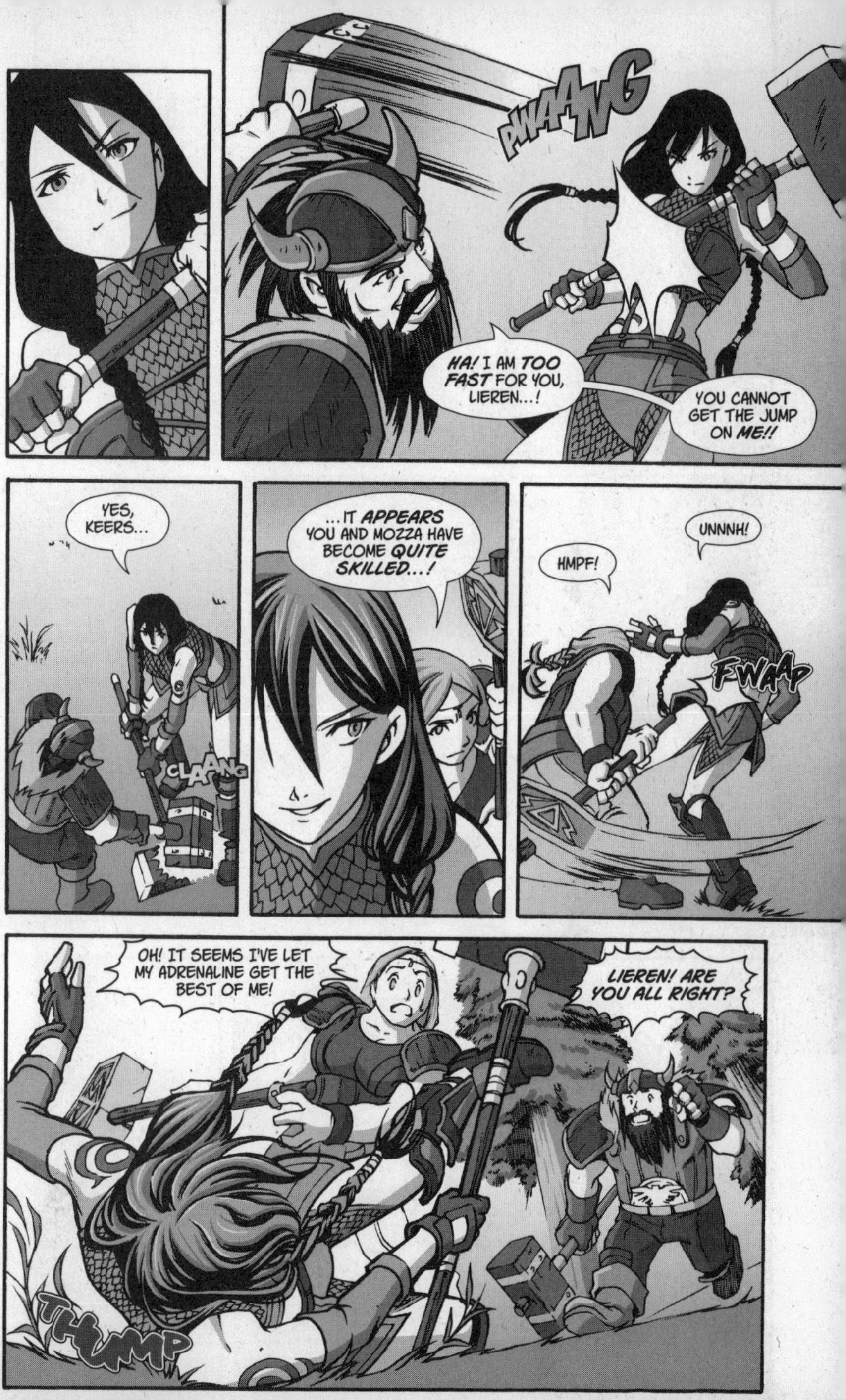
PWAANG
HA! I AM TOO FAST FOR YOU, LIEREN...!
YOU CANNOT GET THE JUMP ON ME!!
YES, KEERS...
CLAANG
...IT APPEARS YOU AND MOZZA HAVE BECOME QUITE SKILLED...!
UNNNH!
HMPF!
FWAAP
OH! IT SEEMS I'VE LET MY ADRENALINE GET THE BEST OF ME!
LIEREN! ARE YOU ALL RIGHT?
THUMP

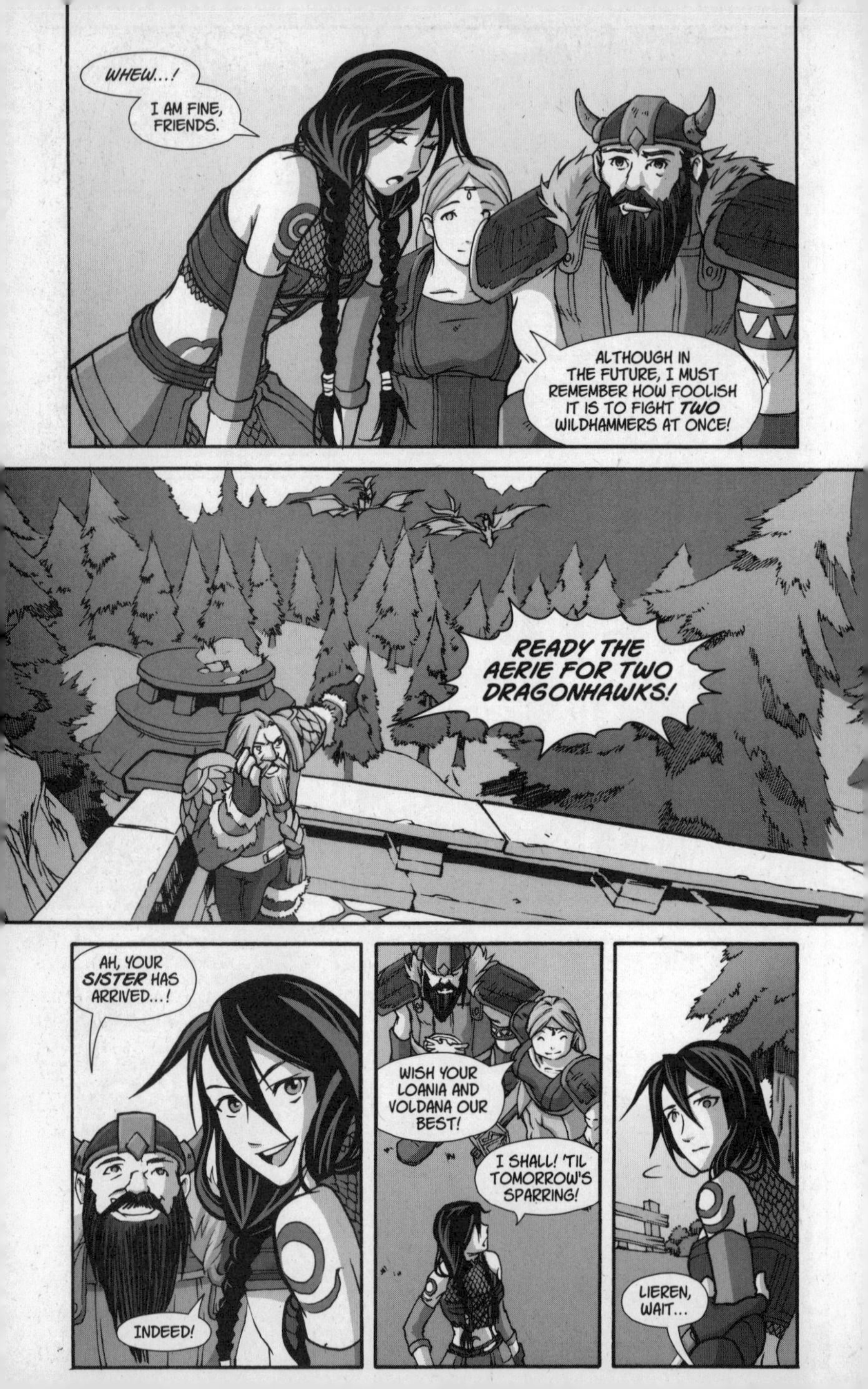
WHEW...!
I AM FINE, FRIENDS.
ALTHOUGH IN THE FUTURE, I MUST REMEMBER HOW FOOLISH IT IS TO FIGHT TWO WILDHAMMERS AT ONCE!
READY THE AERIE FOR TWO DRAGONHAWKS!
AH, YOUR SISTER HAS ARRIVED...!
INDEED!
WISH YOUR LOANIA AND VOLDANA OUR BEST!
I SHALL! 'TIL TOMORROW'S SPARRING!
LIEREN, WAIT...

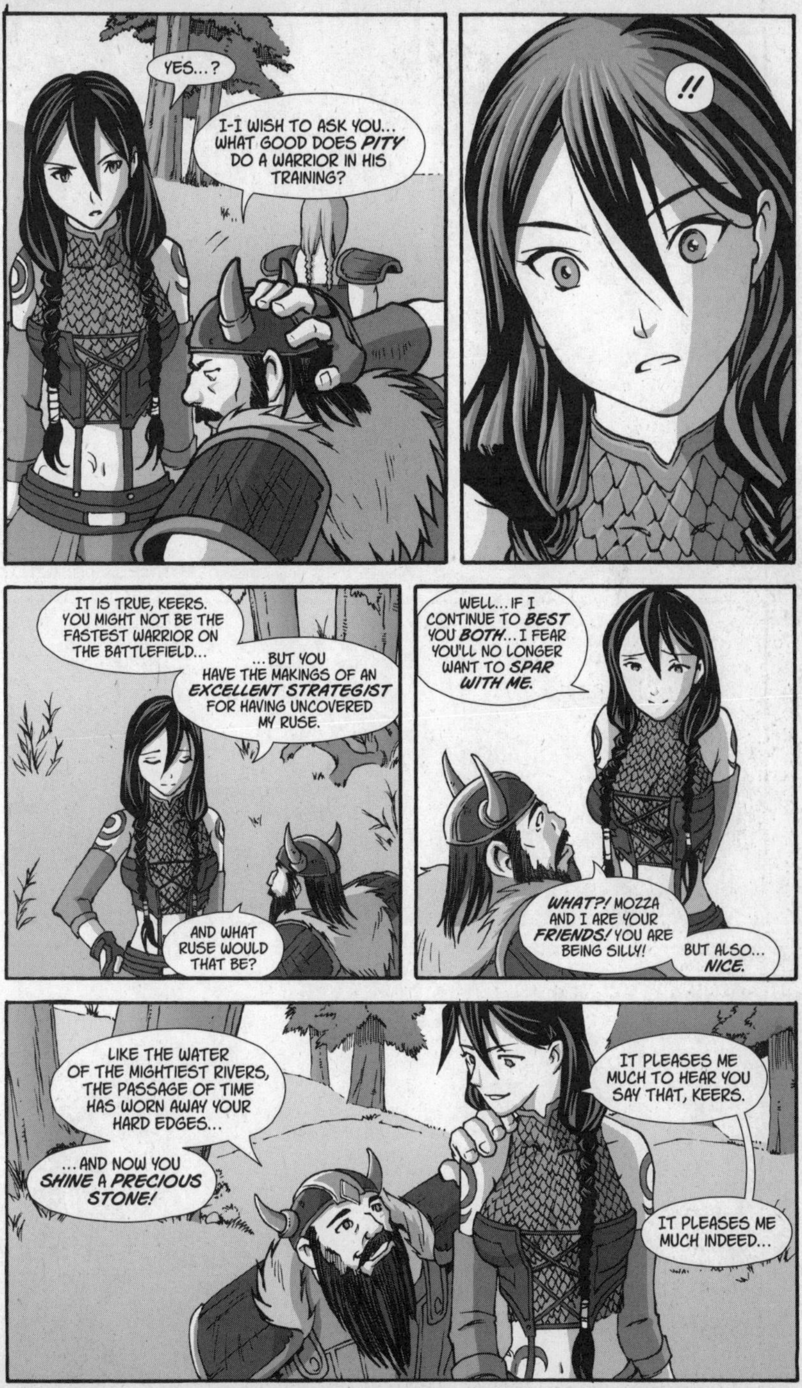
YES...?
I-I WISH TO ASK YOU... WHAT GOOD DOES *PITY* DO A WARRIOR IN HIS TRAINING?
!!
IT IS TRUE, KEERS. YOU MIGHT NOT BE THE FASTEST WARRIOR ON THE BATTLEFIELD...
...BUT YOU HAVE THE MAKINGS OF AN ***EXCELLENT STRATEGIST*** FOR HAVING UNCOVERED MY RUSE.
AND WHAT RUSE WOULD THAT BE?
WELL... IF I CONTINUE TO ***BEST*** YOU ***BOTH***... I FEAR YOU'LL NO LONGER WANT TO ***SPAR WITH ME.***
WHAT?! MOZZA AND I ARE YOUR ***FRIENDS!*** YOU ARE BEING SILLY!
BUT ALSO... ***NICE.***
LIKE THE WATER OF THE MIGHTIEST RIVERS, THE PASSAGE OF TIME HAS WORN AWAY YOUR HARD EDGES...
...AND NOW YOU ***SHINE*** A ***PRECIOUS STONE!***
IT PLEASES ME MUCH TO HEAR YOU SAY THAT, KEERS.
IT PLEASES ME MUCH INDEED...

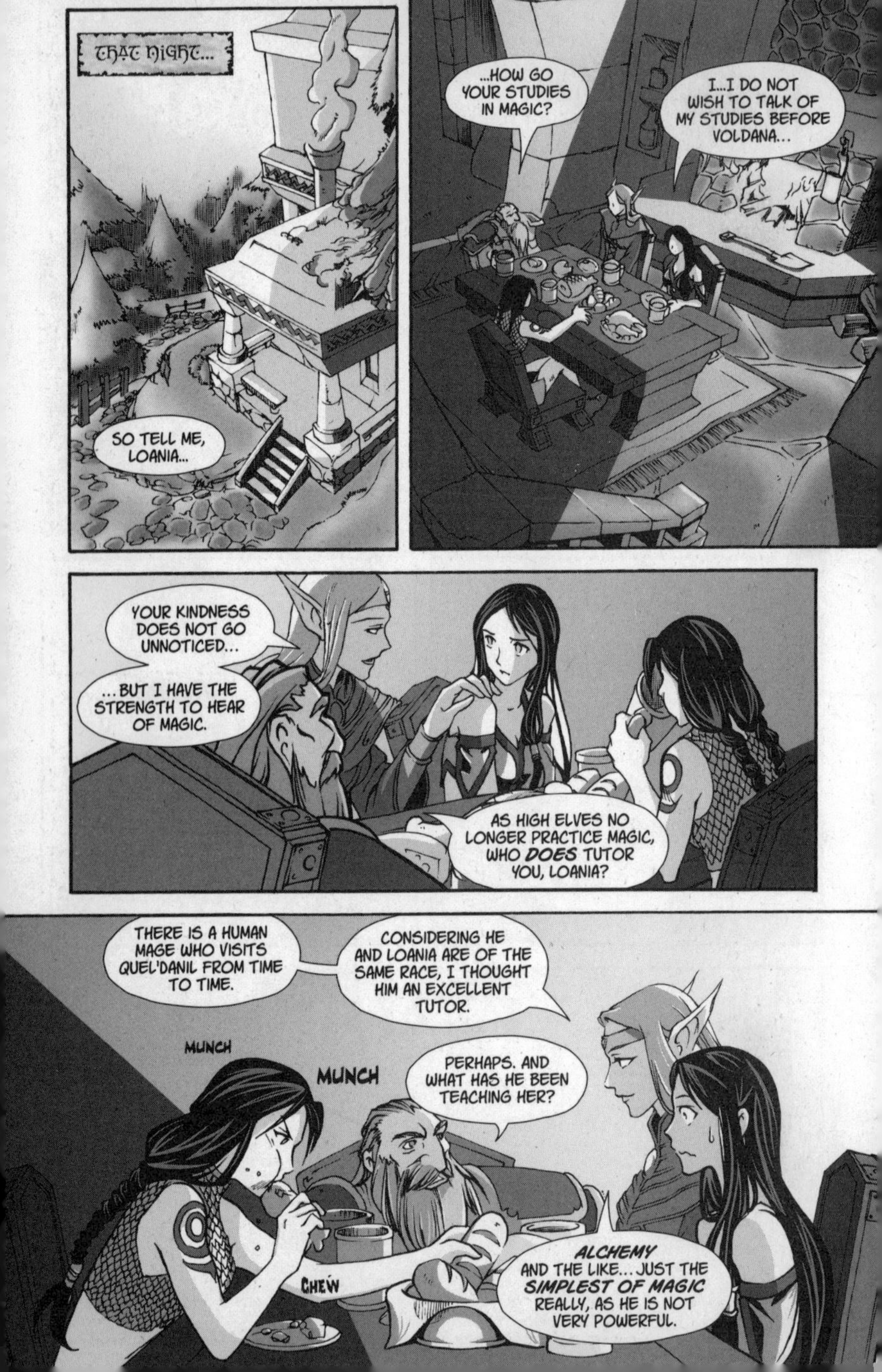
THAT NIGHT...
SO TELL ME, LOANIA...
...HOW GO YOUR STUDIES IN MAGIC?
I...I DO NOT WISH TO TALK OF MY STUDIES BEFORE VOLDANA...
YOUR KINDNESS DOES NOT GO UNNOTICED...
...BUT I HAVE THE STRENGTH TO HEAR OF MAGIC.
AS HIGH ELVES NO LONGER PRACTICE MAGIC, WHO *DOES* TUTOR YOU, LOANIA?
THERE IS A HUMAN MAGE WHO VISITS QUEL'DANIL FROM TIME TO TIME.
CONSIDERING HE AND LOANIA ARE OF THE SAME RACE, I THOUGHT HIM AN EXCELLENT TUTOR.
MUNCH
MUNCH
PERHAPS. AND WHAT HAS HE BEEN TEACHING HER?
CHEW
ALCHEMY AND THE LIKE... JUST THE *SIMPLEST OF MAGIC* REALLY, AS HE IS NOT VERY POWERFUL.

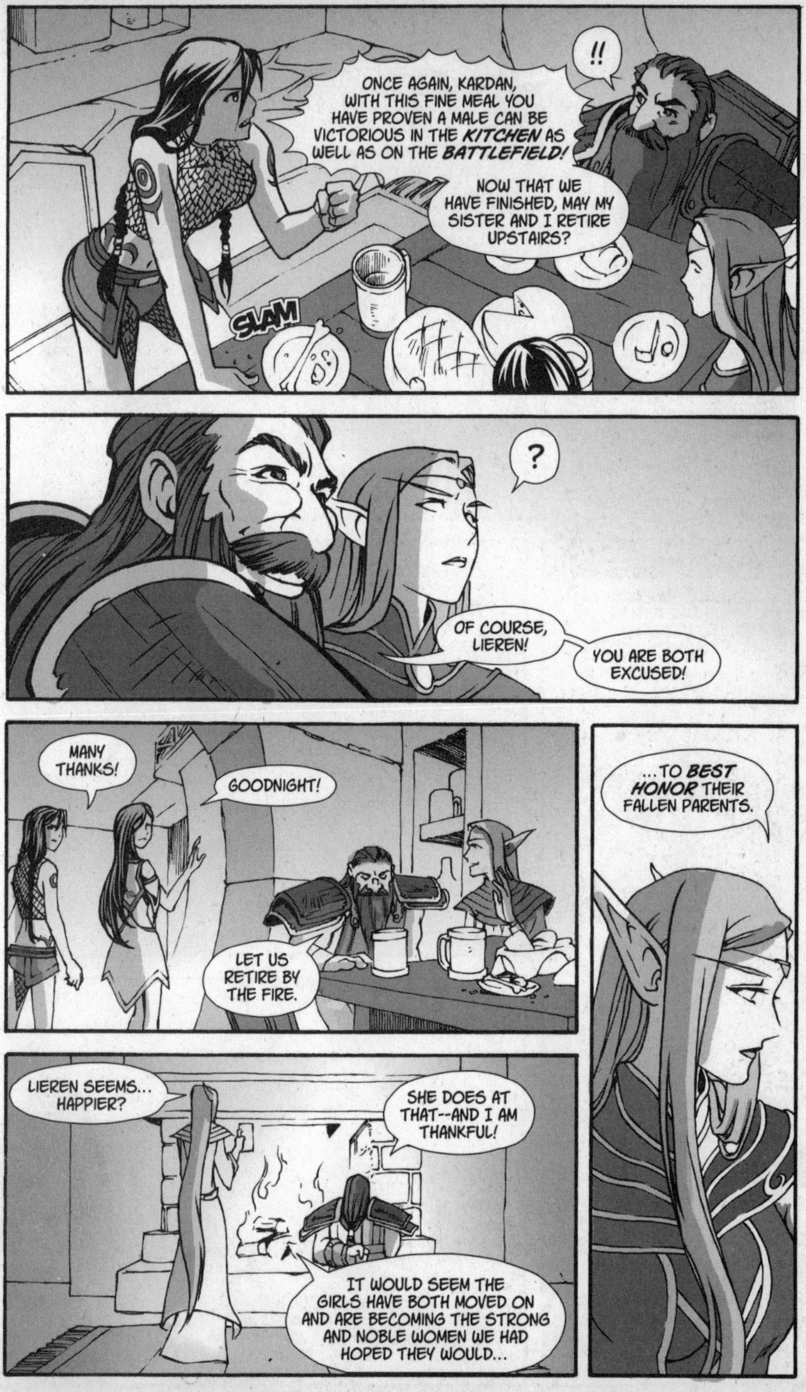

ONCE AGAIN, KARDAN, WITH THIS FINE MEAL YOU HAVE PROVEN A MALE CAN BE VICTORIOUS IN THE *KITCHEN* AS WELL AS ON THE *BATTLEFIELD!*
!!
NOW THAT WE HAVE FINISHED, MAY MY SISTER AND I RETIRE UPSTAIRS?
SLAM
?
OF COURSE, LIEREN!
YOU ARE BOTH EXCUSED!
MANY THANKS!
GOODNIGHT!
LET US RETIRE BY THE FIRE.
LIEREN SEEMS... HAPPIER?
SHE DOES AT THAT--AND I AM THANKFUL!
IT WOULD SEEM THE GIRLS HAVE BOTH MOVED ON AND ARE BECOMING THE STRONG AND NOBLE WOMEN WE HAD HOPED THEY WOULD...
...TO *BEST HONOR* THEIR FALLEN PARENTS.

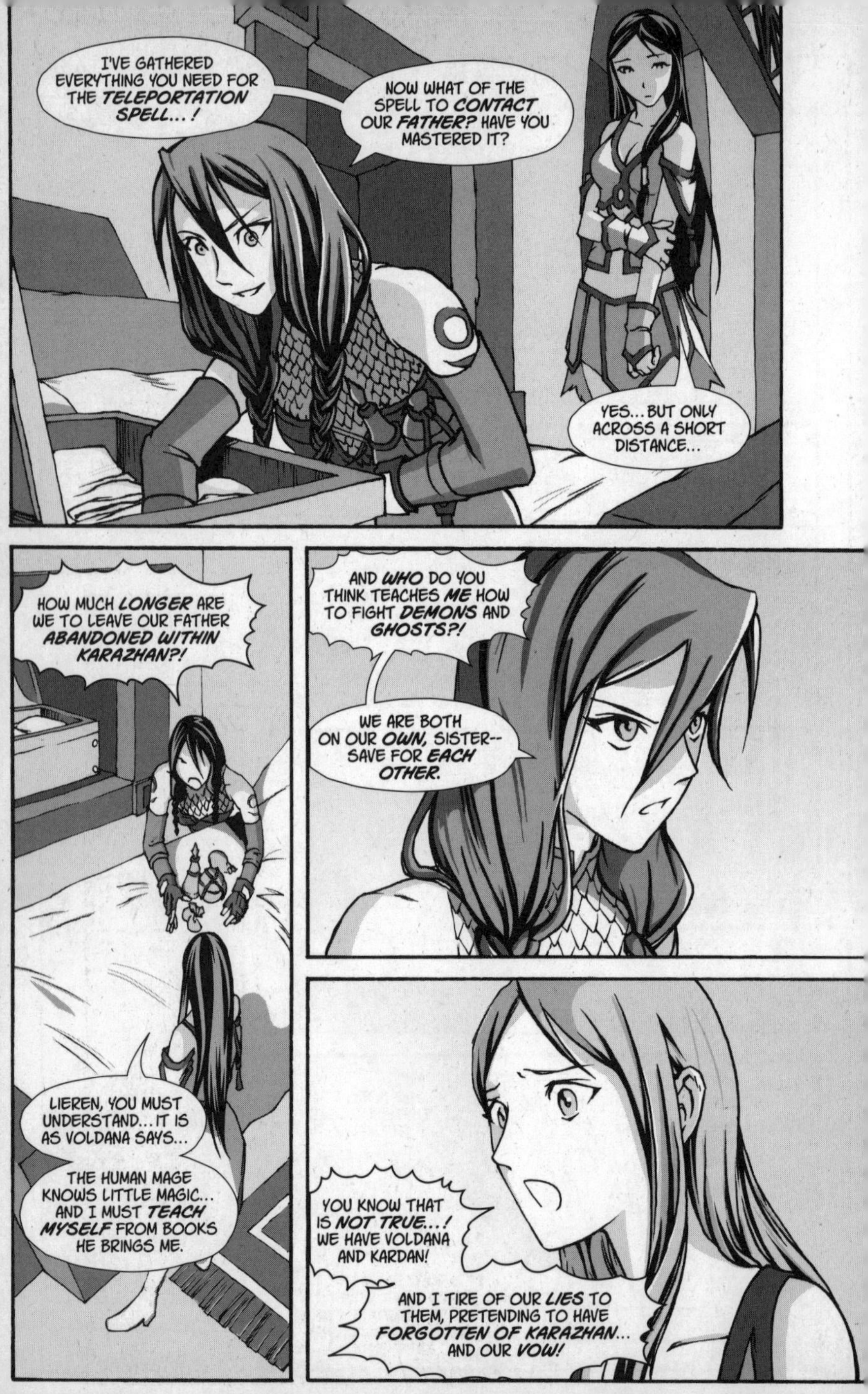
I'VE GATHERED EVERYTHING YOU NEED FOR THE *TELEPORTATION SPELL...!*
NOW WHAT OF THE SPELL TO *CONTACT* OUR *FATHER?* HAVE YOU MASTERED IT?
YES... BUT ONLY ACROSS A SHORT DISTANCE...
HOW MUCH *LONGER* ARE WE TO LEAVE OUR FATHER *ABANDONED WITHIN KARAZHAN?!*
LIEREN, YOU MUST UNDERSTAND... IT IS AS VOLDANA SAYS...
THE HUMAN MAGE KNOWS LITTLE MAGIC... AND I MUST *TEACH MYSELF* FROM BOOKS HE BRINGS ME.
AND *WHO* DO YOU THINK TEACHES *ME* HOW TO FIGHT *DEMONS* AND *GHOSTS?!*
WE ARE BOTH ON OUR *OWN,* SISTER-- SAVE FOR *EACH OTHER.*
YOU KNOW THAT IS *NOT TRUE...!* WE HAVE VOLDANA AND KARDAN!
AND I TIRE OF OUR *LIES* TO THEM, PRETENDING TO HAVE *FORGOTTEN OF KARAZHAN*... AND OUR *VOW!*

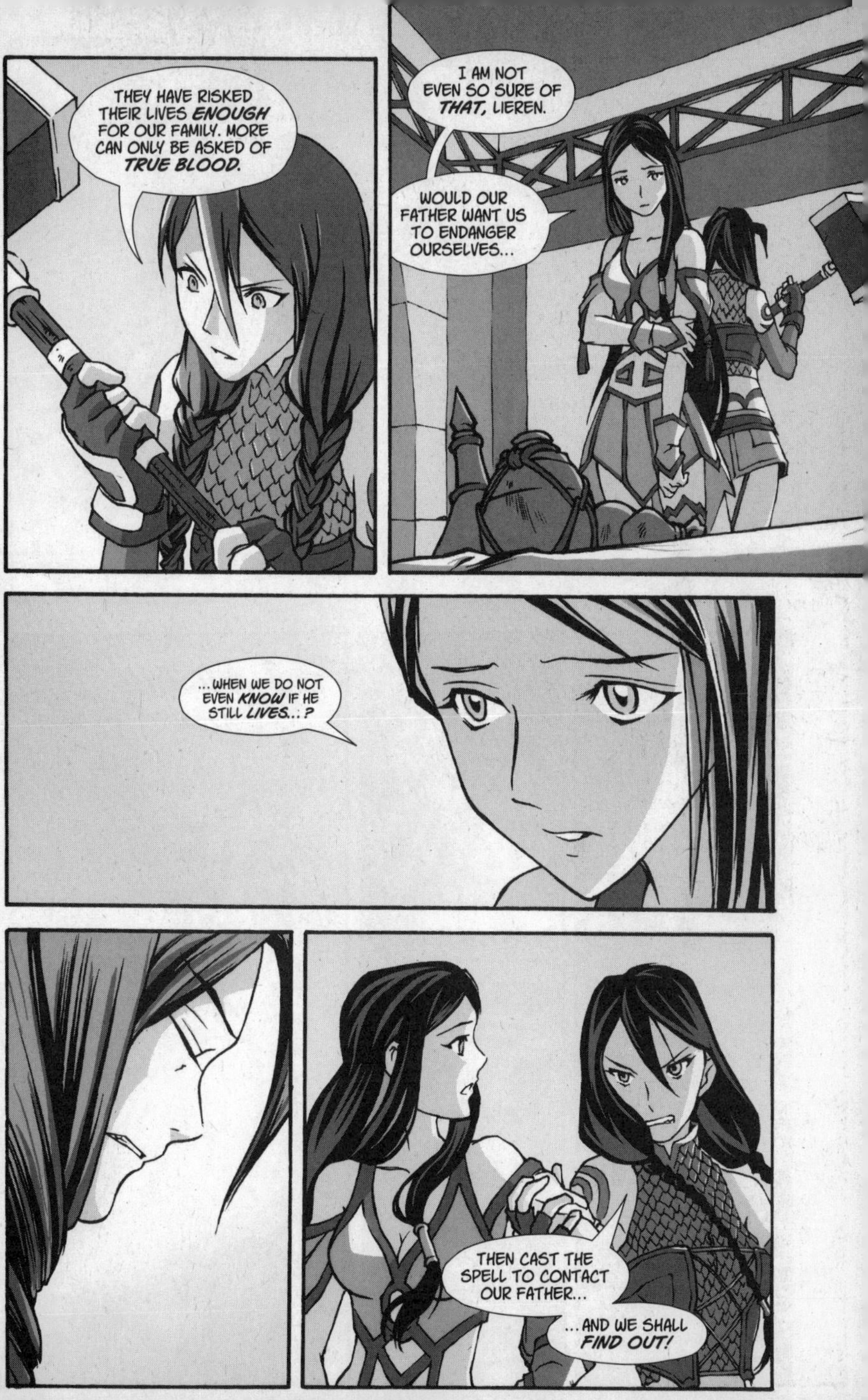
THEY HAVE RISKED THEIR LIVES ENOUGH FOR OUR FAMILY. MORE CAN ONLY BE ASKED OF TRUE BLOOD.
I AM NOT EVEN SO SURE OF THAT, LIEREN.
WOULD OUR FATHER WANT US TO ENDANGER OURSELVES...
...WHEN WE DO NOT EVEN KNOW IF HE STILL LIVES...?
THEN CAST THE SPELL TO CONTACT OUR FATHER...
...AND WE SHALL FIND OUT!

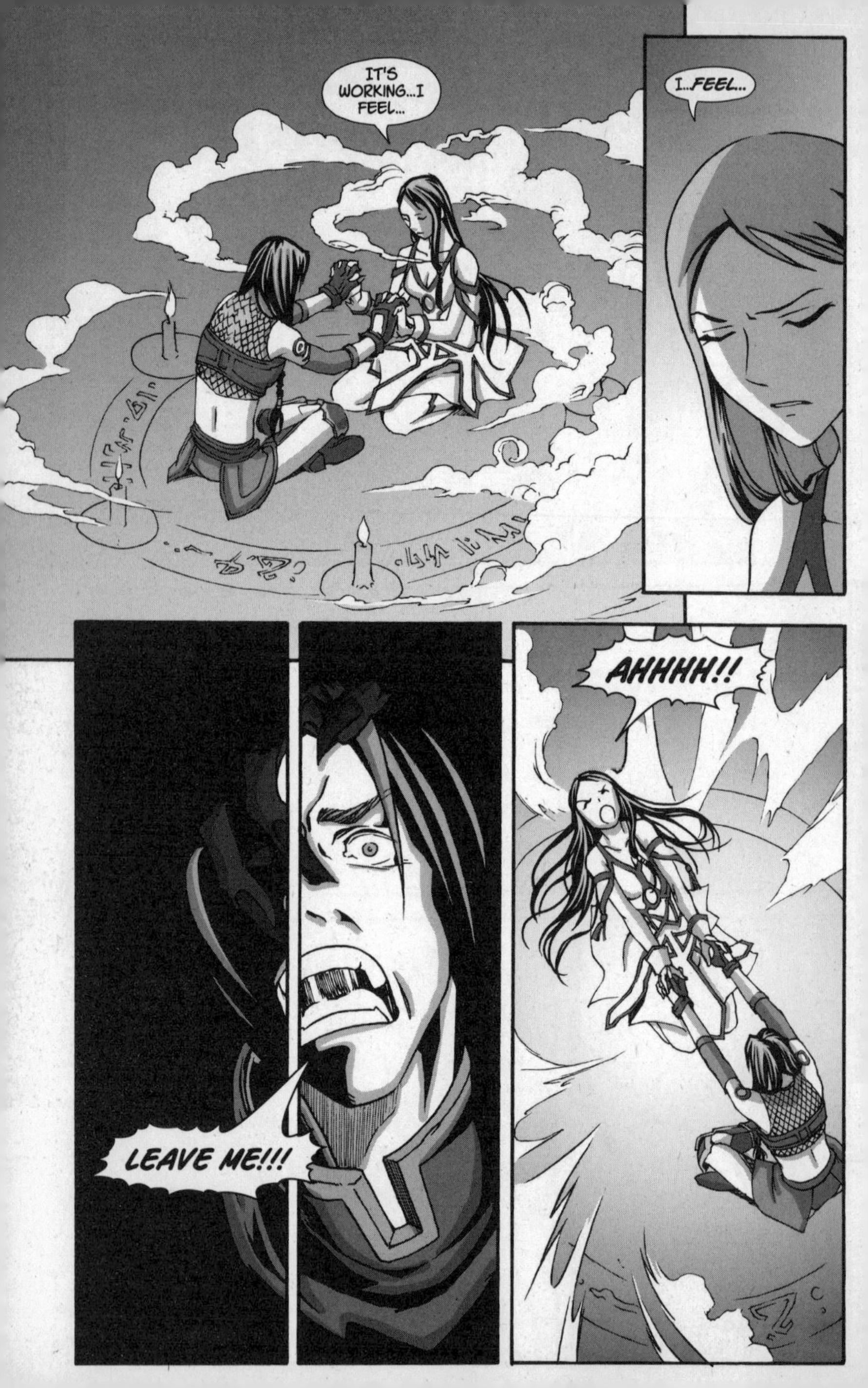
IT'S WORKING...I FEEL...
I...FEEL...
LEAVE ME!!!
AHHHH!!

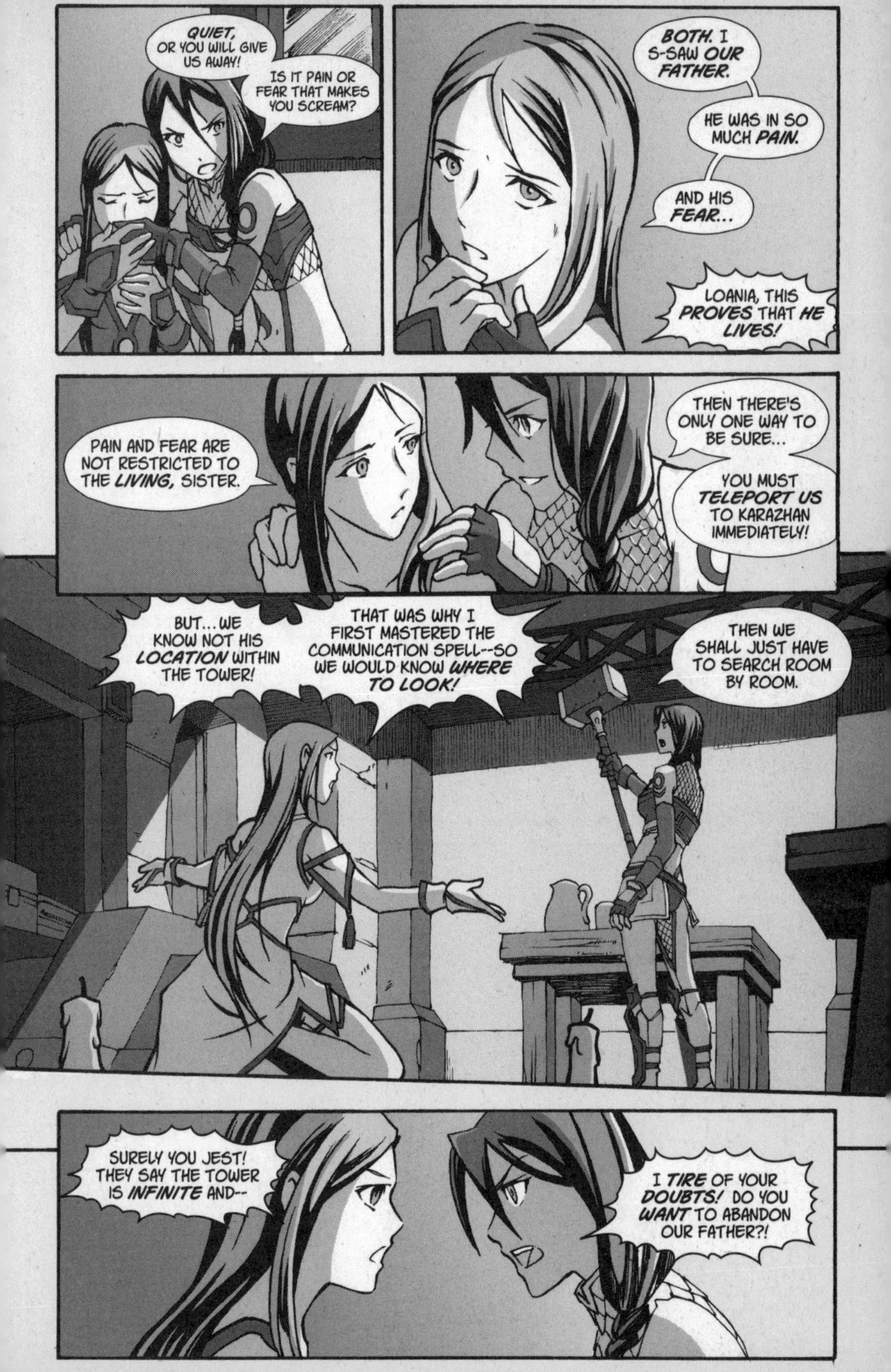
QUIET, OR YOU WILL GIVE US AWAY!
IS IT PAIN OR FEAR THAT MAKES YOU SCREAM?
BOTH. I S-SAW OUR FATHER.
HE WAS IN SO MUCH PAIN.
AND HIS FEAR...
LOANIA, THIS PROVES THAT HE LIVES!
PAIN AND FEAR ARE NOT RESTRICTED TO THE LIVING, SISTER.
THEN THERE'S ONLY ONE WAY TO BE SURE...
YOU MUST TELEPORT US TO KARAZHAN IMMEDIATELY!
BUT... WE KNOW NOT HIS LOCATION WITHIN THE TOWER!
THAT WAS WHY I FIRST MASTERED THE COMMUNICATION SPELL--SO WE WOULD KNOW WHERE TO LOOK!
THEN WE SHALL JUST HAVE TO SEARCH ROOM BY ROOM.
SURELY YOU JEST! THEY SAY THE TOWER IS INFINITE AND--
I TIRE OF YOUR DOUBTS! DO YOU WANT TO ABANDON OUR FATHER?!

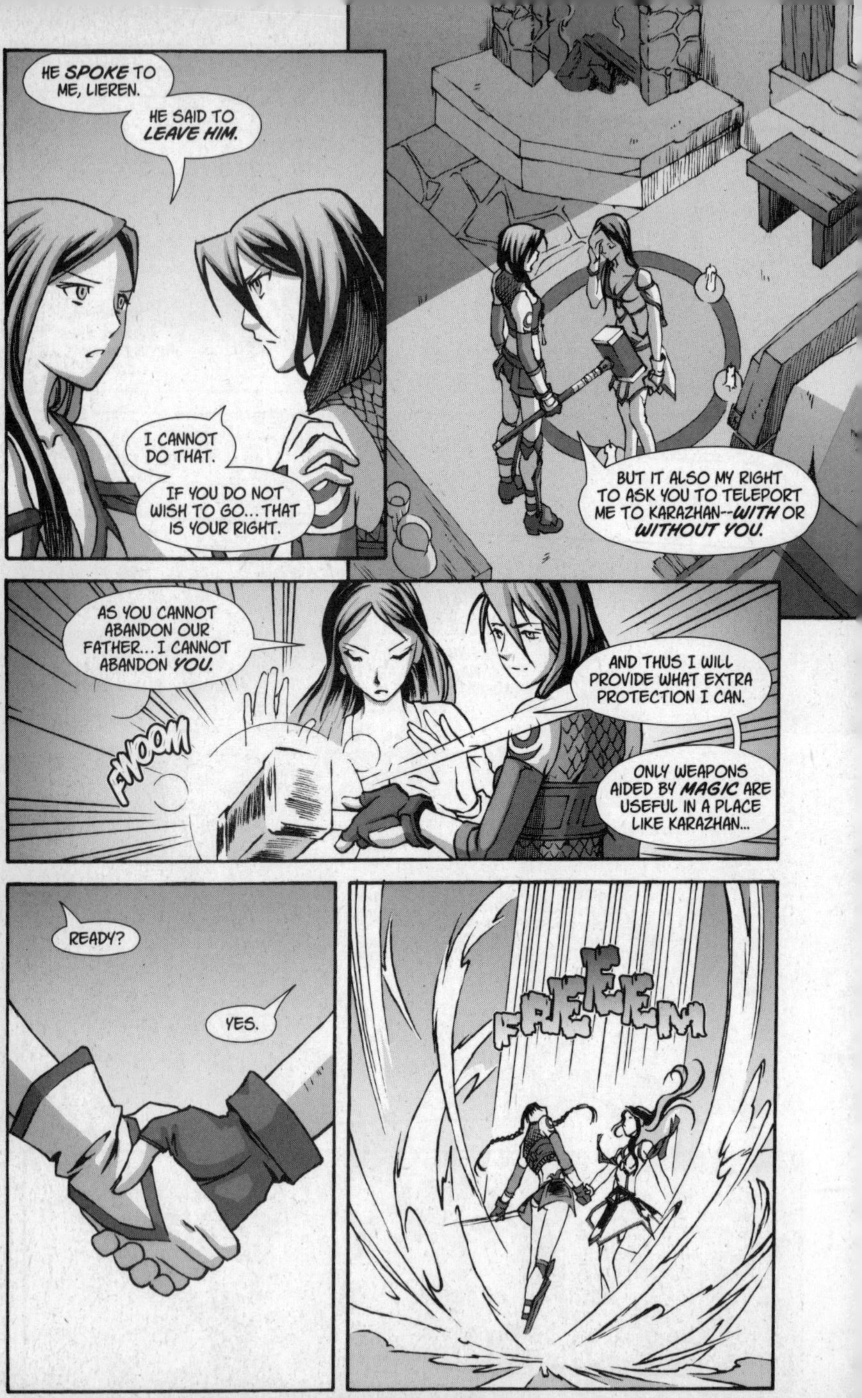
HE *SPOKE* TO ME, LIEREN.
HE SAID TO *LEAVE HIM.*
I CANNOT DO THAT.
IF YOU DO NOT WISH TO GO... THAT IS YOUR RIGHT.
BUT IT ALSO MY RIGHT TO ASK YOU TO TELEPORT ME TO KARAZHAN--*WITH* OR *WITHOUT YOU.*
AS YOU CANNOT ABANDON OUR FATHER... I CANNOT ABANDON *YOU.*
FWOOM
AND THUS I WILL PROVIDE WHAT EXTRA PROTECTION I CAN.
ONLY WEAPONS AIDED BY *MAGIC* ARE USEFUL IN A PLACE LIKE KARAZHAN...
READY?
YES.
FREEEEM

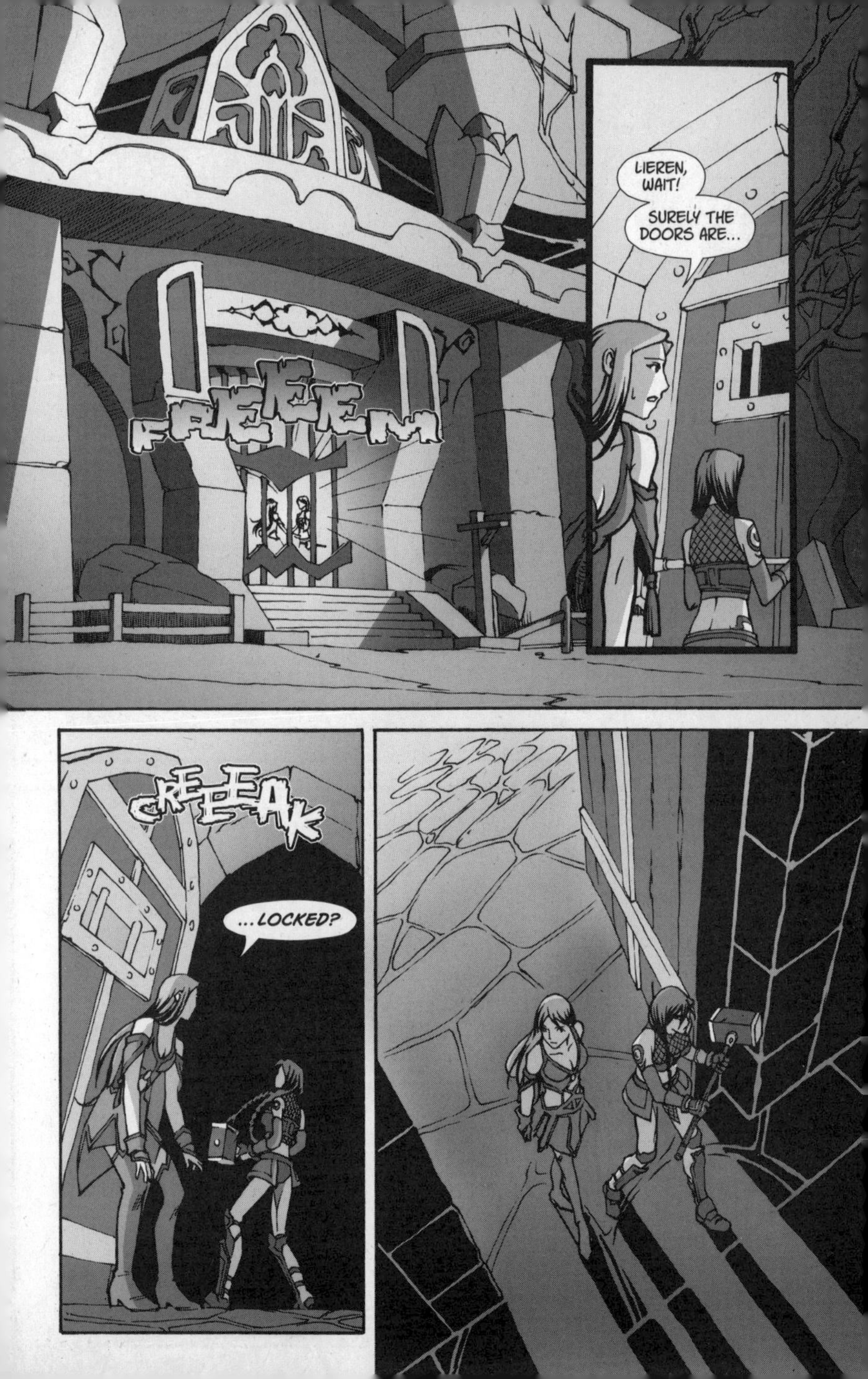
FREEEEEM
LIEREN, WAIT!
SURELY THE DOORS ARE...
CREEEEAK
...LOCKED?

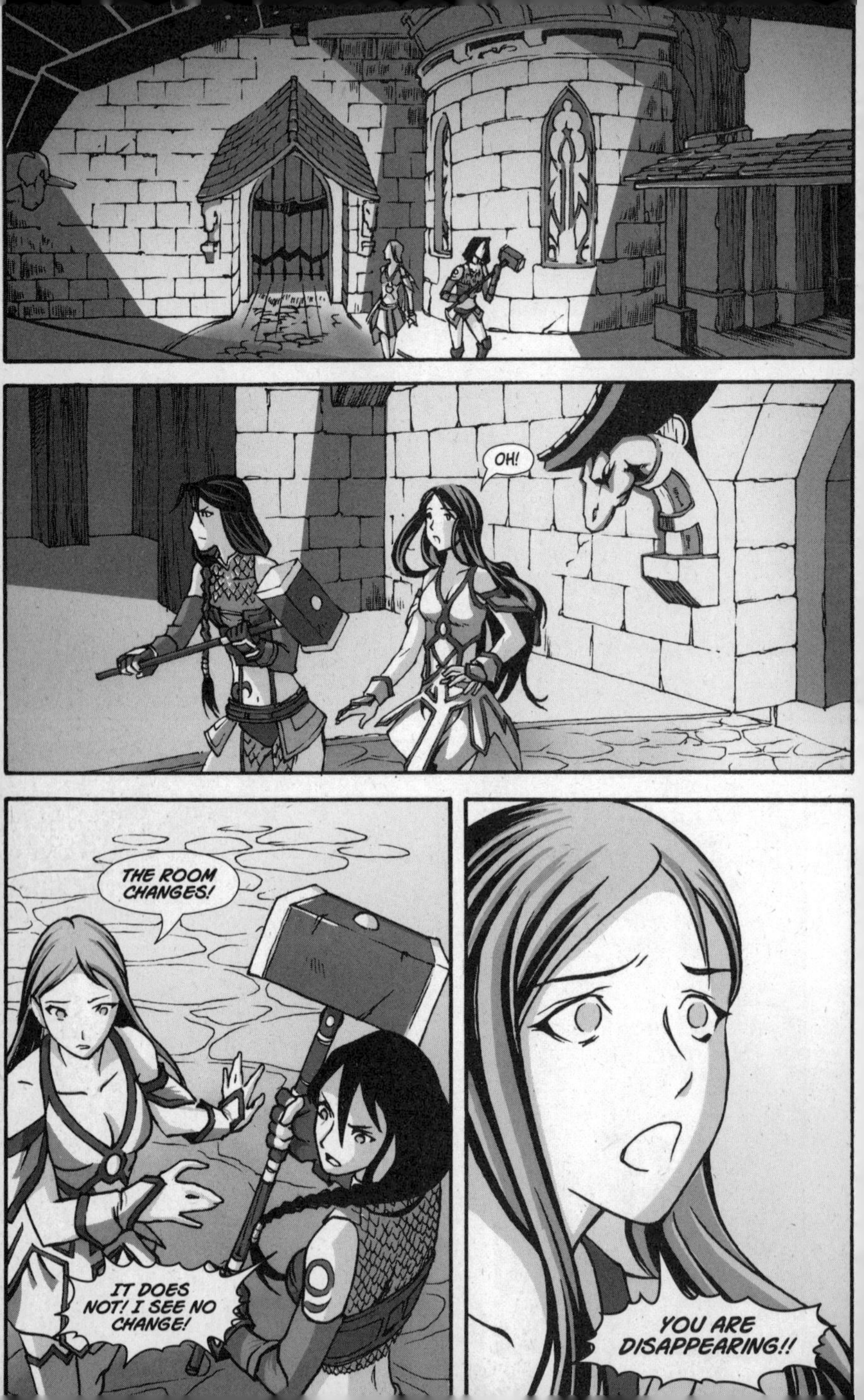
OH!
THE ROOM CHANGES!
IT DOES NOT! I SEE NO CHANGE!
YOU ARE DISAPPEARING!!

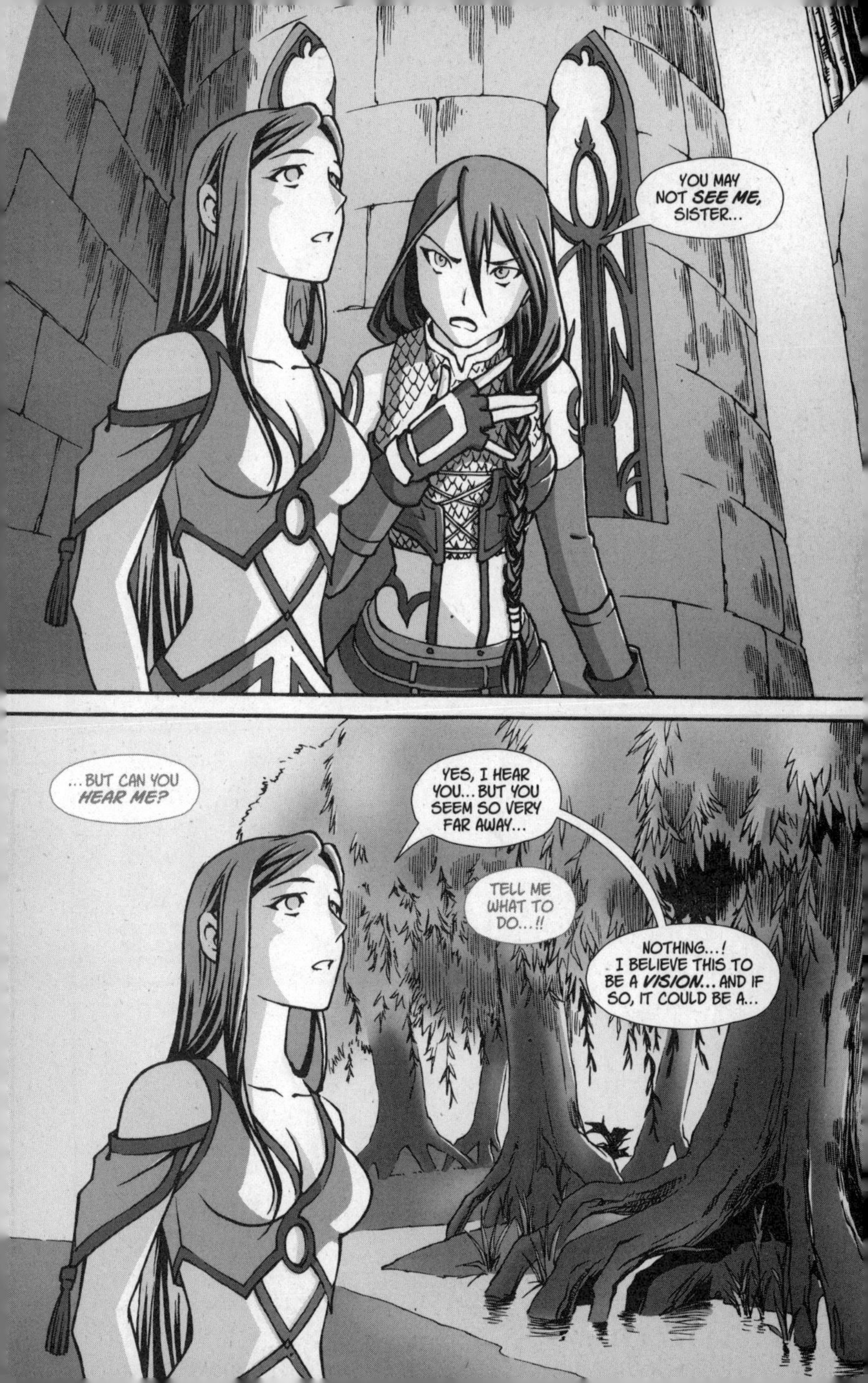
YOU MAY NOT SEE ME, SISTER...
...BUT CAN YOU HEAR ME?
YES, I HEAR YOU... BUT YOU SEEM SO VERY FAR AWAY...
TELL ME WHAT TO DO...!!
NOTHING...! I BELIEVE THIS TO BE A VISION... AND IF SO, IT COULD BE A...

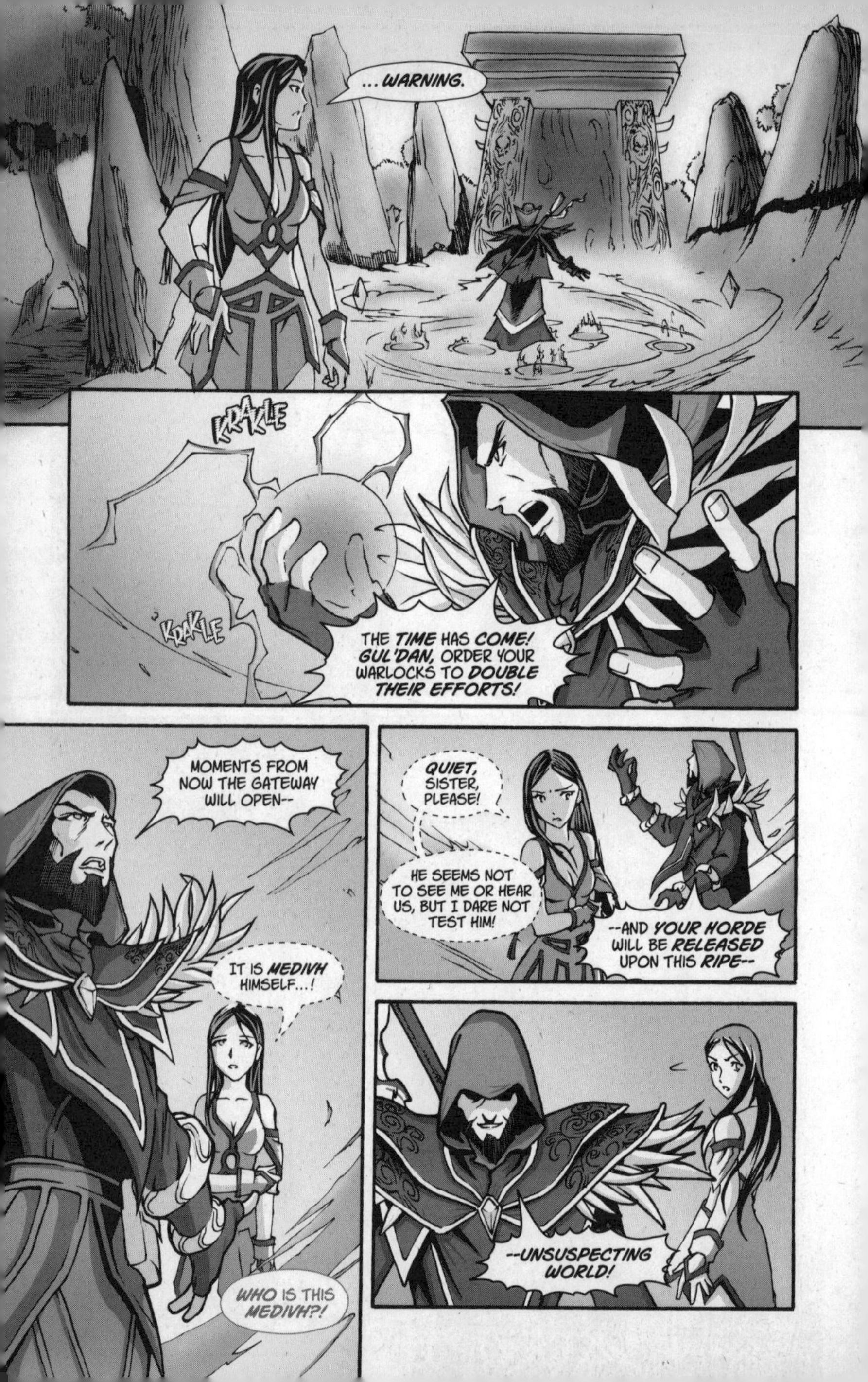

...WARNING.
KRAKLE
KRAKLE
THE TIME HAS COME! GUL'DAN, ORDER YOUR WARLOCKS TO DOUBLE THEIR EFFORTS!
MOMENTS FROM NOW THE GATEWAY WILL OPEN--
IT IS MEDIVH HIMSELF...!
WHO IS THIS MEDIVH?!
QUIET, SISTER, PLEASE!
HE SEEMS NOT TO SEE ME OR HEAR US, BUT I DARE NOT TEST HIM!
--AND YOUR HORDE WILL BE RELEASED UPON THIS RIPE--
--UNSUSPECTING WORLD!

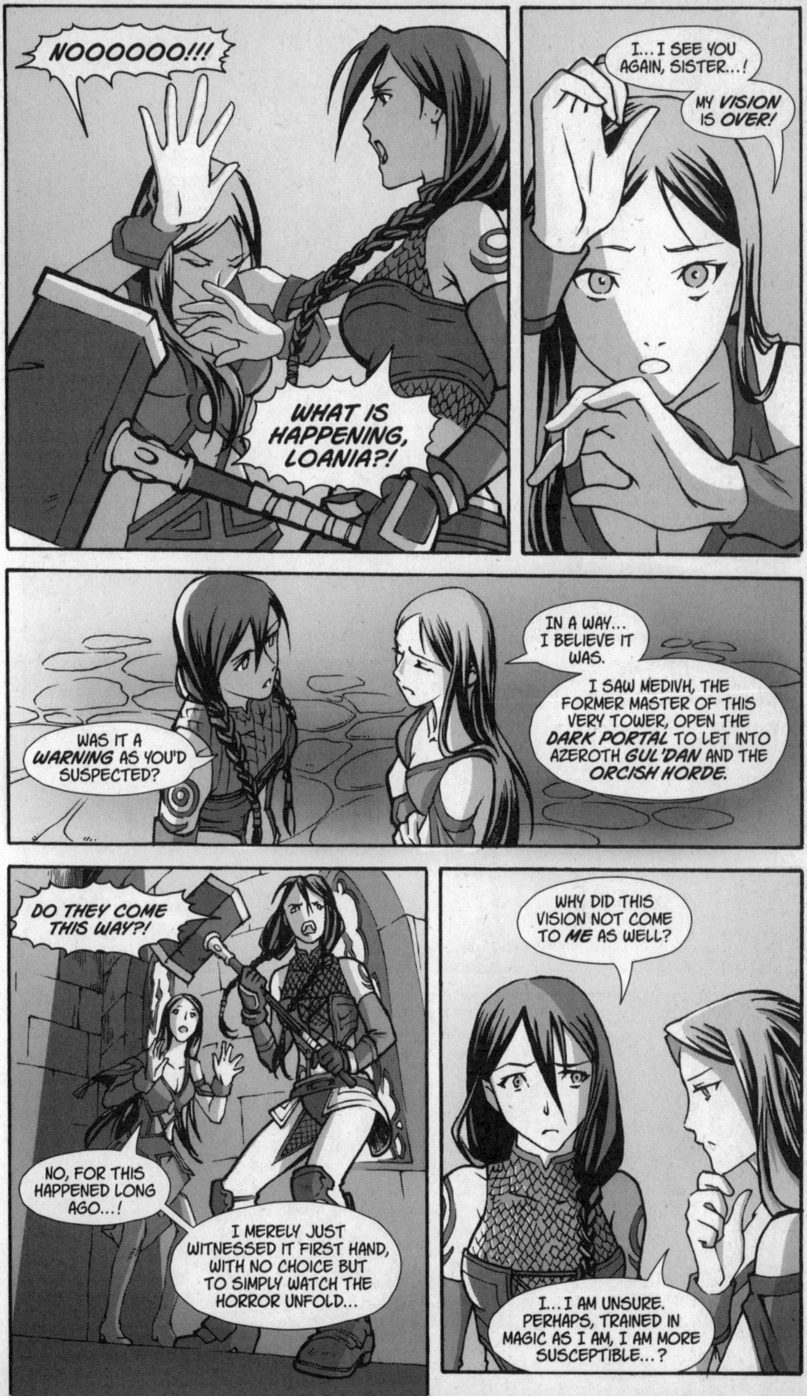
NOOOOOO!!!
WHAT IS HAPPENING, LOANIA?!
I... I SEE YOU AGAIN, SISTER...!
MY VISION IS OVER!
WAS IT A WARNING AS YOU'D SUSPECTED?
IN A WAY... I BELIEVE IT WAS.
I SAW MEDIVH, THE FORMER MASTER OF THIS VERY TOWER, OPEN THE DARK PORTAL TO LET INTO AZEROTH GUL'DAN AND THE ORCISH HORDE.
DO THEY COME THIS WAY?!
NO, FOR THIS HAPPENED LONG AGO...!
I MERELY JUST WITNESSED IT FIRST HAND, WITH NO CHOICE BUT TO SIMPLY WATCH THE HORROR UNFOLD...
WHY DID THIS VISION NOT COME TO ME AS WELL?
I... I AM UNSURE. PERHAPS, TRAINED IN MAGIC AS I AM, I AM MORE SUSCEPTIBLE...?

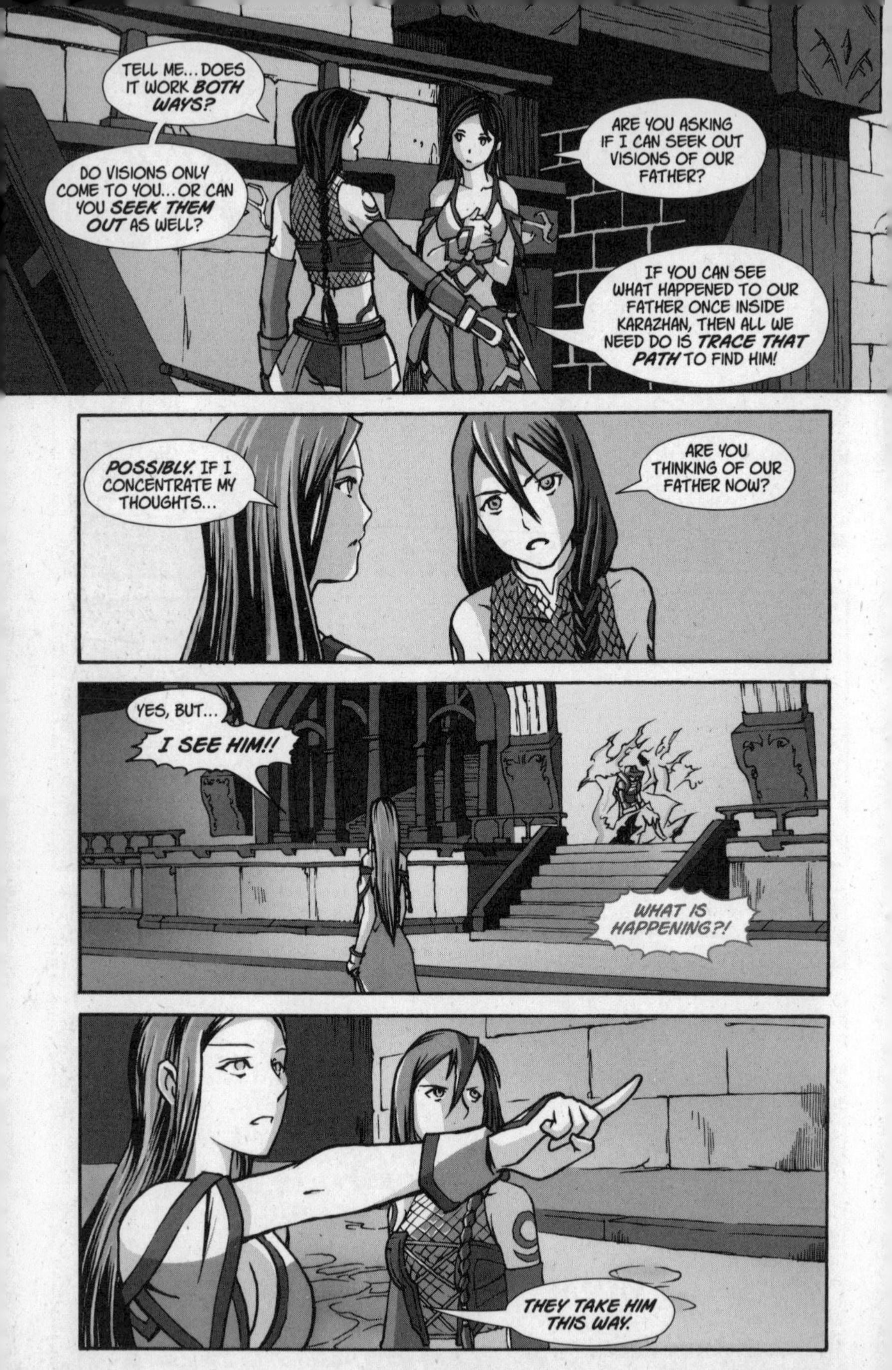
TELL ME... DOES IT WORK BOTH WAYS?
DO VISIONS ONLY COME TO YOU... OR CAN YOU SEEK THEM OUT AS WELL?
ARE YOU ASKING IF I CAN SEEK OUT VISIONS OF OUR FATHER?
IF YOU CAN SEE WHAT HAPPENED TO OUR FATHER ONCE INSIDE KARAZHAN, THEN ALL WE NEED DO IS TRACE THAT PATH TO FIND HIM!
POSSIBLY. IF I CONCENTRATE MY THOUGHTS...
ARE YOU THINKING OF OUR FATHER NOW?
YES, BUT...
I SEE HIM!!
WHAT IS HAPPENING?!
THEY TAKE HIM THIS WAY.

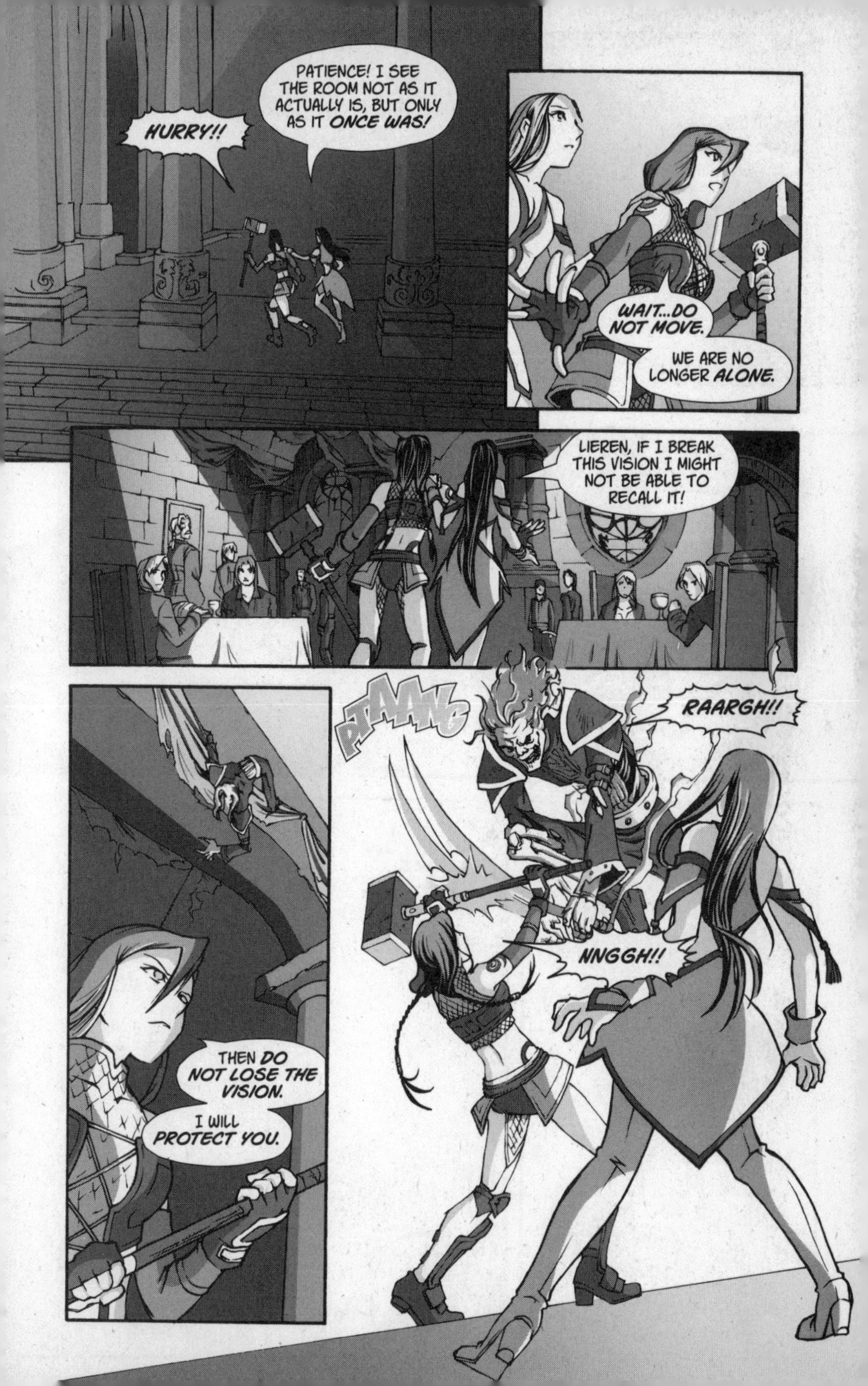
HURRY!!
PATIENCE! I SEE THE ROOM NOT AS IT ACTUALLY IS, BUT ONLY AS IT ONCE WAS!
WAIT...DO NOT MOVE.
WE ARE NO LONGER ALONE.
LIEREN, IF I BREAK THIS VISION I MIGHT NOT BE ABLE TO RECALL IT!
THEN DO NOT LOSE THE VISION.
I WILL PROTECT YOU.
PTAAANG
RAARGH!!
NNGGH!!

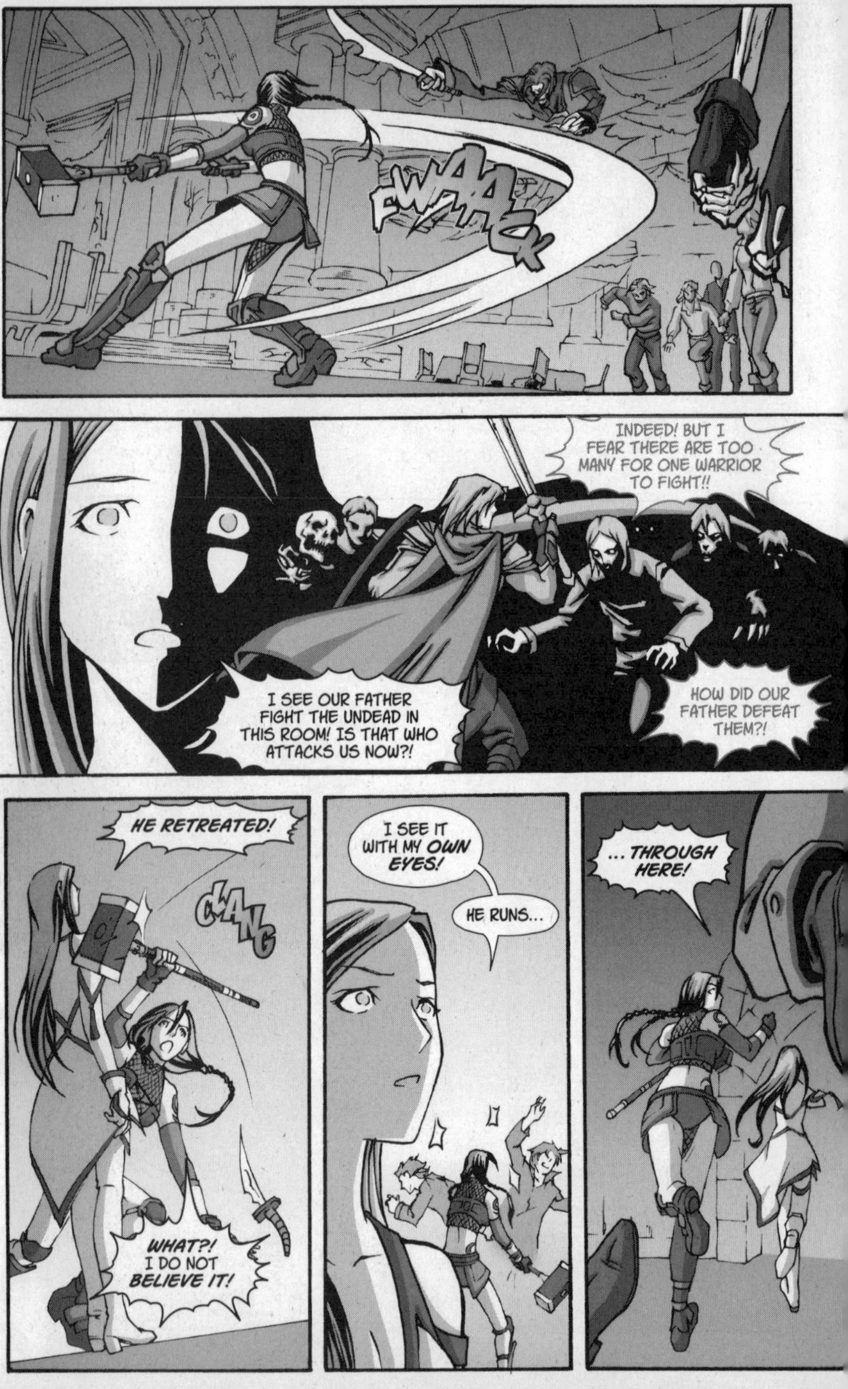
FWAAACK
I SEE OUR FATHER FIGHT THE UNDEAD IN THIS ROOM! IS THAT WHO ATTACKS US NOW?!
INDEED! BUT I FEAR THERE ARE TOO MANY FOR ONE WARRIOR TO FIGHT!!
HOW DID OUR FATHER DEFEAT THEM?!
HE RETREATED!
CLANG
WHAT?! I DO NOT *BELIEVE IT!*
I SEE IT WITH MY *OWN EYES!*
HE RUNS...
...THROUGH HERE!

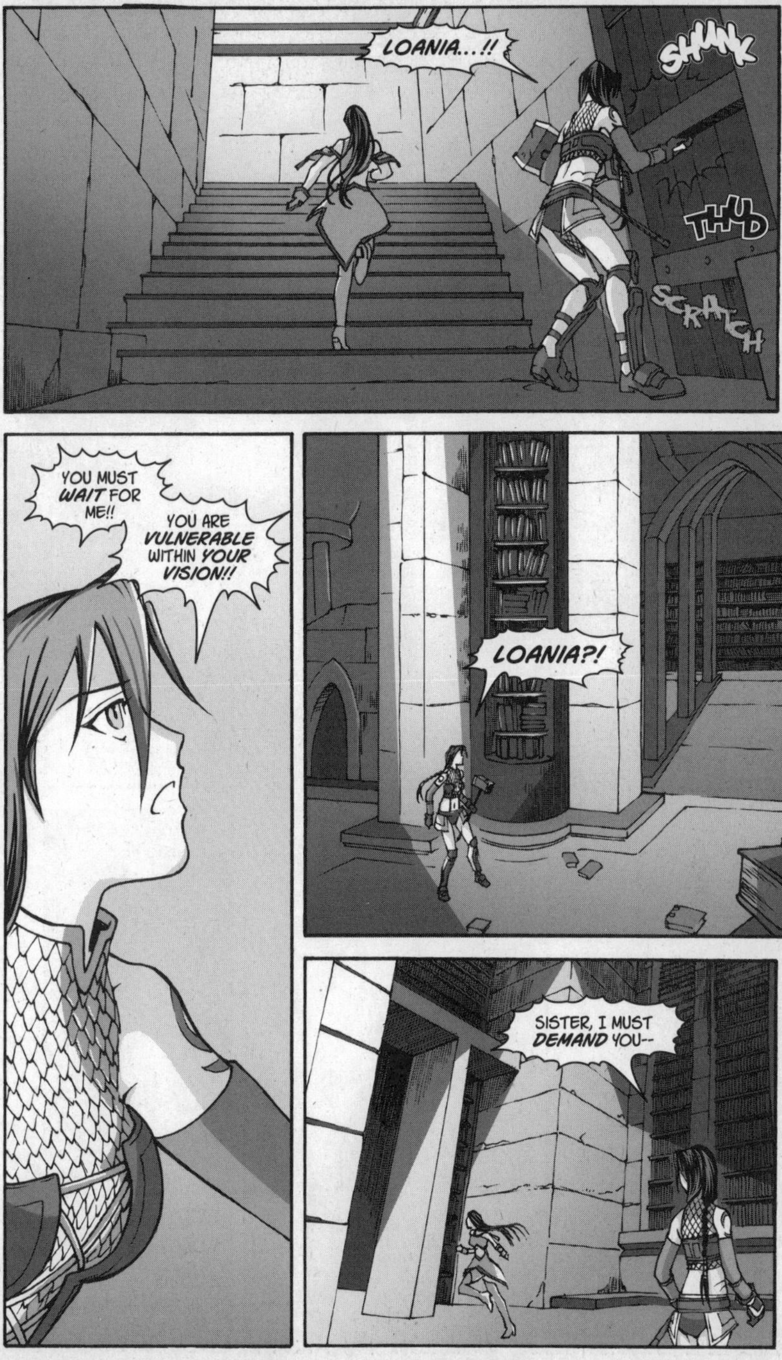
LOANIA...!!
SHUNK
THUD
SCRATCH
YOU MUST WAIT FOR ME!!
YOU ARE VULNERABLE WITHIN YOUR VISION!!
LOANIA?!
SISTER, I MUST DEMAND YOU--

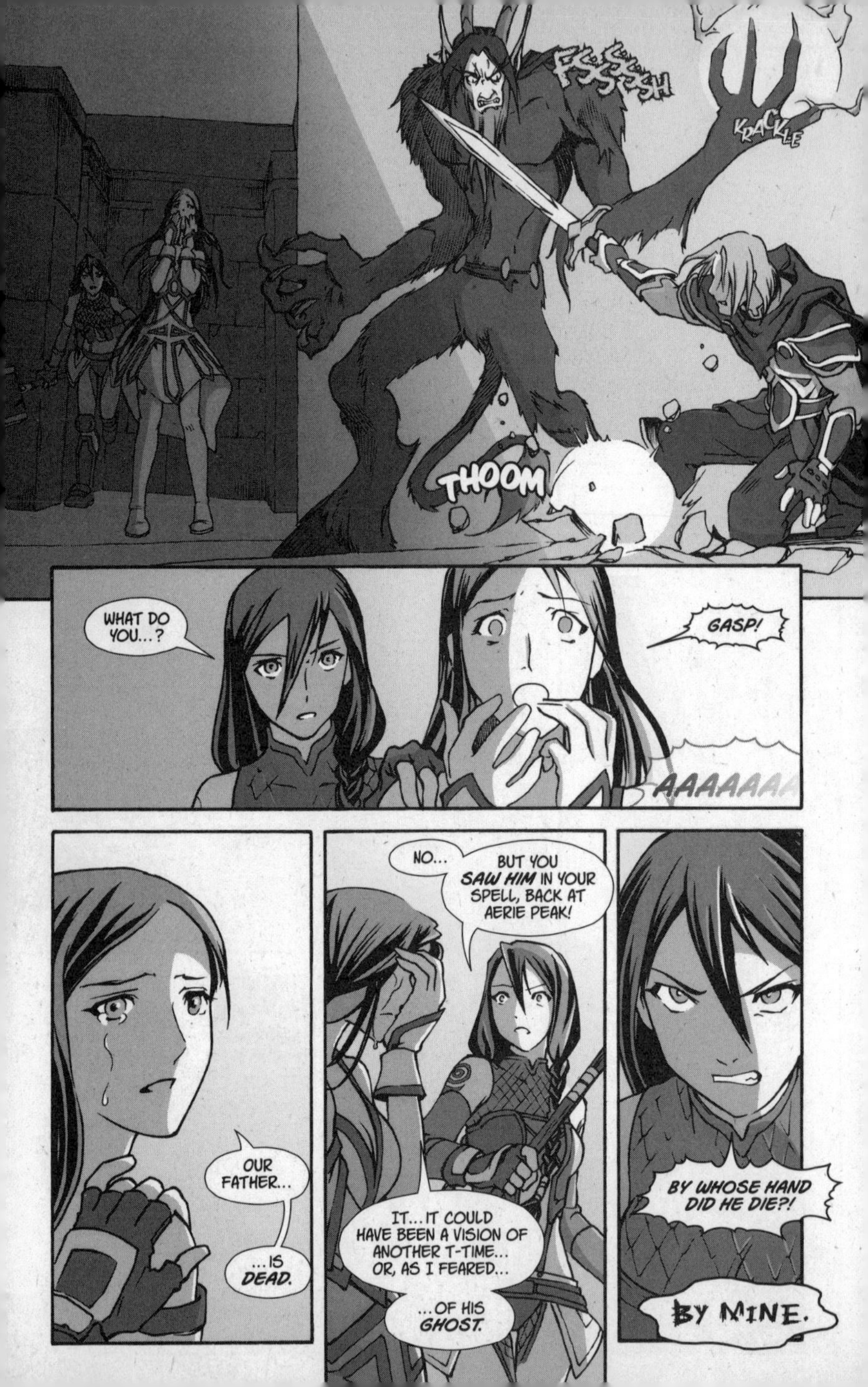
FSSSSSH
KRACKLE
THOOM
WHAT DO YOU...?
GASP!
AAAAAAA
OUR FATHER...
...IS *DEAD.*
NO...
BUT YOU *SAW HIM* IN YOUR SPELL, BACK AT AERIE PEAK!
IT... IT COULD HAVE BEEN A VISION OF ANOTHER T-TIME... OR, AS I FEARED...
...OF HIS *GHOST.*
BY WHOSE HAND DID HE DIE?!
BY MINE.

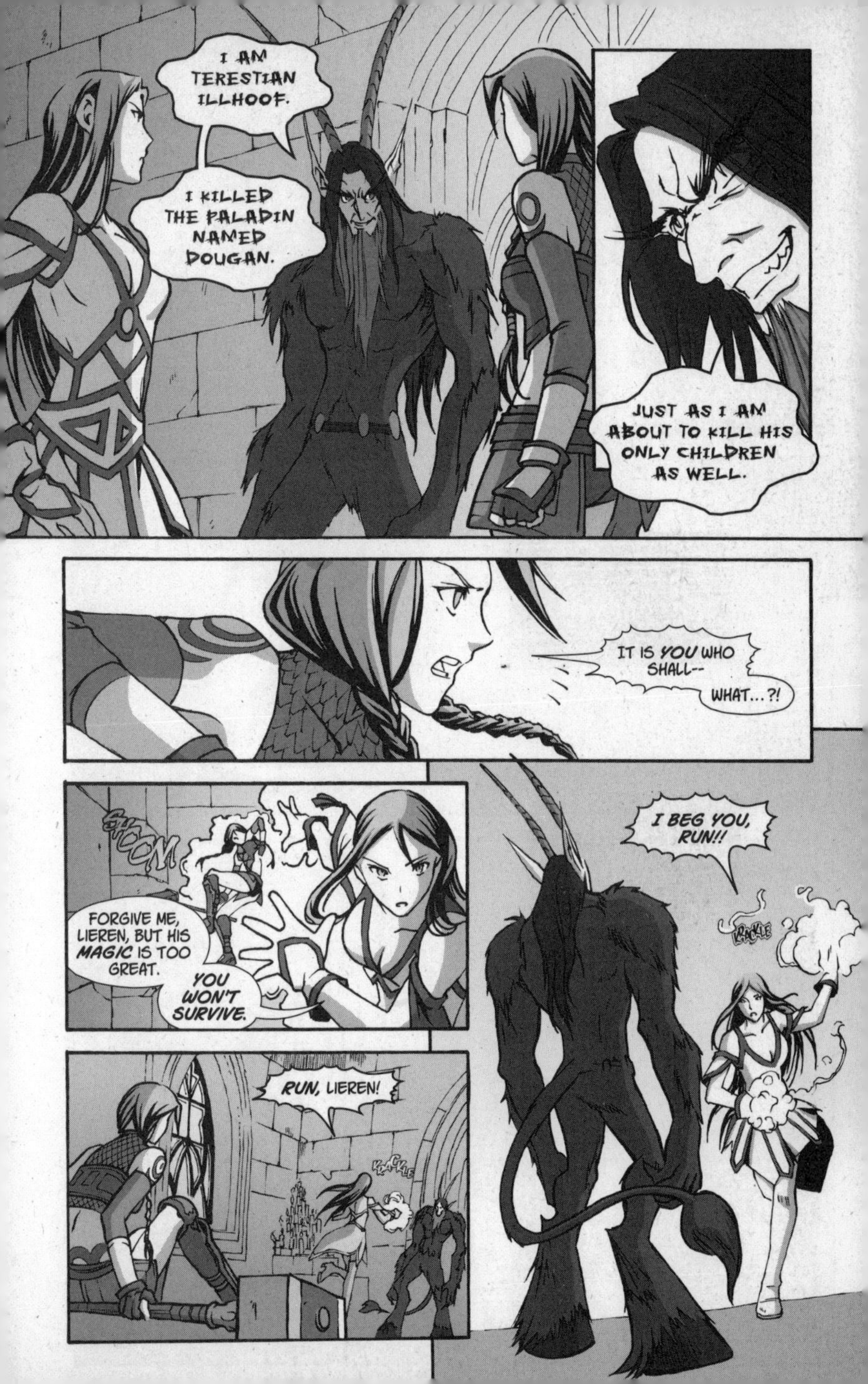
I AM TERESTIAN ILLHOOF.
I KILLED THE PALADIN NAMED DOUGAN.
JUST AS I AM ABOUT TO KILL HIS ONLY CHILDREN AS WELL.
IT IS *YOU* WHO SHALL--
WHAT...?!
SHOOM
FORGIVE ME, LIEREN, BUT HIS *MAGIC* IS TOO GREAT.
YOU WON'T SURVIVE.
RUN, LIEREN!
KRACKLE
I BEG YOU, RUN!!
KRACKLE

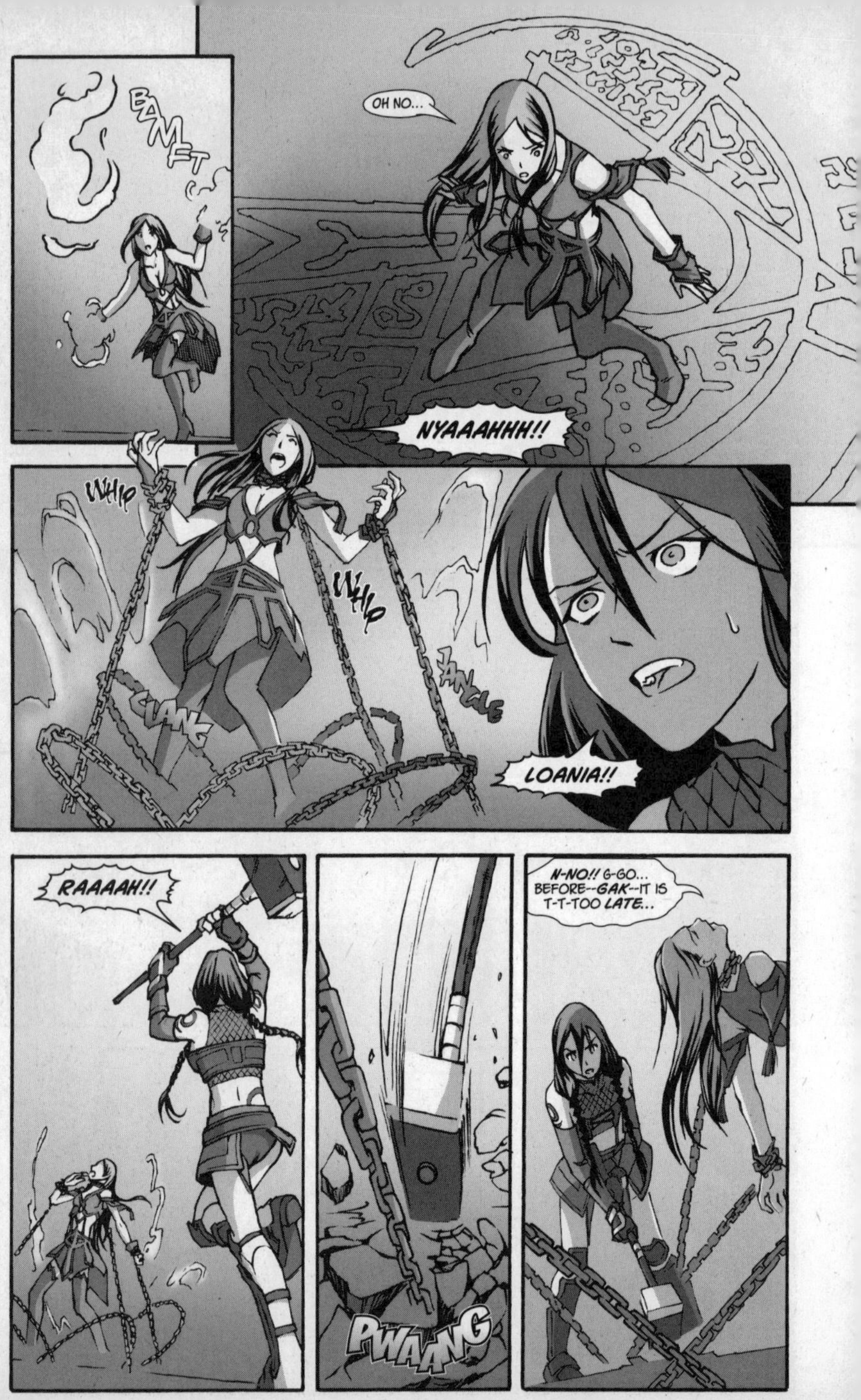
BAMFT
OH NO...
NYAAAHHH!!
WHIP
WHIP
JANGLE
CLANK
LOANIA!!
RAAAAH!!
PWAAANG
N-NO!! G-GO... BEFORE--GAK--IT IS T-T-TOO LATE...

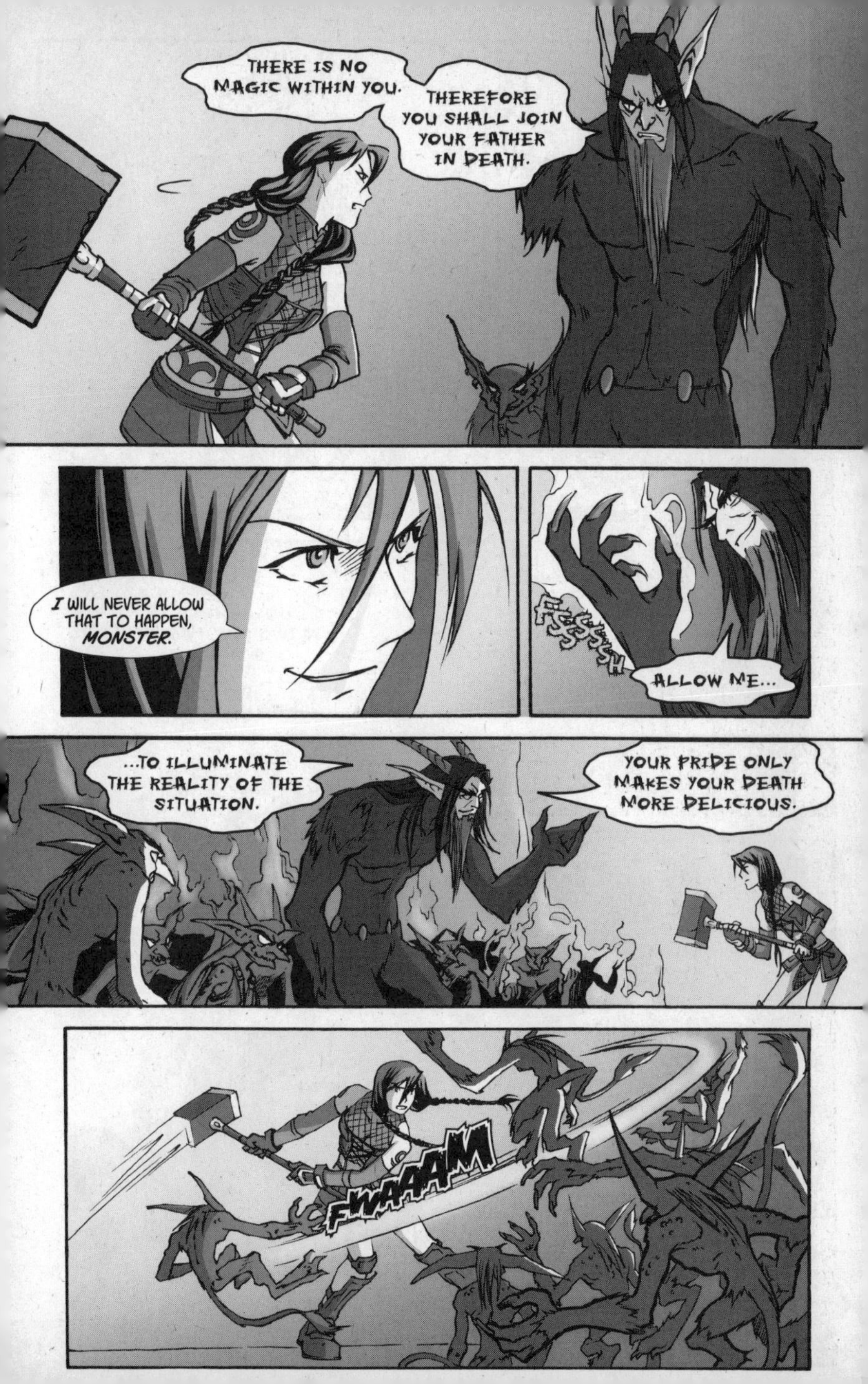
THERE IS NO MAGIC WITHIN YOU.
THEREFORE YOU SHALL JOIN YOUR FATHER IN DEATH.
I WILL NEVER ALLOW THAT TO HAPPEN, MONSTER.
FSSSSH
ALLOW ME...
...TO ILLUMINATE THE REALITY OF THE SITUATION.
YOUR PRIDE ONLY MAKES YOUR DEATH MORE DELICIOUS.
FWAAAM

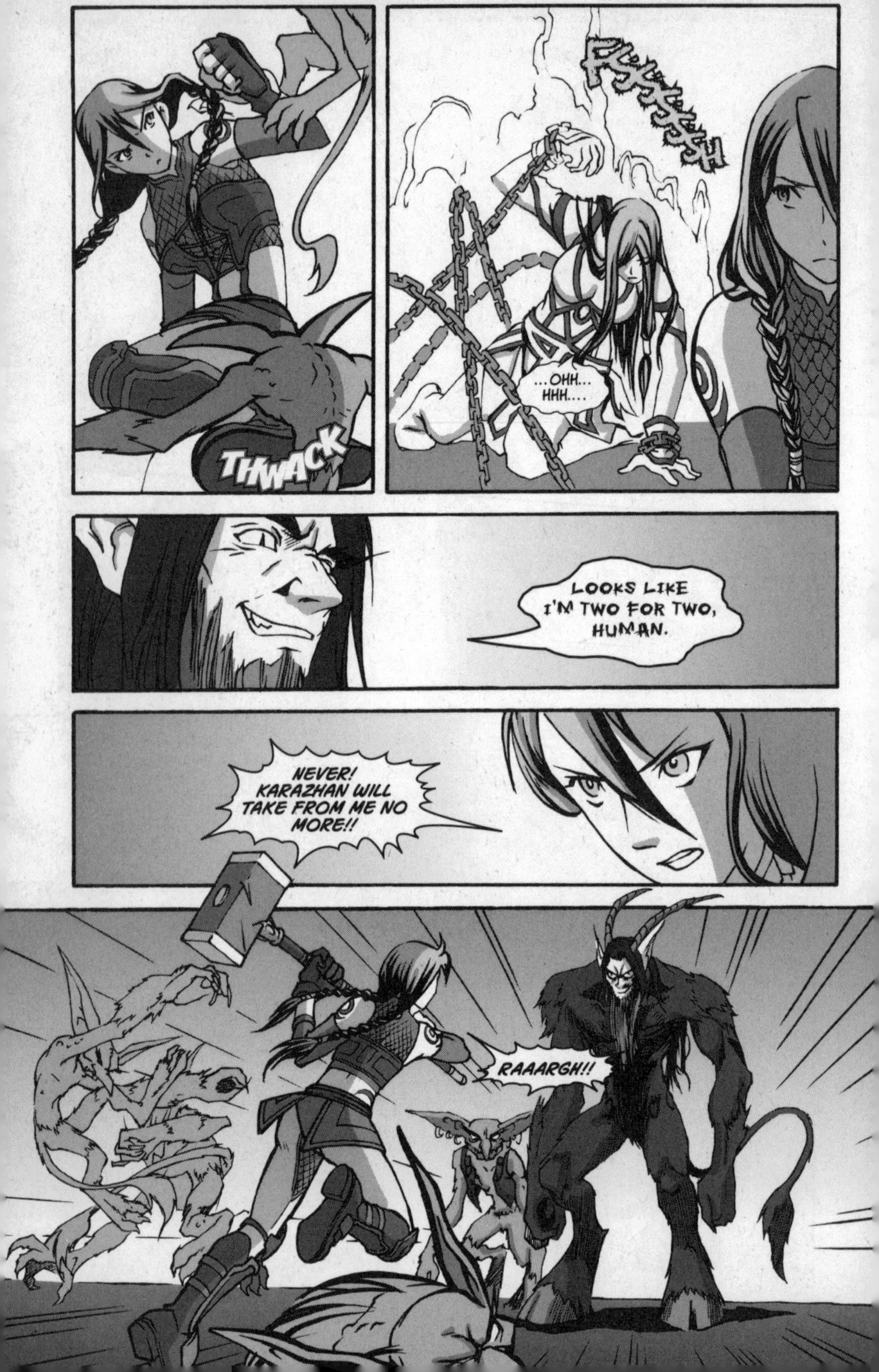
THWACK
PKSSSSH
...OHH... HHH....
LOOKS LIKE I'M TWO FOR TWO, HUMAN.
NEVER! KARAZHAN WILL TAKE FROM ME NO MORE!!
RAAARGH!!

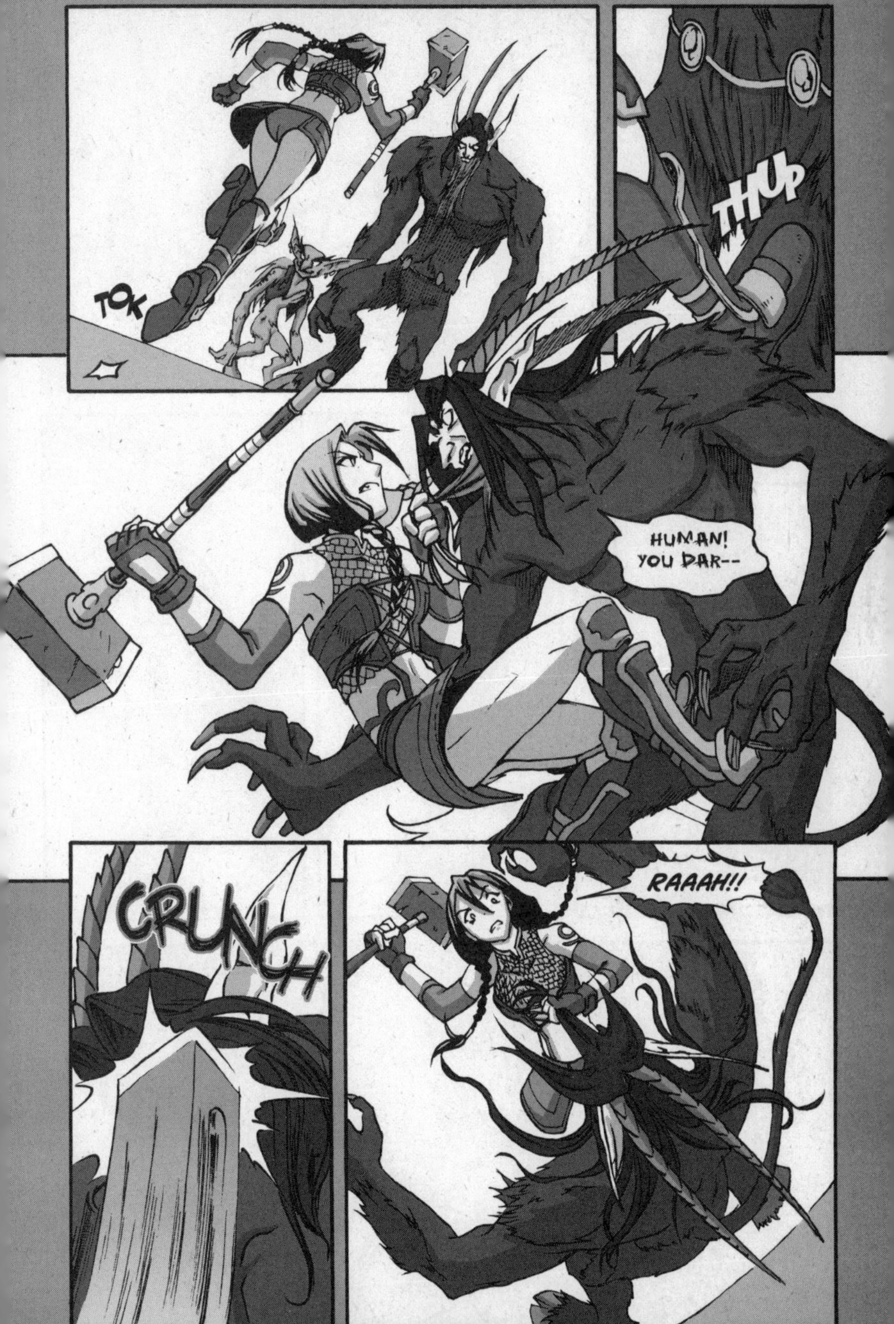
TOK
THUP
HUMAN! YOU DAR--
CRUNCH
RAAAH!!

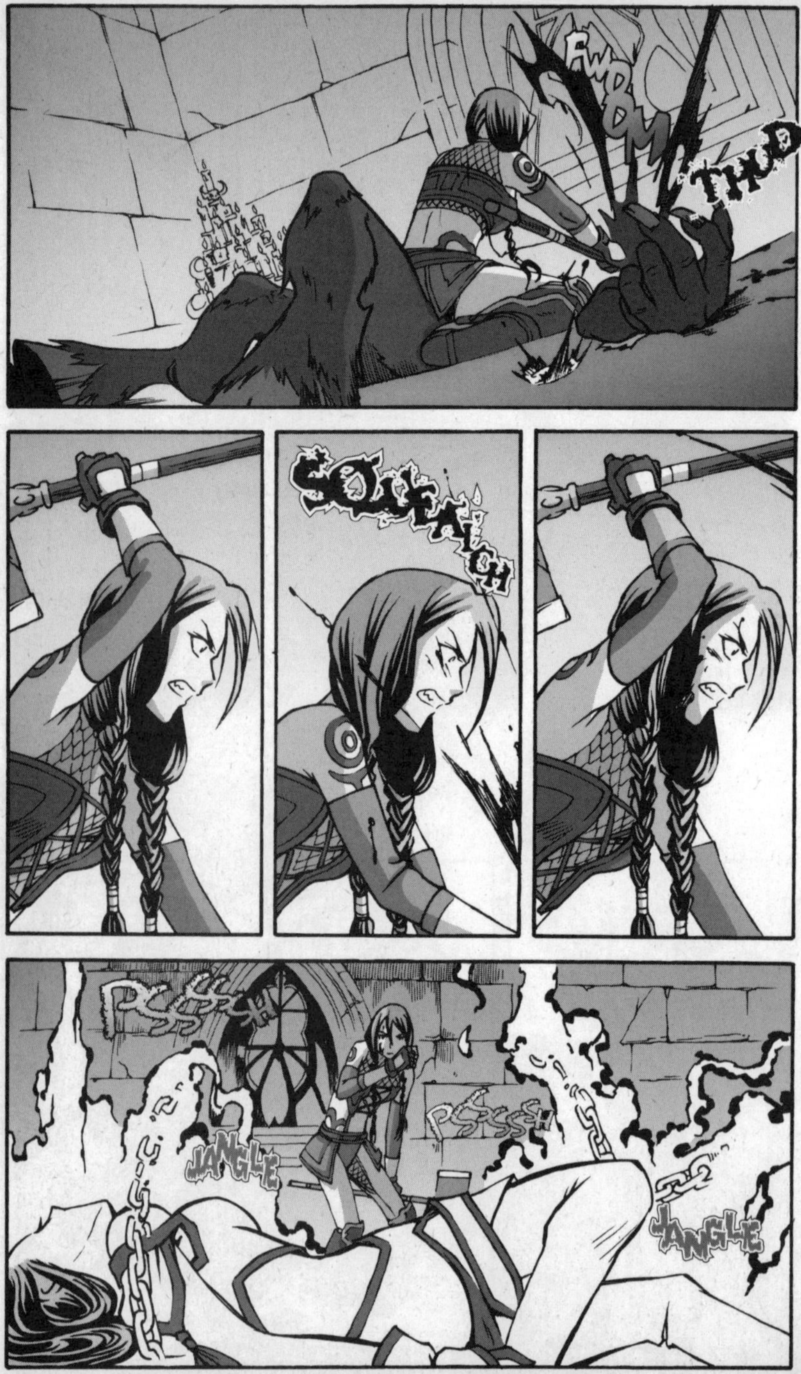
FWOOM
THUD
SQUELCH
PSSSH
JANGLE
PSSSH
JANGLE

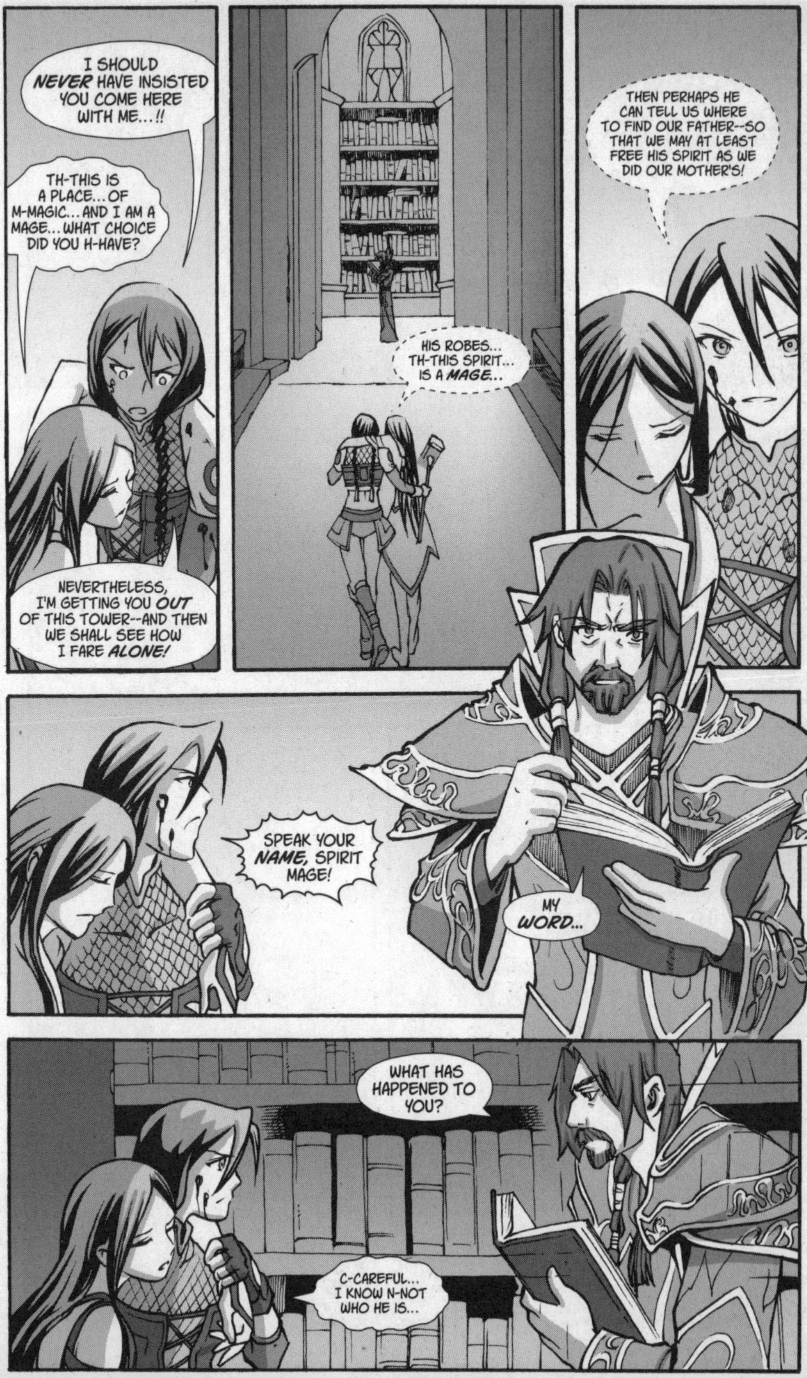
I SHOULD NEVER HAVE INSISTED YOU COME HERE WITH ME...!!
TH-THIS IS A PLACE... OF M-MAGIC... AND I AM A MAGE... WHAT CHOICE DID YOU H-HAVE?
NEVERTHELESS, I'M GETTING YOU OUT OF THIS TOWER--AND THEN WE SHALL SEE HOW I FARE ALONE!
HIS ROBES... TH-THIS SPIRIT... IS A MAGE...
THEN PERHAPS HE CAN TELL US WHERE TO FIND OUR FATHER--SO THAT WE MAY AT LEAST FREE HIS SPIRIT AS WE DID OUR MOTHER'S!
SPEAK YOUR NAME, SPIRIT MAGE!
MY WORD...
WHAT HAS HAPPENED TO YOU?
C-CAREFUL... I KNOW N-NOT WHO HE IS...

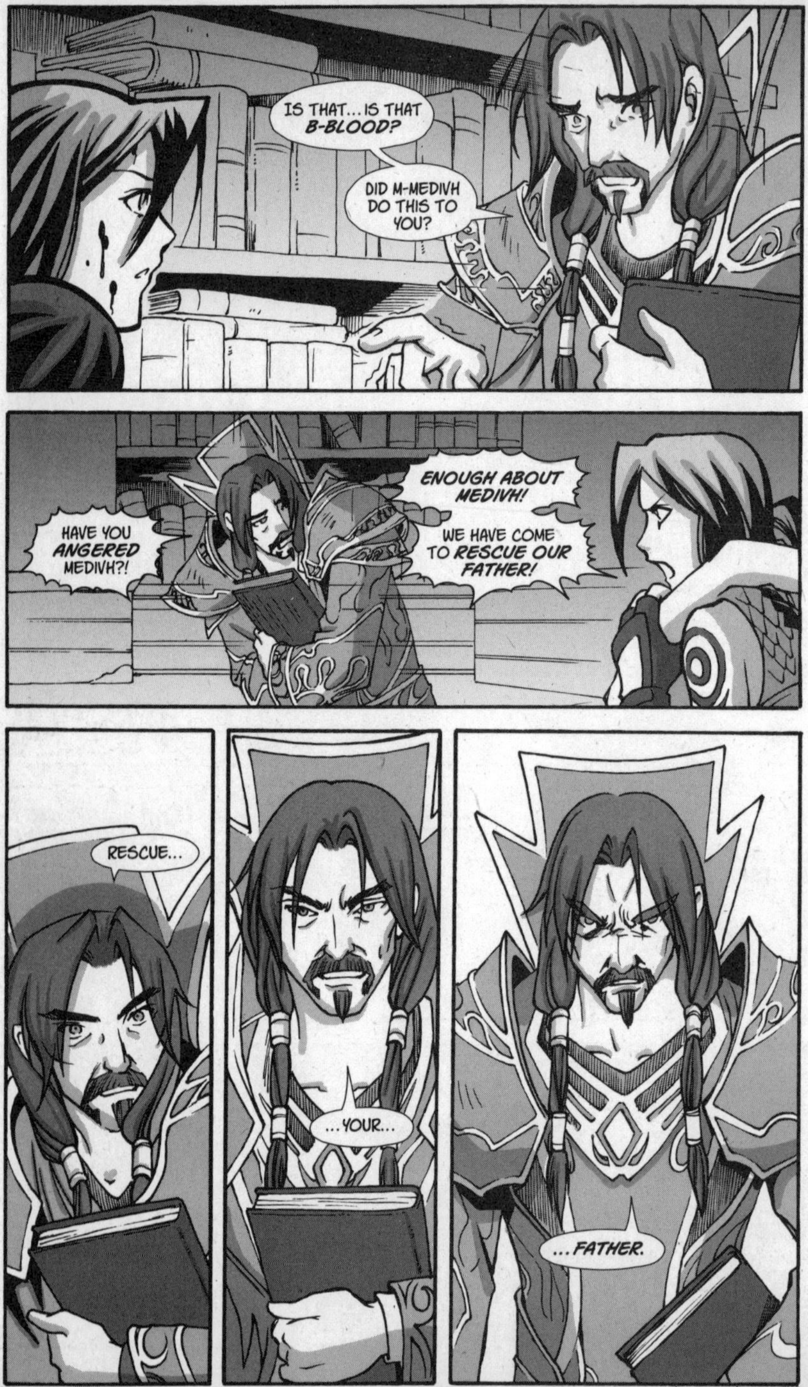
IS THAT... IS THAT *B-BLOOD?*
DID M-MEDIVH DO THIS TO YOU?
HAVE YOU *ANGERED* MEDIVH?!
ENOUGH ABOUT MEDIVH!
WE HAVE COME TO *RESCUE OUR FATHER!*
RESCUE...
...YOUR...
...*FATHER.*

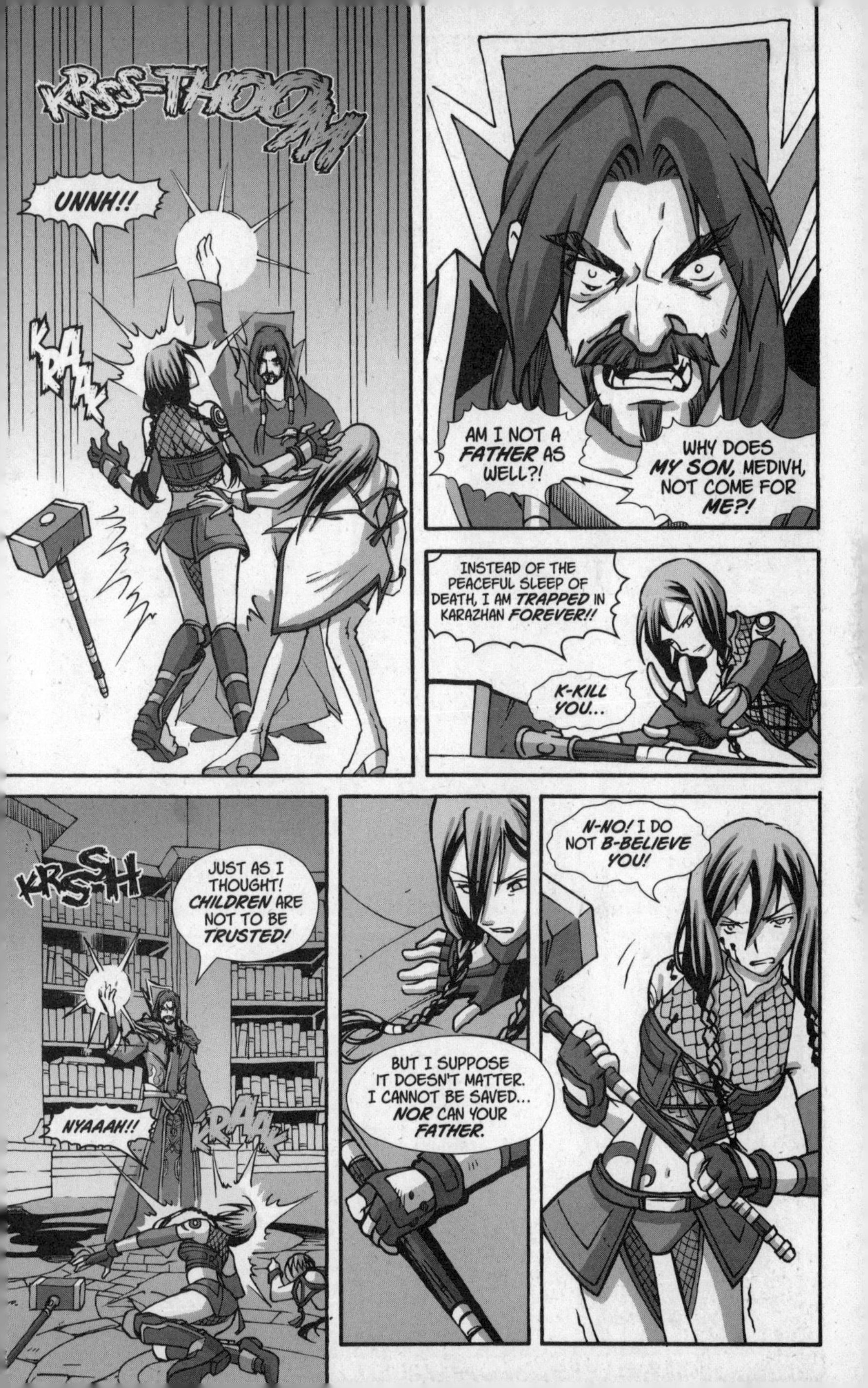
KRSS-THOOM
UNNH!!
KRAAK
AM I NOT A FATHER AS WELL?!
WHY DOES MY SON, MEDIVH, NOT COME FOR ME?!
INSTEAD OF THE PEACEFUL SLEEP OF DEATH, I AM TRAPPED IN KARAZHAN FOREVER!!
K-KILL YOU...
KRSSH
JUST AS I THOUGHT! CHILDREN ARE NOT TO BE TRUSTED!
NYAAAH!!
KRAAK
BUT I SUPPOSE IT DOESN'T MATTER. I CANNOT BE SAVED... NOR CAN YOUR FATHER.
N-NO! I DO NOT B-BELIEVE YOU!

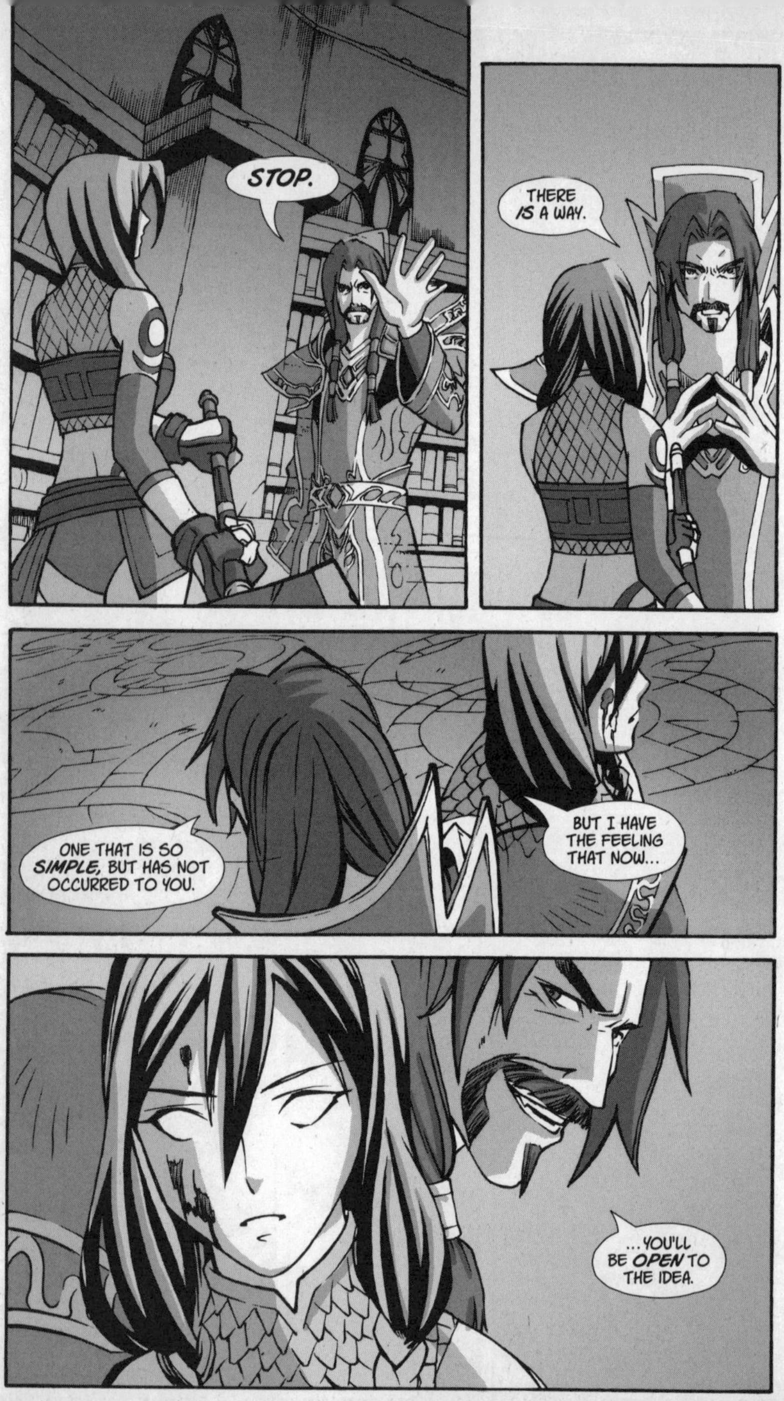
STOP.
THERE *IS* A WAY.
ONE THAT IS SO *SIMPLE,* BUT HAS NOT OCCURRED TO YOU.
BUT I HAVE THE FEELING THAT NOW...
...YOU'LL BE *OPEN* TO THE IDEA.

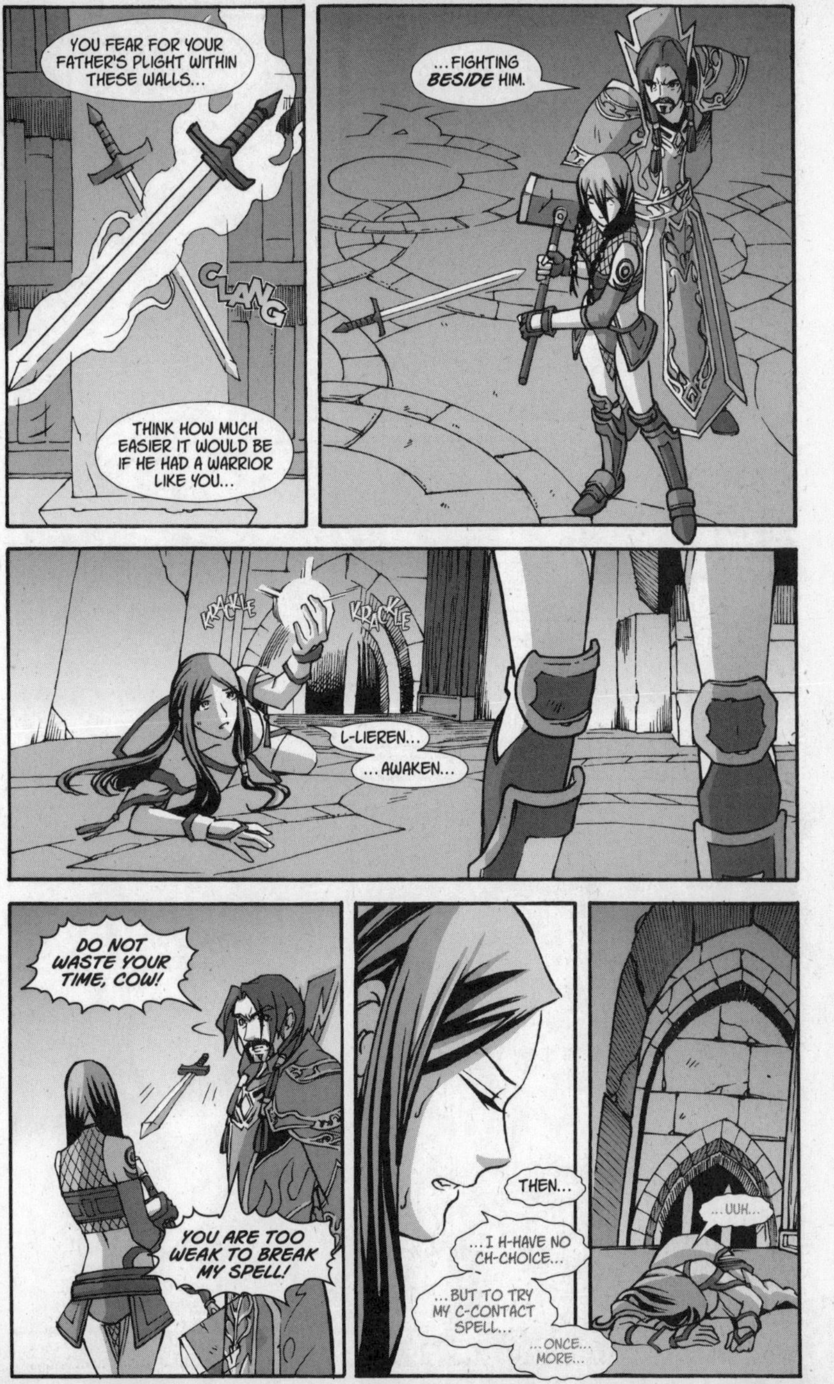
YOU FEAR FOR YOUR FATHER'S PLIGHT WITHIN THESE WALLS...
CLANG
THINK HOW MUCH EASIER IT WOULD BE IF HE HAD A WARRIOR LIKE YOU...
...FIGHTING **BESIDE** HIM.
KRACKLE
KRACKLE
L-LIEREN...
...AWAKEN...
DO NOT WASTE YOUR TIME, COW!
YOU ARE TOO WEAK TO BREAK MY SPELL!
THEN...
...I H-HAVE NO CH-CHOICE...
...BUT TO TRY MY C-CONTACT SPELL...
...ONCE... MORE...
...UUH...

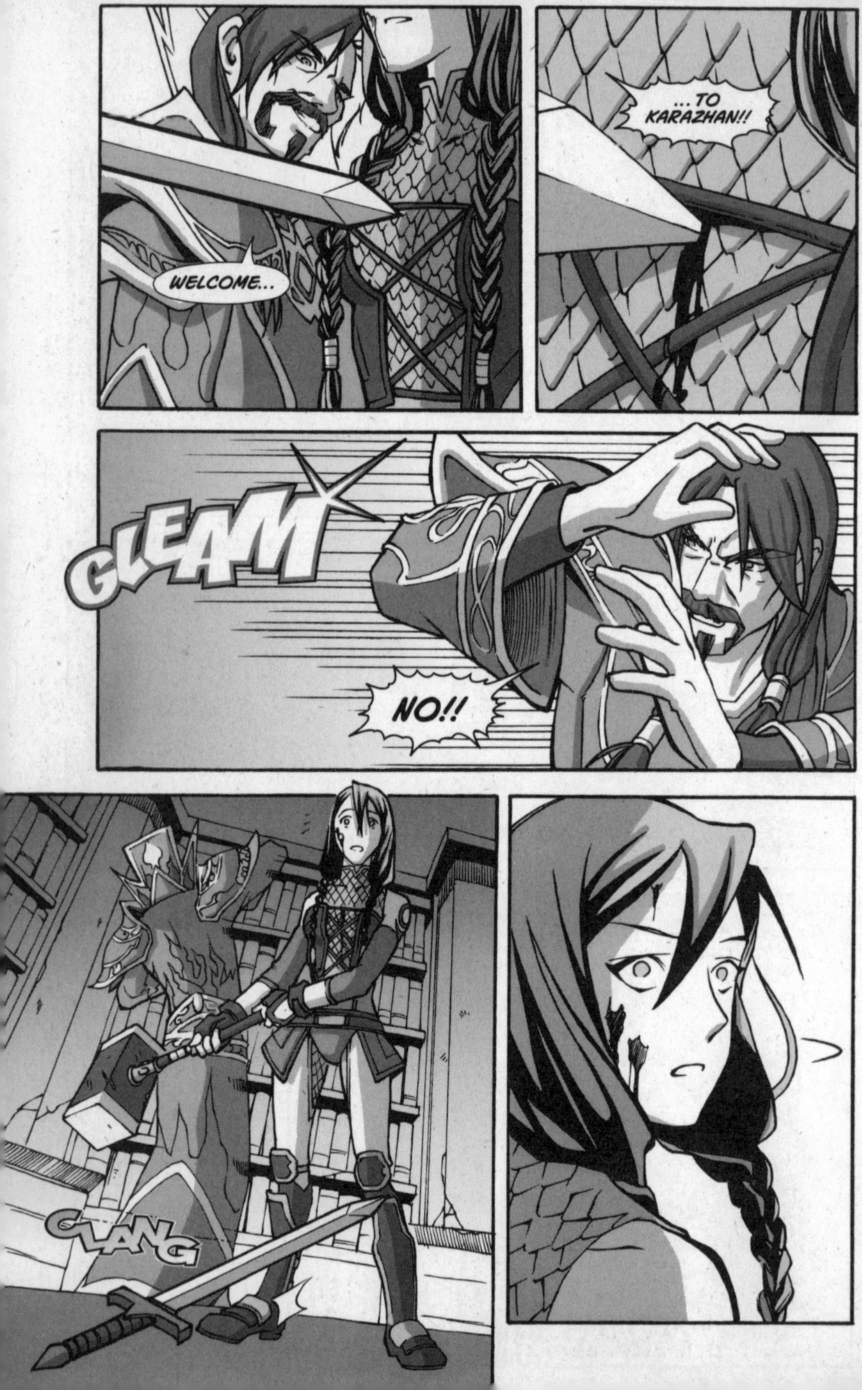
WELCOME...
...TO KARAZHAN!!
GLEAM
NO!!
CLANG

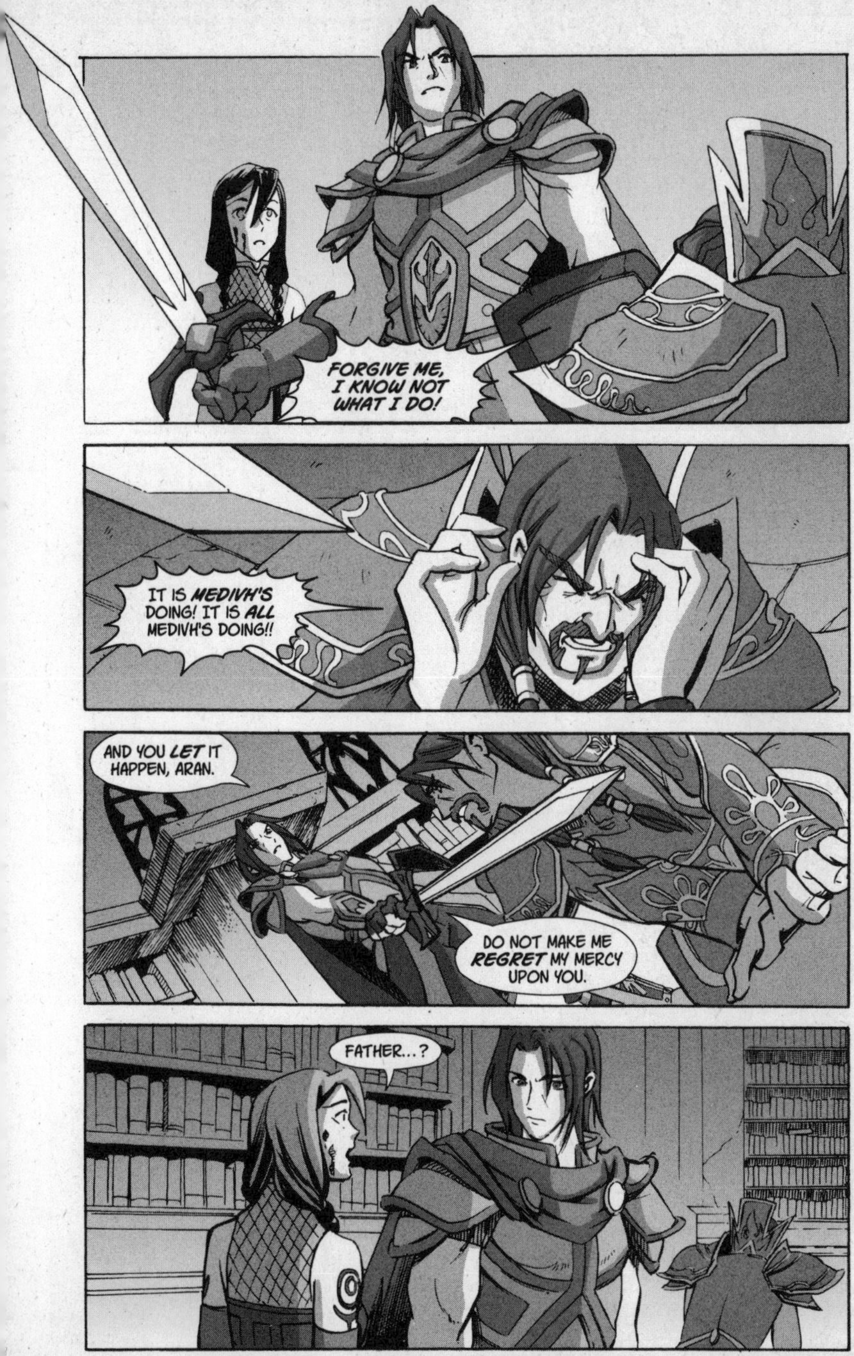
FORGIVE ME, I KNOW NOT WHAT I DO!
IT IS MEDIVH'S DOING! IT IS ALL MEDIVH'S DOING!!
AND YOU LET IT HAPPEN, ARAN.
DO NOT MAKE ME REGRET MY MERCY UPON YOU.
FATHER...?

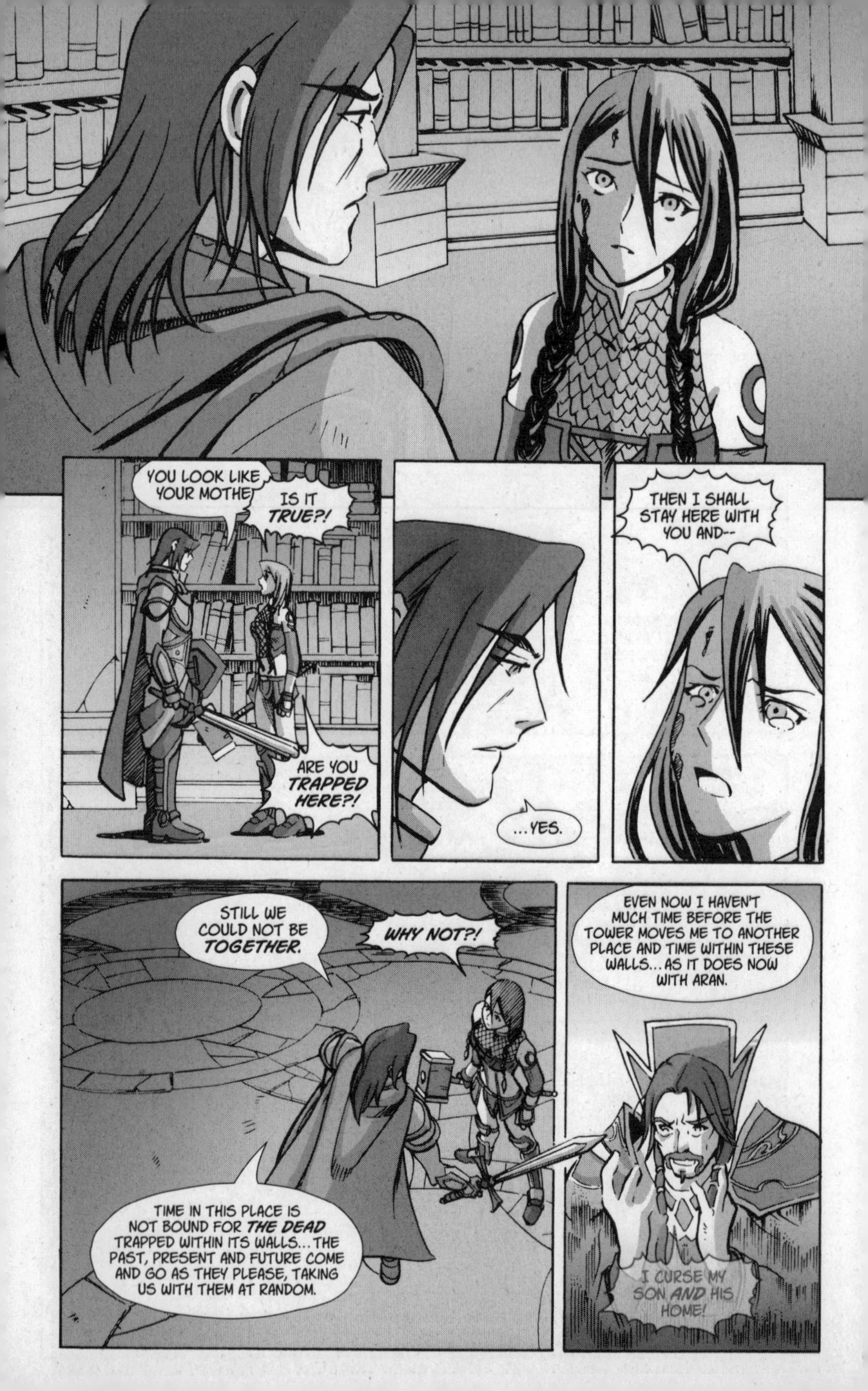

YOU LOOK LIKE YOUR MOTHE
IS IT TRUE?!
ARE YOU TRAPPED HERE?!
...YES.
THEN I SHALL STAY HERE WITH YOU AND--
STILL WE COULD NOT BE TOGETHER.
WHY NOT?!
TIME IN THIS PLACE IS NOT BOUND FOR THE DEAD TRAPPED WITHIN ITS WALLS... THE PAST, PRESENT AND FUTURE COME AND GO AS THEY PLEASE, TAKING US WITH THEM AT RANDOM.
EVEN NOW I HAVEN'T MUCH TIME BEFORE THE TOWER MOVES ME TO ANOTHER PLACE AND TIME WITHIN THESE WALLS... AS IT DOES NOW WITH ARAN.
I CURSE MY SON AND HIS HOME!

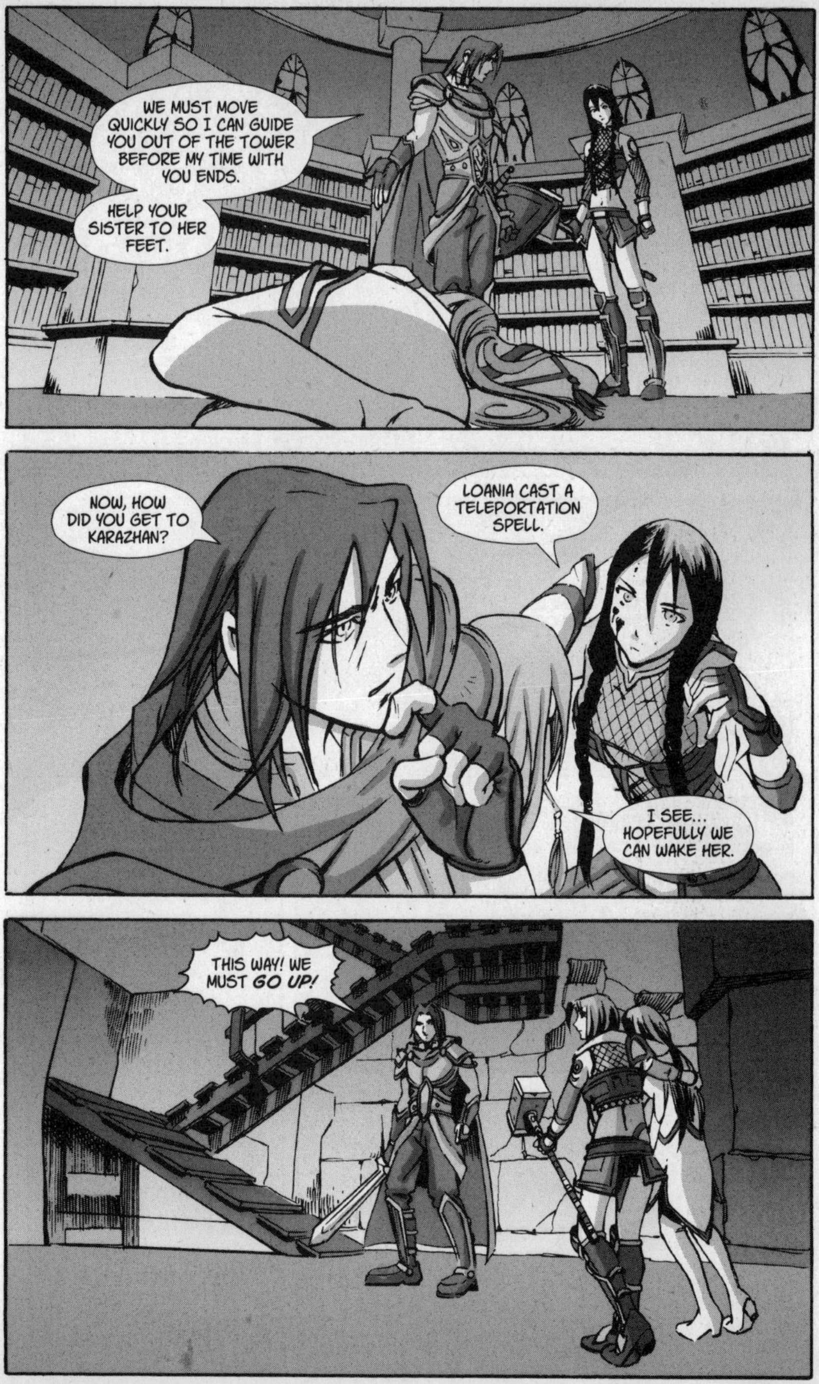
WE MUST MOVE QUICKLY SO I CAN GUIDE YOU OUT OF THE TOWER BEFORE MY TIME WITH YOU ENDS.
HELP YOUR SISTER TO HER FEET.
NOW, HOW DID YOU GET TO KARAZHAN?
LOANIA CAST A TELEPORTATION SPELL.
I SEE... HOPEFULLY WE CAN WAKE HER.
THIS WAY! WE MUST *GO UP*!

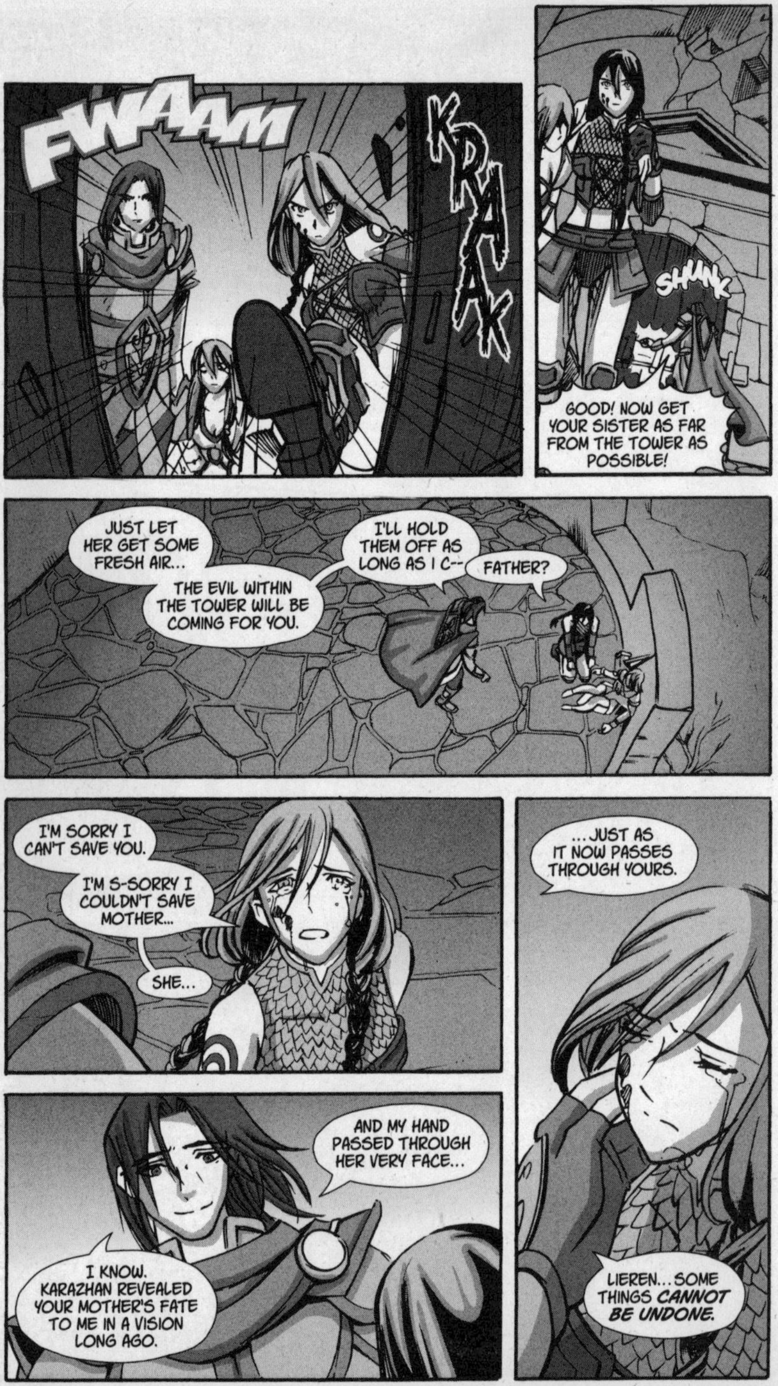
FWAAAM
KRAAK
SHUNK
GOOD! NOW GET YOUR SISTER AS FAR FROM THE TOWER AS POSSIBLE!
JUST LET HER GET SOME FRESH AIR...
THE EVIL WITHIN THE TOWER WILL BE COMING FOR YOU.
I'LL HOLD THEM OFF AS LONG AS I C--
FATHER?
I'M SORRY I CAN'T SAVE YOU.
I'M S-SORRY I COULDN'T SAVE MOTHER...
SHE...
...JUST AS IT NOW PASSES THROUGH YOURS.
AND MY HAND PASSED THROUGH HER VERY FACE...
I KNOW. KARAZHAN REVEALED YOUR MOTHER'S FATE TO ME IN A VISION LONG AGO.
LIEREN... SOME THINGS *CANNOT BE UNDONE.*

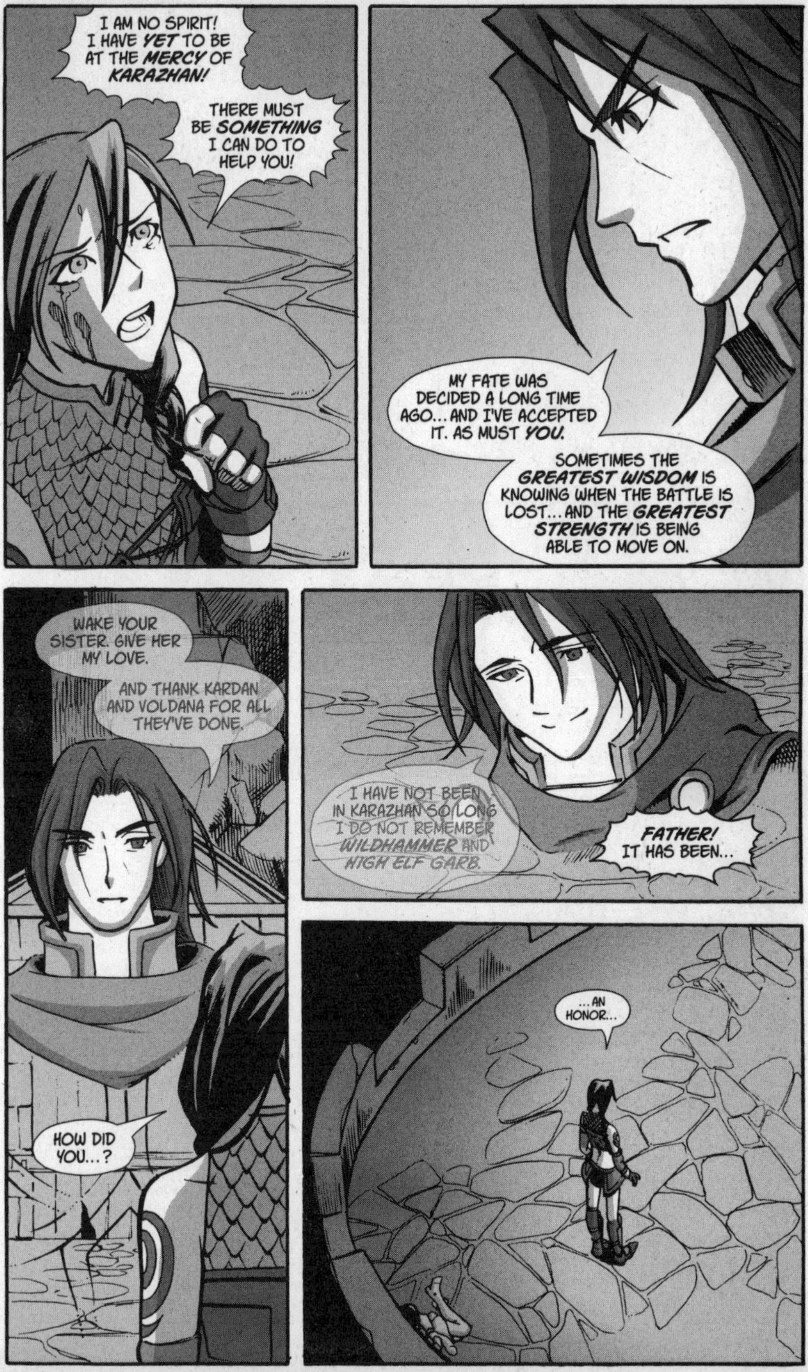
I AM NO SPIRIT! I HAVE *YET* TO BE AT THE *MERCY* OF *KARAZHAN!*
THERE MUST BE *SOMETHING* I CAN DO TO HELP YOU!
MY FATE WAS DECIDED A LONG TIME AGO... AND I'VE ACCEPTED IT. AS MUST *YOU.*
SOMETIMES THE *GREATEST WISDOM* IS KNOWING WHEN THE BATTLE IS LOST... AND THE *GREATEST STRENGTH* IS BEING ABLE TO MOVE ON.
WAKE YOUR SISTER. GIVE HER MY LOVE.
AND THANK KARDAN AND VOLDANA FOR ALL THEY'VE DONE.
HOW DID YOU...?
I HAVE NOT BEEN IN KARAZHAN SO LONG I DO NOT REMEMBER *WILDHAMMER* AND *HIGH ELF GARB.*
FATHER! IT HAS BEEN...
...AN HONOR...

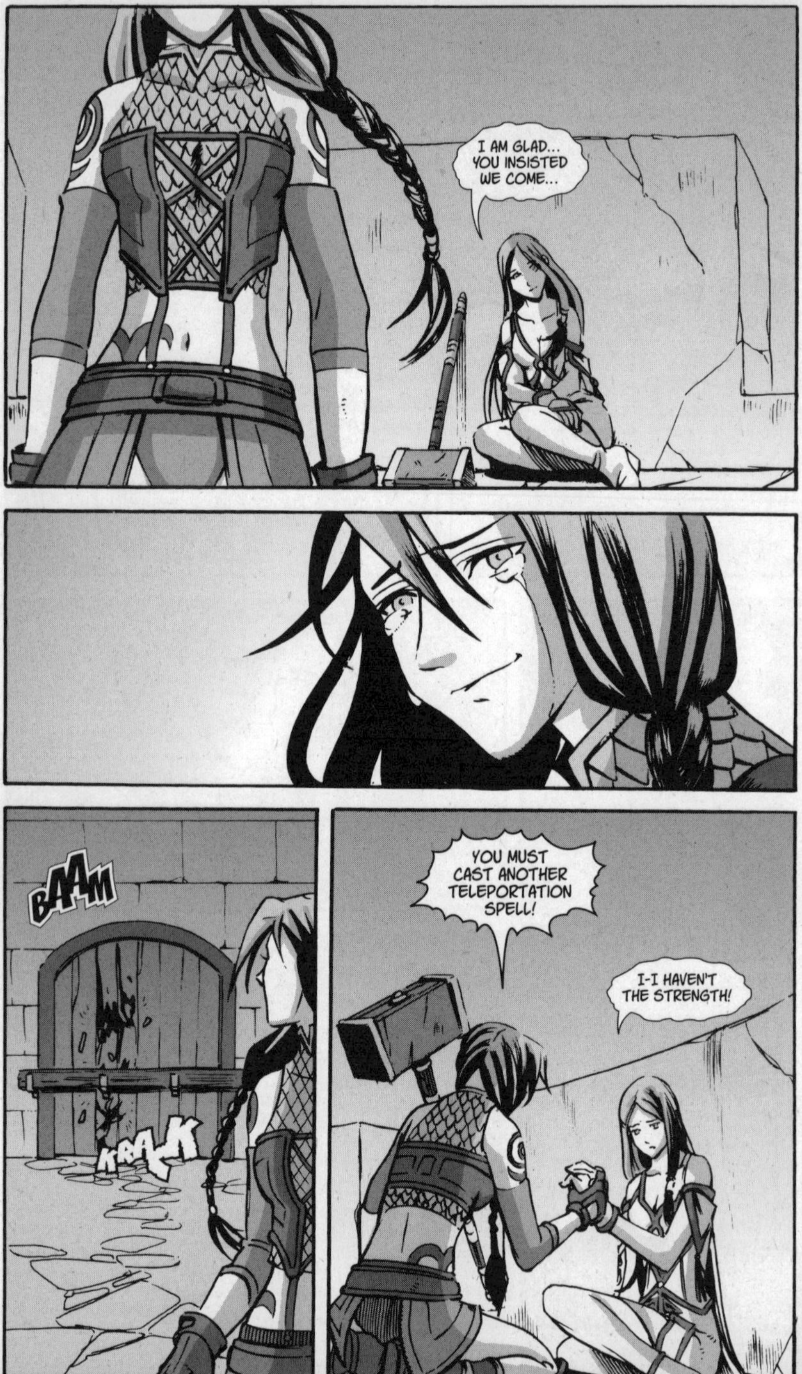
I AM GLAD... YOU INSISTED WE COME...
BAAAM
KRAK
YOU MUST CAST ANOTHER TELEPORTATION SPELL!
I-I HAVEN'T THE STRENGTH!

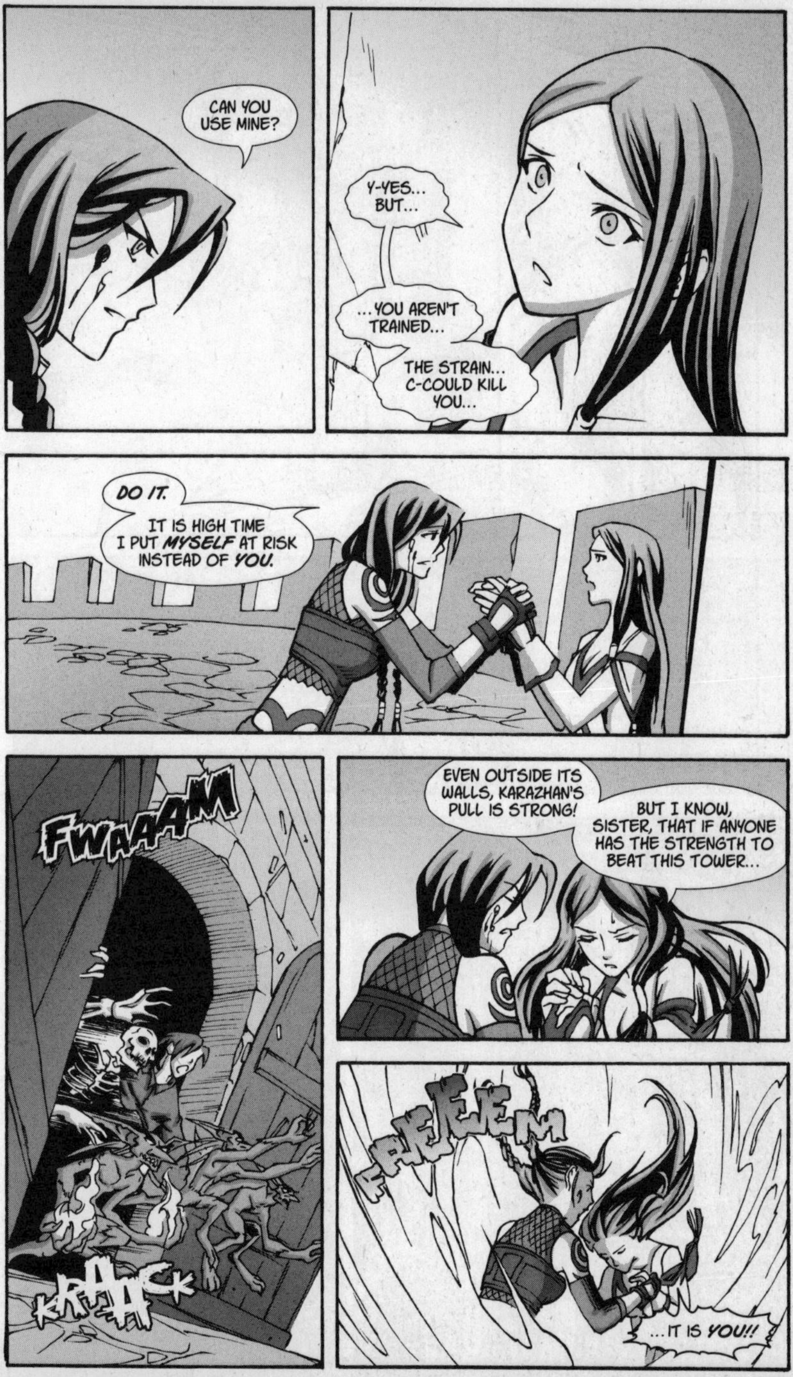
CAN YOU USE MINE?
Y-YES... BUT...
...YOU AREN'T TRAINED...
THE STRAIN... C-COULD KILL YOU...
DO IT.
IT IS HIGH TIME I PUT *MYSELF* AT RISK INSTEAD OF *YOU.*
FWAAAAM
KRAAK*
EVEN OUTSIDE ITS WALLS, KARAZHAN'S PULL IS STRONG!
BUT I KNOW, SISTER, THAT IF ANYONE HAS THE STRENGTH TO BEAT THIS TOWER...
FREEEEM
...IT IS *YOU!!*

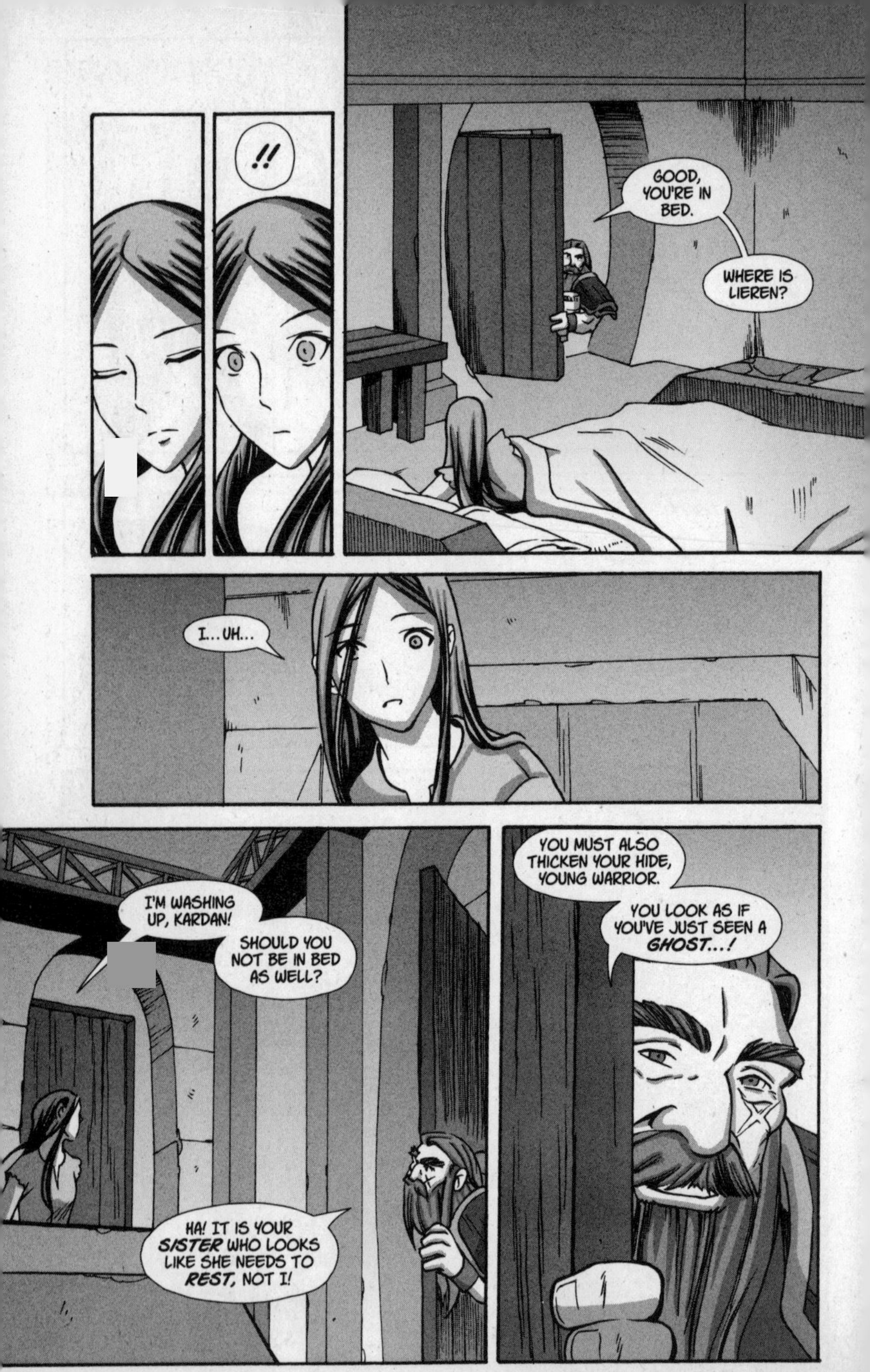
!!
GOOD, YOU'RE IN BED.
WHERE IS LIEREN?
I... UH...
I'M WASHING UP, KARDAN!
SHOULD YOU NOT BE IN BED AS WELL?
HA! IT IS YOUR *SISTER* WHO LOOKS LIKE SHE NEEDS TO *REST,* NOT I!
YOU MUST ALSO THICKEN YOUR HIDE, YOUNG WARRIOR.
YOU LOOK AS IF YOU'VE JUST SEEN A *GHOST...!*

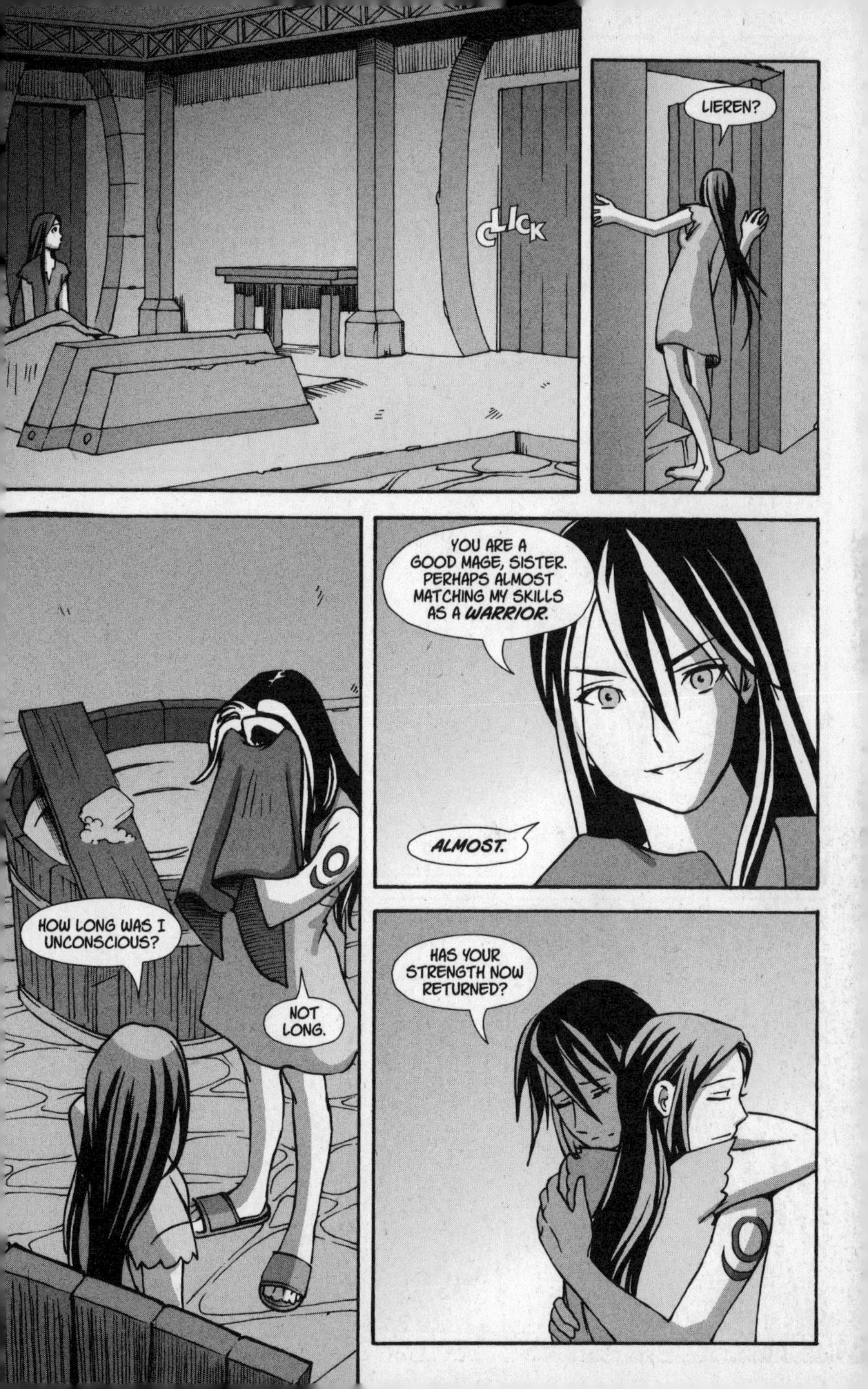
CLICK
LIEREN?
HOW LONG WAS I UNCONSCIOUS?
NOT LONG.
YOU ARE A GOOD MAGE, SISTER. PERHAPS ALMOST MATCHING MY SKILLS AS A *WARRIOR*.
ALMOST.
HAS YOUR STRENGTH NOW RETURNED?

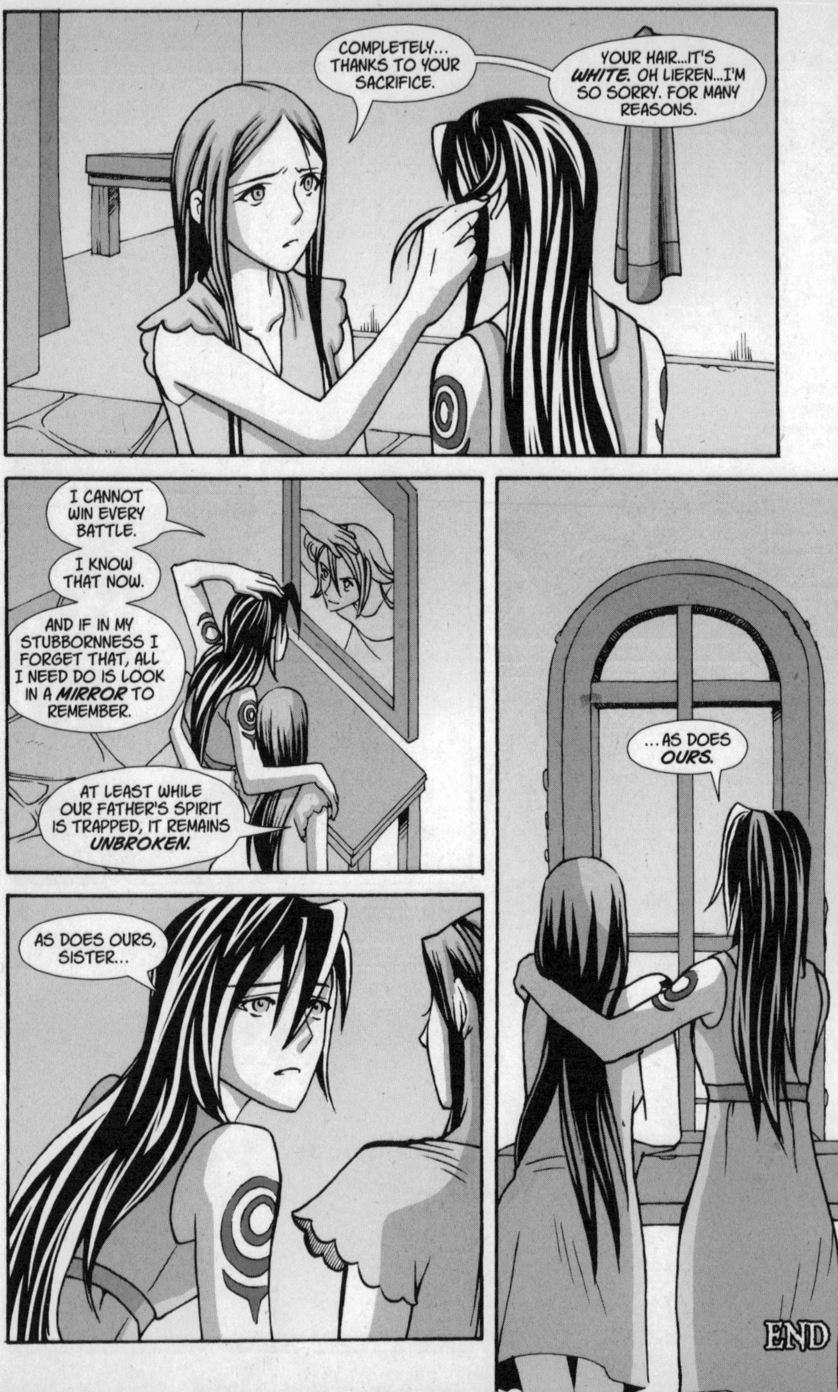
COMPLETELY... THANKS TO YOUR SACRIFICE.
YOUR HAIR...IT'S WHITE. OH LIEREN...I'M SO SORRY. FOR MANY REASONS.
I CANNOT WIN EVERY BATTLE.
I KNOW THAT NOW.
AND IF IN MY STUBBORNNESS I FORGET THAT, ALL I NEED DO IS LOOK IN A MIRROR TO REMEMBER.
AT LEAST WHILE OUR FATHER'S SPIRIT IS TRAPPED, IT REMAINS UNBROKEN.
AS DOES OURS, SISTER...
...AS DOES OURS.
END

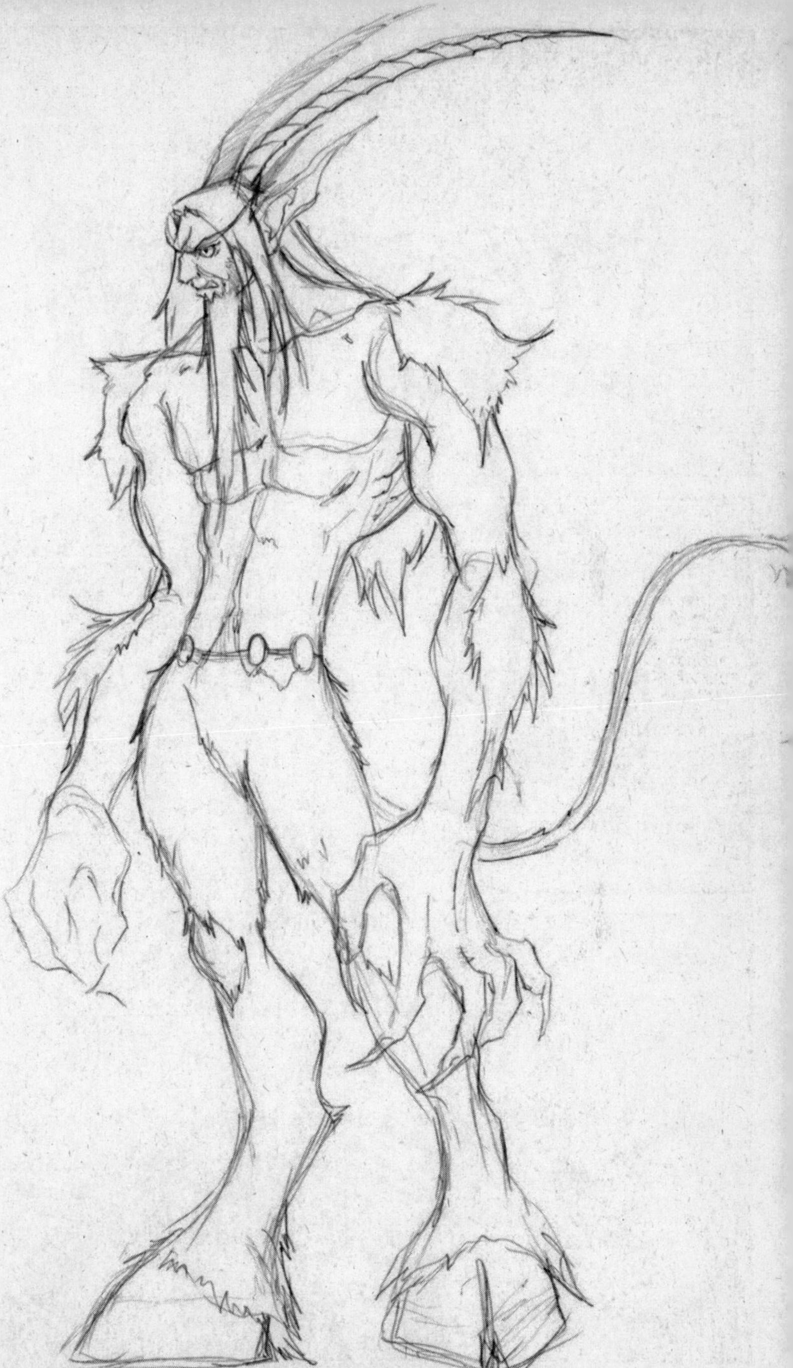

WARCRAFT
LEGENDS
VOLUME FIVE

THE FIRST GUARDIAN

WRITTEN BY LOUISE SIMONSON

PENCILS BY SEUNG-HUI KYE
INKS BY SEUNG-HUI KYE, ARIEL IACCI
& FERNANDO MELEK
TONES BY GONZALO DUARTE

RETOUCH ARTIST & LETTERER: MICHAEL PAOLILLI

DALARAN: A BRIEF HISTORY

Almost 3,000 years ago, a group of human magi, feeling fettered by
strict laws governing magic in Strom, journeyed north to Lordaeron.
On the southern shore of Lordamere Lake, these magi founded the
city-state of Dalaran, where they hoped to practice their craft with less
restraint.

The ruling archmagi, called Magocrats, eagerly devoted themselves to
the arcane. They housed their growing libraries and research laborato-
ries in the Violet Citadel, a towering spire raised by magic in the heart
of the city.

Magi flocked to Dalaran in ever-increasing numbers to study at its
schools, do research in its vast libraries and practice their craft freely
in the company of their peers. Soon non-magical beings moved to
Dalaran to provide necessary services for the residents of the thriving
magocracy.

The citizens of Dalaran thought that their shining city was impreg-
nable and that its glory would never end.

But, in time, the constant and ungoverned use of magic began to tear
the fabric of reality around the city. These tears sent bright beacons
out into the Twisting Nether and drew the attention of the banished
denizens of the Burning Legion. Through these rents, demons began
to slip back into Azeroth, bringing with them conflict and cruelty,
misery and corruption.

Consulting the high elves, the Magocrats learned that as long as they
used magic, they would need to protect their citizenry from the
Legion's agents. Yet mankind could not be allowed to learn of this
threat lest the people riot in fear. Thus, the elves and Magocrats
formed a secret order known as the Council of Tirisfal.

The order began to experiment, trying to discover the most effective
way to deal with the demon incursions.

One group held that the magi should work together as a team of
equals. Another group believed that their magic should be funneled
through a single head, though how that should be managed was
another challenge.

In time, the solution was found by... THE FIRST GUARDIAN.

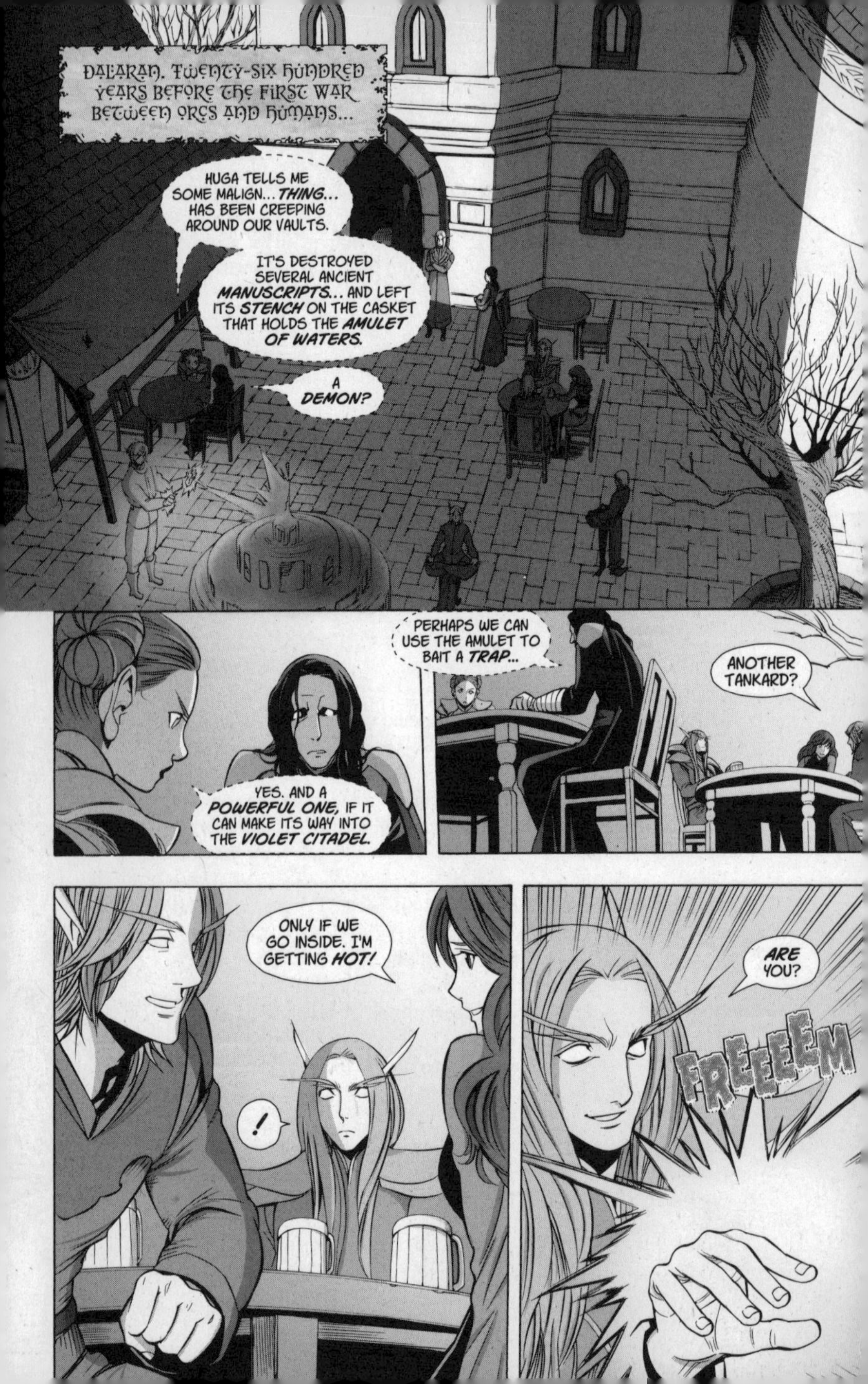
DALARAN. TWENTY-SIX HUNDRED YEARS BEFORE THE FIRST WAR BETWEEN ORCS AND HUMANS...
HUGA TELLS ME SOME MALIGN... THING... HAS BEEN CREEPING AROUND OUR VAULTS.
IT'S DESTROYED SEVERAL ANCIENT MANUSCRIPTS... AND LEFT ITS STENCH ON THE CASKET THAT HOLDS THE AMULET OF WATERS.
A DEMON?
YES. AND A POWERFUL ONE, IF IT CAN MAKE ITS WAY INTO THE VIOLET CITADEL.
PERHAPS WE CAN USE THE AMULET TO BAIT A TRAP...
ANOTHER TANKARD?
ONLY IF WE GO INSIDE. I'M GETTING HOT!
!
ARE YOU?
FREEEEM

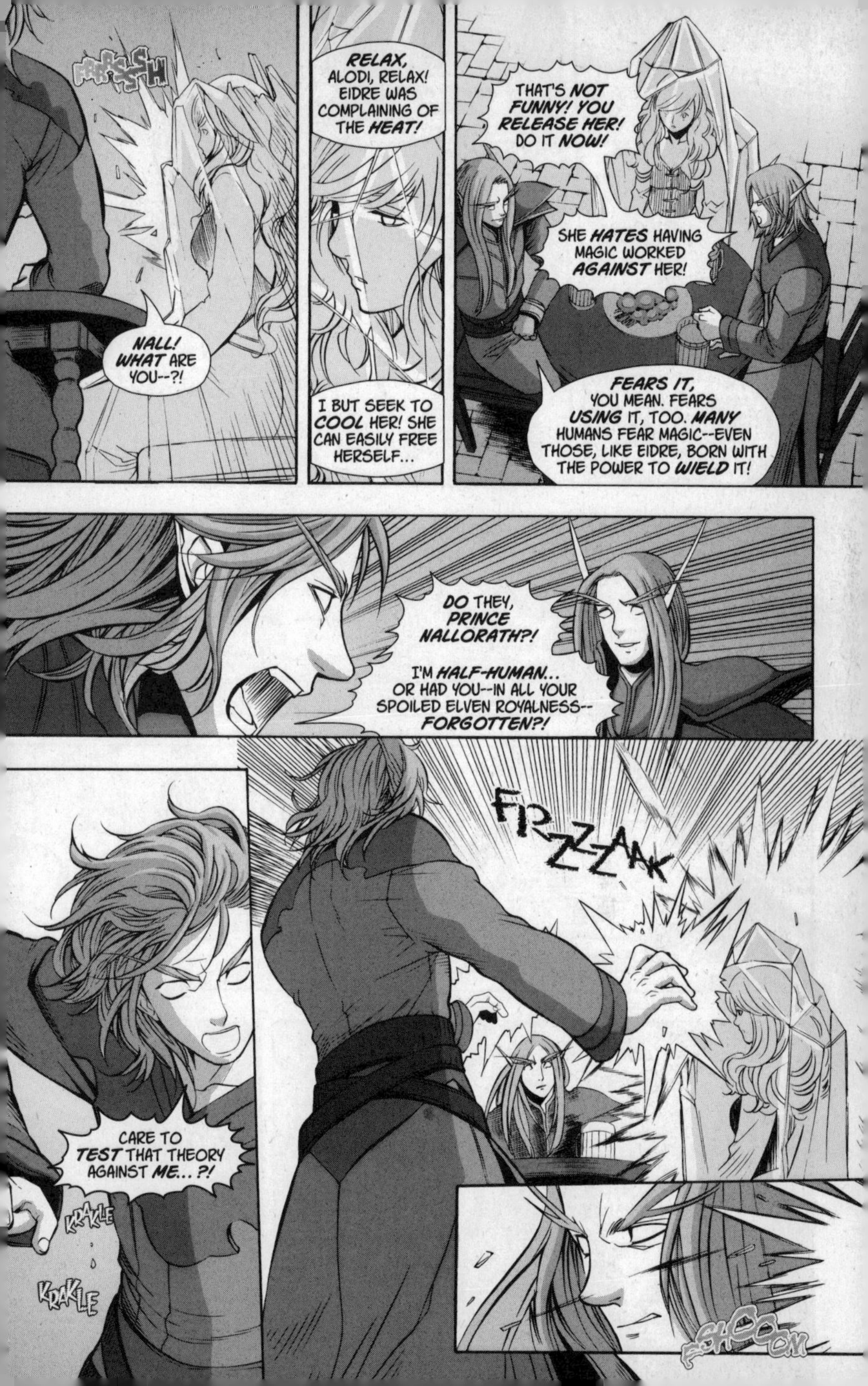
FRRSSSH
NALL! WHAT ARE YOU--?!
RELAX, ALODI, RELAX! EIDRE WAS COMPLAINING OF THE HEAT!
I BUT SEEK TO COOL HER! SHE CAN EASILY FREE HERSELF...
THAT'S NOT FUNNY! YOU RELEASE HER! DO IT NOW!
SHE HATES HAVING MAGIC WORKED AGAINST HER!
FEARS IT, YOU MEAN. FEARS USING IT, TOO. MANY HUMANS FEAR MAGIC--EVEN THOSE, LIKE EIDRE, BORN WITH THE POWER TO WIELD IT!
DO THEY, PRINCE NALLORATH?!
I'M HALF-HUMAN... OR HAD YOU--IN ALL YOUR SPOILED ELVEN ROYALNESS--FORGOTTEN?!
CARE TO TEST THAT THEORY AGAINST ME...?!
KRAKLE
KRAKLE
FIZZZAAK
FSHOOOM

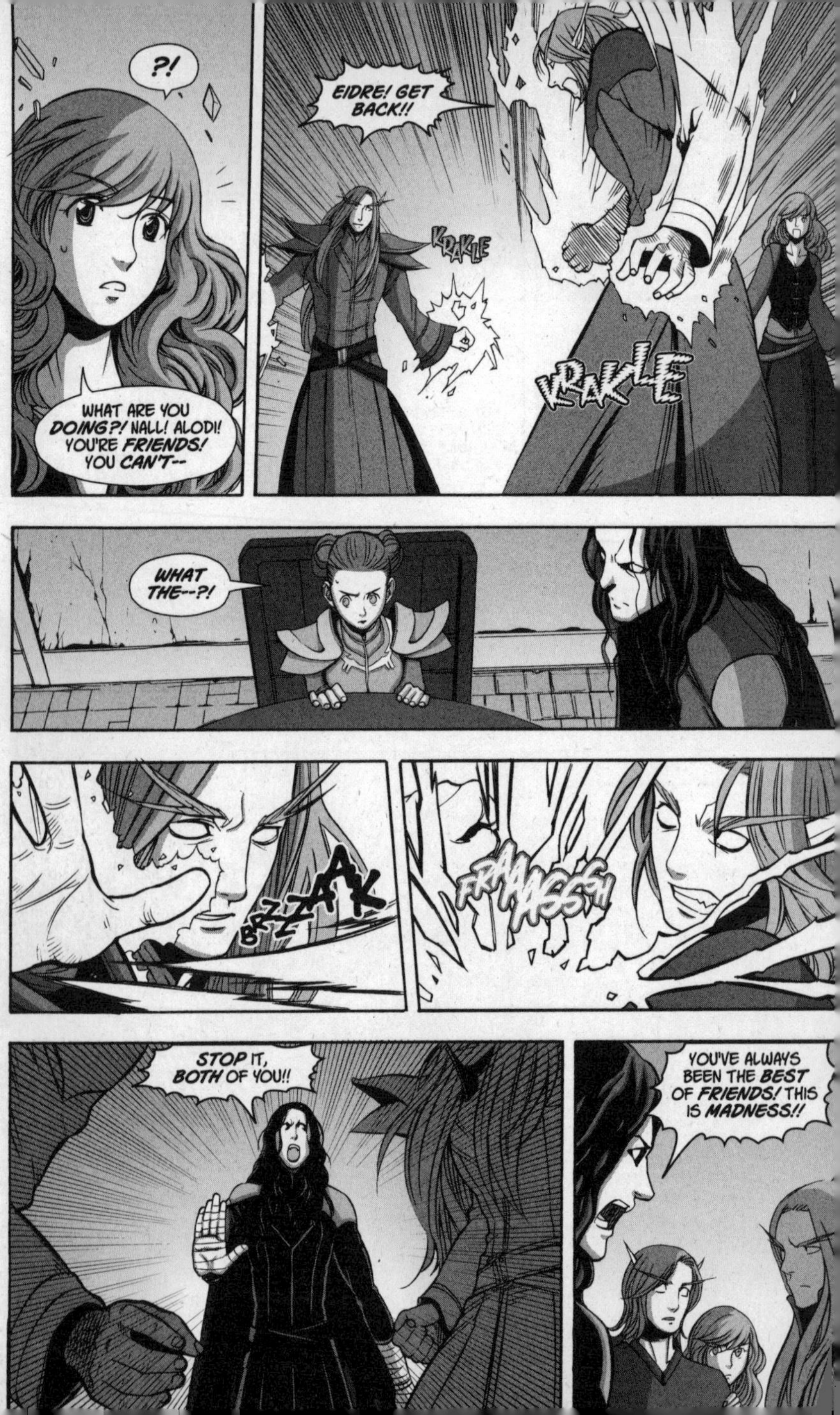
?!
WHAT ARE YOU DOING?! NALL! ALODI! YOU'RE FRIENDS! YOU CAN'T--
EIDRE! GET BACK!!
KRAKLE
VRAKLE
WHAT THE--?!
BRZZZAK
FRAAAASSSH
STOP IT, BOTH OF YOU!!
YOU'VE ALWAYS BEEN THE BEST OF FRIENDS! THIS IS MADNESS!!

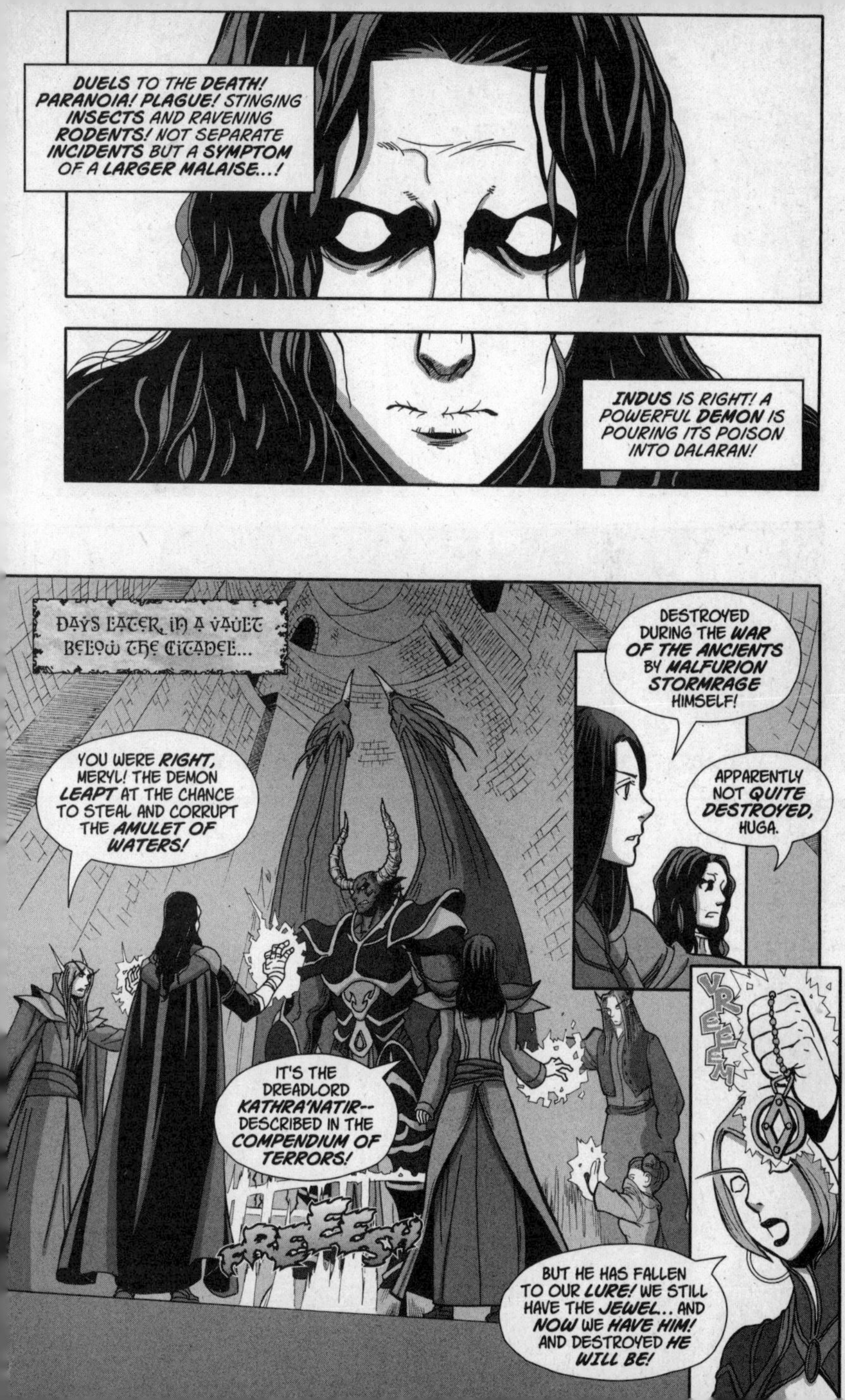
DUELS TO THE DEATH! PARANOIA! PLAGUE! STINGING INSECTS AND RAVENING RODENTS! NOT SEPARATE INCIDENTS BUT A SYMPTOM OF A LARGER MALAISE...!
INDUS IS RIGHT! A POWERFUL DEMON IS POURING ITS POISON INTO DALARAN!
DAYS LATER, IN A VAULT BELOW THE CITADEL...
YOU WERE RIGHT, MERYL! THE DEMON LEAPT AT THE CHANCE TO STEAL AND CORRUPT THE AMULET OF WATERS!
IT'S THE DREADLORD KATHRA'NATIR-- DESCRIBED IN THE COMPENDIUM OF TERRORS!
DESTROYED DURING THE WAR OF THE ANCIENTS BY MALFURION STORMRAGE HIMSELF!
APPARENTLY NOT QUITE DESTROYED, HUGA.
VREEEM
BUT HE HAS FALLEN TO OUR LURE! WE STILL HAVE THE JEWEL... AND NOW WE HAVE HIM! AND DESTROYED HE WILL BE!

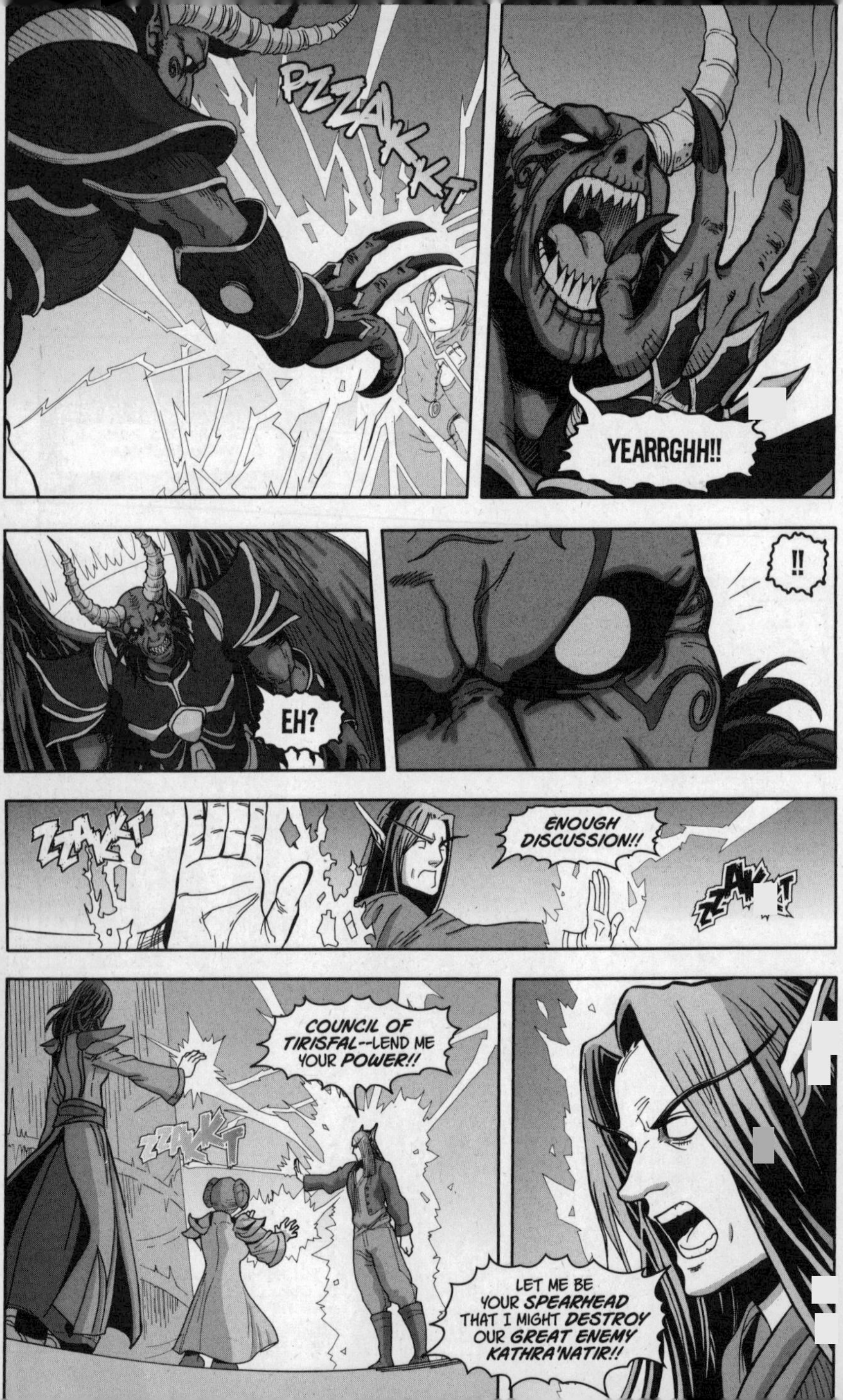
PZZAKKT
YEARRGHH!!
EH?
!!
ZZAKT
ENOUGH DISCUSSION!!
COUNCIL OF TIRISFAL--LEND ME YOUR *POWER!!*
ZZAKT
LET ME BE YOUR *SPEARHEAD* THAT I MIGHT *DESTROY* OUR *GREAT ENEMY KATHRA'NATIR!!*

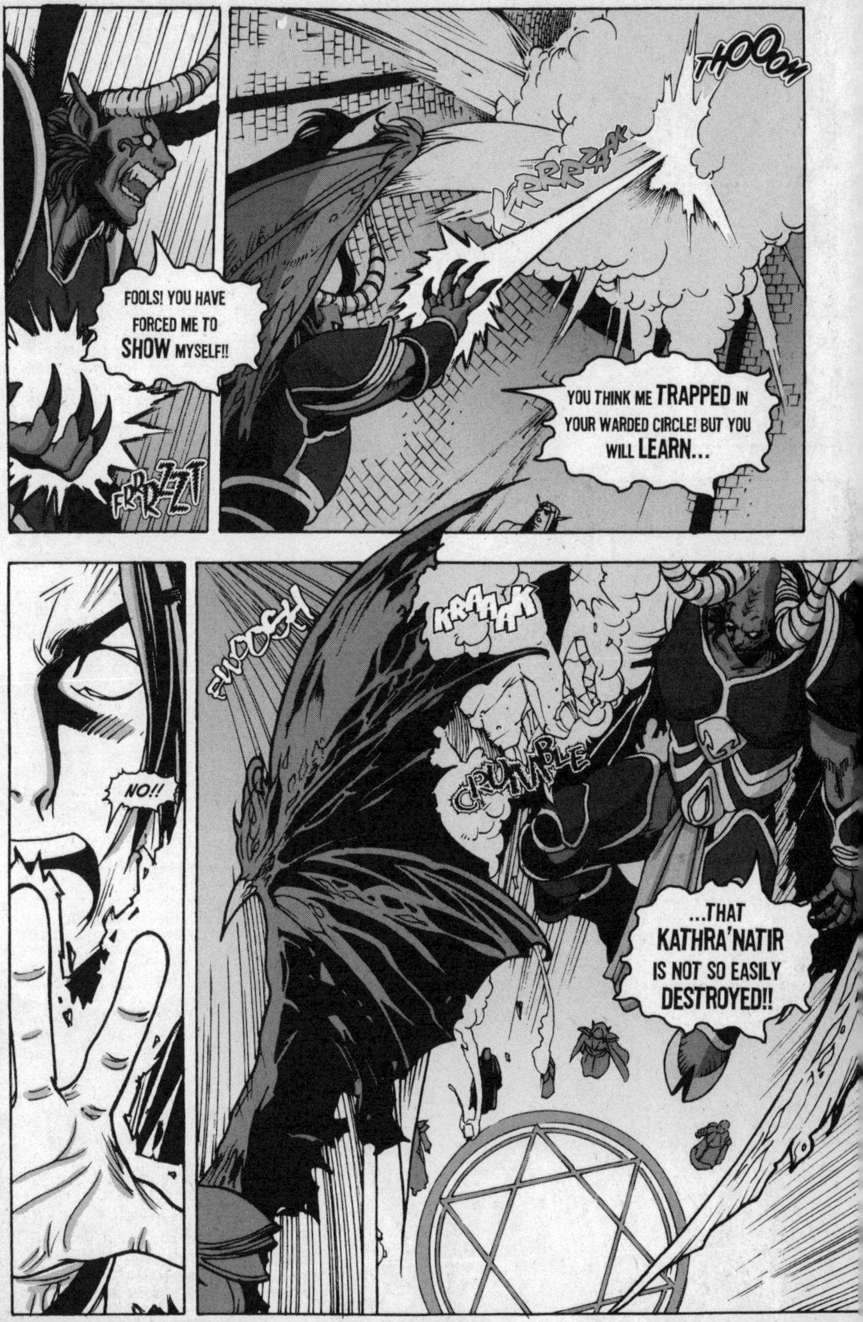
FOOLS! YOU HAVE FORCED ME TO SHOW MYSELF!!
THOOOM
KRRRZAAK
YOU THINK ME TRAPPED IN YOUR WARDED CIRCLE! BUT YOU WILL LEARN...
NO!!
FWOOSH
KRAAAAK
CRUMBLE
...THAT KATHRA'NATIR IS NOT SO EASILY DESTROYED!!

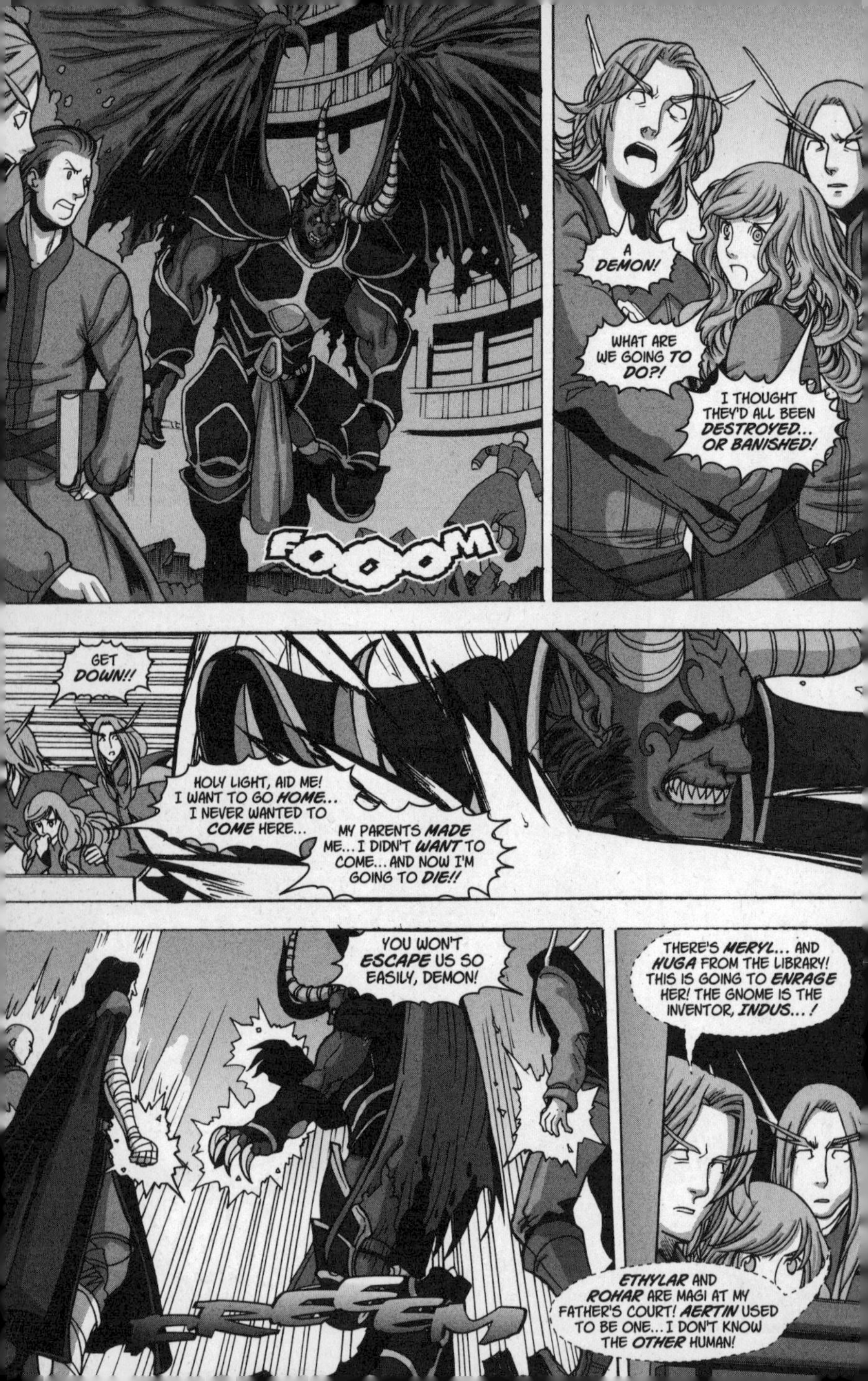
FOOOM
A DEMON!
WHAT ARE WE GOING TO DO?!
I THOUGHT THEY'D ALL BEEN DESTROYED... OR BANISHED!
GET DOWN!!
HOLY LIGHT, AID ME! I WANT TO GO HOME... I NEVER WANTED TO COME HERE...
MY PARENTS MADE ME... I DIDN'T WANT TO COME... AND NOW I'M GOING TO DIE!!
YOU WON'T ESCAPE US SO EASILY, DEMON!
THERE'S MERYL... AND HUGA FROM THE LIBRARY! THIS IS GOING TO ENRAGE HER! THE GNOME IS THE INVENTOR, INDUS...!
ETHYLAR AND ROHAR ARE MAGI AT MY FATHER'S COURT! AERTIN USED TO BE ONE... I DON'T KNOW THE OTHER HUMAN!

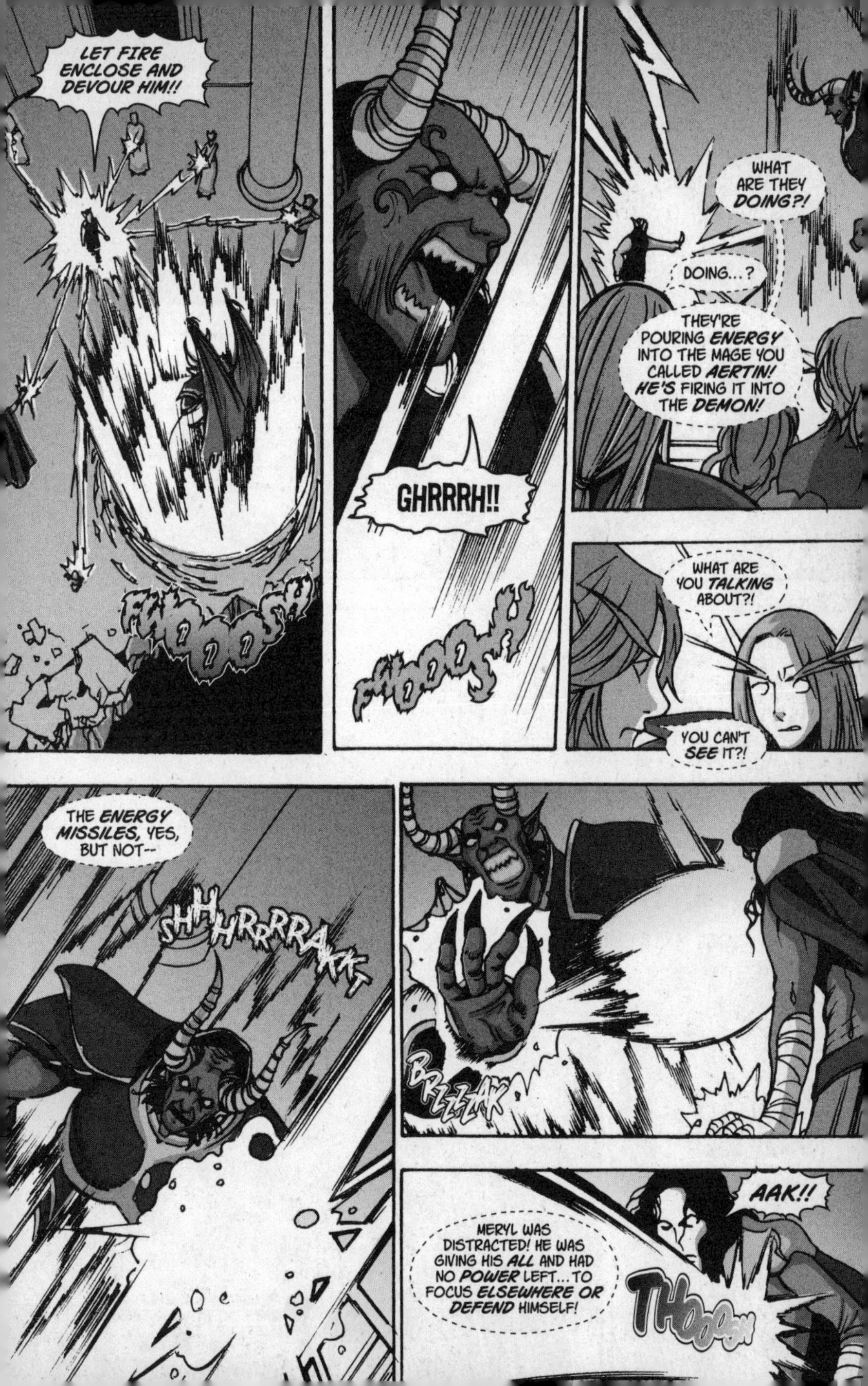
LET FIRE ENCLOSE AND DEVOUR HIM!!
FWOOSH
GHRRRH!!
FWOOSH
WHAT ARE THEY DOING?!
DOING...?
THEY'RE POURING ENERGY INTO THE MAGE YOU CALLED AERTIN! HE'S FIRING IT INTO THE DEMON!
WHAT ARE YOU TALKING ABOUT?!
YOU CAN'T SEE IT?!
THE ENERGY MISSILES, YES, BUT NOT--
SHHHRRRRAKKT
BRZZZAK
MERYL WAS DISTRACTED! HE WAS GIVING HIS ALL AND HAD NO POWER LEFT... TO FOCUS ELSEWHERE OR DEFEND HIMSELF!
AAK!!
THOOOSH

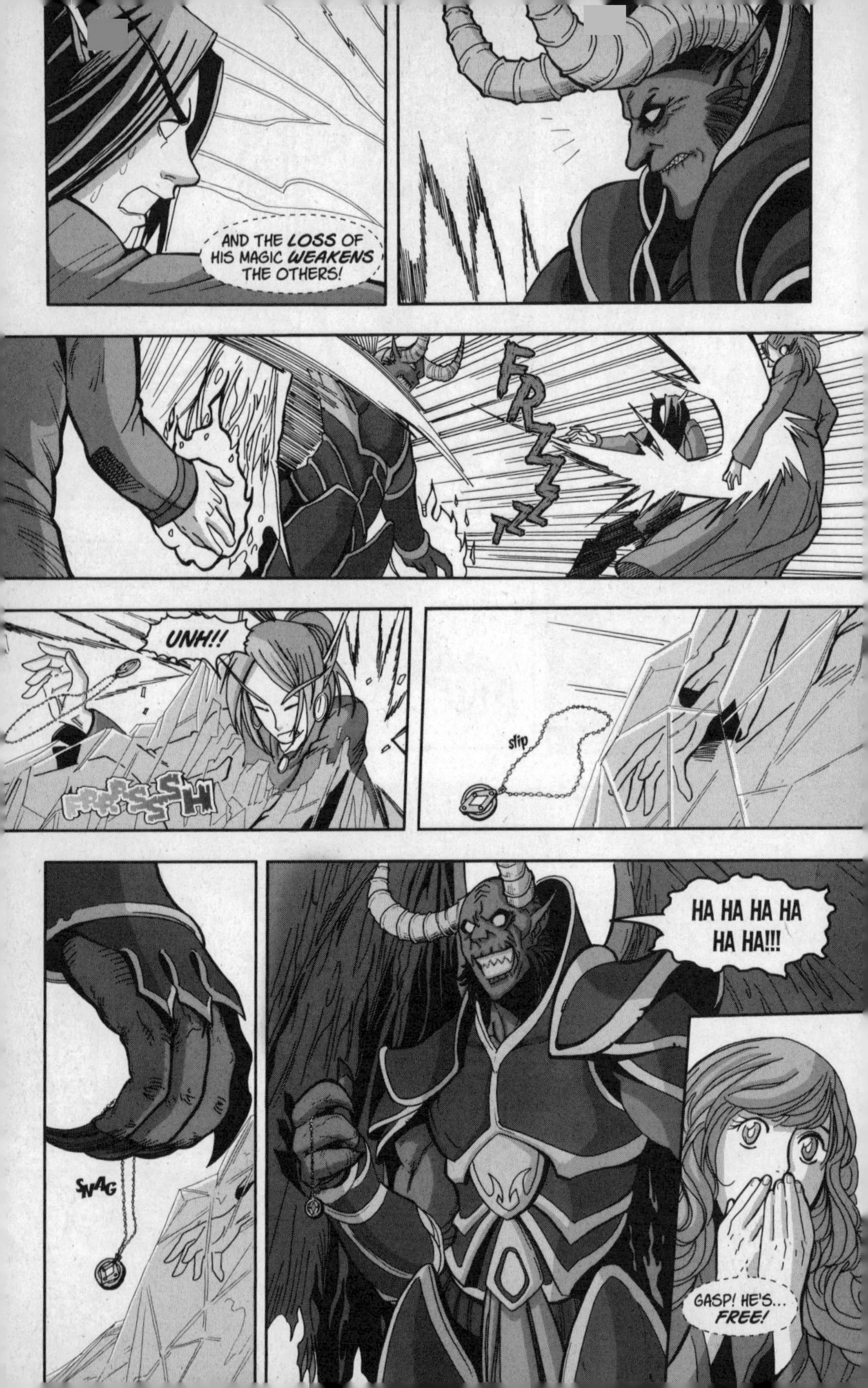
AND THE *LOSS* OF HIS MAGIC *WEAKENS* THE OTHERS!
FRZZZT
UNH!!
FRASSSH
slip
SNAG
HA HA HA HA HA HA!!!
GASP! HE'S... *FREE!*

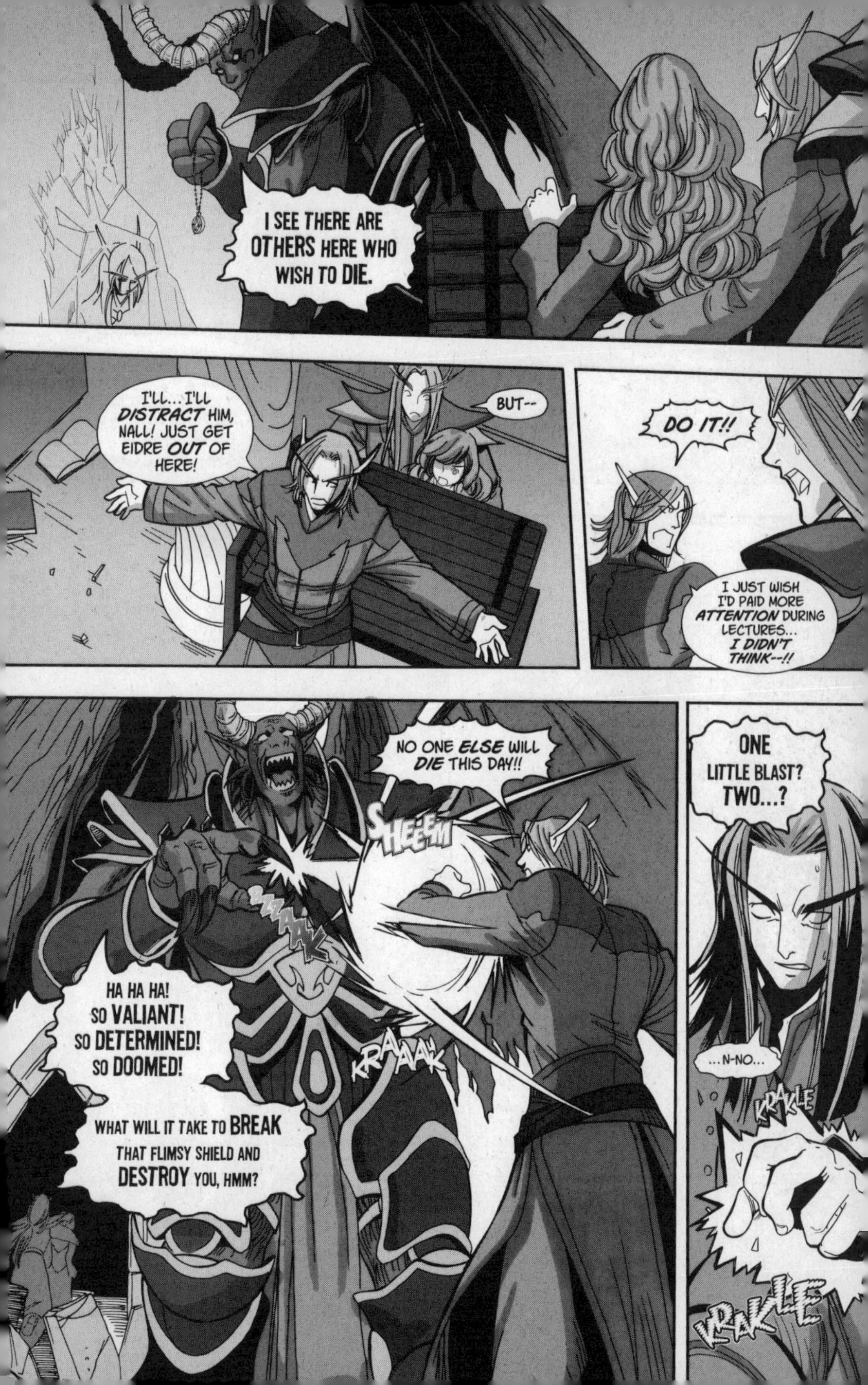
I SEE THERE ARE OTHERS HERE WHO WISH TO DIE.
I'LL... I'LL DISTRACT HIM, NALL! JUST GET EIDRE OUT OF HERE!
BUT--
DO IT!!
I JUST WISH I'D PAID MORE ATTENTION DURING LECTURES... I DIDN'T THINK--!!
NO ONE ELSE WILL DIE THIS DAY!!
SHEEEM
HA HA HA! SO VALIANT! SO DETERMINED! SO DOOMED!
KRAAAAK
WHAT WILL IT TAKE TO BREAK THAT FLIMSY SHIELD AND DESTROY YOU, HMM?
ONE LITTLE BLAST? TWO...?
...N-NO...
KRAKLE
KRAKLE

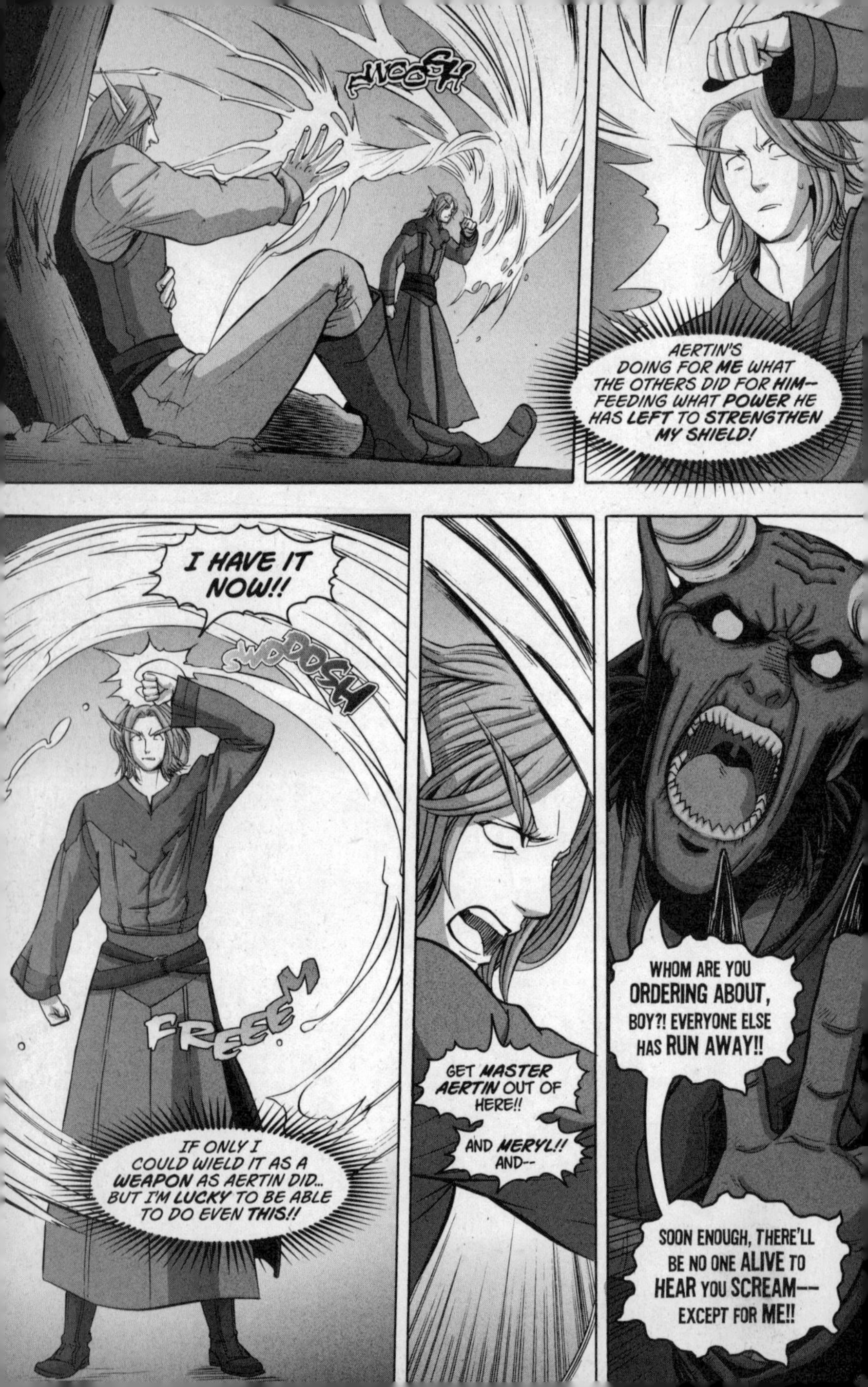
WOOSH
AERTIN'S DOING FOR ME WHAT THE OTHERS DID FOR HIM— FEEDING WHAT POWER HE HAS LEFT TO STRENGTHEN MY SHIELD!
I HAVE IT NOW!!
SWOOOSH
FREEEM
IF ONLY I COULD WIELD IT AS A WEAPON AS AERTIN DID... BUT I'M LUCKY TO BE ABLE TO DO EVEN THIS!!
GET MASTER AERTIN OUT OF HERE!!
AND MERYL!! AND--
WHOM ARE YOU ORDERING ABOUT, BOY?! EVERYONE ELSE HAS RUN AWAY!!
SOON ENOUGH, THERE'LL BE NO ONE ALIVE TO HEAR YOU SCREAM—— EXCEPT FOR ME!!

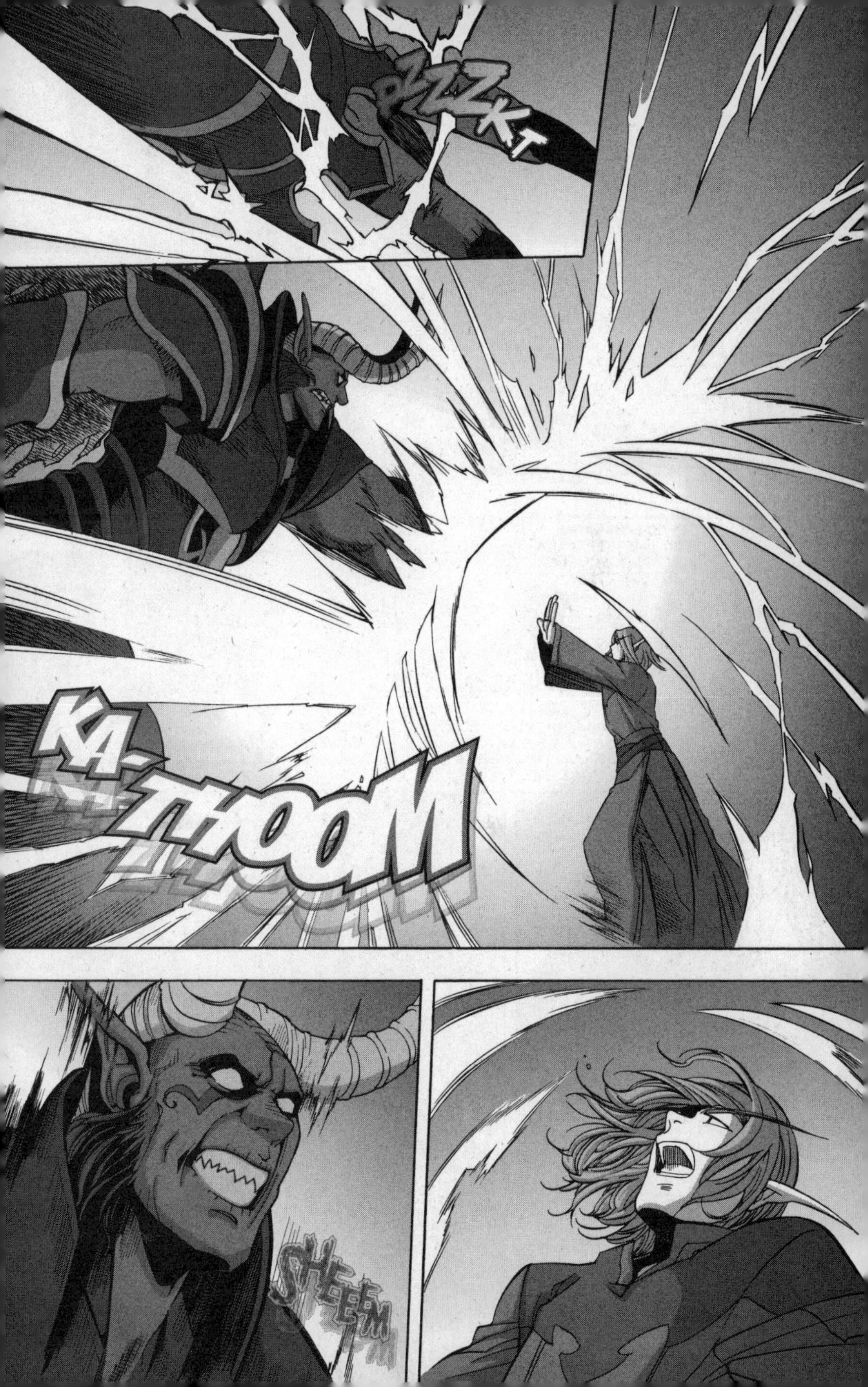
BZZZKT
KA-THOOM
SHEEEM

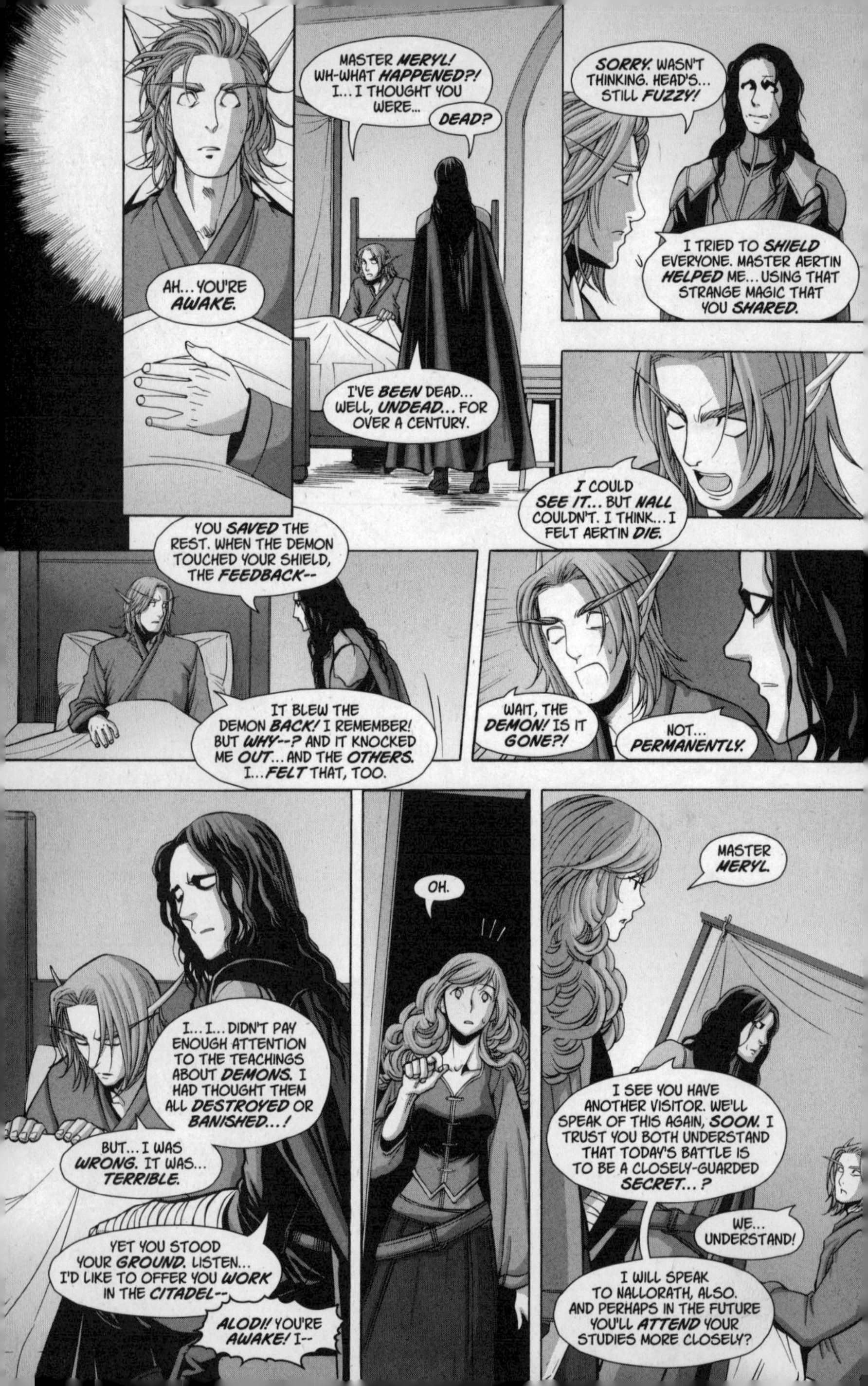
AH... YOU'RE **AWAKE.**
MASTER **MERYL!** WH-WHAT **HAPPENED?!** I... I THOUGHT YOU WERE...
DEAD?
I'VE **BEEN** DEAD... WELL, **UNDEAD...** FOR OVER A CENTURY.
SORRY. WASN'T THINKING. HEAD'S... STILL **FUZZY!**
I TRIED TO **SHIELD** EVERYONE. MASTER AERTIN **HELPED** ME... USING THAT STRANGE MAGIC THAT YOU **SHARED.**
I COULD **SEE IT...** BUT **NALL** COULDN'T. I THINK... I FELT AERTIN **DIE.**
YOU **SAVED** THE REST. WHEN THE DEMON TOUCHED YOUR SHIELD, THE **FEEDBACK--**
IT BLEW THE DEMON **BACK!** I REMEMBER! BUT **WHY--?** AND IT KNOCKED ME **OUT**... AND THE **OTHERS.** I... **FELT** THAT, TOO.
WAIT, THE **DEMON!** IS IT **GONE?!**
NOT... **PERMANENTLY.**
I... I... DIDN'T PAY ENOUGH ATTENTION TO THE TEACHINGS ABOUT **DEMONS.** I HAD THOUGHT THEM ALL **DESTROYED** OR **BANISHED...!**
BUT... I WAS **WRONG.** IT WAS... **TERRIBLE.**
YET YOU STOOD YOUR **GROUND.** LISTEN... I'D LIKE TO OFFER YOU **WORK** IN THE **CITADEL--**
ALODI! YOU'RE **AWAKE!** I--
OH.
MASTER **MERYL.**
I SEE YOU HAVE ANOTHER VISITOR. WE'LL SPEAK OF THIS AGAIN, **SOON.** I TRUST YOU BOTH UNDERSTAND THAT TODAY'S BATTLE IS TO BE A CLOSELY-GUARDED **SECRET...?**
WE... UNDERSTAND!
I WILL SPEAK TO NALLORATH, ALSO. AND PERHAPS IN THE FUTURE YOU'LL **ATTEND** YOUR STUDIES MORE CLOSELY?

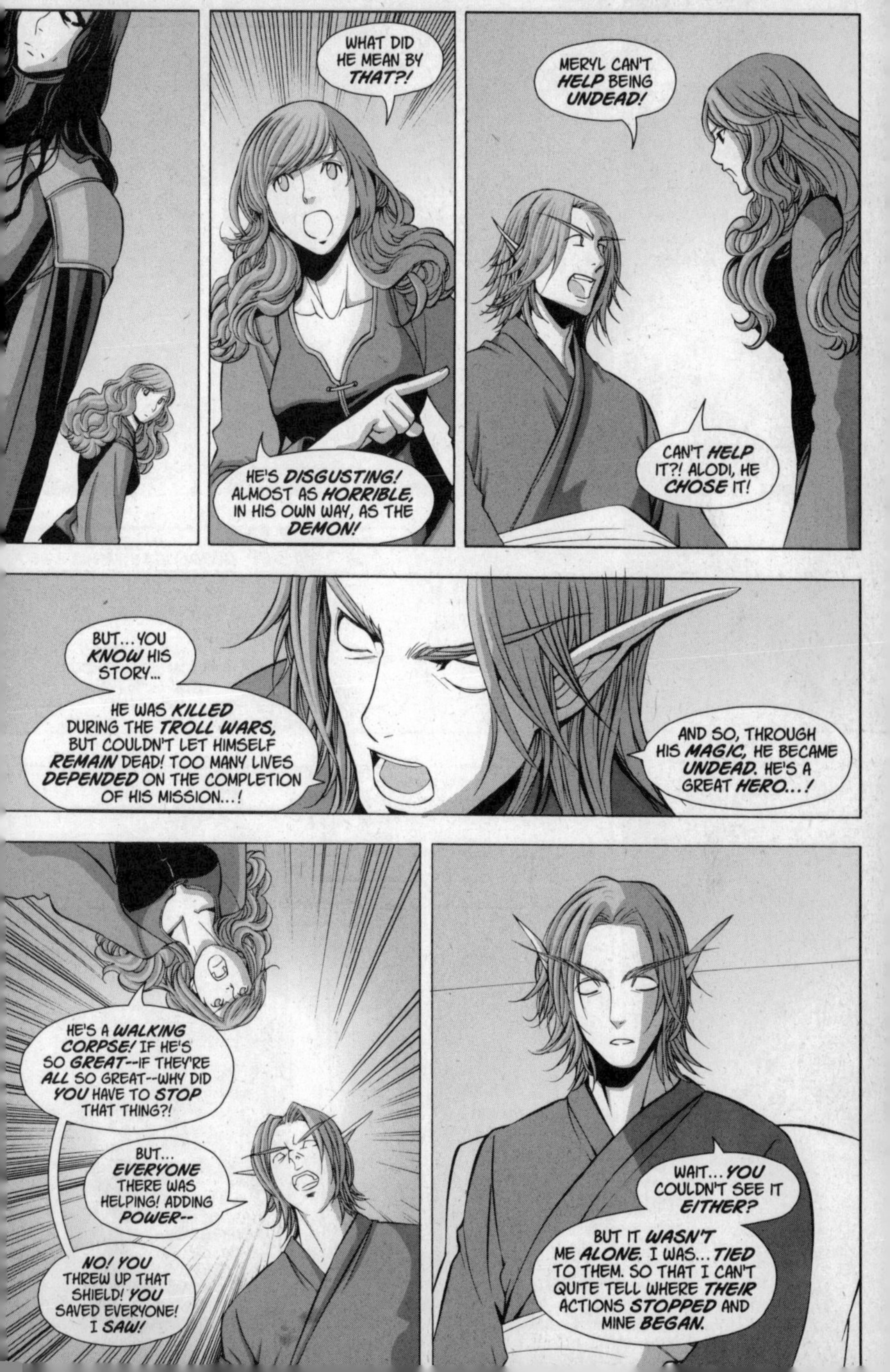
WHAT DID HE MEAN BY THAT?!
HE'S DISGUSTING! ALMOST AS HORRIBLE, IN HIS OWN WAY, AS THE DEMON!
MERYL CAN'T HELP BEING UNDEAD!
CAN'T HELP IT?! ALODI, HE CHOSE IT!
BUT... YOU KNOW HIS STORY...
HE WAS KILLED DURING THE TROLL WARS, BUT COULDN'T LET HIMSELF REMAIN DEAD! TOO MANY LIVES DEPENDED ON THE COMPLETION OF HIS MISSION...!
AND SO, THROUGH HIS MAGIC, HE BECAME UNDEAD. HE'S A GREAT HERO...!
HE'S A WALKING CORPSE! IF HE'S SO GREAT--IF THEY'RE ALL SO GREAT--WHY DID YOU HAVE TO STOP THAT THING?!
BUT... EVERYONE THERE WAS HELPING! ADDING POWER--
NO! YOU THREW UP THAT SHIELD! YOU SAVED EVERYONE! I SAW!
WAIT... YOU COULDN'T SEE IT EITHER?
BUT IT WASN'T ME ALONE. I WAS... TIED TO THEM. SO THAT I CAN'T QUITE TELL WHERE THEIR ACTIONS STOPPED AND MINE BEGAN.

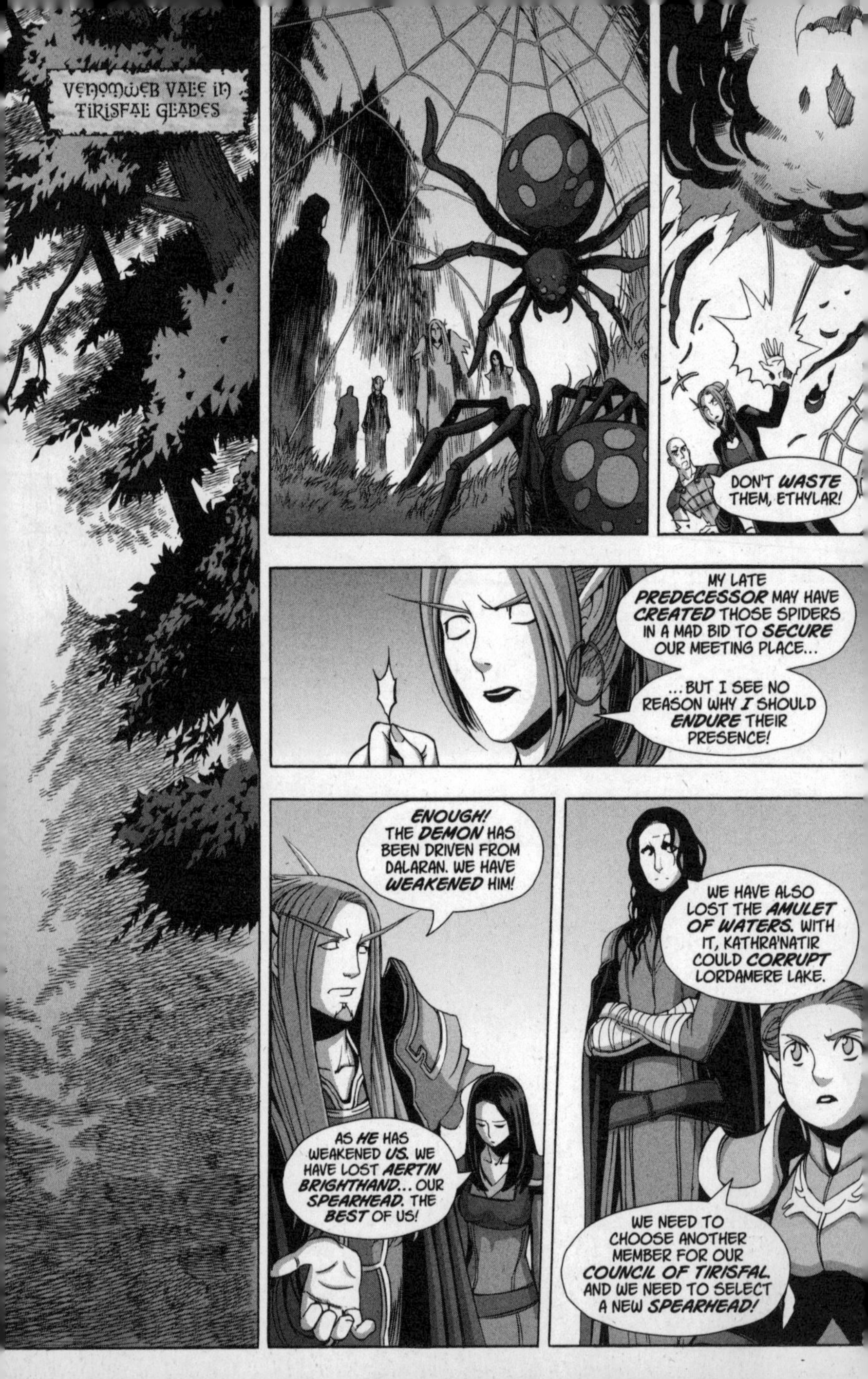
VENOMWEB VALE IN TIRISFAL GLADES
DON'T WASTE THEM, ETHYLAR!
MY LATE PREDECESSOR MAY HAVE CREATED THOSE SPIDERS IN A MAD BID TO SECURE OUR MEETING PLACE...
...BUT I SEE NO REASON WHY I SHOULD ENDURE THEIR PRESENCE!
ENOUGH! THE DEMON HAS BEEN DRIVEN FROM DALARAN. WE HAVE WEAKENED HIM!
AS HE HAS WEAKENED US. WE HAVE LOST AERTIN BRIGHTHAND... OUR SPEARHEAD. THE BEST OF US!
WE HAVE ALSO LOST THE AMULET OF WATERS. WITH IT, KATHRA'NATIR COULD CORRUPT LORDAMERE LAKE.
WE NEED TO CHOOSE ANOTHER MEMBER FOR OUR COUNCIL OF TIRISFAL. AND WE NEED TO SELECT A NEW SPEARHEAD!

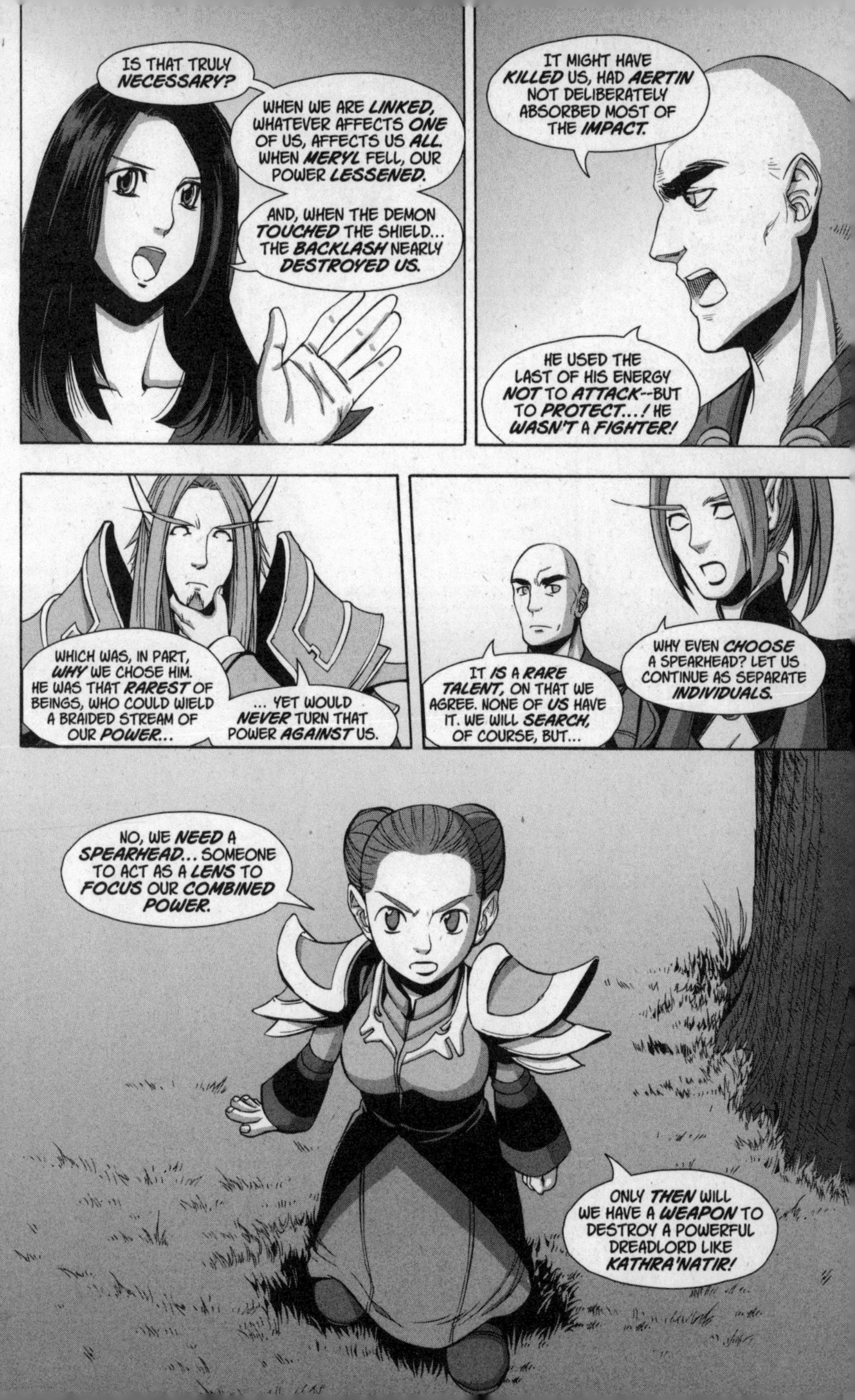
IS THAT TRULY NECESSARY?
WHEN WE ARE LINKED, WHATEVER AFFECTS ONE OF US, AFFECTS US ALL. WHEN MERYL FELL, OUR POWER LESSENED.
AND, WHEN THE DEMON TOUCHED THE SHIELD... THE BACKLASH NEARLY DESTROYED US.
IT MIGHT HAVE KILLED US, HAD AERTIN NOT DELIBERATELY ABSORBED MOST OF THE IMPACT.
HE USED THE LAST OF HIS ENERGY NOT TO ATTACK--BUT TO PROTECT...! HE WASN'T A FIGHTER!
WHICH WAS, IN PART, WHY WE CHOSE HIM. HE WAS THAT RAREST OF BEINGS, WHO COULD WIELD A BRAIDED STREAM OF OUR POWER...
... YET WOULD NEVER TURN THAT POWER AGAINST US.
IT IS A RARE TALENT, ON THAT WE AGREE. NONE OF US HAVE IT. WE WILL SEARCH, OF COURSE, BUT...
WHY EVEN CHOOSE A SPEARHEAD? LET US CONTINUE AS SEPARATE INDIVIDUALS.
NO, WE NEED A SPEARHEAD... SOMEONE TO ACT AS A LENS TO FOCUS OUR COMBINED POWER.
ONLY THEN WILL WE HAVE A WEAPON TO DESTROY A POWERFUL DREADLORD LIKE KATHRA'NATIR!

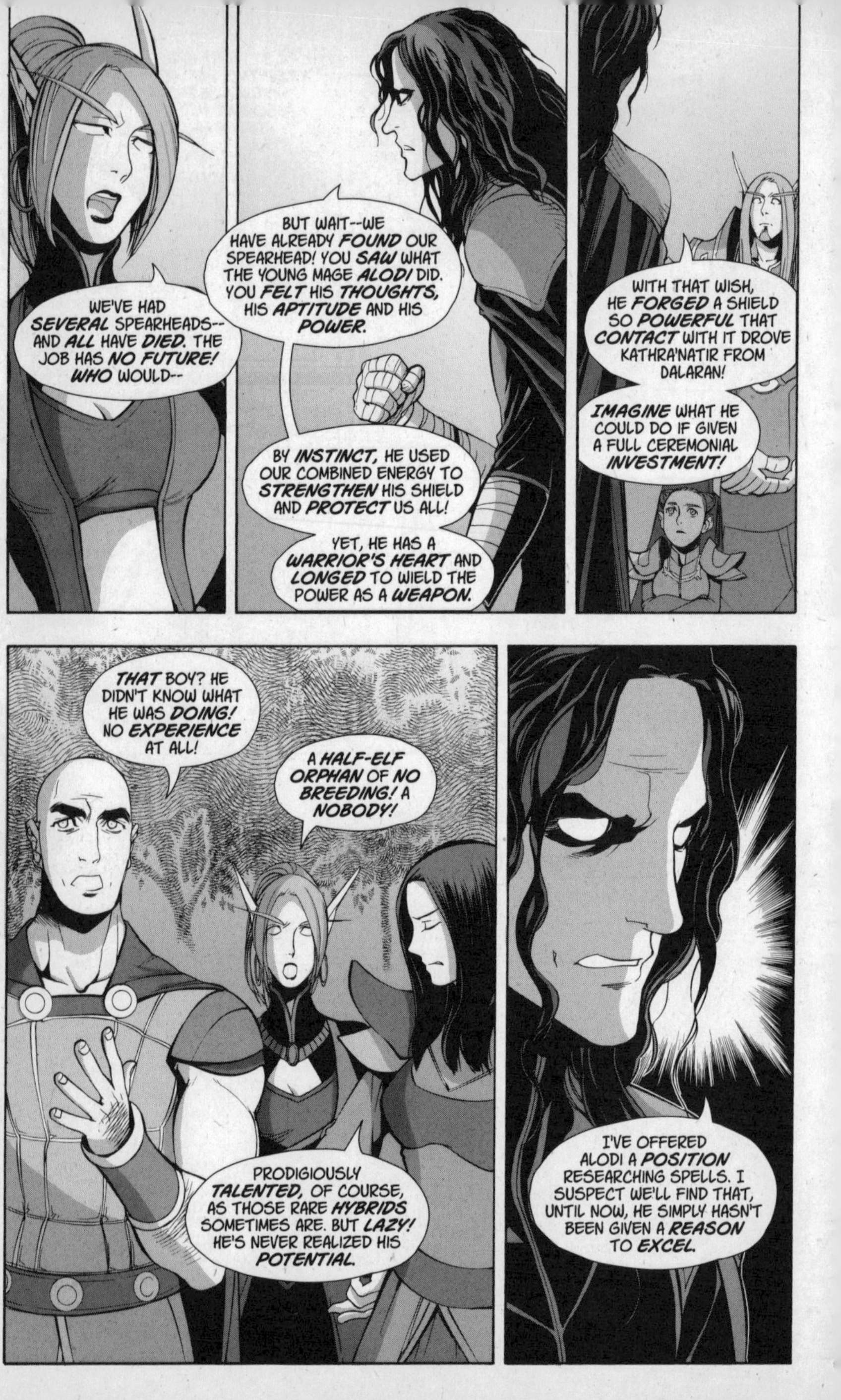
WE'VE HAD SEVERAL SPEARHEADS-- AND ALL HAVE DIED. THE JOB HAS NO FUTURE! WHO WOULD--
BUT WAIT--WE HAVE ALREADY FOUND OUR SPEARHEAD! YOU SAW WHAT THE YOUNG MAGE ALODI DID. YOU FELT HIS THOUGHTS, HIS APTITUDE AND HIS POWER.
BY INSTINCT, HE USED OUR COMBINED ENERGY TO STRENGTHEN HIS SHIELD AND PROTECT US ALL!
YET, HE HAS A WARRIOR'S HEART AND LONGED TO WIELD THE POWER AS A WEAPON.
WITH THAT WISH, HE FORGED A SHIELD SO POWERFUL THAT CONTACT WITH IT DROVE KATHRA'NATIR FROM DALARAN!
IMAGINE WHAT HE COULD DO IF GIVEN A FULL CEREMONIAL INVESTMENT!
THAT BOY? HE DIDN'T KNOW WHAT HE WAS DOING! NO EXPERIENCE AT ALL!
A HALF-ELF ORPHAN OF NO BREEDING! A NOBODY!
PRODIGIOUSLY TALENTED, OF COURSE, AS THOSE RARE HYBRIDS SOMETIMES ARE. BUT LAZY! HE'S NEVER REALIZED HIS POTENTIAL.
I'VE OFFERED ALODI A POSITION RESEARCHING SPELLS. I SUSPECT WE'LL FIND THAT, UNTIL NOW, HE SIMPLY HASN'T BEEN GIVEN A REASON TO EXCEL.

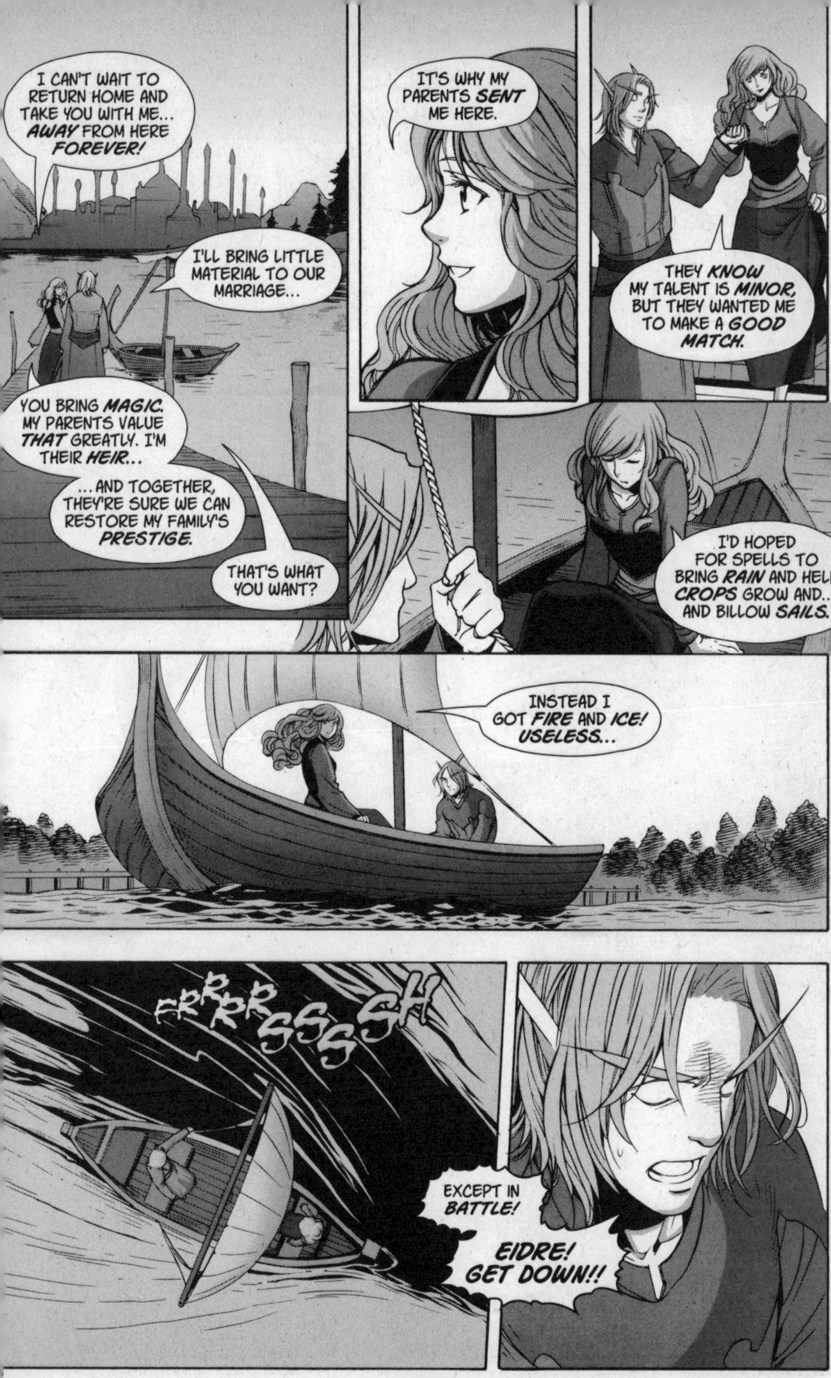
I CAN'T WAIT TO RETURN HOME AND TAKE YOU WITH ME... AWAY FROM HERE FOREVER!
I'LL BRING LITTLE MATERIAL TO OUR MARRIAGE...
YOU BRING MAGIC. MY PARENTS VALUE THAT GREATLY. I'M THEIR HEIR...
...AND TOGETHER, THEY'RE SURE WE CAN RESTORE MY FAMILY'S PRESTIGE.
THAT'S WHAT YOU WANT?
IT'S WHY MY PARENTS SENT ME HERE.
THEY KNOW MY TALENT IS MINOR, BUT THEY WANTED ME TO MAKE A GOOD MATCH.
I'D HOPED FOR SPELLS TO BRING RAIN AND HELP CROPS GROW AND... AND BILLOW SAILS.
INSTEAD I GOT FIRE AND ICE! USELESS...
FRRRRSSSSH
EXCEPT IN BATTLE!
EIDRE! GET DOWN!!

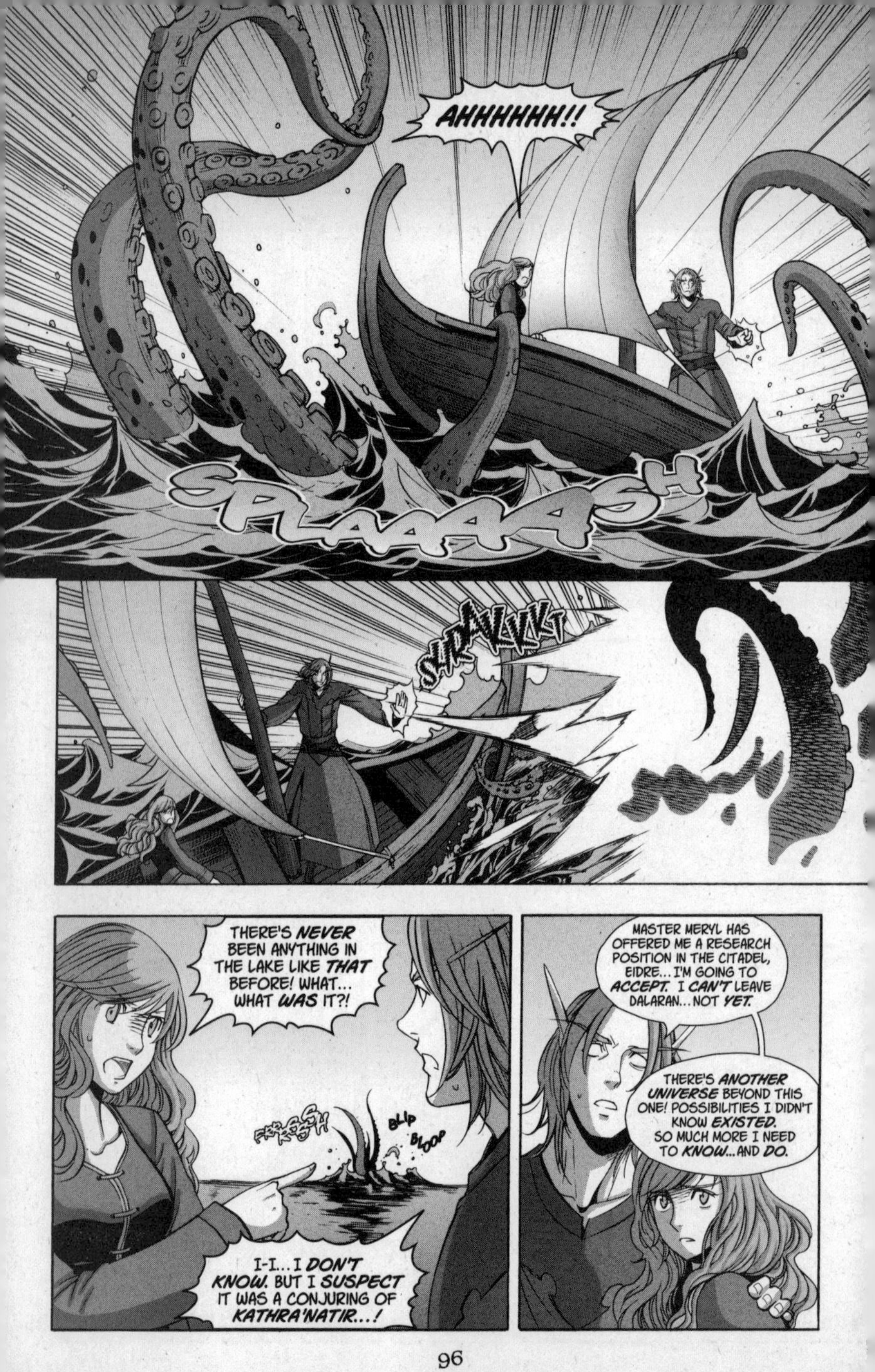
AHHHHHH!!
SPLAAAASH
THERE'S NEVER BEEN ANYTHING IN THE LAKE LIKE THAT BEFORE! WHAT... WHAT WAS IT?!
BLIP
BLOOP
I-I... I DON'T KNOW. BUT I SUSPECT IT WAS A CONJURING OF KATHRA'NATIR...!
MASTER MERYL HAS OFFERED ME A RESEARCH POSITION IN THE CITADEL, EIDRE... I'M GOING TO ACCEPT. I CAN'T LEAVE DALARAN... NOT YET.
THERE'S ANOTHER UNIVERSE BEYOND THIS ONE! POSSIBILITIES I DIDN'T KNOW EXISTED. SO MUCH MORE I NEED TO KNOW... AND DO.

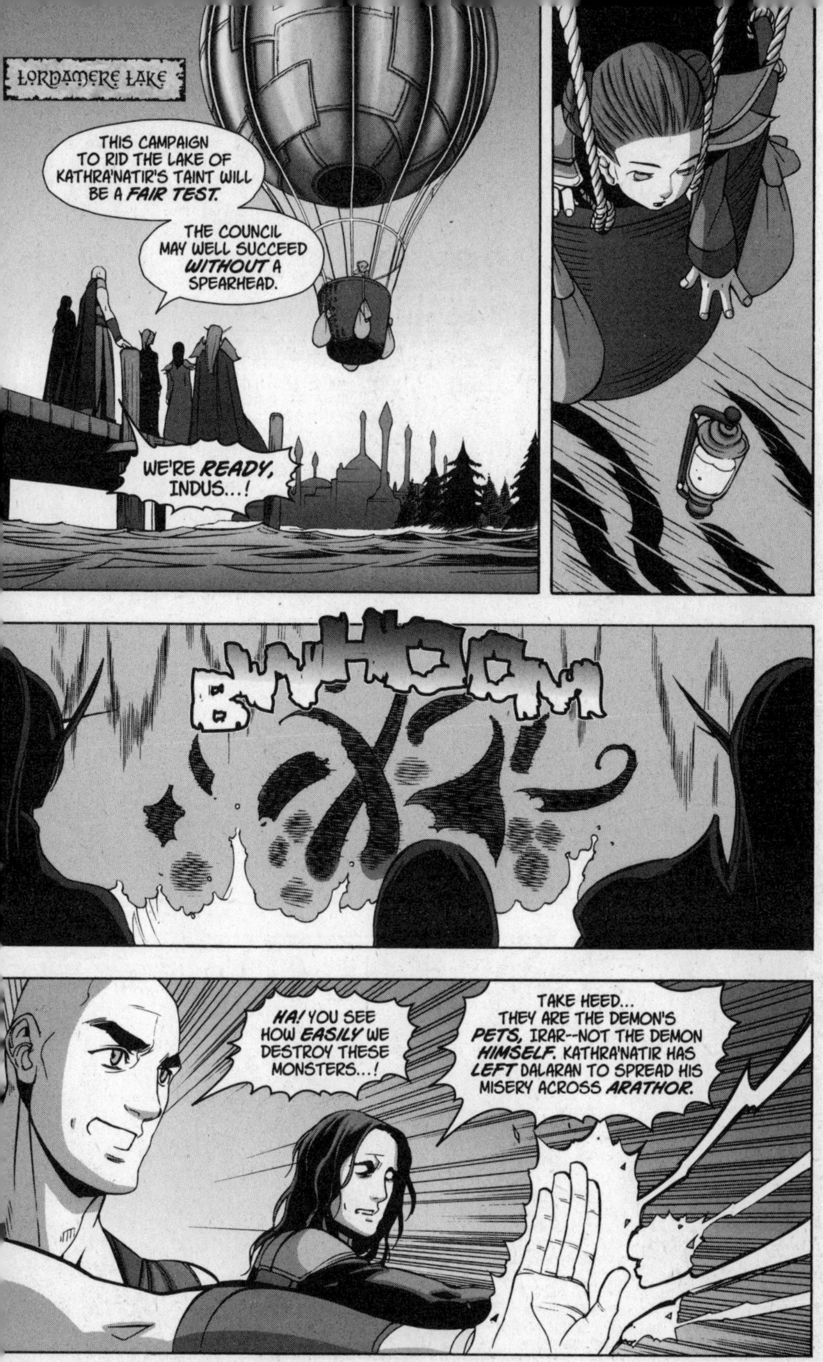
LORDAMERE LAKE
THIS CAMPAIGN TO RID THE LAKE OF KATHRA'NATIR'S TAINT WILL BE A FAIR TEST.
THE COUNCIL MAY WELL SUCCEED WITHOUT A SPEARHEAD.
WE'RE READY, INDUS...!
HA! YOU SEE HOW EASILY WE DESTROY THESE MONSTERS...!
TAKE HEED... THEY ARE THE DEMON'S PETS, IRAR--NOT THE DEMON HIMSELF. KATHRA'NATIR HAS LEFT DALARAN TO SPREAD HIS MISERY ACROSS ARATHOR.

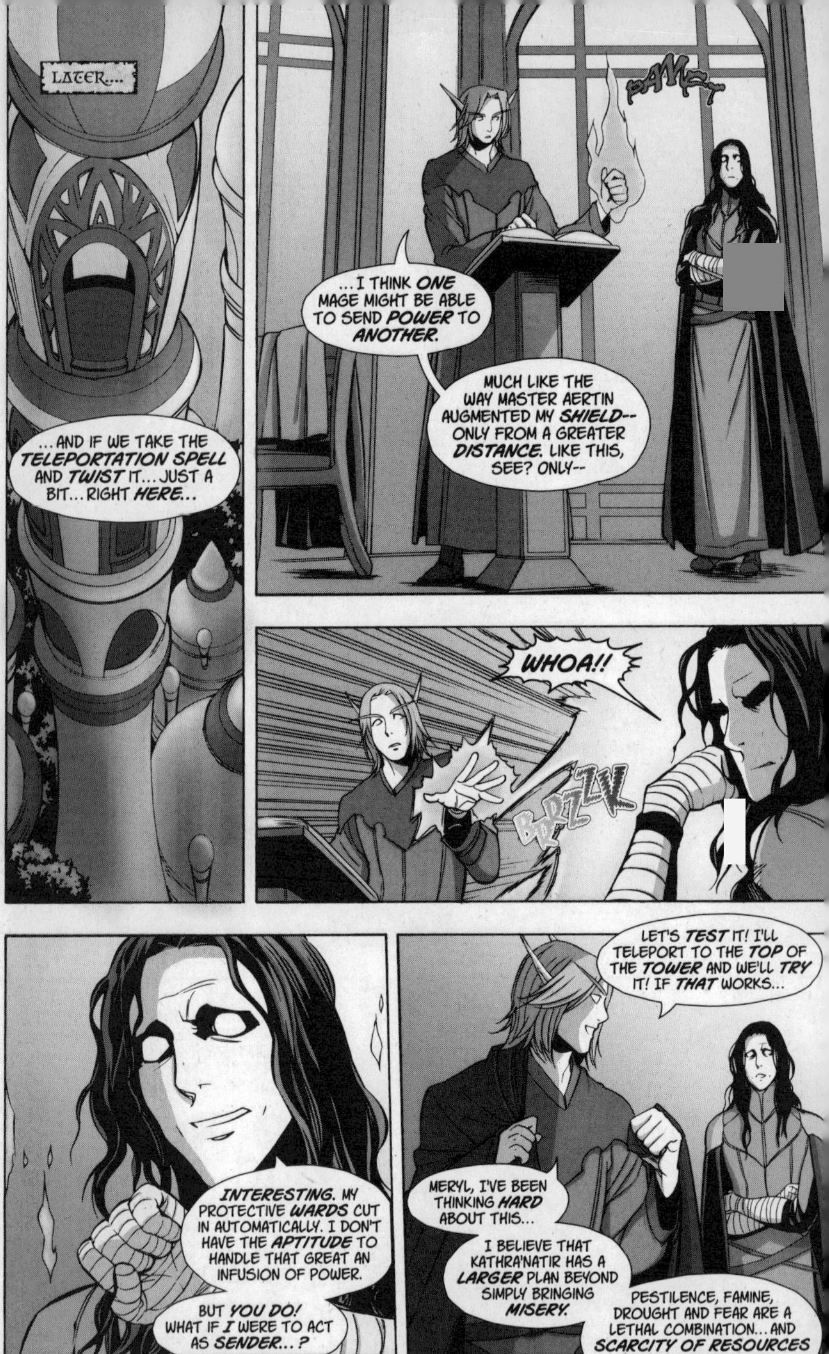
LATER....
...AND IF WE TAKE THE TELEPORTATION SPELL AND TWIST IT... JUST A BIT... RIGHT HERE...
...I THINK ONE MAGE MIGHT BE ABLE TO SEND POWER TO ANOTHER.
MUCH LIKE THE WAY MASTER AERTIN AUGMENTED MY SHIELD-- ONLY FROM A GREATER DISTANCE. LIKE THIS, SEE? ONLY--
WHOA!!
INTERESTING. MY PROTECTIVE WARDS CUT IN AUTOMATICALLY. I DON'T HAVE THE APTITUDE TO HANDLE THAT GREAT AN INFUSION OF POWER.
BUT YOU DO! WHAT IF I WERE TO ACT AS SENDER...?
LET'S TEST IT! I'LL TELEPORT TO THE TOP OF THE TOWER AND WE'LL TRY IT! IF THAT WORKS...
MERYL, I'VE BEEN THINKING HARD ABOUT THIS...
I BELIEVE THAT KATHRA'NATIR HAS A LARGER PLAN BEYOND SIMPLY BRINGING MISERY.
PESTILENCE, FAMINE, DROUGHT AND FEAR ARE A LETHAL COMBINATION... AND SCARCITY OF RESOURCES CAN SO EASILY LEAD TO WAR.

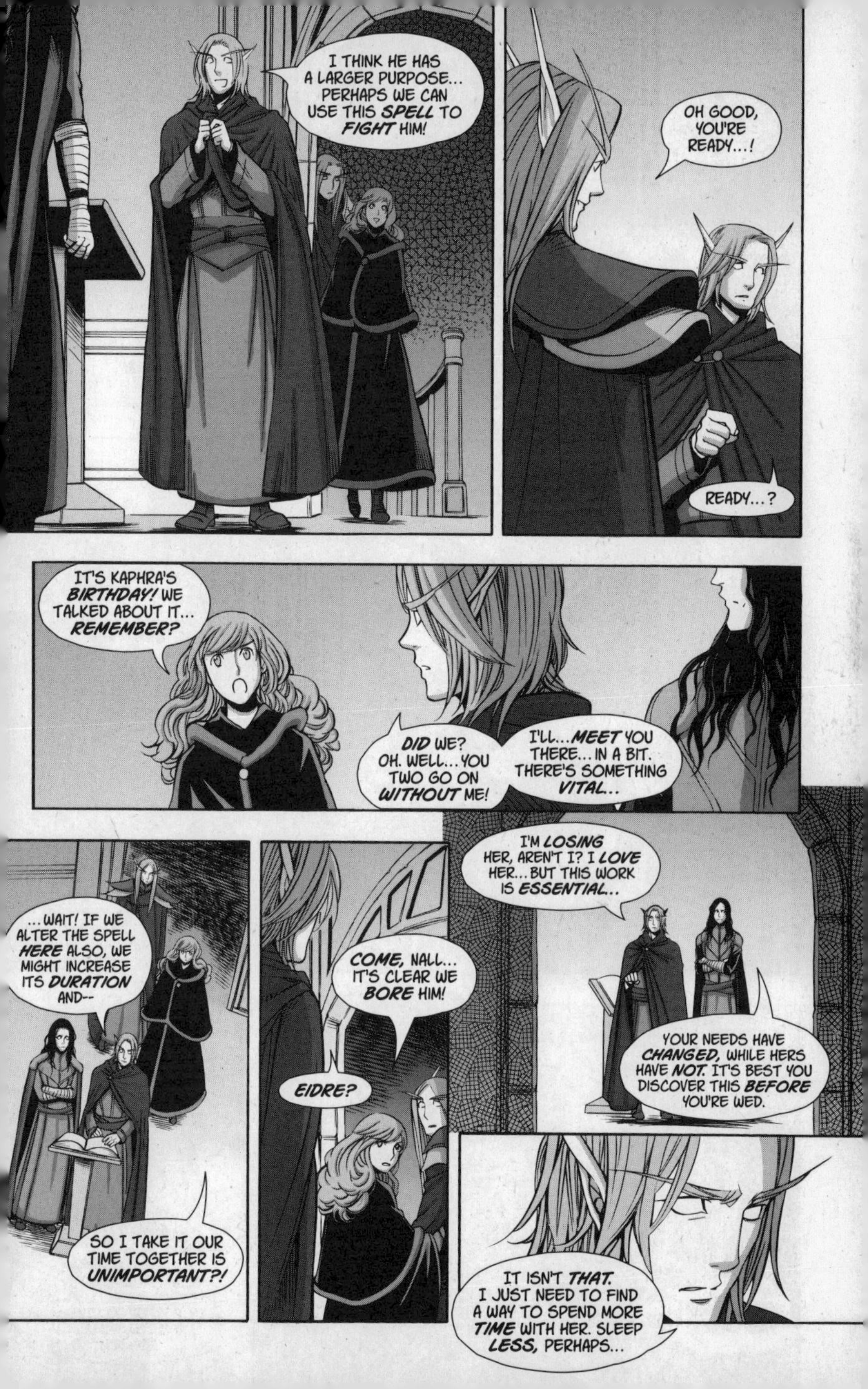
I THINK HE HAS A LARGER PURPOSE... PERHAPS WE CAN USE THIS SPELL TO FIGHT HIM!
OH GOOD, YOU'RE READY...!
READY...?
IT'S KAPHRA'S BIRTHDAY! WE TALKED ABOUT IT... REMEMBER?
DID WE? OH. WELL... YOU TWO GO ON WITHOUT ME!
I'LL... MEET YOU THERE... IN A BIT. THERE'S SOMETHING VITAL...
...WAIT! IF WE ALTER THE SPELL HERE ALSO, WE MIGHT INCREASE ITS DURATION AND--
SO I TAKE IT OUR TIME TOGETHER IS UNIMPORTANT?!
COME, NALL... IT'S CLEAR WE BORE HIM!
EIDRE?
I'M LOSING HER, AREN'T I? I LOVE HER... BUT THIS WORK IS ESSENTIAL...
YOUR NEEDS HAVE CHANGED, WHILE HERS HAVE NOT. IT'S BEST YOU DISCOVER THIS BEFORE YOU'RE WED.
IT ISN'T THAT. I JUST NEED TO FIND A WAY TO SPEND MORE TIME WITH HER. SLEEP LESS, PERHAPS...

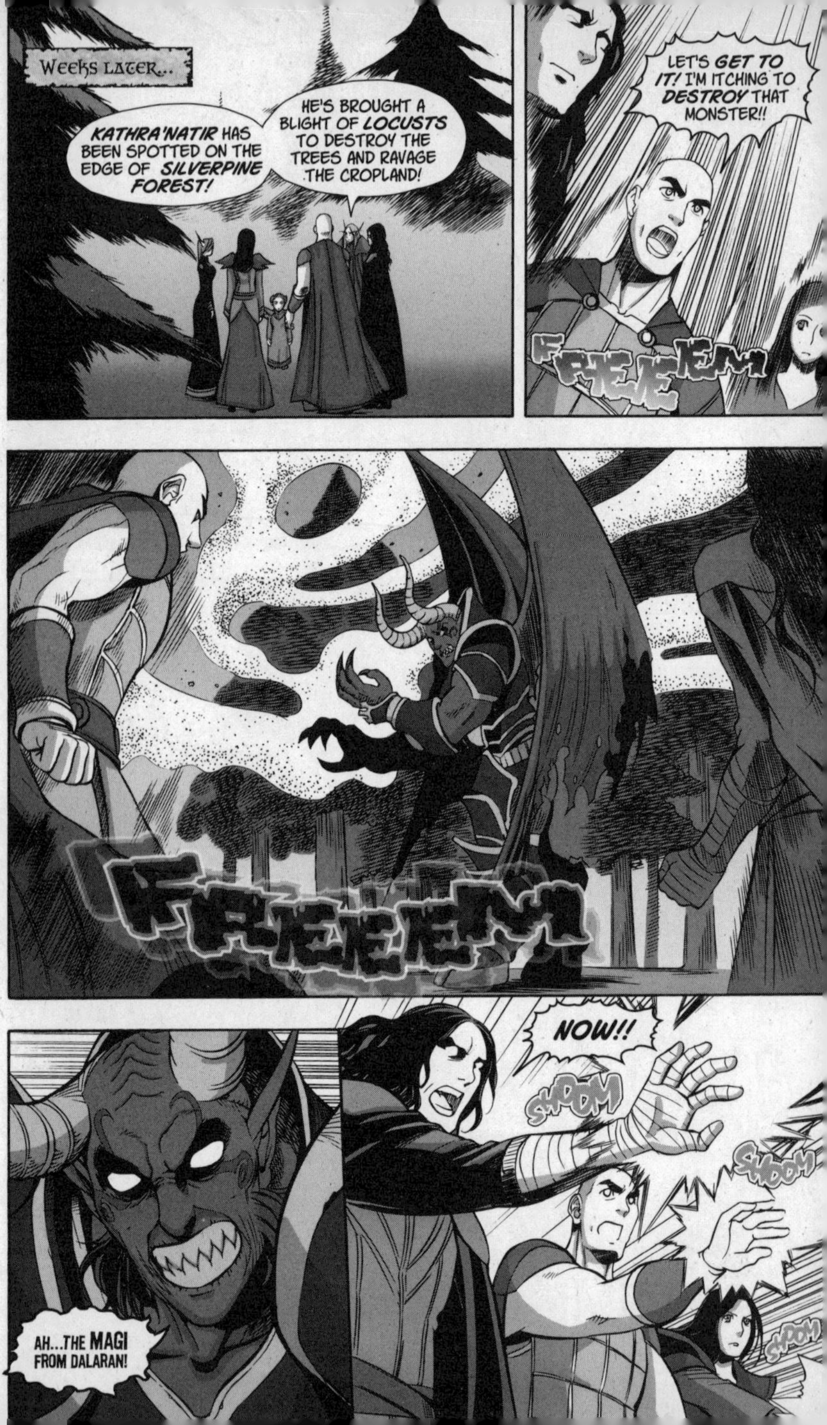
WEEKS LATER...
KATHRA'NATIR HAS BEEN SPOTTED ON THE EDGE OF SILVERPINE FOREST!
HE'S BROUGHT A BLIGHT OF LOCUSTS TO DESTROY THE TREES AND RAVAGE THE CROPLAND!
LET'S GET TO IT! I'M ITCHING TO DESTROY THAT MONSTER!!
FRREEEM
FRREEEEM
AH...THE MAGI FROM DALARAN!
NOW!!
SHOOM
SHOOM
SHOOM

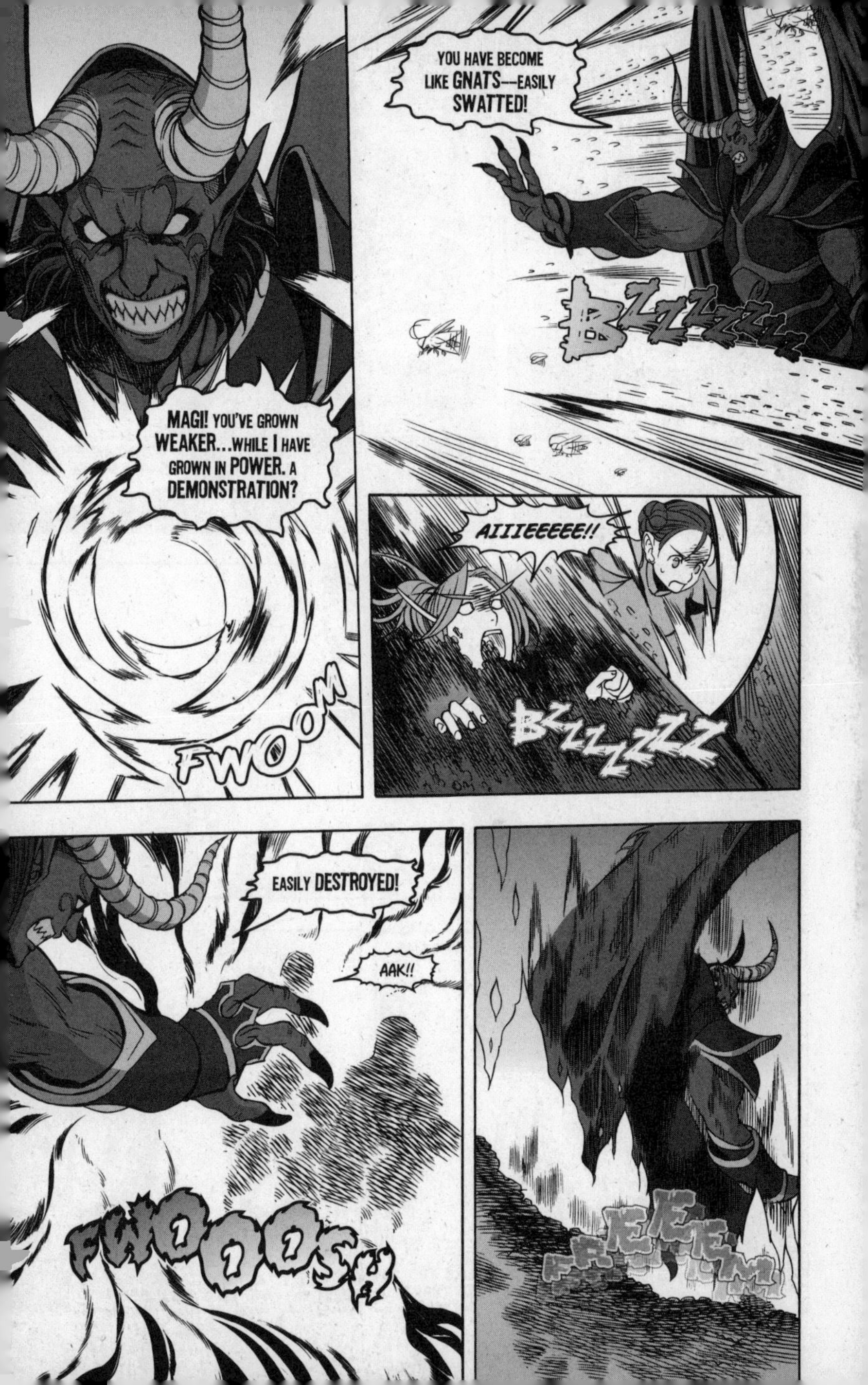
MAGI! YOU'VE GROWN WEAKER...WHILE I HAVE GROWN IN POWER. A DEMONSTRATION?
FWOOM
YOU HAVE BECOME LIKE GNATS--EASILY SWATTED!
BZZZZZZZ
AIIIEEEEE!!
BZZZZZZZ
EASILY DESTROYED!
AAK!!
FWOOOOSH

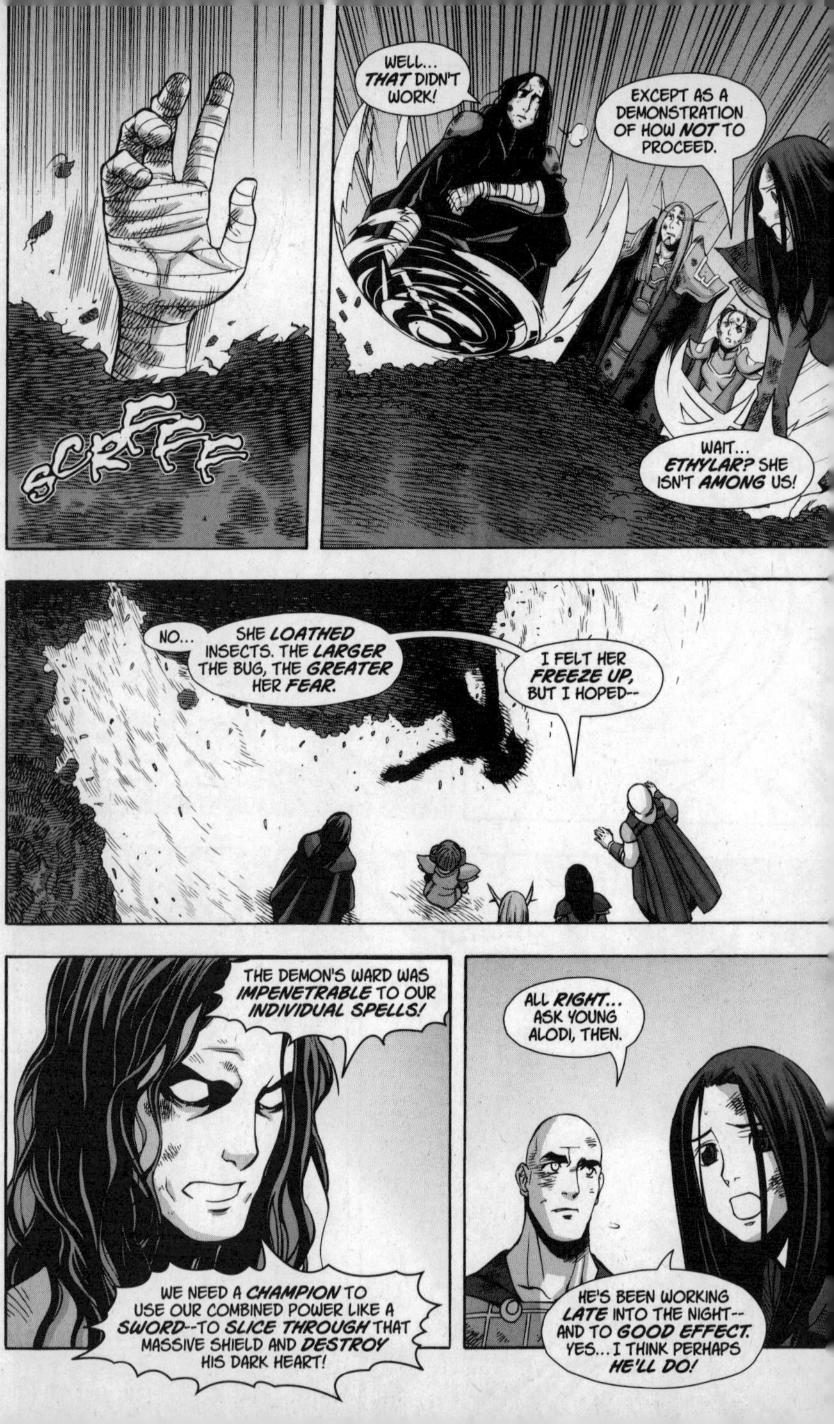
SCRFFF
WELL... *THAT* DIDN'T WORK!
EXCEPT AS A DEMONSTRATION OF HOW *NOT* TO PROCEED.
WAIT... *ETHYLAR?* SHE ISN'T *AMONG* US!
NO...
SHE *LOATHED* INSECTS. THE *LARGER* THE BUG, THE *GREATER* HER *FEAR.*
I FELT HER *FREEZE UP,* BUT I HOPED--
THE DEMON'S WARD WAS *IMPENETRABLE* TO OUR *INDIVIDUAL SPELLS!*
WE NEED A *CHAMPION* TO USE OUR COMBINED POWER LIKE A *SWORD*--TO *SLICE THROUGH* THAT MASSIVE SHIELD AND *DESTROY* HIS DARK HEART!
ALL *RIGHT*... ASK YOUNG ALODI, THEN.
HE'S BEEN WORKING *LATE* INTO THE NIGHT-- AND TO *GOOD EFFECT.* YES... I THINK PERHAPS *HE'LL DO!*

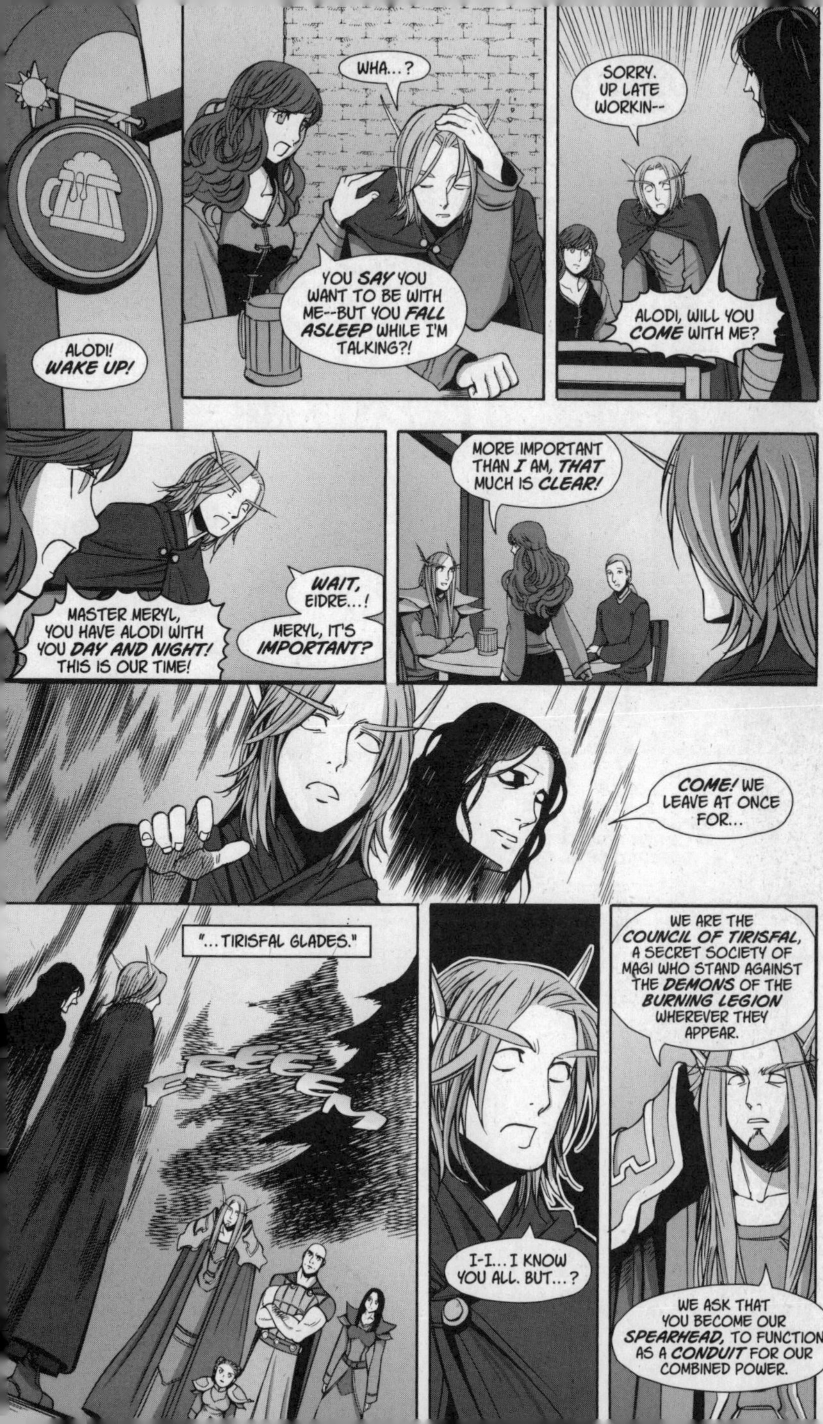
ALODI! WAKE UP!
WHA...?
YOU SAY YOU WANT TO BE WITH ME--BUT YOU FALL ASLEEP WHILE I'M TALKING?!
SORRY. UP LATE WORKIN--
ALODI, WILL YOU COME WITH ME?
MASTER MERYL, YOU HAVE ALODI WITH YOU DAY AND NIGHT! THIS IS OUR TIME!
WAIT, EIDRE...!
MERYL, IT'S IMPORTANT?
MORE IMPORTANT THAN I AM, THAT MUCH IS CLEAR!
COME! WE LEAVE AT ONCE FOR...
"...TIRISFAL GLADES."
I-I... I KNOW YOU ALL. BUT...?
WE ARE THE COUNCIL OF TIRISFAL, A SECRET SOCIETY OF MAGI WHO STAND AGAINST THE DEMONS OF THE BURNING LEGION WHEREVER THEY APPEAR.
WE ASK THAT YOU BECOME OUR SPEARHEAD, TO FUNCTION AS A CONDUIT FOR OUR COMBINED POWER.

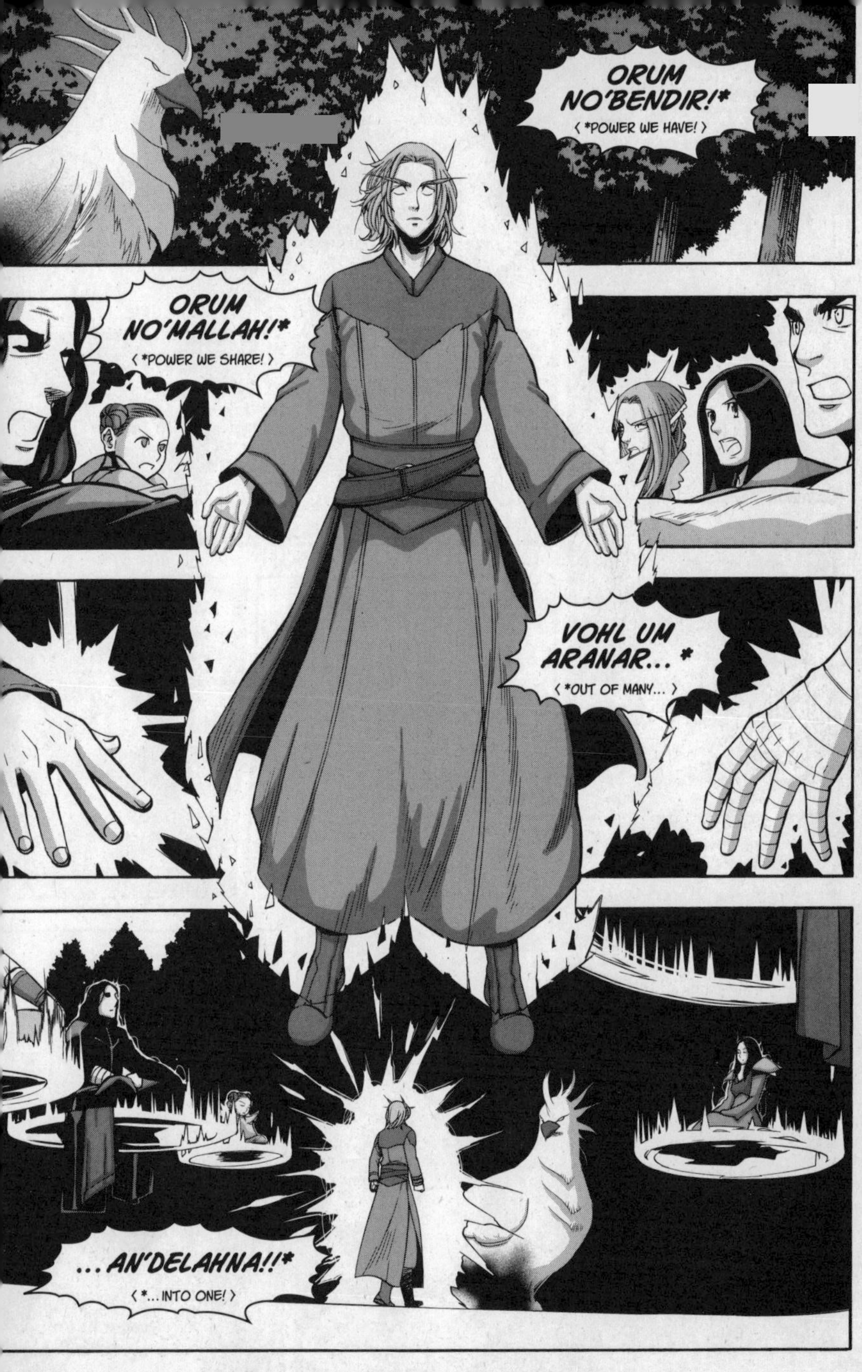
ORUM NO'BENDIR!*
‹ *POWER WE HAVE! ›
ORUM NO'MALLAH!*
‹ *POWER WE SHARE! ›
VOHL UM ARANAR... *
‹ *OUT OF MANY... ›
... AN'DELAHNA!!*
‹ *... INTO ONE! ›

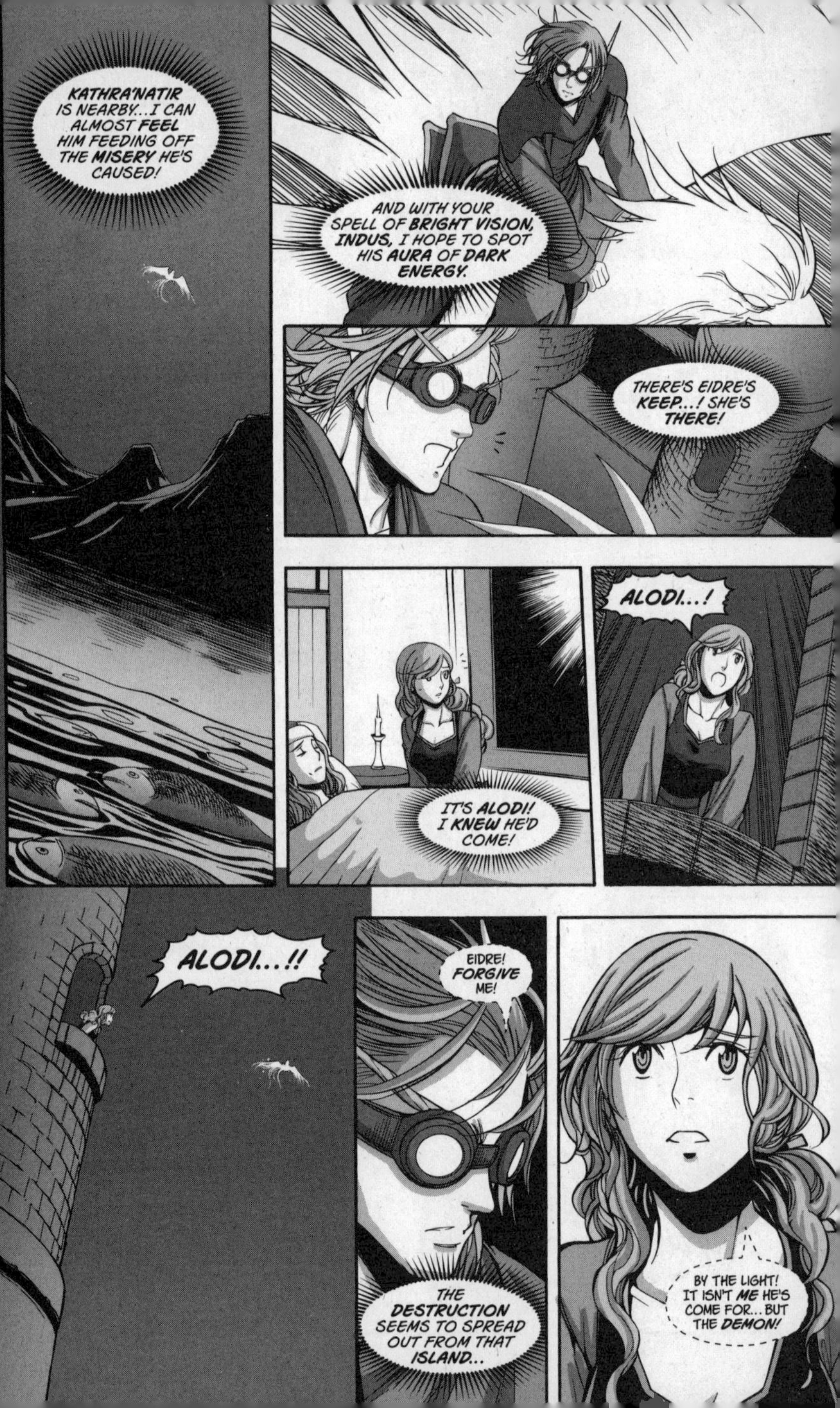
KATHRA'NATIR IS NEARBY...I CAN ALMOST FEEL HIM FEEDING OFF THE MISERY HE'S CAUSED!
AND WITH YOUR SPELL OF BRIGHT VISION, INDUS, I HOPE TO SPOT HIS AURA OF DARK ENERGY.
THERE'S EIDRE'S KEEP...! SHE'S THERE!
IT'S ALODI! I KNEW HE'D COME!
ALODI...!
ALODI...!!
EIDRE! FORGIVE ME!
THE DESTRUCTION SEEMS TO SPREAD OUT FROM THAT ISLAND...
BY THE LIGHT! IT ISN'T ME HE'S COME FOR... BUT THE DEMON!

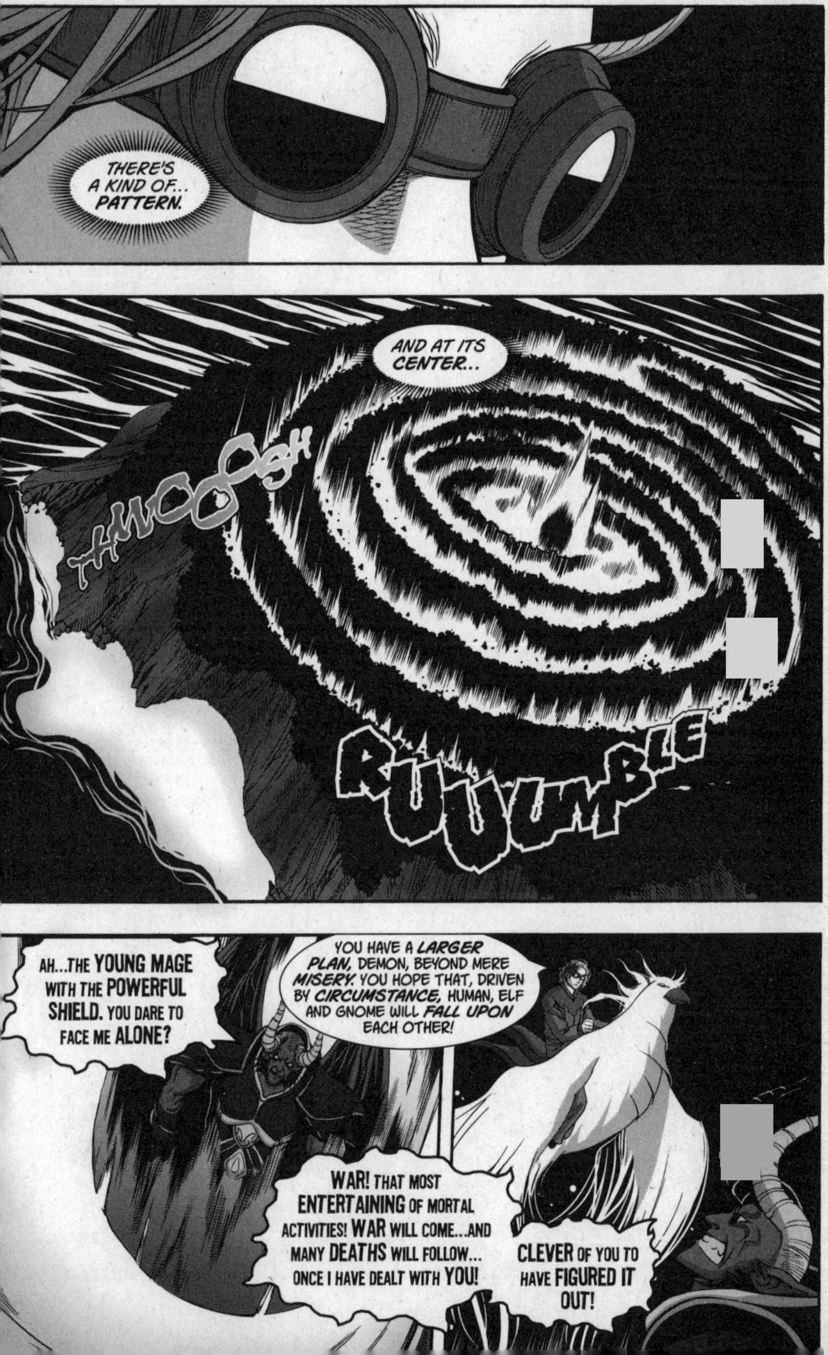

THERE'S A KIND OF... PATTERN.
AND AT ITS CENTER...
THWOOOSH
RUUUMBLE
AH...THE YOUNG MAGE WITH THE POWERFUL SHIELD. YOU DARE TO FACE ME ALONE?
YOU HAVE A LARGER PLAN, DEMON, BEYOND MERE MISERY. YOU HOPE THAT, DRIVEN BY CIRCUMSTANCE, HUMAN, ELF AND GNOME WILL FALL UPON EACH OTHER!
WAR! THAT MOST ENTERTAINING OF MORTAL ACTIVITIES! WAR WILL COME...AND MANY DEATHS WILL FOLLOW... ONCE I HAVE DEALT WITH YOU!
CLEVER OF YOU TO HAVE FIGURED IT OUT!

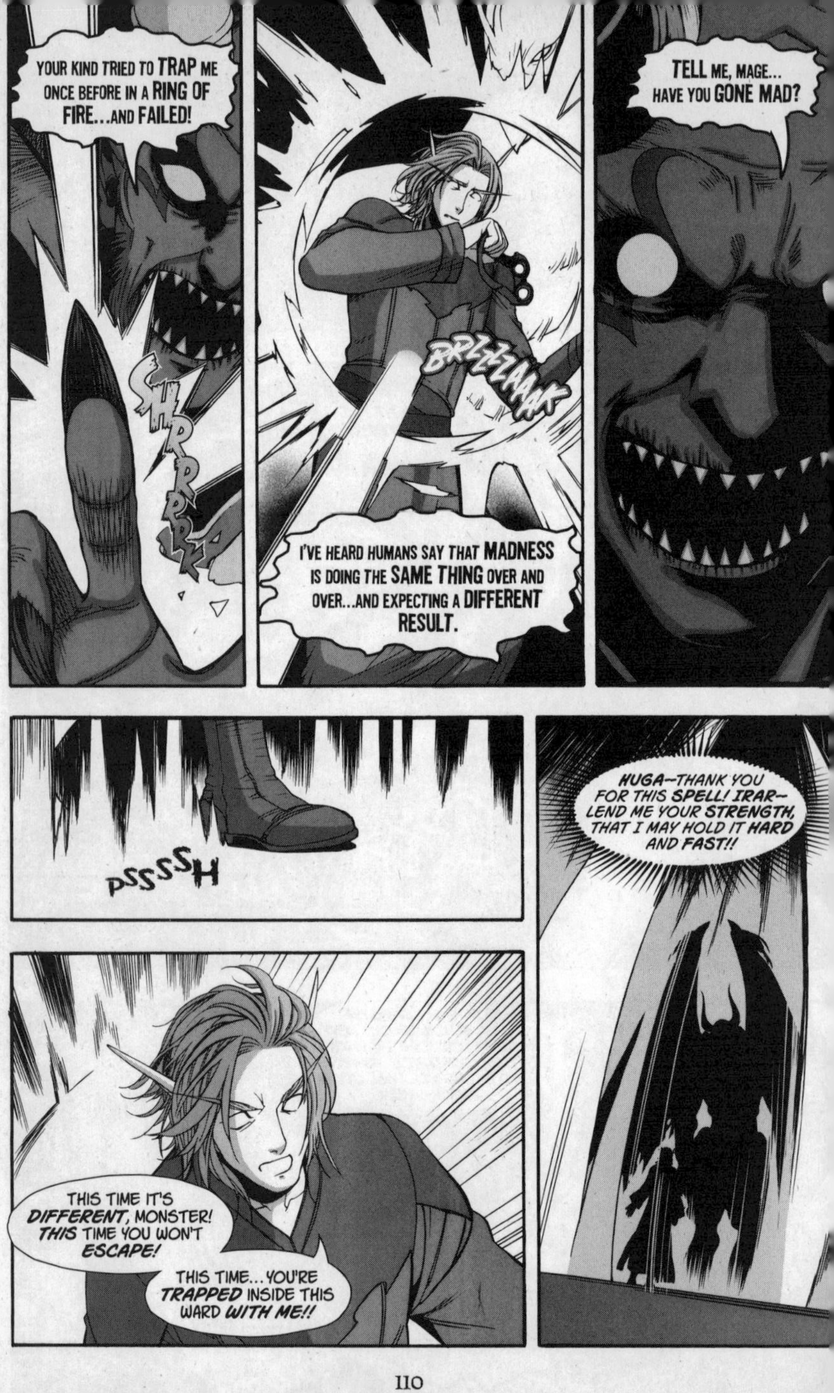
YOUR KIND TRIED TO **TRAP** ME ONCE BEFORE IN A **RING OF FIRE**...AND **FAILED!**
SHRRRRK
BRZZZAAAK
I'VE HEARD HUMANS SAY THAT **MADNESS** IS DOING THE **SAME THING** OVER AND OVER...AND EXPECTING A **DIFFERENT RESULT.**
TELL ME, MAGE... HAVE YOU **GONE MAD?**
PSSSSH
THIS TIME IT'S ***DIFFERENT***, MONSTER! ***THIS*** TIME YOU WON'T ***ESCAPE!***
THIS TIME... YOU'RE ***TRAPPED*** INSIDE THIS WARD ***WITH ME!!***
*HUGA—THANK YOU FOR THIS **SPELL!** IRAR—LEND ME YOUR **STRENGTH**, THAT I MAY HOLD IT **HARD AND FAST!!***

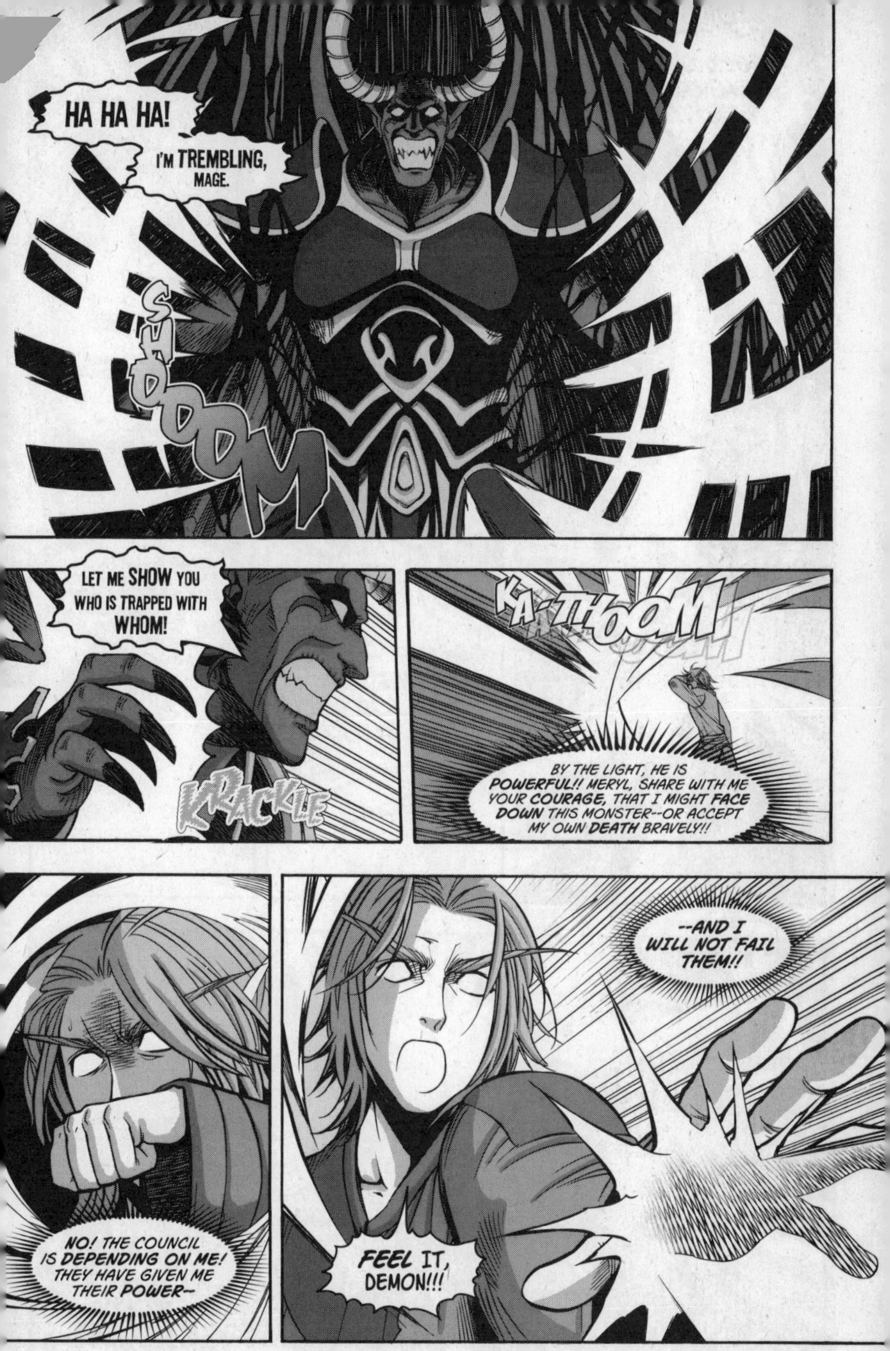
HA HA HA!
I'M TREMBLING, MAGE.
SHADOOM
LET ME SHOW YOU WHO IS TRAPPED WITH WHOM!
KRACKLE
KA-THOOM
BY THE LIGHT, HE IS POWERFUL!! MERYL, SHARE WITH ME YOUR COURAGE, THAT I MIGHT FACE DOWN THIS MONSTER--OR ACCEPT MY OWN DEATH BRAVELY!!
NO! THE COUNCIL IS DEPENDING ON ME! THEY HAVE GIVEN ME THEIR POWER--
--AND I WILL NOT FAIL THEM!!
FEEL IT, DEMON!!!

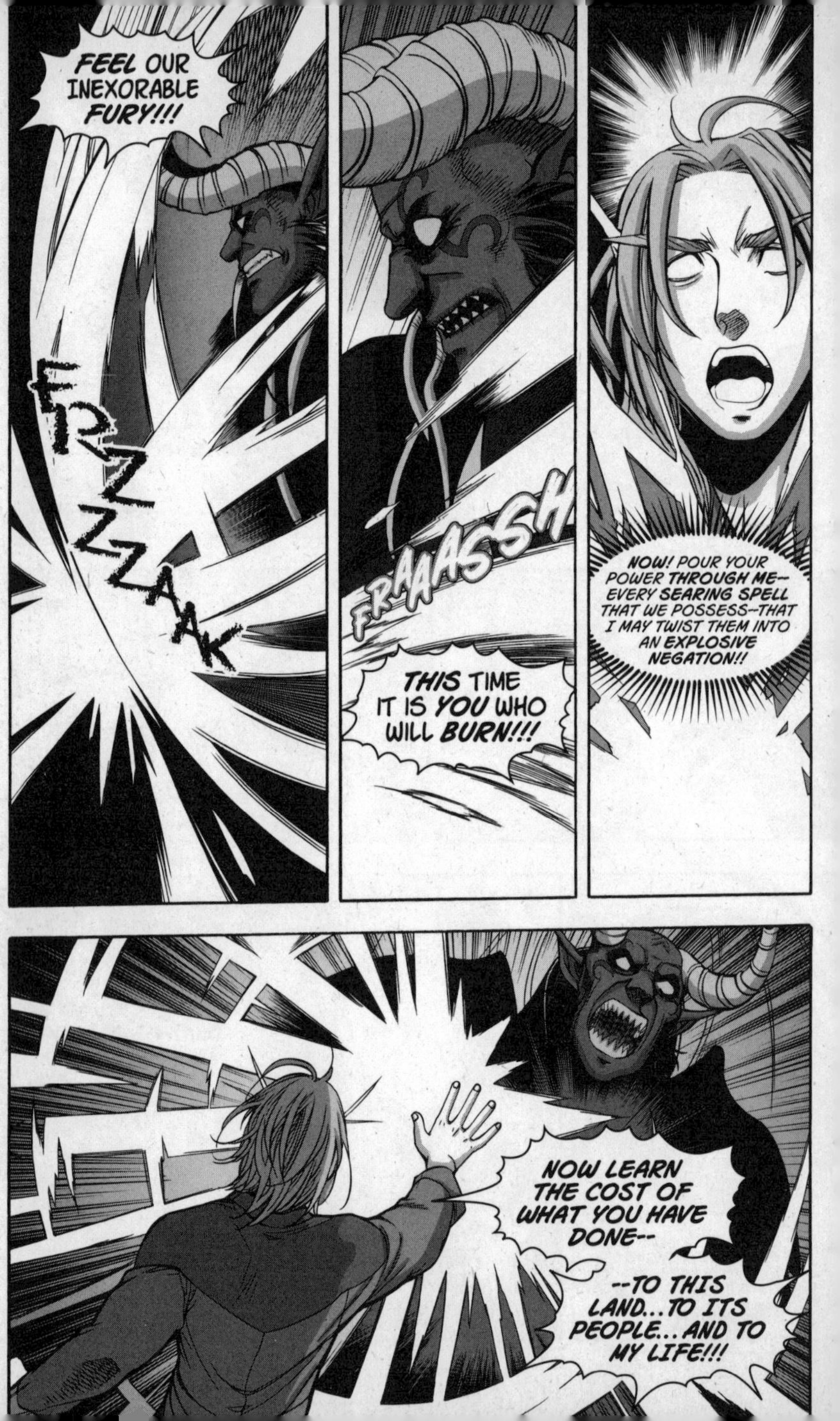
FEEL OUR INEXORABLE FURY!!!
FRZZZZAAK
FRAAASSH
THIS TIME IT IS YOU WHO WILL BURN!!!
NOW! POUR YOUR POWER THROUGH ME-- EVERY SEARING SPELL THAT WE POSSESS--THAT I MAY TWIST THEM INTO AN EXPLOSIVE NEGATION!!
NOW LEARN THE COST OF WHAT YOU HAVE DONE--
--TO THIS LAND...TO ITS PEOPLE...AND TO MY LIFE!!!

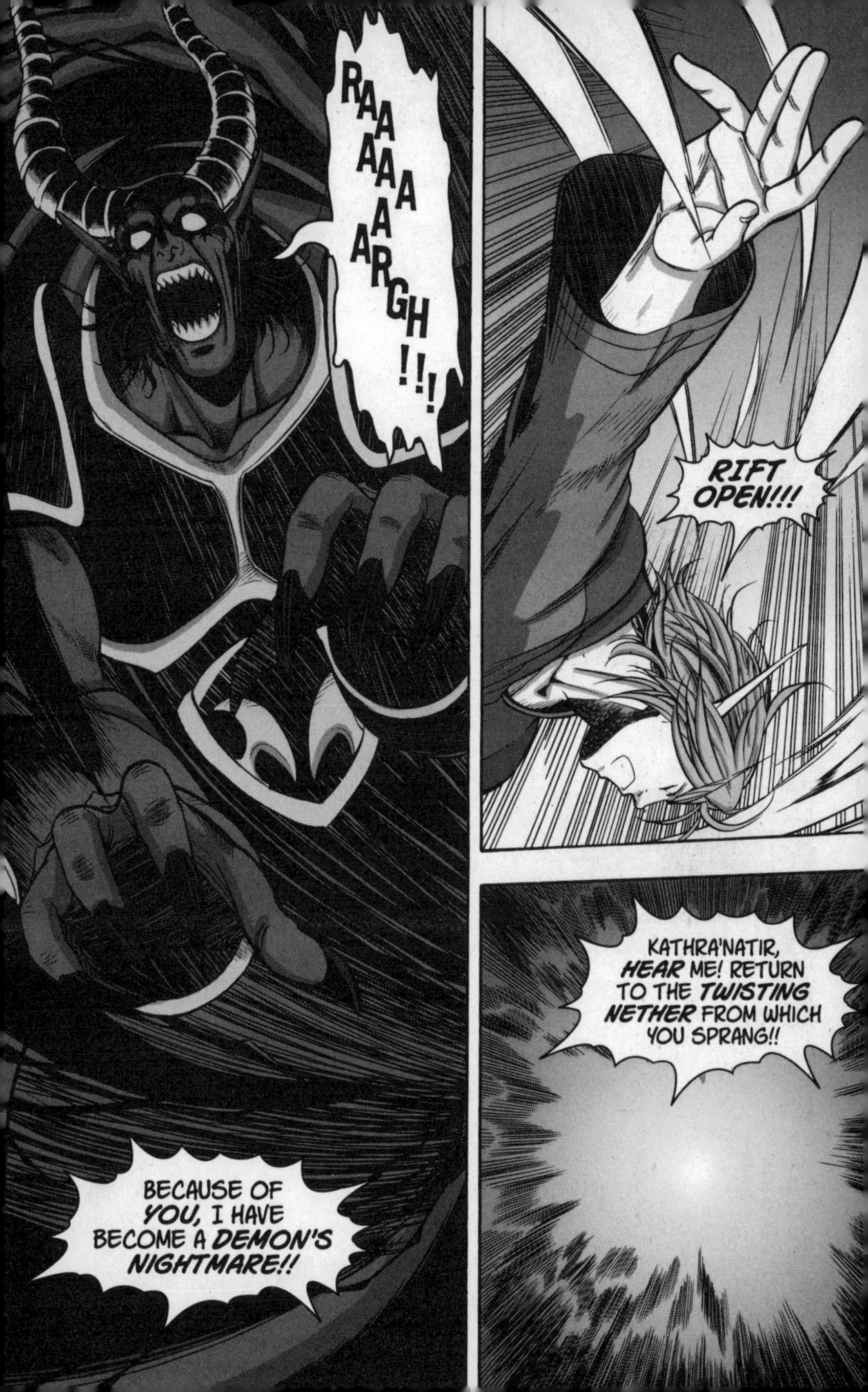
RAAAAAAARGH!!!
BECAUSE OF YOU, I HAVE BECOME A DEMON'S NIGHTMARE!!
RIFT OPEN!!!
KATHRA'NATIR, HEAR ME! RETURN TO THE TWISTING NETHER FROM WHICH YOU SPRANG!!

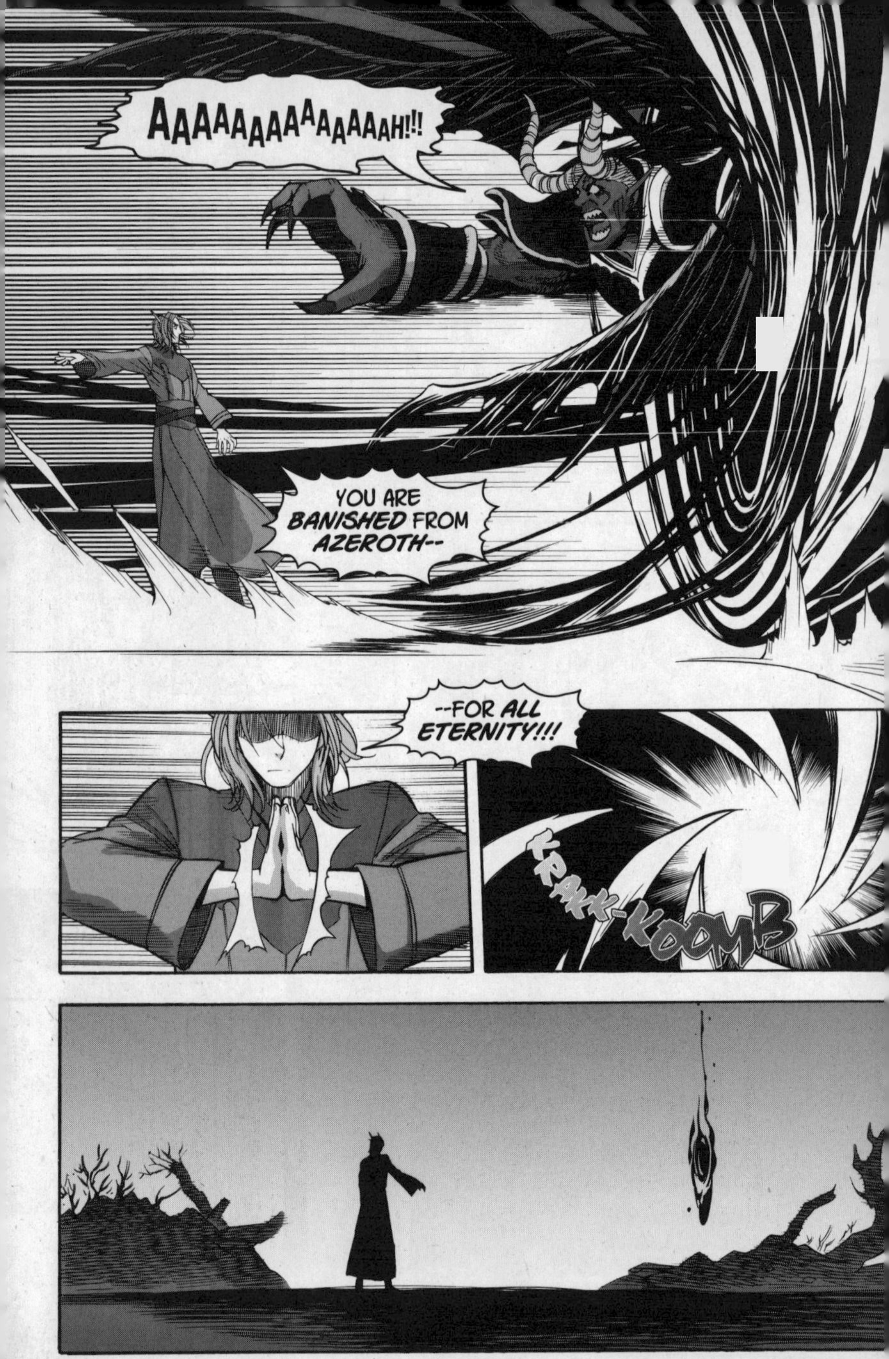

AAAAAAAAAAAAAH!!!
YOU ARE BANISHED FROM AZEROTH--
--FOR ALL ETERNITY!!!
KRAKK-KOOMB

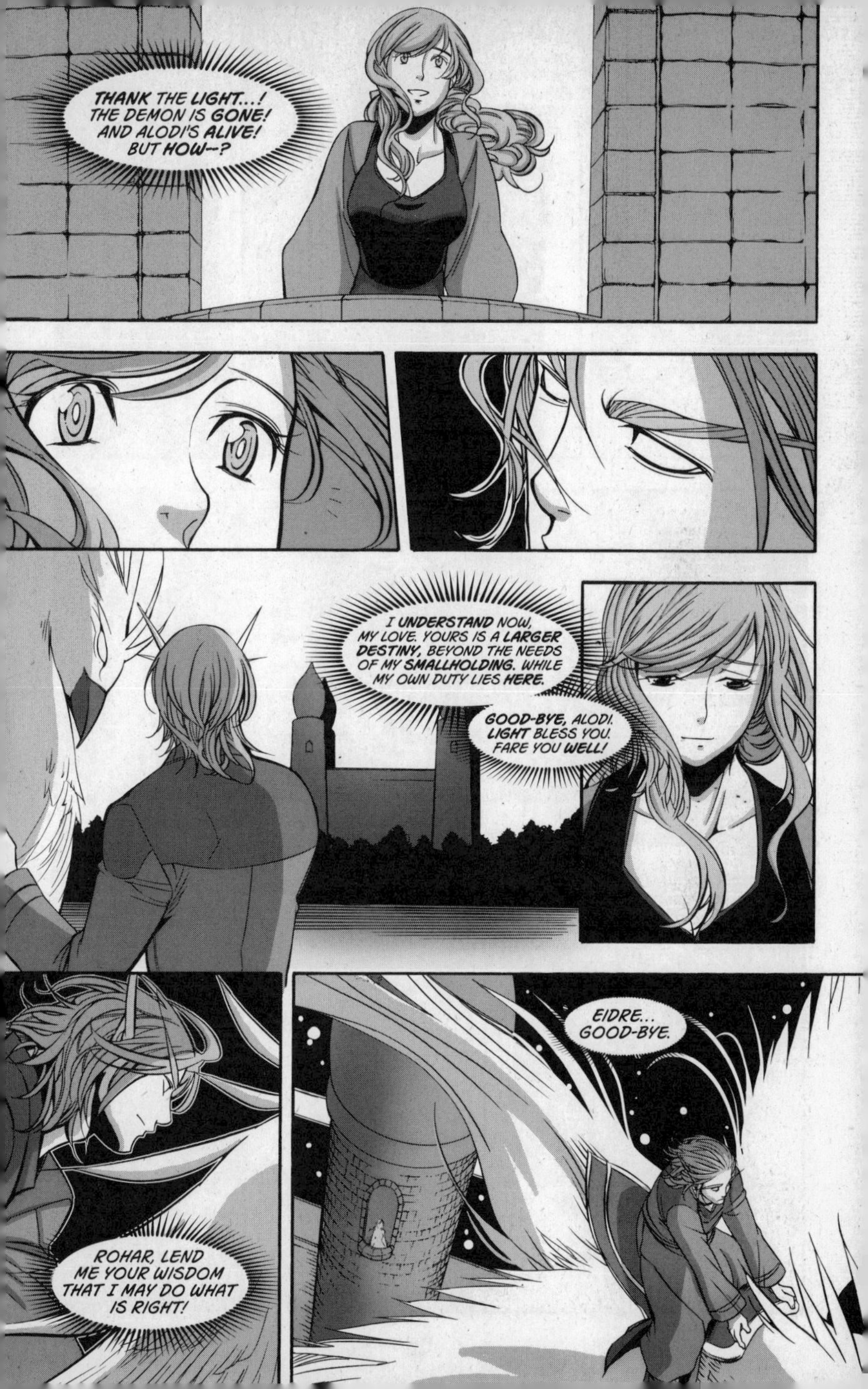
THANK THE LIGHT...! THE DEMON IS GONE! AND ALODI'S ALIVE! BUT HOW--?
I UNDERSTAND NOW, MY LOVE. YOURS IS A LARGER DESTINY, BEYOND THE NEEDS OF MY SMALLHOLDING. WHILE MY OWN DUTY LIES HERE.
GOOD-BYE, ALODI. LIGHT BLESS YOU. FARE YOU WELL!
ROHAR, LEND ME YOUR WISDOM THAT I MAY DO WHAT IS RIGHT!
EIDRE... GOOD-BYE.

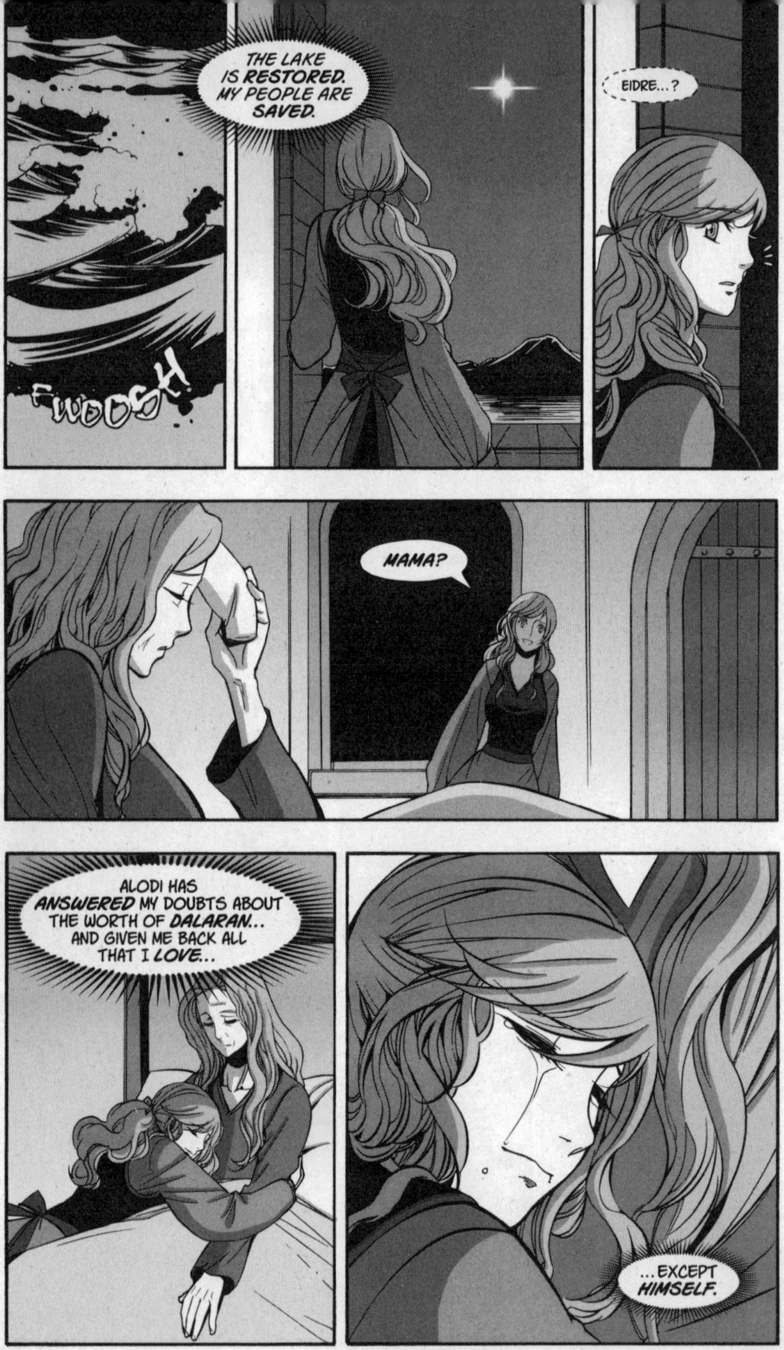
FWOOSH!
THE LAKE IS RESTORED. MY PEOPLE ARE SAVED.
EIDRE...?
MAMA?
ALODI HAS ANSWERED MY DOUBTS ABOUT THE WORTH OF DALARAN... AND GIVEN ME BACK ALL THAT I LOVE...
...EXCEPT HIMSELF.

AT LEAST UNTIL THE *NEXT* DEMON THREATENS AZEROTH. IS OUR MAGIC SO *IRKSOME* THAT YOU ARE *EAGER* TO BE *RID* OF IT?

KATHRA'NATIR IS *BANISHED* TO THE TWISTING NETHER. HE WILL TROUBLE AZEROTH *NO LONGER!*

AND NOW... I MUST *RETURN* YOUR *POWER.*

I BOTH *LOVE* AND *HATE* WHAT I'VE BECOME. WHAT THIS SHARED POWER *MAKES* ME.

YOU *ARE* WHAT YOU WERE *BORN* TO BE--THE FIRST *GUARDIAN OF TIRISFAL.*

I HOPE THAT, IN THE END, ITS *VALUE* WILL BE GREATER THAN WHAT YOU HAVE *SACRIFICED...* LIKE *EIDRE.*

IT'S BETTER THIS WAY, INDUS. EIDRE *HATED* LIVING IN DALARAN. SHE WAS COMFORTABLE WORKING ONLY THE MOST *HUMBLE SPELLS.* AND SHE WAS *TERRIFIED* OF DEMONS.

THIS WAY IS *WISEST.* SHE WOULD HAVE ENDED UP *HATING* OUR LIFE TOGETHER. WE... WOULD HAVE HATED *EACH OTHER.*

BUT NOW, I HAVE A LARGER *DUTY...* TO PROTECT *ALL* OF AZEROTH!

EIDRE'S FIRST DUTY WAS ALWAYS TO *HER PEOPLE.* I ACCEPTED THAT. BEFORE KATHRA'NATIR, I WOULD HAVE *JOINED* HER.

END

WARCRAFT

LEGENDS

VOLUME FIVE

A CLEANSING FIRE

WRITTEN BY EVELYN FREDERICKSEN

PENCILS & TONES BY RYO KAWAKAMI
INKS BY FERNANDO MELEK

LETTERER: MICHAEL PAOLILLI

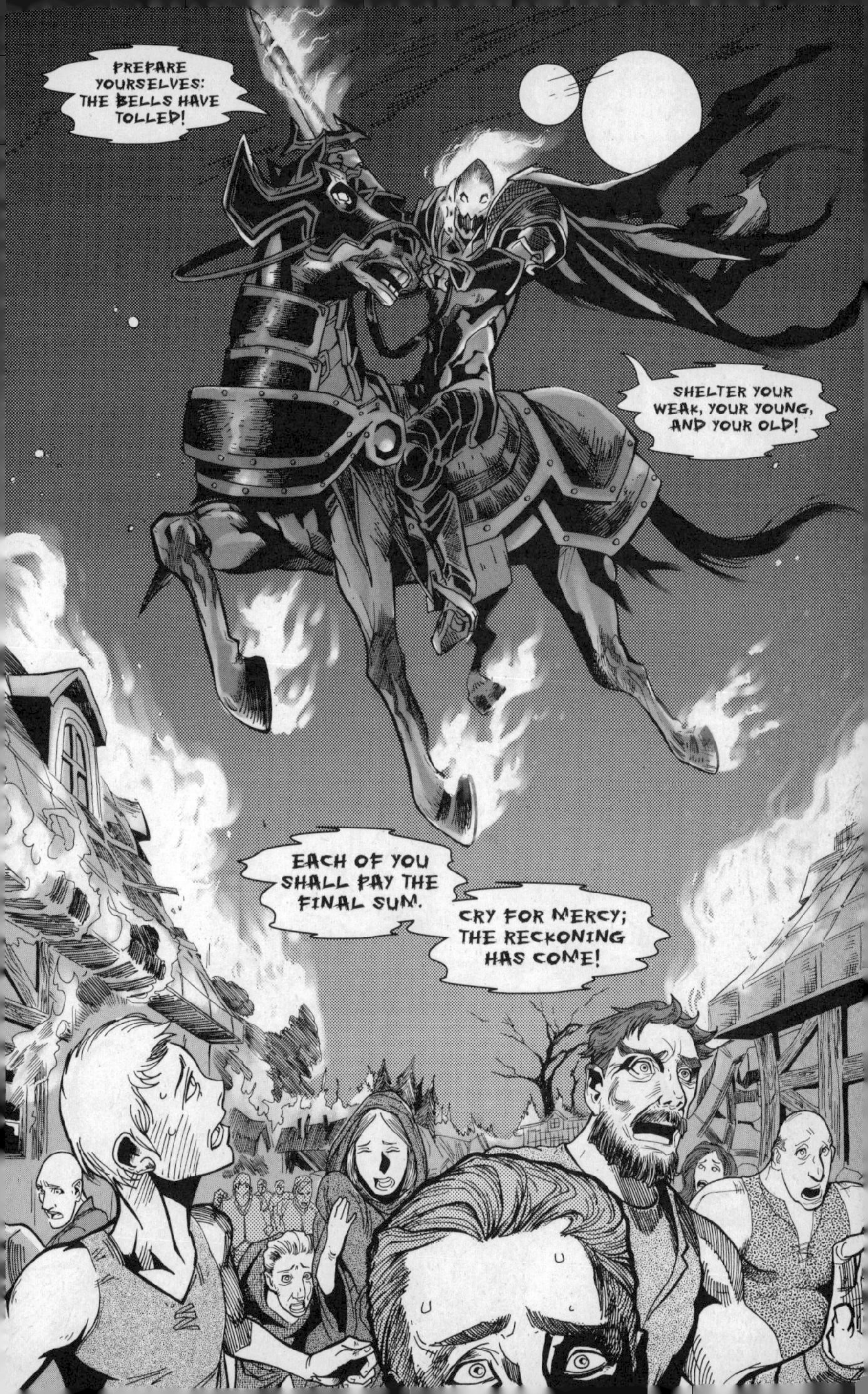
PREPARE YOURSELVES: THE BELLS HAVE TOLLED!
SHELTER YOUR WEAK, YOUR YOUNG, AND YOUR OLD!
EACH OF YOU SHALL PAY THE FINAL SUM.
CRY FOR MERCY; THE RECKONING HAS COME!

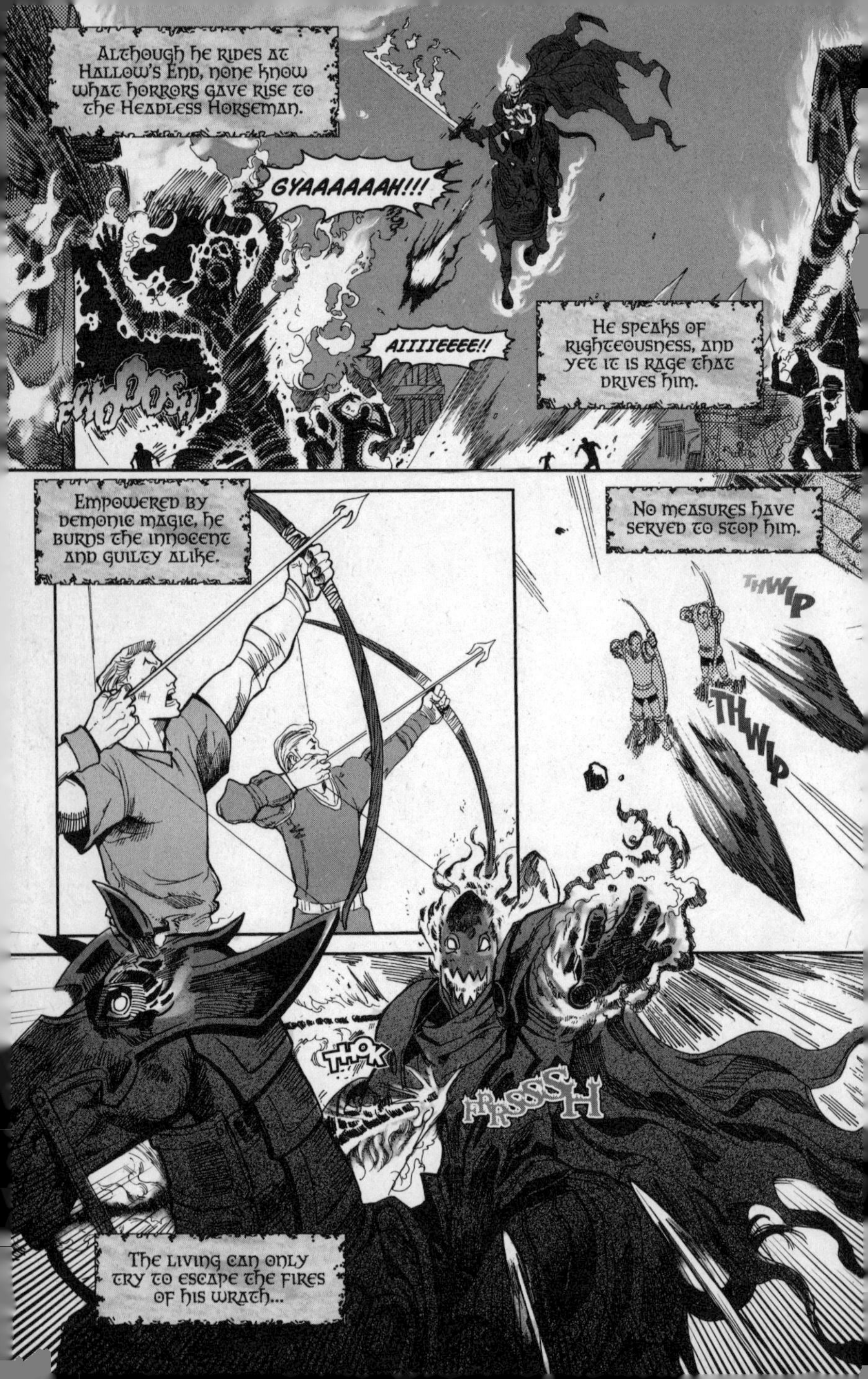

Although he rides at Hallow's End, none know what horrors gave rise to the Headless Horseman.
GYAAAAAAH!!!
AIIIIEEEE!!
FWOOSH
He speaks of righteousness, and yet it is rage that drives him.
Empowered by demonic magic, he burns the innocent and guilty alike.
No measures have served to stop him.
THWIP
THWIP
THOK
FRRSSSH
The living can only try to escape the fires of his wrath...

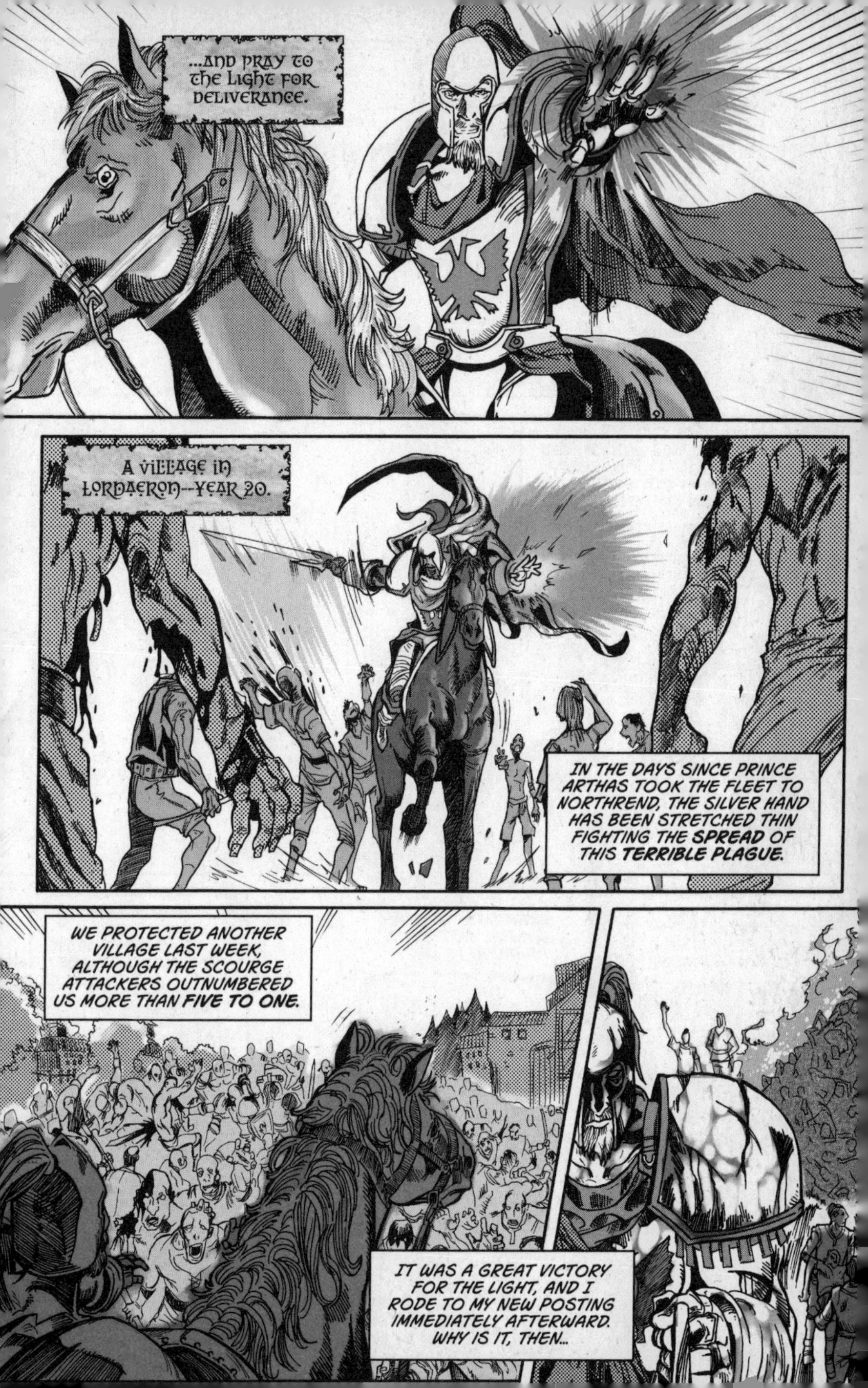

...AND PRAY TO THE LIGHT FOR DELIVERANCE.
A VILLAGE IN LORDAERON--YEAR 20.
IN THE DAYS SINCE PRINCE ARTHAS TOOK THE FLEET TO NORTHREND, THE SILVER HAND HAS BEEN STRETCHED THIN FIGHTING THE SPREAD OF THIS TERRIBLE PLAGUE.
WE PROTECTED ANOTHER VILLAGE LAST WEEK, ALTHOUGH THE SCOURGE ATTACKERS OUTNUMBERED US MORE THAN FIVE TO ONE.
IT WAS A GREAT VICTORY FOR THE LIGHT, AND I RODE TO MY NEW POSTING IMMEDIATELY AFTERWARD. WHY IS IT, THEN...

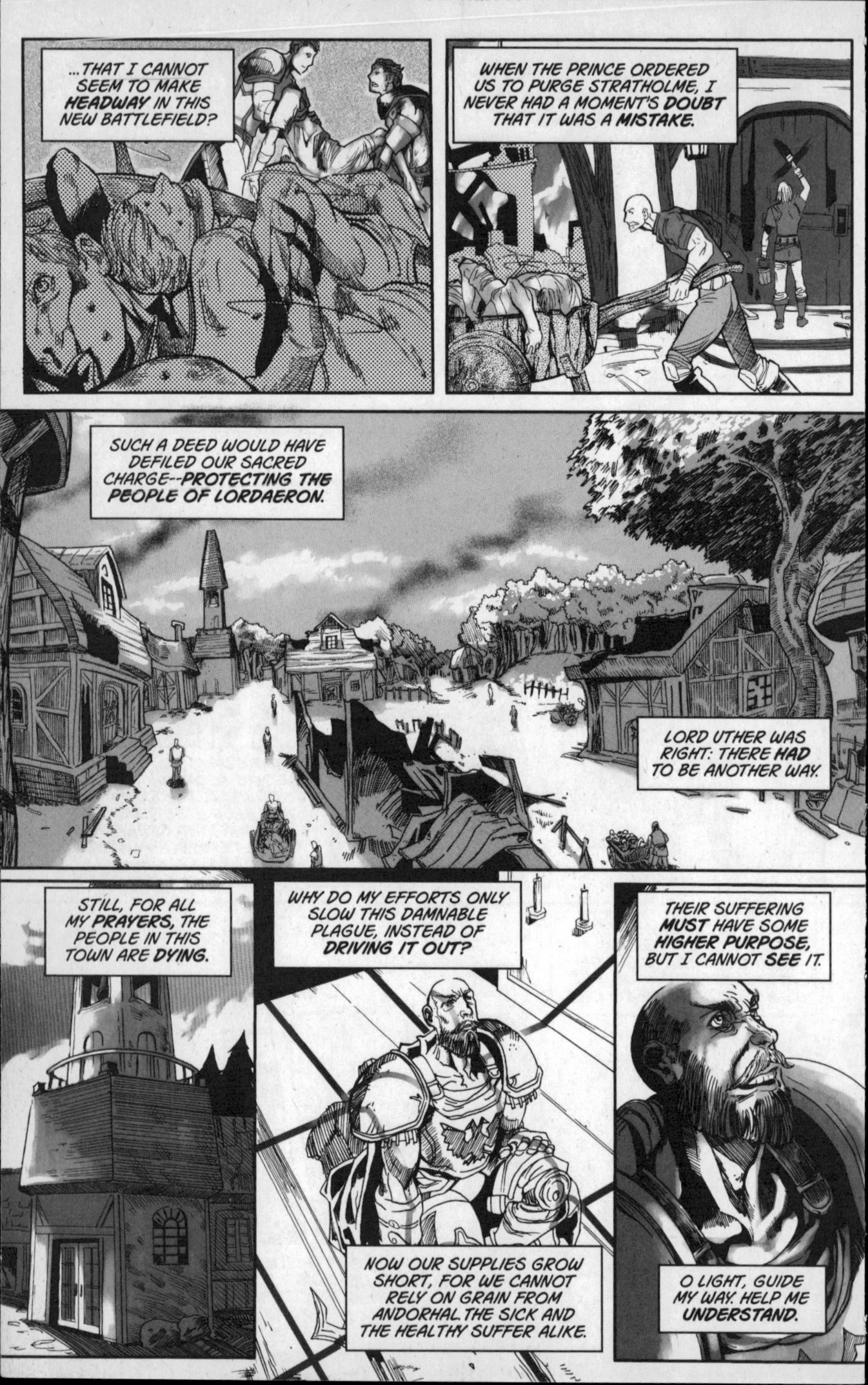
...THAT I CANNOT SEEM TO MAKE **HEADWAY** IN THIS NEW BATTLEFIELD?
WHEN THE PRINCE ORDERED US TO PURGE STRATHOLME, I NEVER HAD A MOMENT'S **DOUBT** THAT IT WAS A **MISTAKE**.
SUCH A DEED WOULD HAVE DEFILED OUR SACRED CHARGE--**PROTECTING THE PEOPLE OF LORDAERON**.
LORD UTHER WAS RIGHT: THERE **HAD** TO BE ANOTHER WAY.
STILL, FOR ALL MY **PRAYERS**, THE PEOPLE IN THIS TOWN ARE **DYING**.
WHY DO MY EFFORTS ONLY SLOW THIS DAMNABLE PLAGUE, INSTEAD OF **DRIVING IT OUT?**
NOW OUR SUPPLIES GROW SHORT, FOR WE CANNOT RELY ON GRAIN FROM ANDORHAL. THE SICK AND THE HEALTHY SUFFER ALIKE.
THEIR SUFFERING **MUST** HAVE SOME **HIGHER PURPOSE**, BUT I CANNOT **SEE** IT.
O LIGHT, GUIDE MY WAY. HELP ME **UNDERSTAND**.

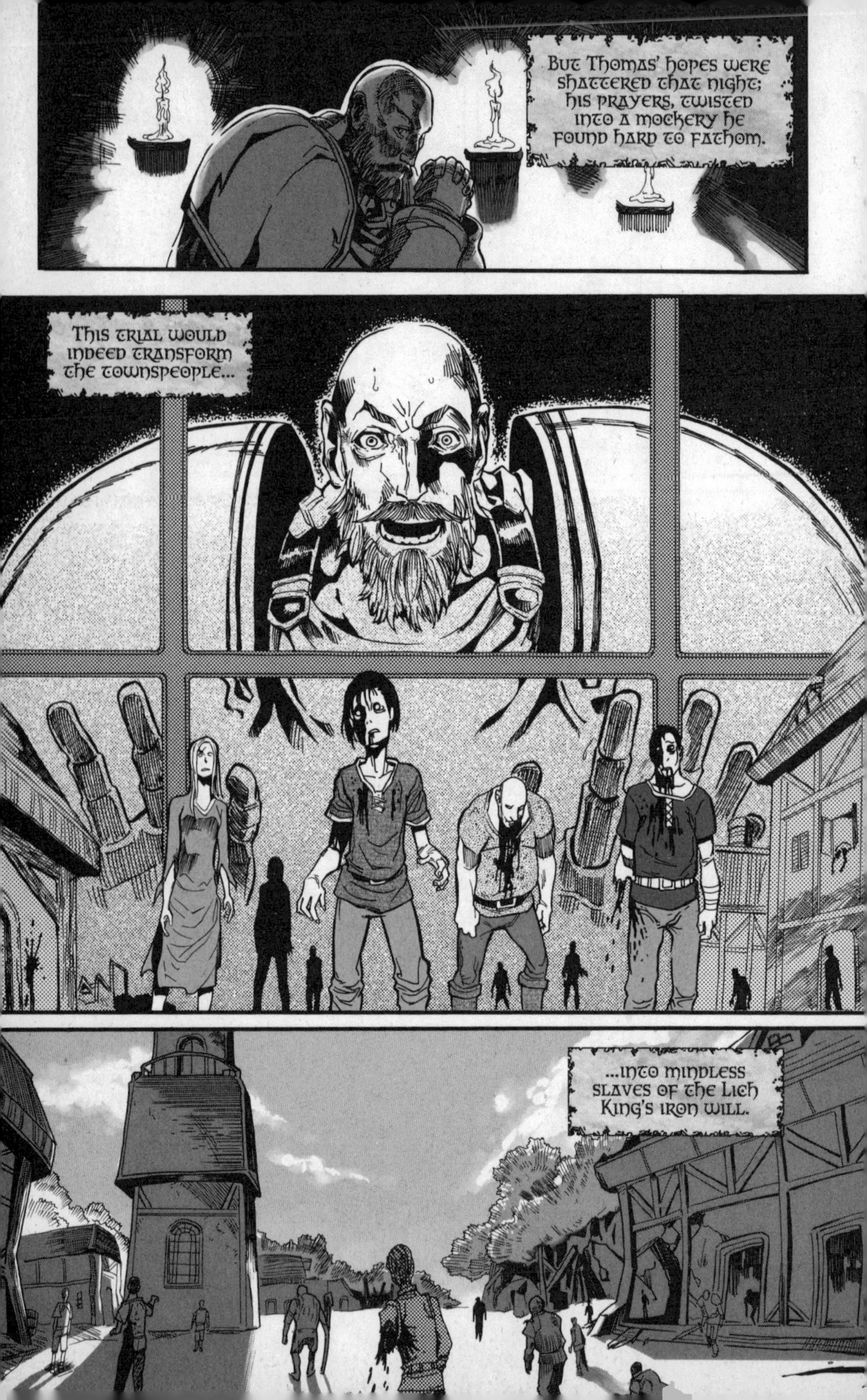
But Thomas' hopes were shattered that night; his prayers, twisted into a mockery he found hard to fathom.
This trial would indeed transform the townspeople...
...into mindless slaves of the Lich King's iron will.

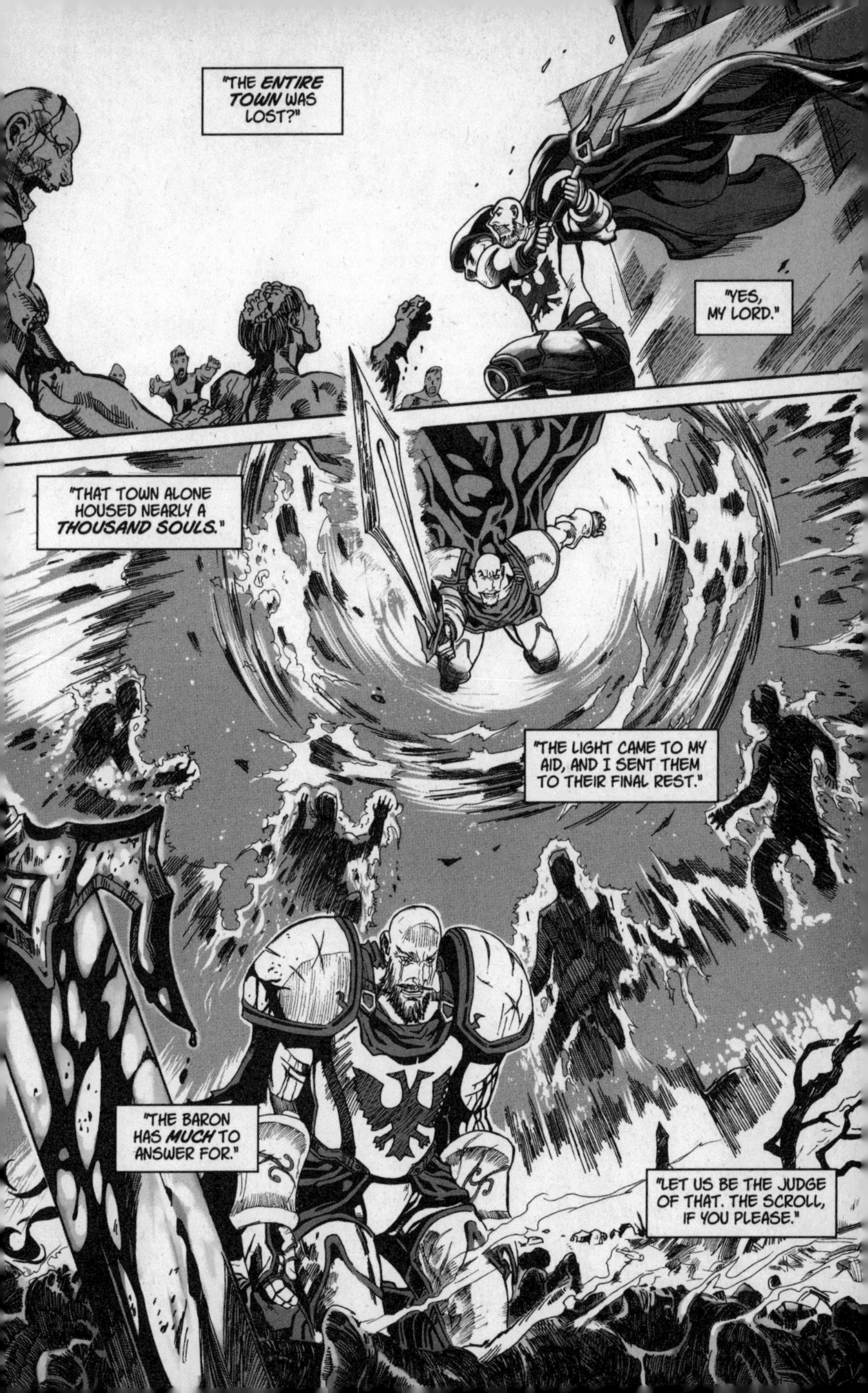
"THE ENTIRE TOWN WAS LOST?"
"YES, MY LORD."
"THAT TOWN ALONE HOUSED NEARLY A THOUSAND SOULS."
"THE LIGHT CAME TO MY AID, AND I SENT THEM TO THEIR FINAL REST."
"THE BARON HAS MUCH TO ANSWER FOR."
"LET US BE THE JUDGE OF THAT. THE SCROLL, IF YOU PLEASE."

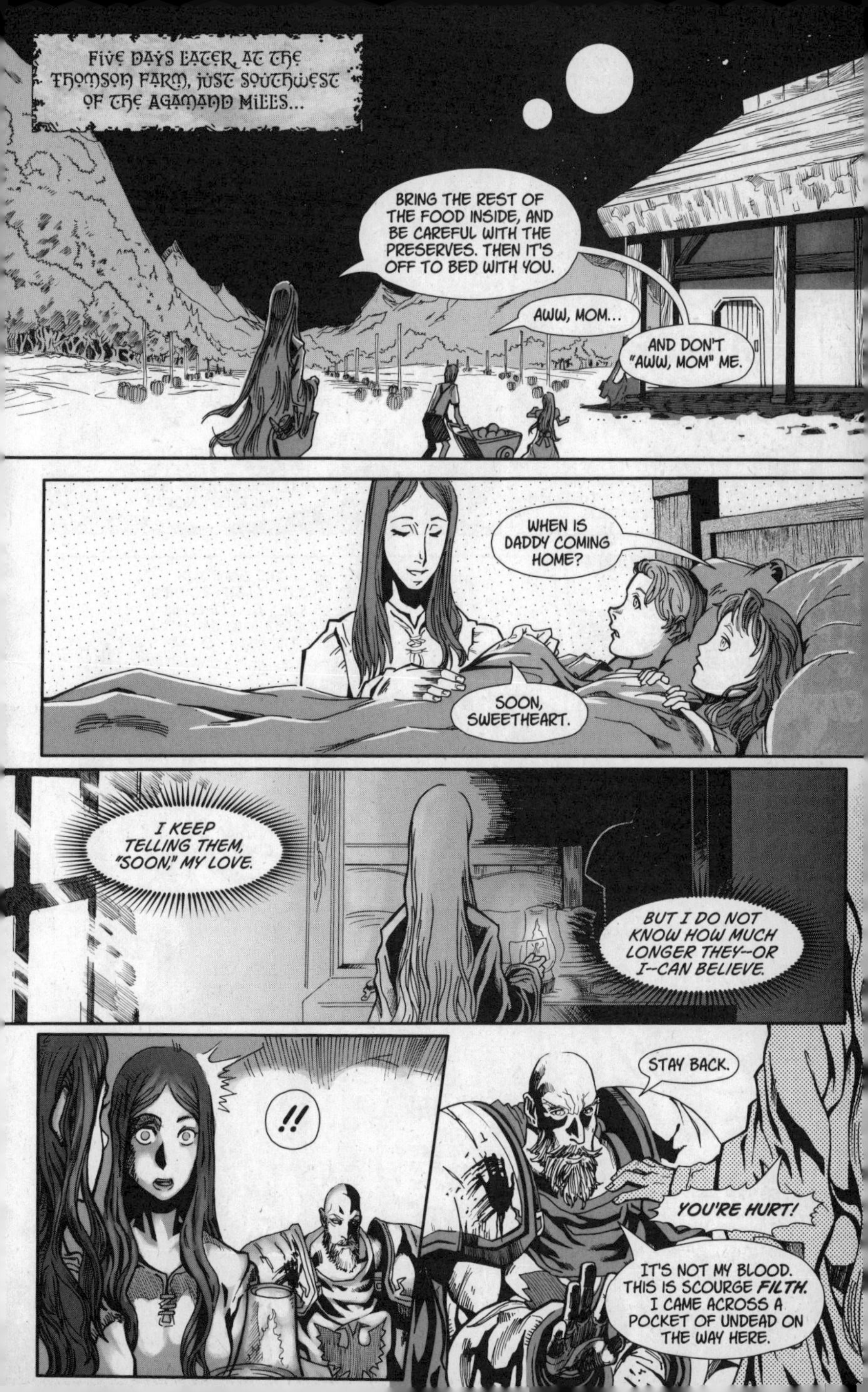
FIVE DAYS LATER, AT THE THOMSON FARM, JUST SOUTHWEST OF THE AGAMAND MILLS...
BRING THE REST OF THE FOOD INSIDE, AND BE CAREFUL WITH THE PRESERVES. THEN IT'S OFF TO BED WITH YOU.
AWW, MOM...
AND DON'T "AWW, MOM" ME.
WHEN IS DADDY COMING HOME?
SOON, SWEETHEART.
I KEEP TELLING THEM, "SOON," MY LOVE.
BUT I DO NOT KNOW HOW MUCH LONGER THEY--OR I--CAN BELIEVE.
!!
STAY BACK.
YOU'RE HURT!
IT'S NOT MY BLOOD. THIS IS SCOURGE FILTH. I CAME ACROSS A POCKET OF UNDEAD ON THE WAY HERE.

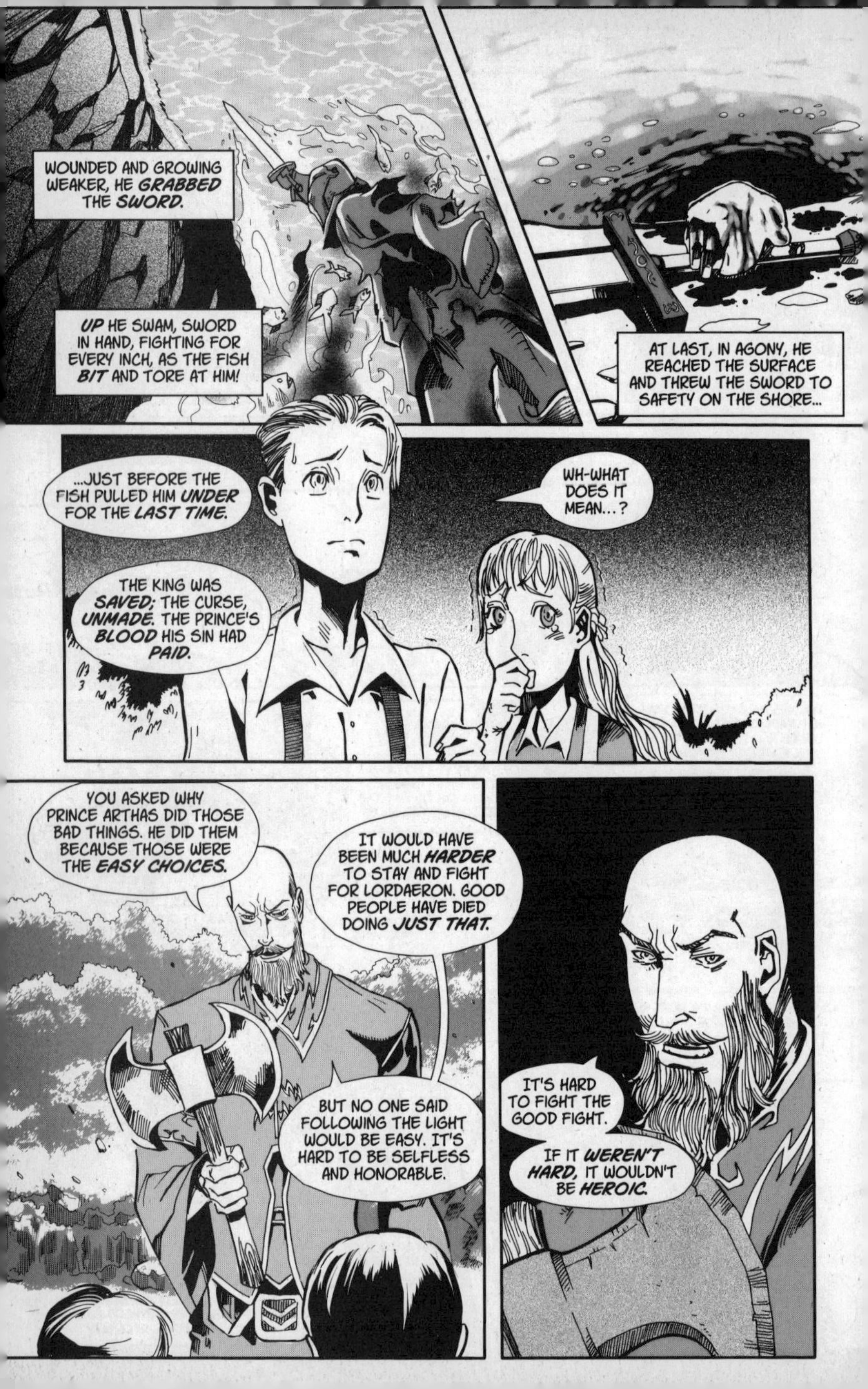
WOUNDED AND GROWING WEAKER, HE GRABBED THE SWORD.
UP HE SWAM, SWORD IN HAND, FIGHTING FOR EVERY INCH, AS THE FISH BIT AND TORE AT HIM!
AT LAST, IN AGONY, HE REACHED THE SURFACE AND THREW THE SWORD TO SAFETY ON THE SHORE...
...JUST BEFORE THE FISH PULLED HIM UNDER FOR THE LAST TIME.
WH-WHAT DOES IT MEAN...?
THE KING WAS SAVED; THE CURSE, UNMADE. THE PRINCE'S BLOOD HIS SIN HAD PAID.
YOU ASKED WHY PRINCE ARTHAS DID THOSE BAD THINGS. HE DID THEM BECAUSE THOSE WERE THE EASY CHOICES.
IT WOULD HAVE BEEN MUCH HARDER TO STAY AND FIGHT FOR LORDAERON. GOOD PEOPLE HAVE DIED DOING JUST THAT.
BUT NO ONE SAID FOLLOWING THE LIGHT WOULD BE EASY. IT'S HARD TO BE SELFLESS AND HONORABLE.
IT'S HARD TO FIGHT THE GOOD FIGHT.
IF IT WEREN'T HARD, IT WOULDN'T BE HEROIC.

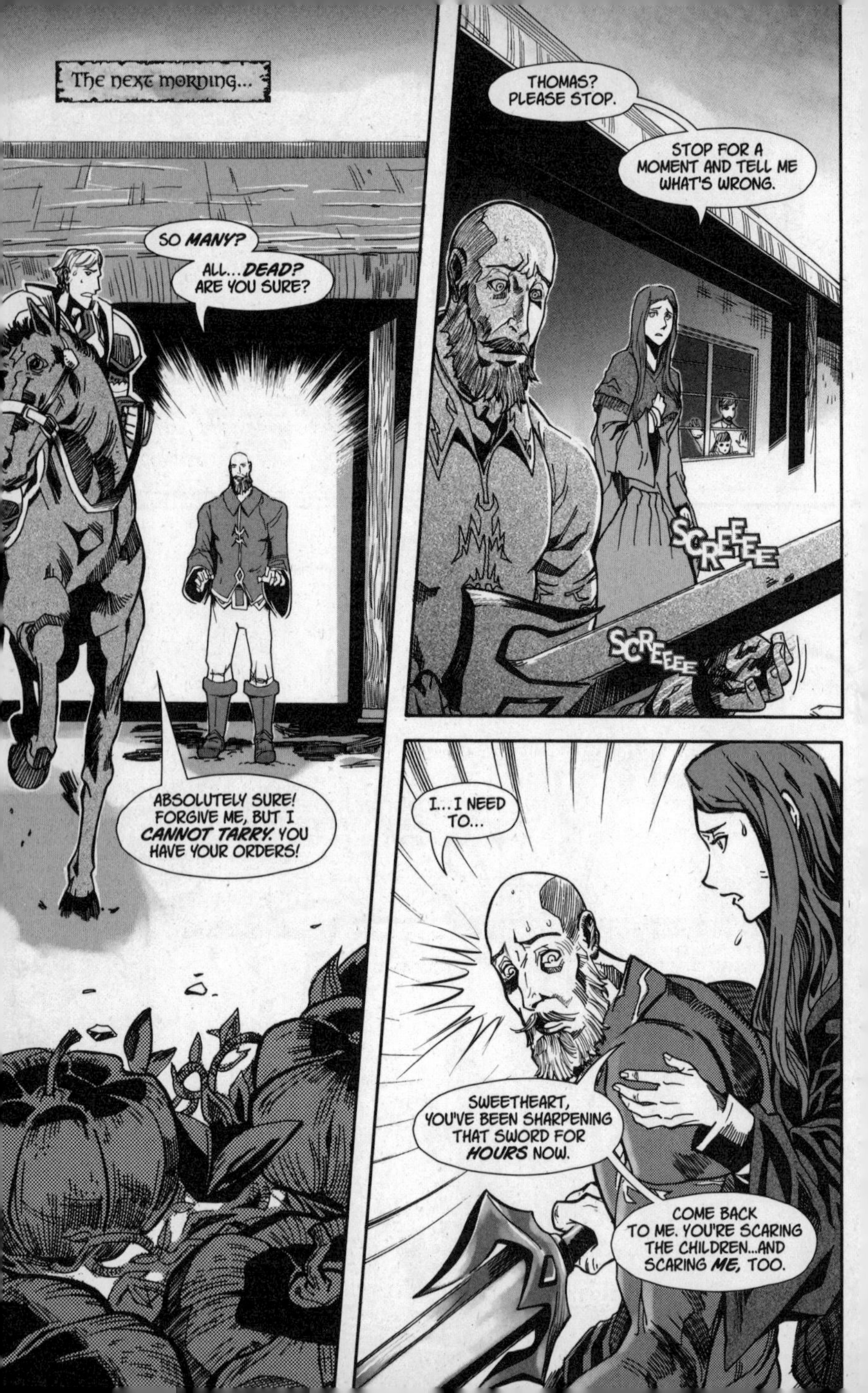

The next morning...
So MANY?
ALL...DEAD? ARE YOU SURE?
ABSOLUTELY SURE! FORGIVE ME, BUT I CANNOT TARRY. YOU HAVE YOUR ORDERS!
THOMAS? PLEASE STOP.
STOP FOR A MOMENT AND TELL ME WHAT'S WRONG.
SCREEEEE
SCREEEEE
I...I NEED TO...
SWEETHEART, YOU'VE BEEN SHARPENING THAT SWORD FOR HOURS NOW.
COME BACK TO ME. YOU'RE SCARING THE CHILDREN...AND SCARING ME, TOO.

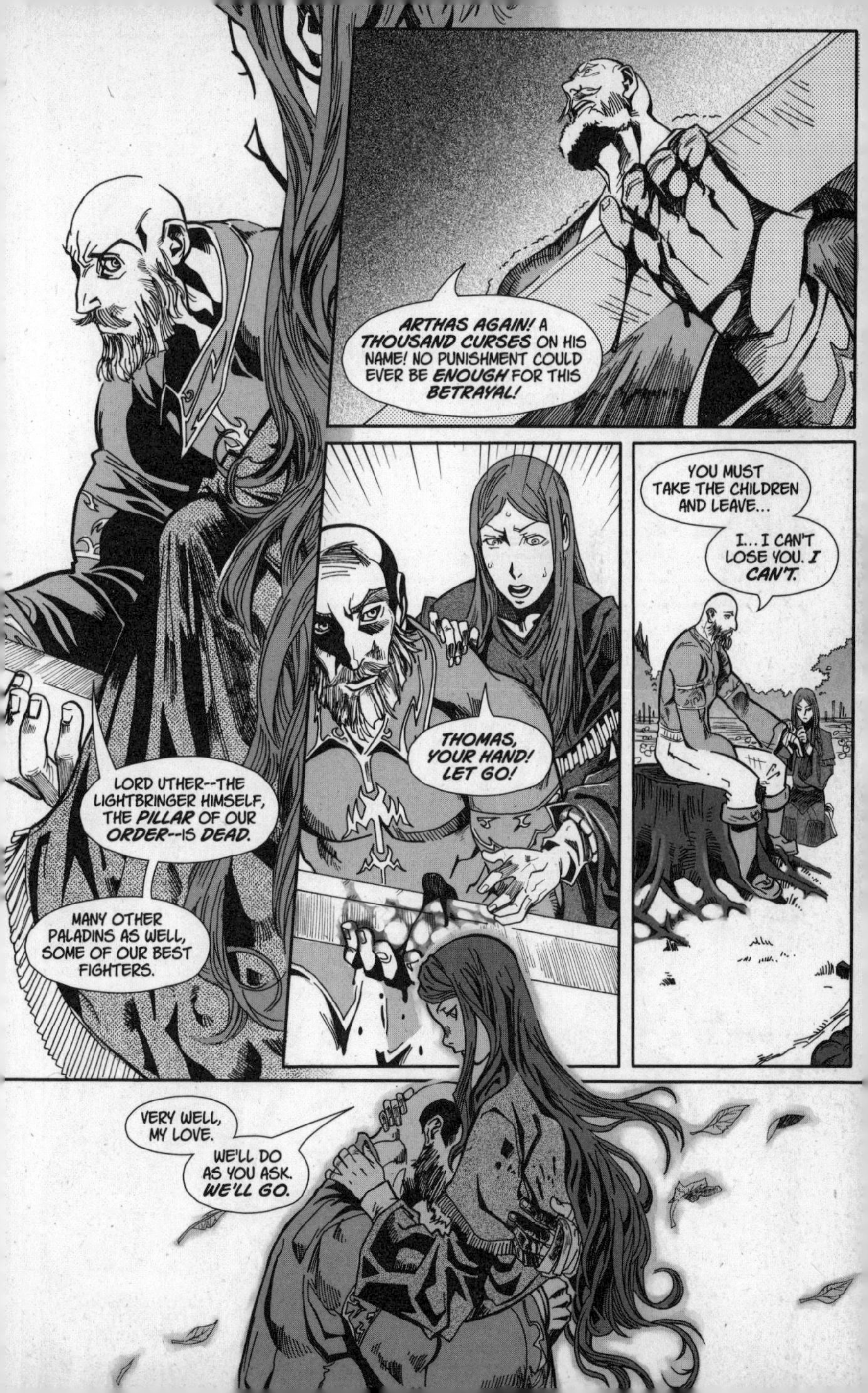
ARTHAS AGAIN! A THOUSAND CURSES ON HIS NAME! NO PUNISHMENT COULD EVER BE ENOUGH FOR THIS BETRAYAL!
LORD UTHER--THE LIGHTBRINGER HIMSELF, THE PILLAR OF OUR ORDER--IS DEAD.
MANY OTHER PALADINS AS WELL, SOME OF OUR BEST FIGHTERS.
THOMAS, YOUR HAND! LET GO!
YOU MUST TAKE THE CHILDREN AND LEAVE...
I... I CAN'T LOSE YOU. I CAN'T.
VERY WELL, MY LOVE.
WE'LL DO AS YOU ASK. WE'LL GO.

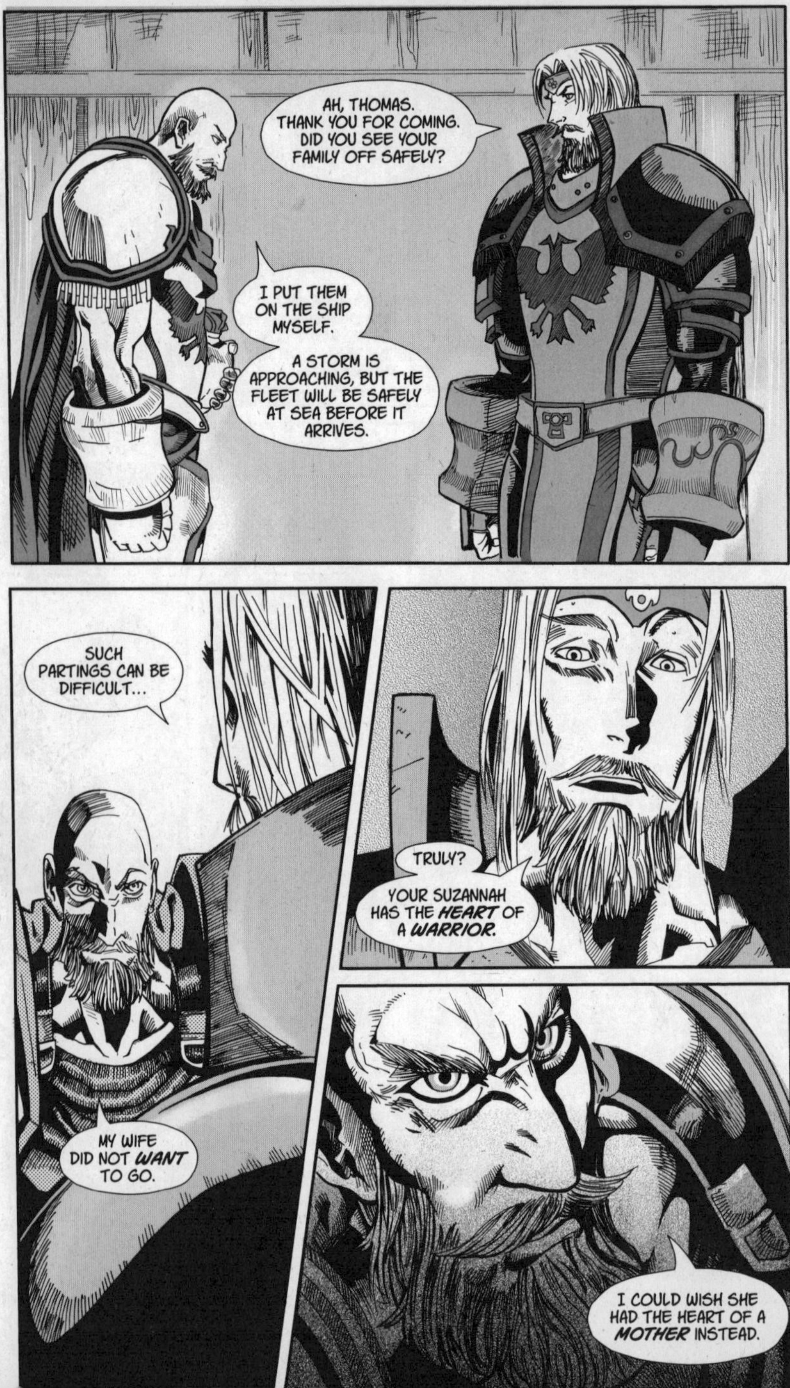
AH, THOMAS. THANK YOU FOR COMING. DID YOU SEE YOUR FAMILY OFF SAFELY?
I PUT THEM ON THE SHIP MYSELF.
A STORM IS APPROACHING, BUT THE FLEET WILL BE SAFELY AT SEA BEFORE IT ARRIVES.
SUCH PARTINGS CAN BE DIFFICULT...
MY WIFE DID NOT *WANT* TO GO.
TRULY?
YOUR SUZANNAH HAS THE *HEART* OF A *WARRIOR*.
I COULD WISH SHE HAD THE HEART OF A *MOTHER* INSTEAD.

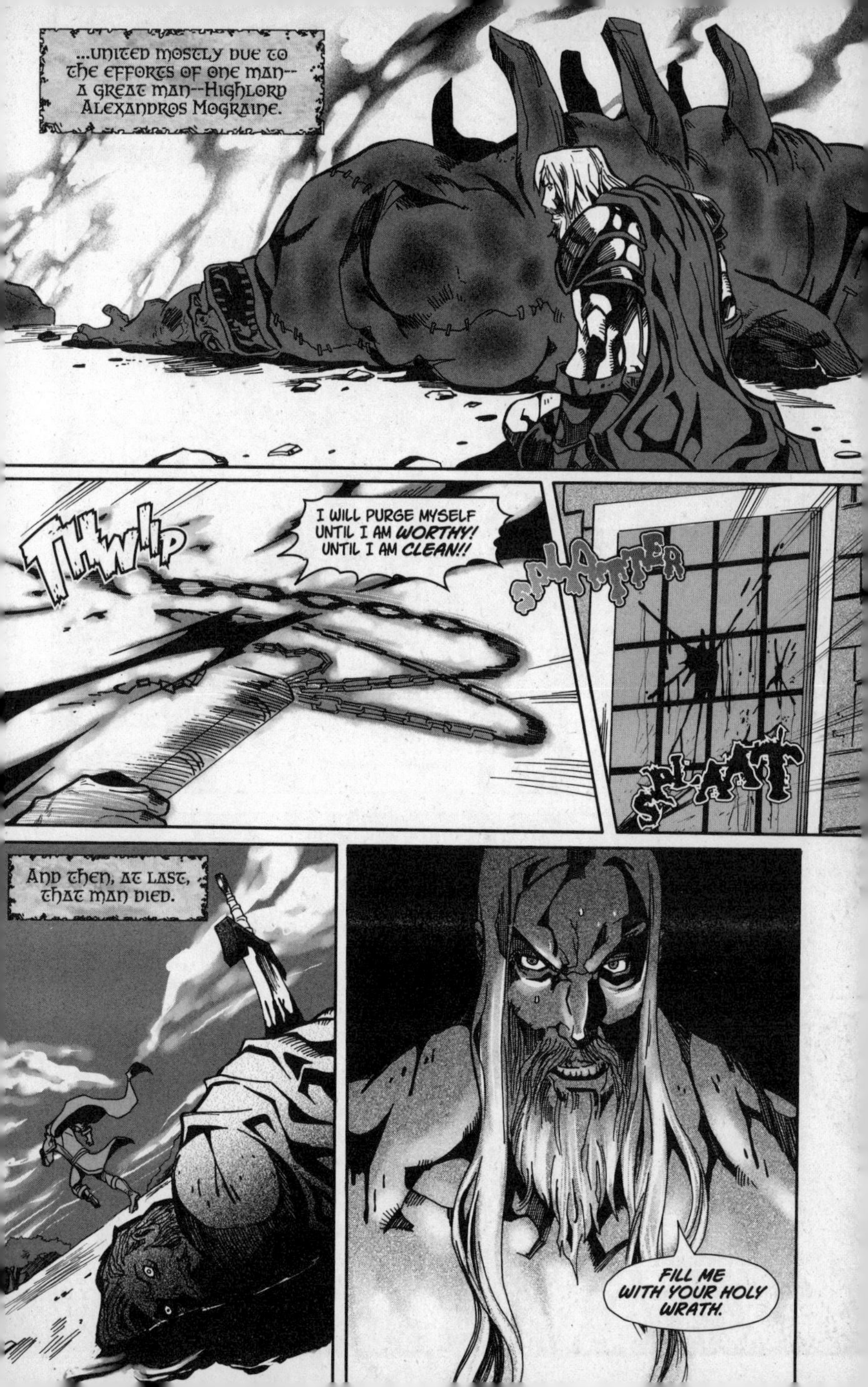
...UNITED MOSTLY DUE TO THE EFFORTS OF ONE MAN--A GREAT MAN--HIGHLORD ALEXANDROS MOGRAINE.
THWIP
I WILL PURGE MYSELF UNTIL I AM *WORTHY!* UNTIL I AM *CLEAN!!*
SPLATTER
SPLAT
AND THEN, AT LAST, THAT MAN DIED.
FILL ME WITH YOUR HOLY WRATH.

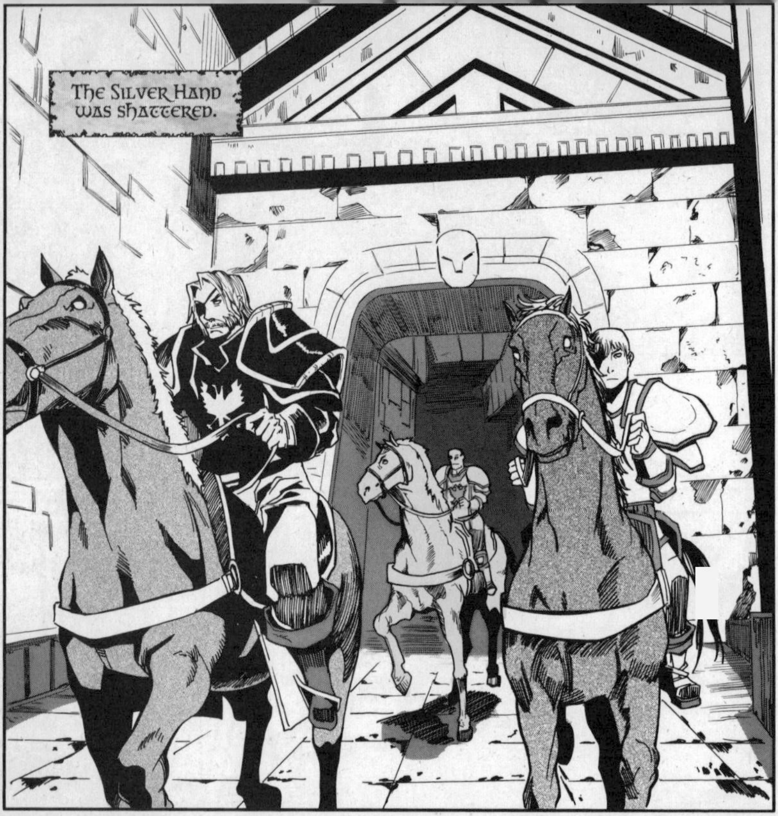
The Silver Hand
was shattered.
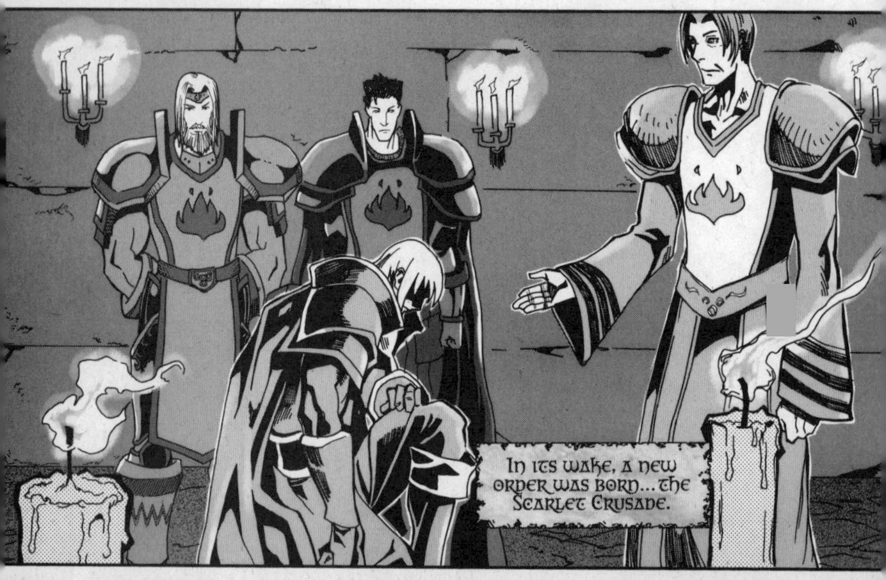
In its wake, a new
order was born... the
Scarlet Crusade.

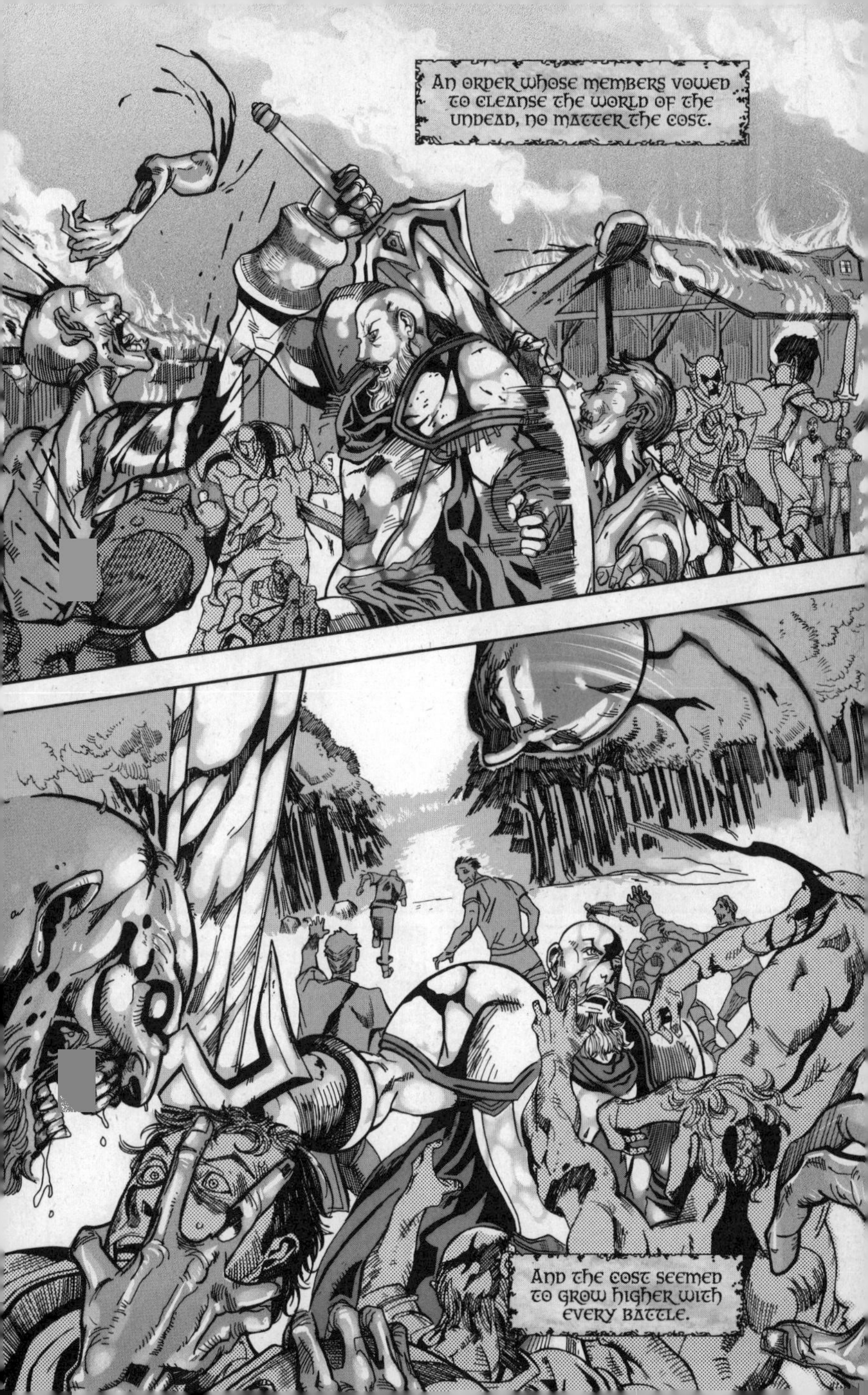
An order whose members vowed to cleanse the world of the undead, no matter the cost.
And the cost seemed to grow higher with every battle.

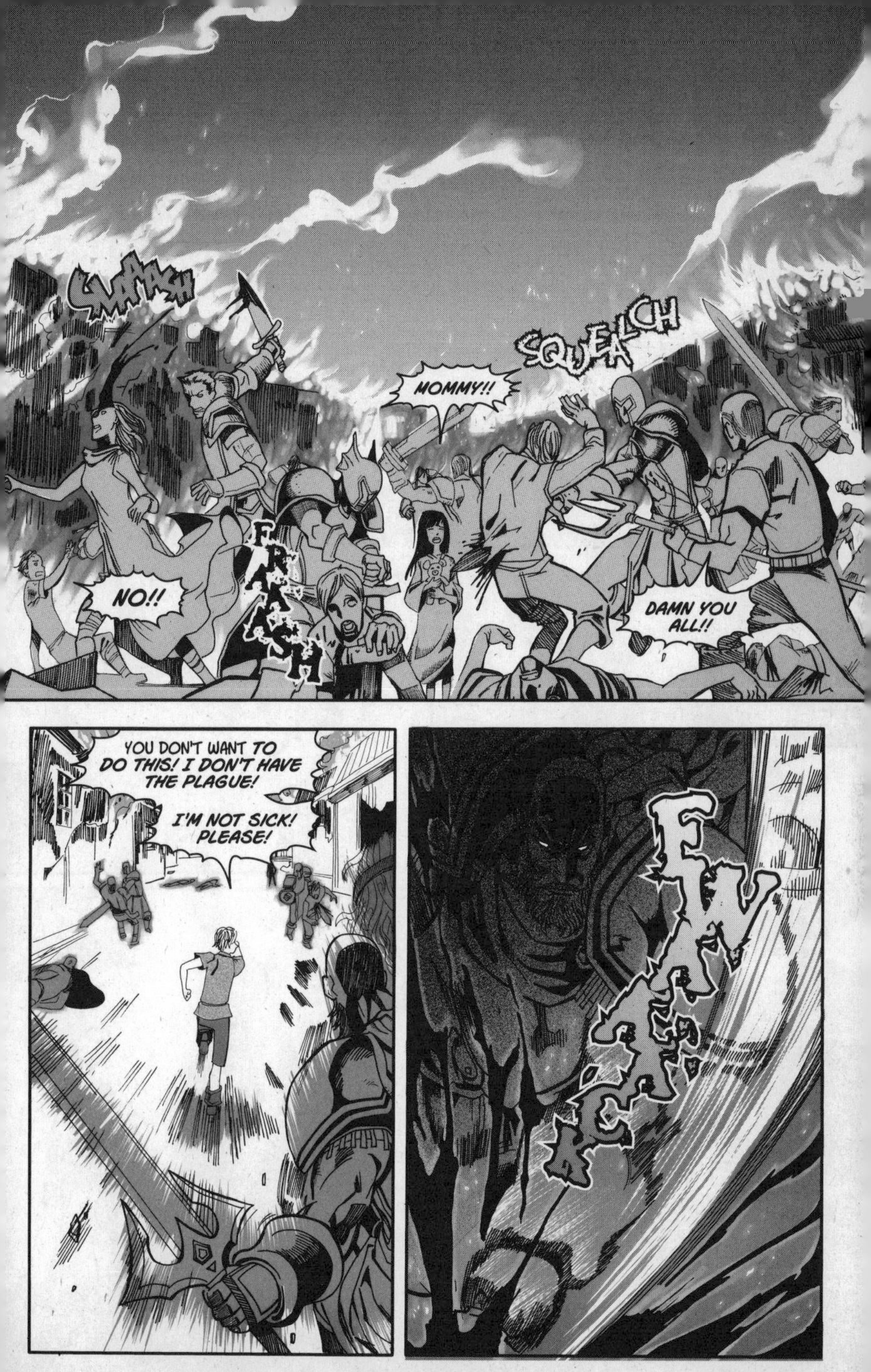
SQUEALCH
MOMMY!!
NO!!
FRAAASH
DAMN YOU ALL!!
YOU DON'T WANT TO DO THIS! I DON'T HAVE THE PLAGUE!
I'M NOT SICK! PLEASE!
FWACK

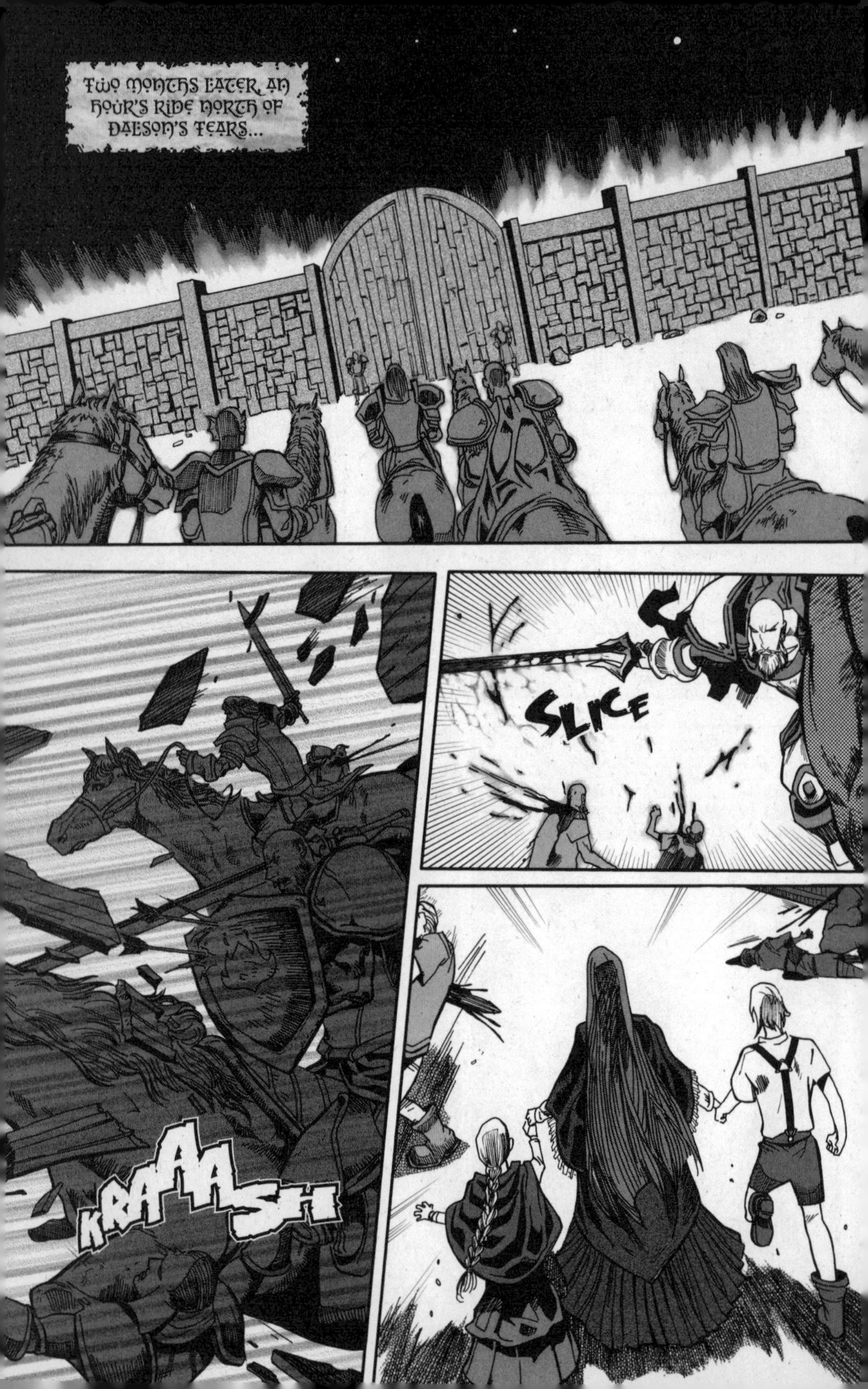
TWO MONTHS LATER, AN HOUR'S RIDE NORTH OF DALSON'S TEARS...
KRAAASH
SLICE

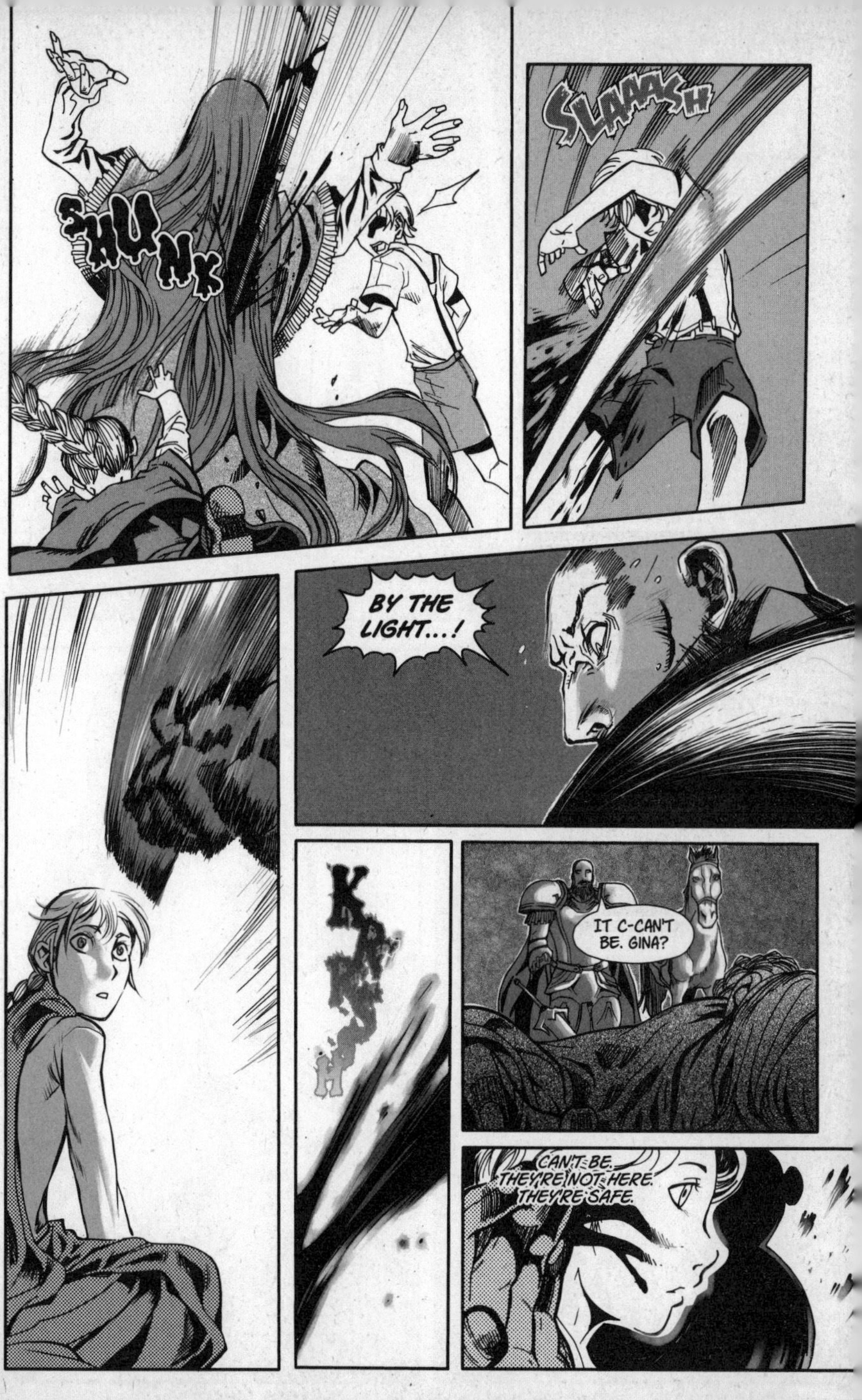
SHUNK
SLAAASH
BY THE LIGHT...!
KRASH
IT C-CAN'T BE. GINA?
CAN'T BE. THEY'RE NOT HERE. THEY'RE SAFE.

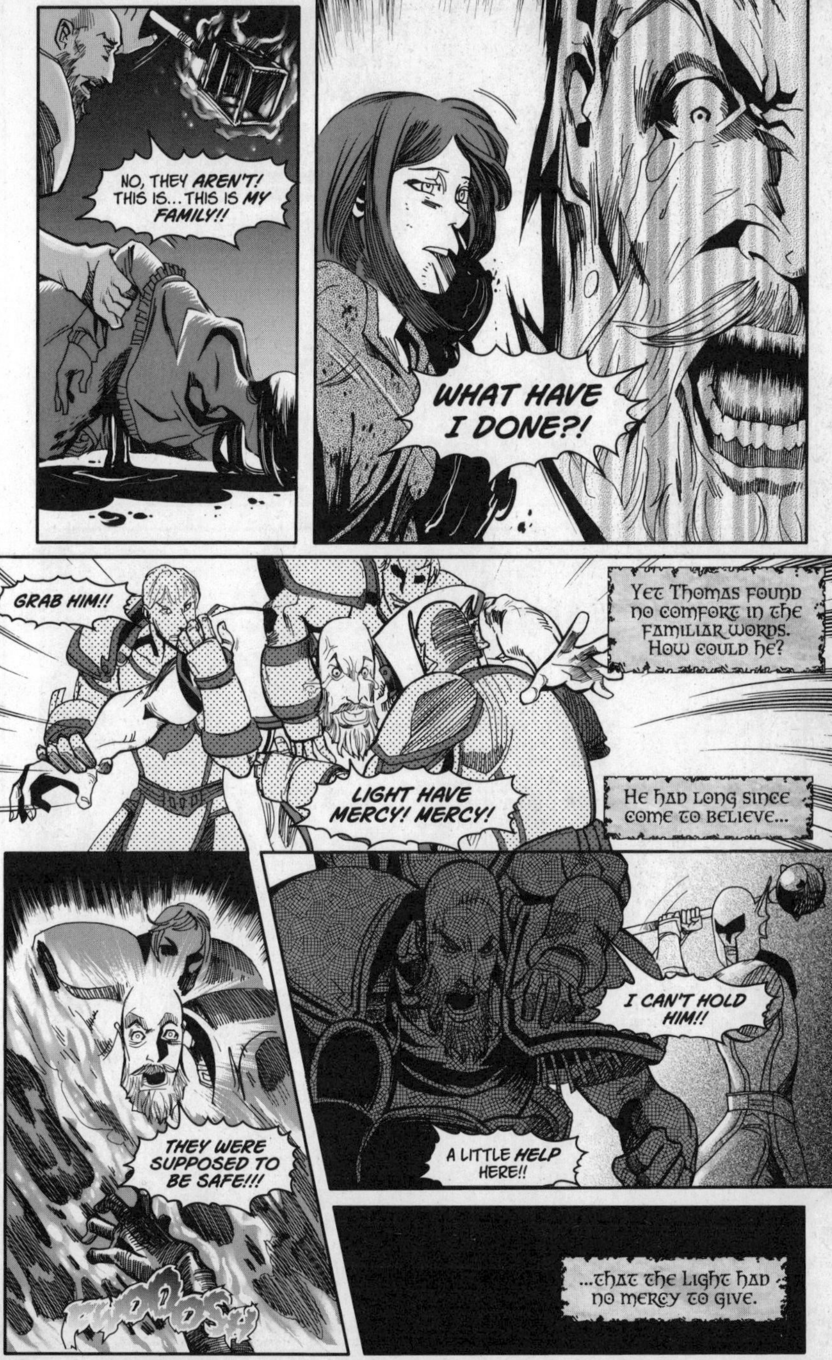

NO, THEY AREN'T! THIS IS... THIS IS MY FAMILY!!
WHAT HAVE I DONE?!
GRAB HIM!!
LIGHT HAVE MERCY! MERCY!
Yet Thomas found no comfort in the familiar words. How could he?
He had long since come to believe...
THEY WERE SUPPOSED TO BE SAFE!!!
I CAN'T HOLD HIM!!
A LITTLE HELP HERE!!
...that the Light had no mercy to give.

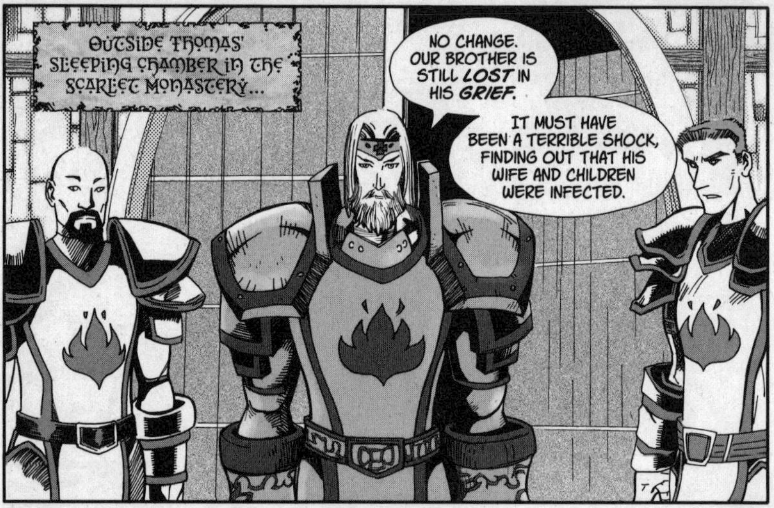
OUTSIDE THOMAS' SLEEPING CHAMBER IN THE SCARLET MONASTERY...
NO CHANGE. OUR BROTHER IS STILL LOST IN HIS GRIEF.
IT MUST HAVE BEEN A TERRIBLE SHOCK, FINDING OUT THAT HIS WIFE AND CHILDREN WERE INFECTED.
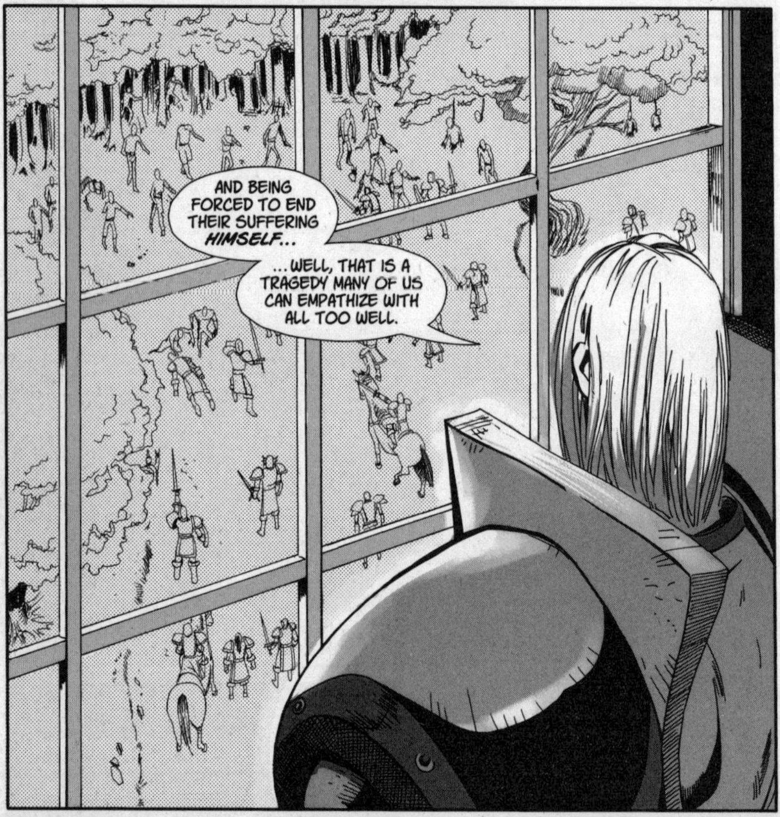
AND BEING FORCED TO END THEIR SUFFERING HIMSELF...
...WELL, THAT IS A TRAGEDY MANY OF US CAN EMPATHIZE WITH ALL TOO WELL.

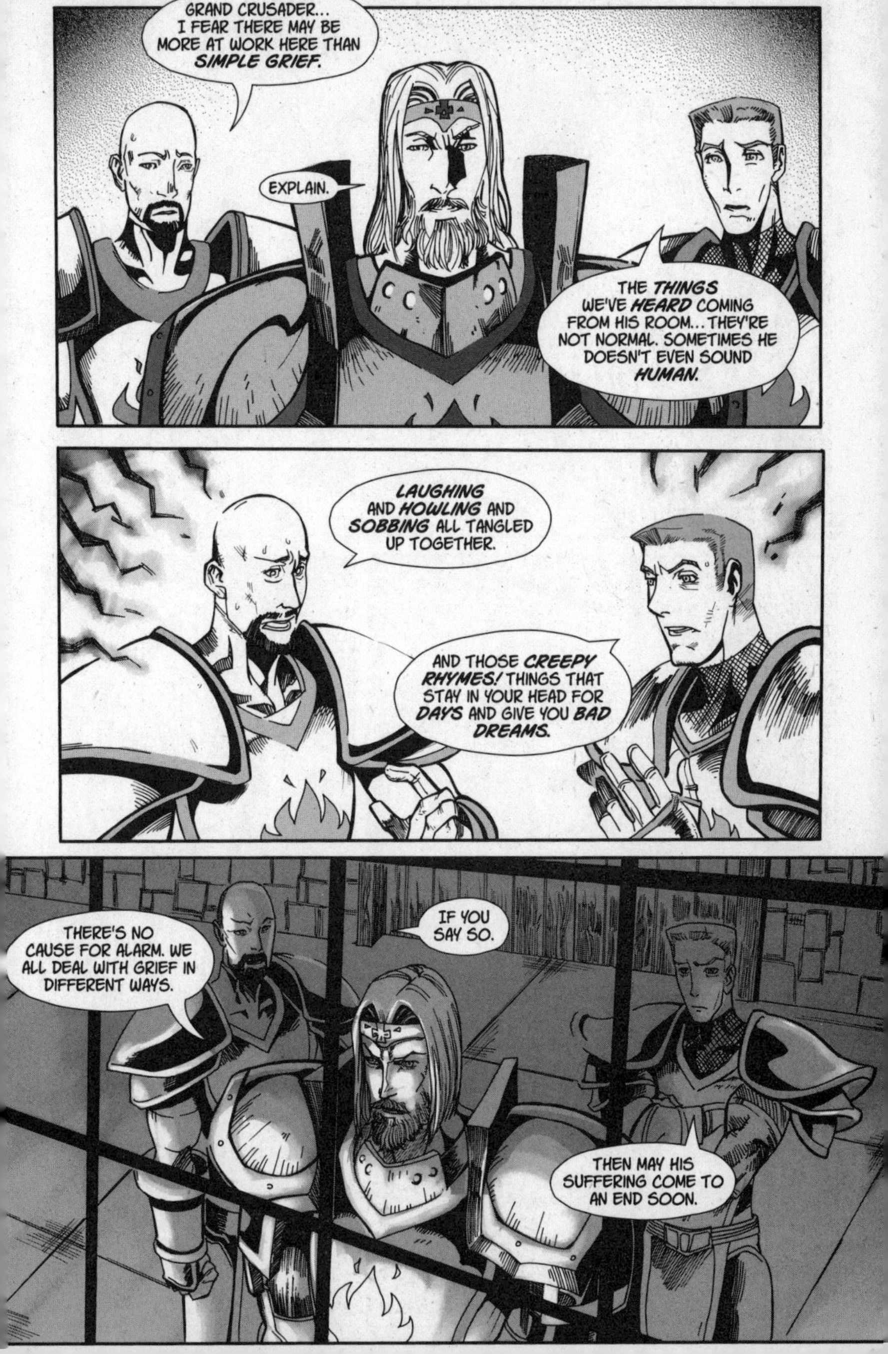
GRAND CRUSADER... I FEAR THERE MAY BE MORE AT WORK HERE THAN SIMPLE GRIEF.
EXPLAIN.
THE THINGS WE'VE HEARD COMING FROM HIS ROOM... THEY'RE NOT NORMAL. SOMETIMES HE DOESN'T EVEN SOUND HUMAN.
LAUGHING AND HOWLING AND SOBBING ALL TANGLED UP TOGETHER.
AND THOSE CREEPY RHYMES! THINGS THAT STAY IN YOUR HEAD FOR DAYS AND GIVE YOU BAD DREAMS.
THERE'S NO CAUSE FOR ALARM. WE ALL DEAL WITH GRIEF IN DIFFERENT WAYS.
IF YOU SAY SO.
THEN MAY HIS SUFFERING COME TO AN END SOON.

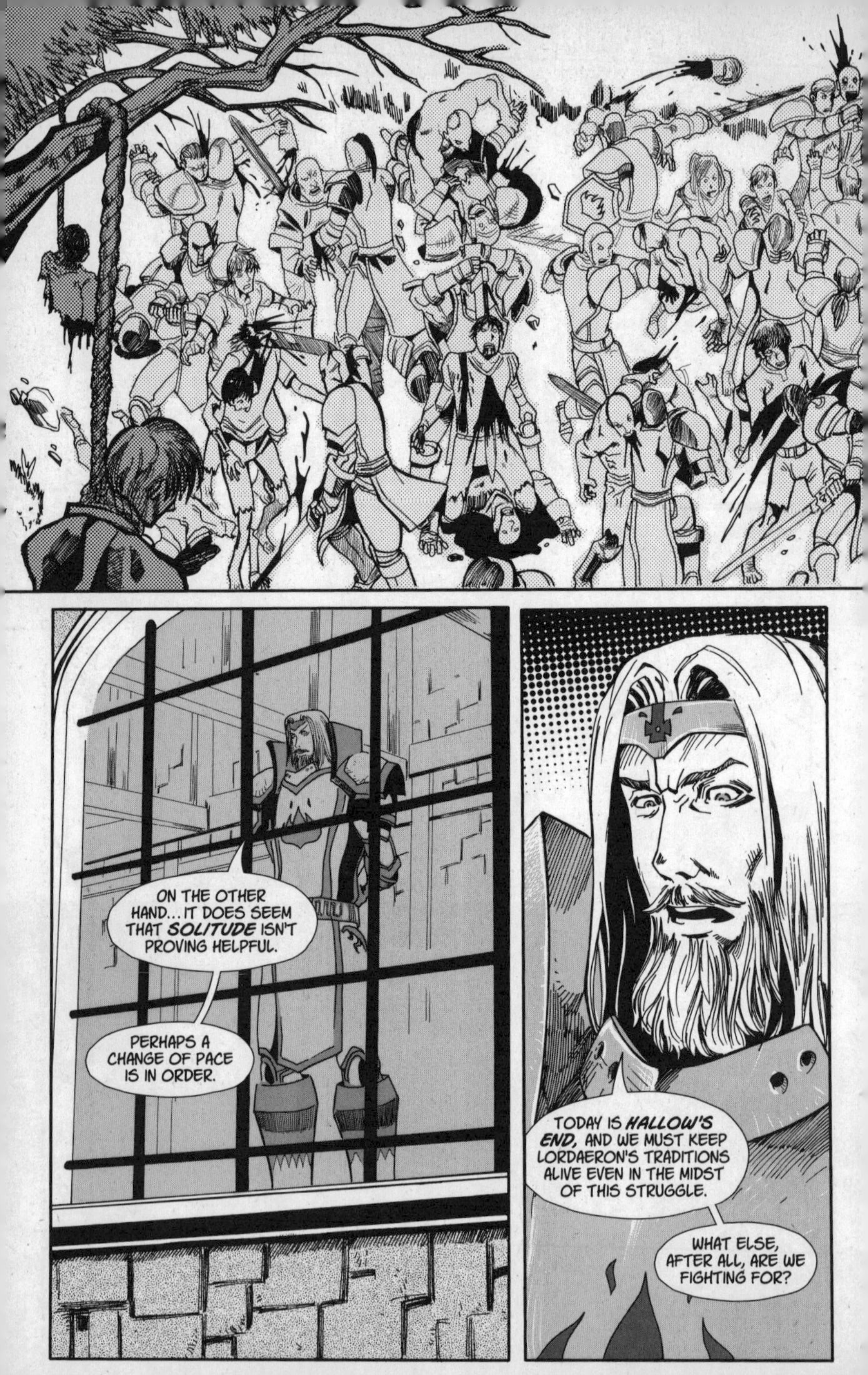
ON THE OTHER HAND... IT DOES SEEM THAT ***SOLITUDE*** ISN'T PROVING HELPFUL.
PERHAPS A CHANGE OF PACE IS IN ORDER.
TODAY IS ***HALLOW'S END,*** AND WE MUST KEEP LORDAERON'S TRADITIONS ALIVE EVEN IN THE MIDST OF THIS STRUGGLE.
WHAT ELSE, AFTER ALL, ARE WE FIGHTING FOR?

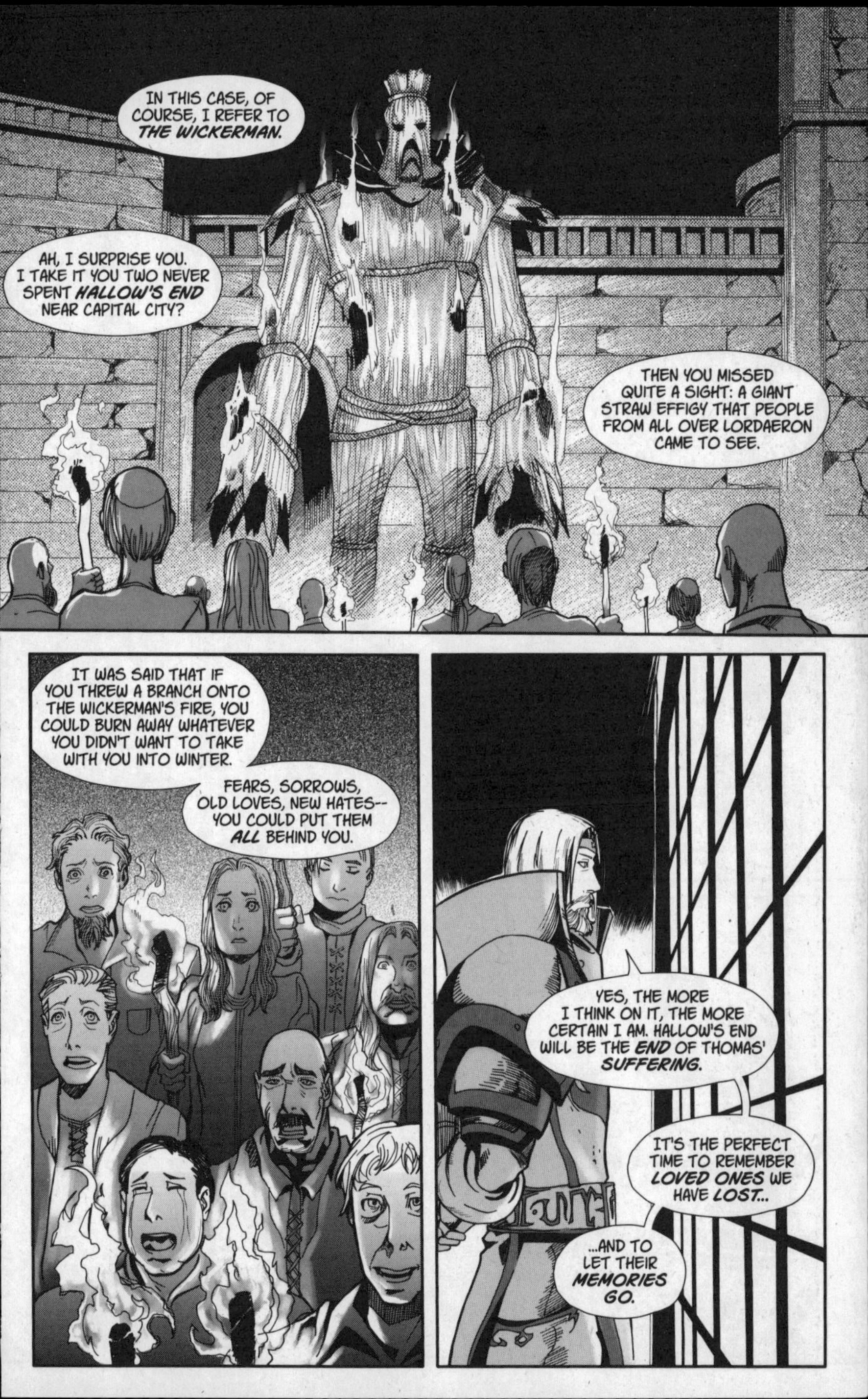

IN THIS CASE, OF COURSE, I REFER TO *THE WICKERMAN.*
AH, I SURPRISE YOU. I TAKE IT YOU TWO NEVER SPENT *HALLOW'S END* NEAR CAPITAL CITY?
THEN YOU MISSED QUITE A SIGHT: A GIANT STRAW EFFIGY THAT PEOPLE FROM ALL OVER LORDAERON CAME TO SEE.
IT WAS SAID THAT IF YOU THREW A BRANCH ONTO THE WICKERMAN'S FIRE, YOU COULD BURN AWAY WHATEVER YOU DIDN'T WANT TO TAKE WITH YOU INTO WINTER.
FEARS, SORROWS, OLD LOVES, NEW HATES--YOU COULD PUT THEM *ALL* BEHIND YOU.
YES, THE MORE I THINK ON IT, THE MORE CERTAIN I AM. HALLOW'S END WILL BE THE *END* OF THOMAS' *SUFFERING.*
IT'S THE PERFECT TIME TO REMEMBER *LOVED ONES* WE HAVE *LOST...*
...AND TO LET THEIR *MEMORIES* GO.

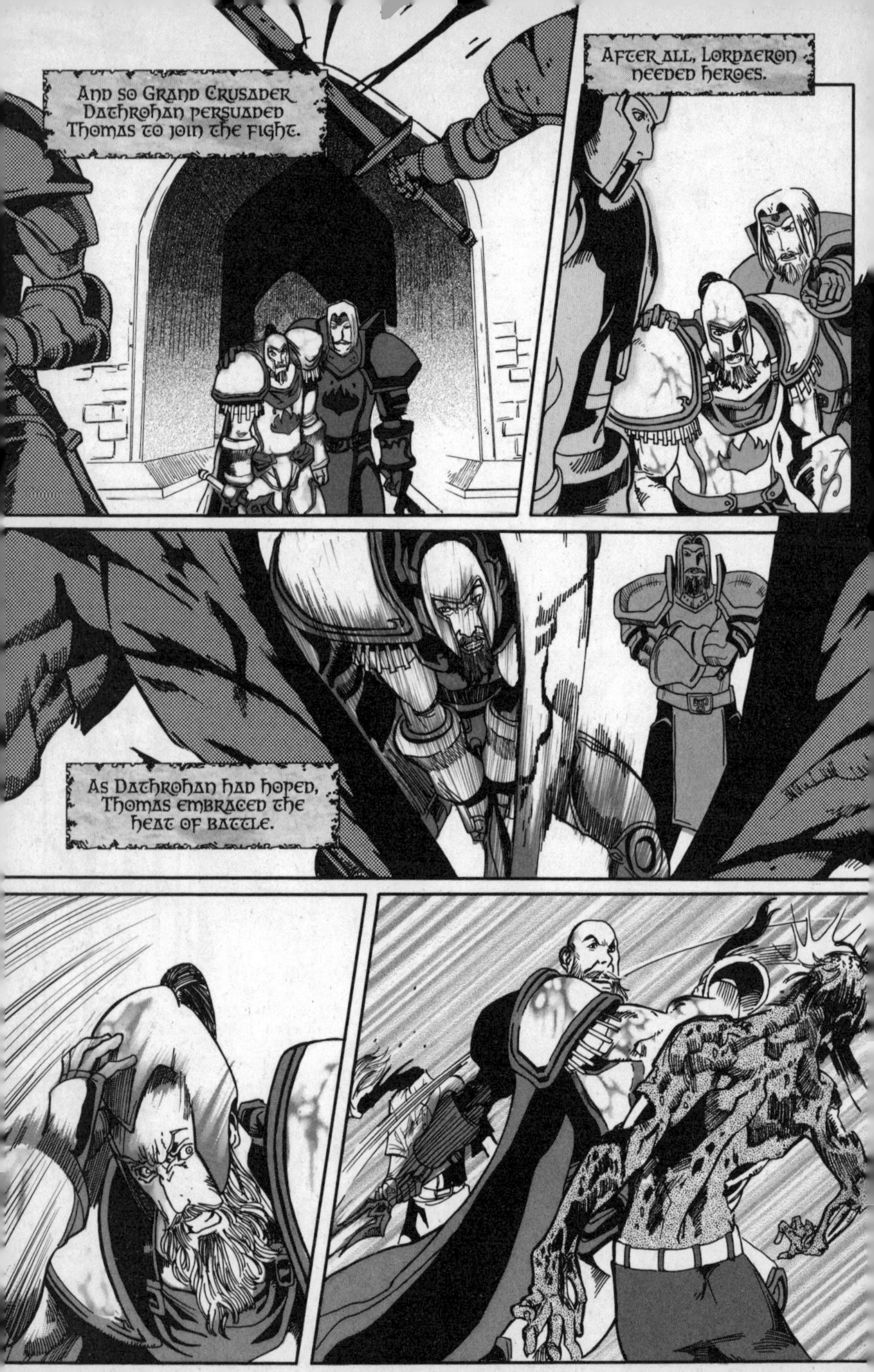
And so Grand Crusader Dathrohan persuaded Thomas to join the fight.
After all, Lordaeron needed heroes.
As Dathrohan had hoped, Thomas embraced the heat of battle.

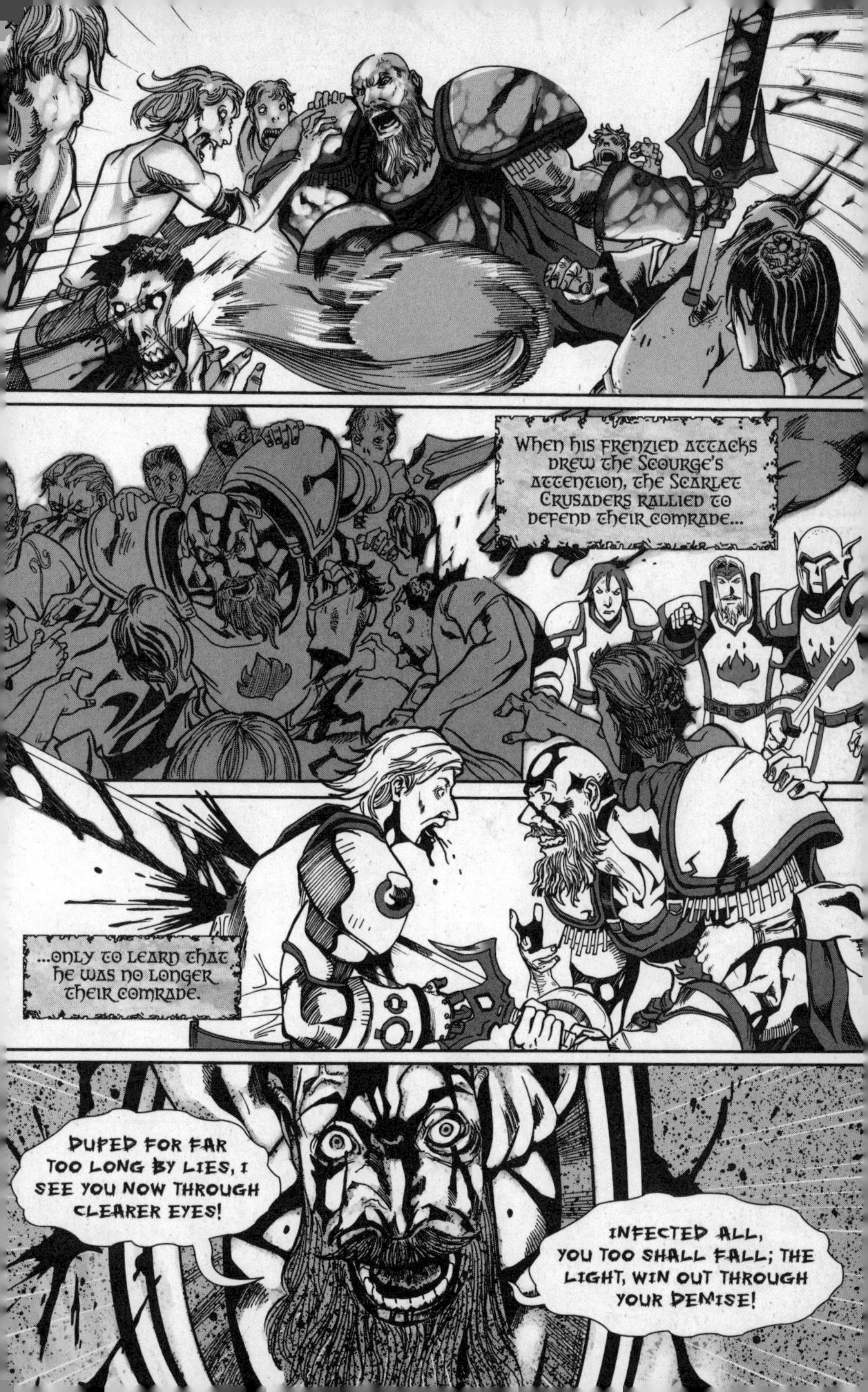
When his frenzied attacks drew the Scourge's attention, the Scarlet Crusaders rallied to defend their comrade...
...only to learn that he was no longer their comrade.
DUPED FOR FAR TOO LONG BY LIES, I SEE YOU NOW THROUGH CLEARER EYES!
INFECTED ALL, YOU TOO SHALL FALL; THE LIGHT, WIN OUT THROUGH YOUR DEMISE!

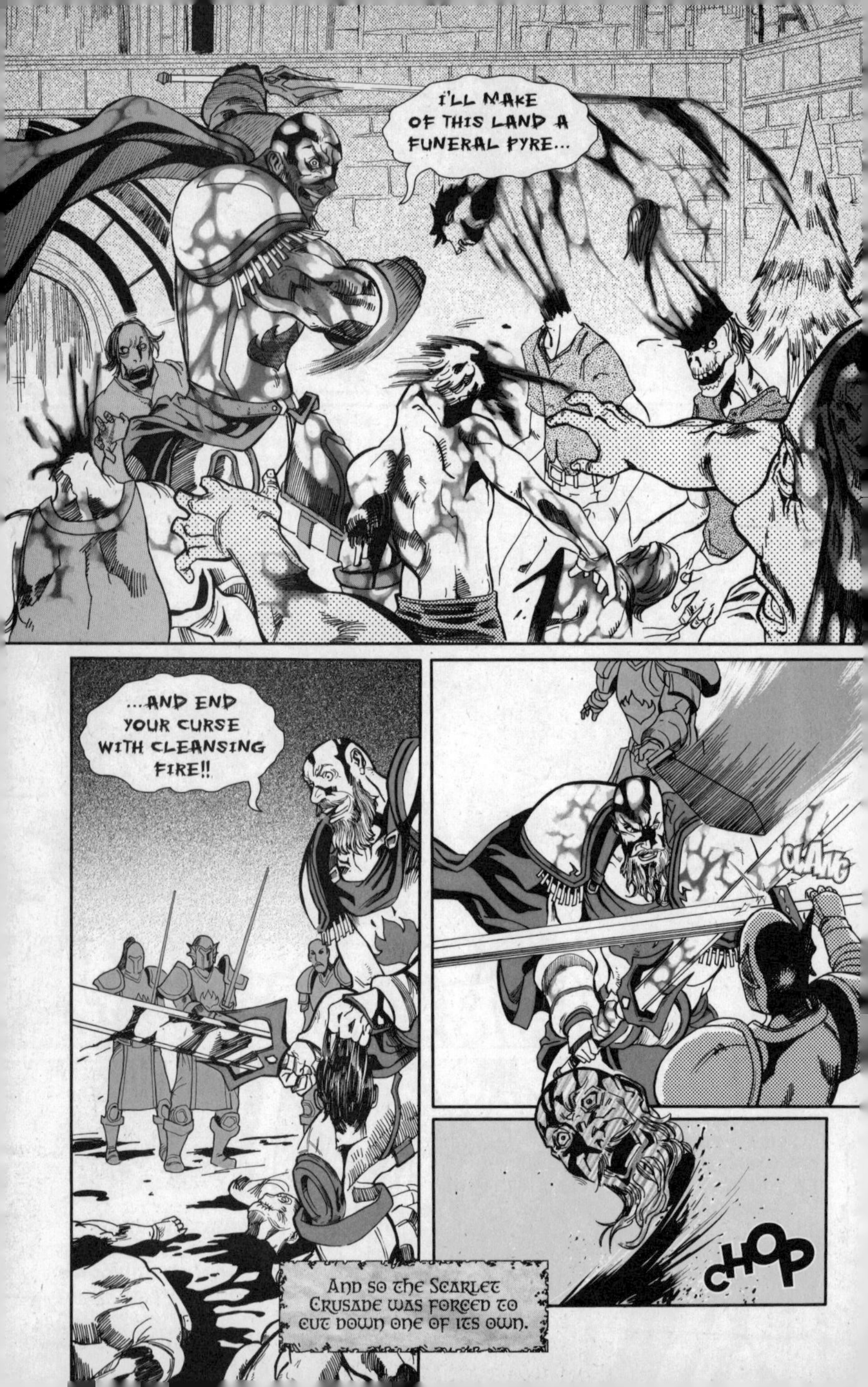
I'LL MAKE OF THIS LAND A FUNERAL PYRE...
...AND END YOUR CURSE WITH CLEANSING FIRE!!
And so the Scarlet Crusade was forced to cut down one of its own.
CLANG
CHOP

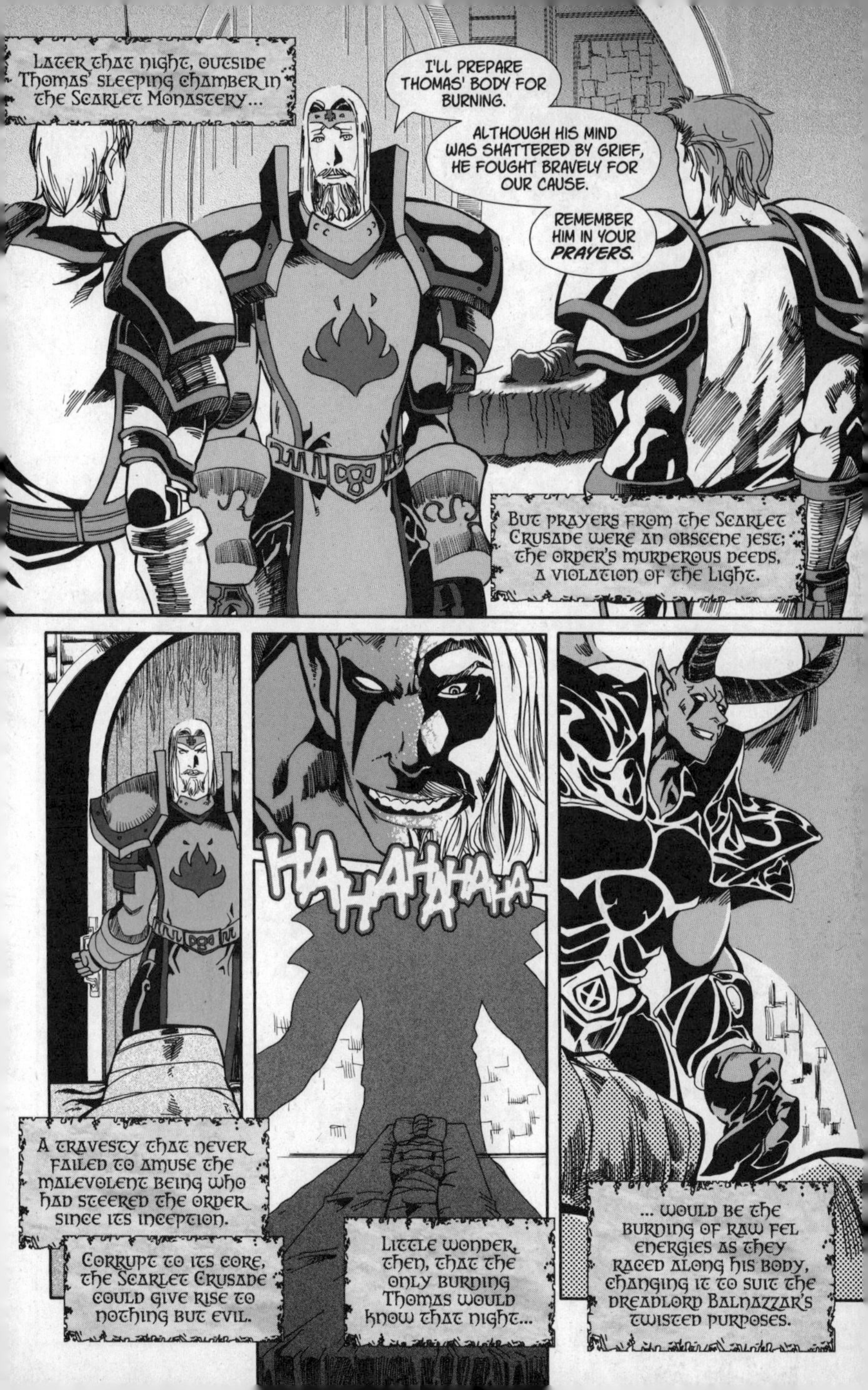
Later that night, outside Thomas' sleeping chamber in the Scarlet Monastery...
I'LL PREPARE THOMAS' BODY FOR BURNING.
ALTHOUGH HIS MIND WAS SHATTERED BY GRIEF, HE FOUGHT BRAVELY FOR OUR CAUSE.
REMEMBER HIM IN YOUR *PRAYERS.*
But prayers from the Scarlet Crusade were an obscene jest; the order's murderous deeds, a violation of the Light.
A travesty that never failed to amuse the malevolent being who had steered the order since its inception.
Corrupt to its core, the Scarlet Crusade could give rise to nothing but evil.
HAHAHAHAHAHAHA
Little wonder, then, that the only burning Thomas would know that night...
... would be the burning of raw fel energies as they raced along his body, changing it to suit the dreadlord Balnazzar's twisted purposes.

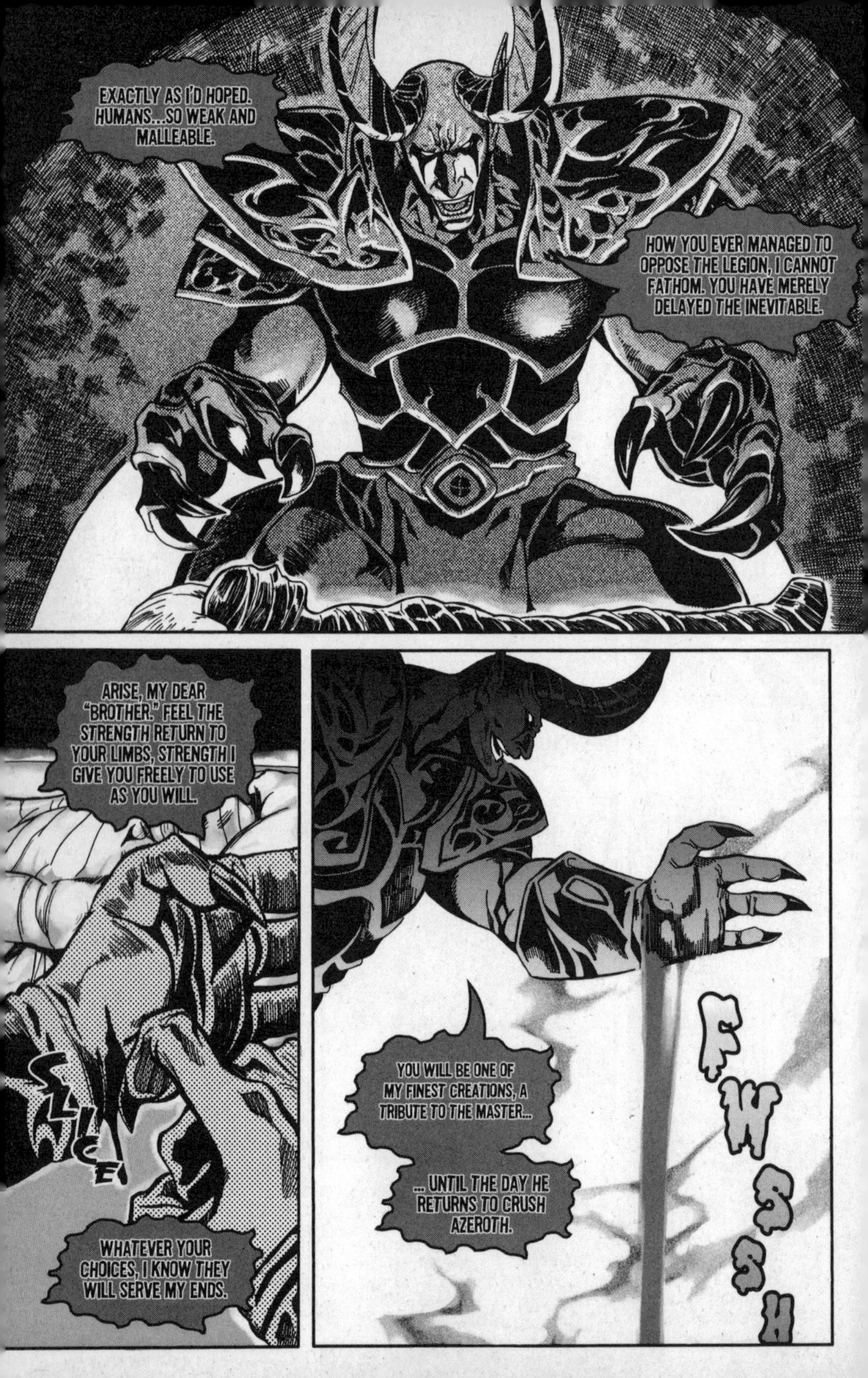
EXACTLY AS I'D HOPED. HUMANS...SO WEAK AND MALLEABLE.
HOW YOU EVER MANAGED TO OPPOSE THE LEGION, I CANNOT FATHOM. YOU HAVE MERELY DELAYED THE INEVITABLE.
ARISE, MY DEAR "BROTHER." FEEL THE STRENGTH RETURN TO YOUR LIMBS, STRENGTH I GIVE YOU FREELY TO USE AS YOU WILL.
SLICE!
WHATEVER YOUR CHOICES, I KNOW THEY WILL SERVE MY ENDS.
YOU WILL BE ONE OF MY FINEST CREATIONS, A TRIBUTE TO THE MASTER...
... UNTIL THE DAY HE RETURNS TO CRUSH AZEROTH.
FWSSH

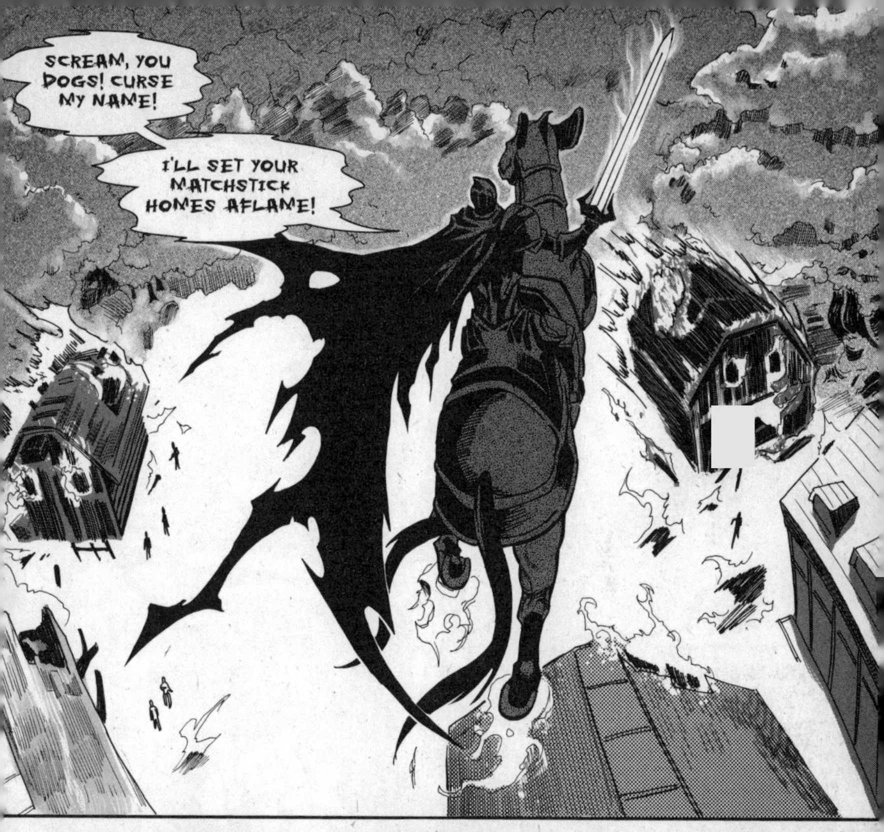
SCREAM, YOU DOGS! CURSE MY NAME!
I'LL SET YOUR MATCHSTICK HOMES AFLAME!
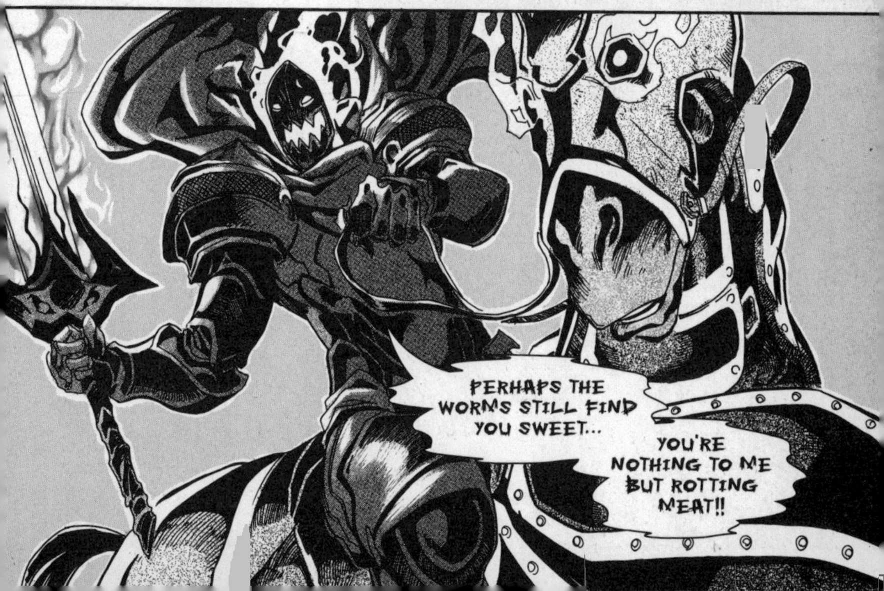
PERHAPS THE WORMS STILL FIND YOU SWEET...
YOU'RE NOTHING TO ME BUT ROTTING MEAT!!

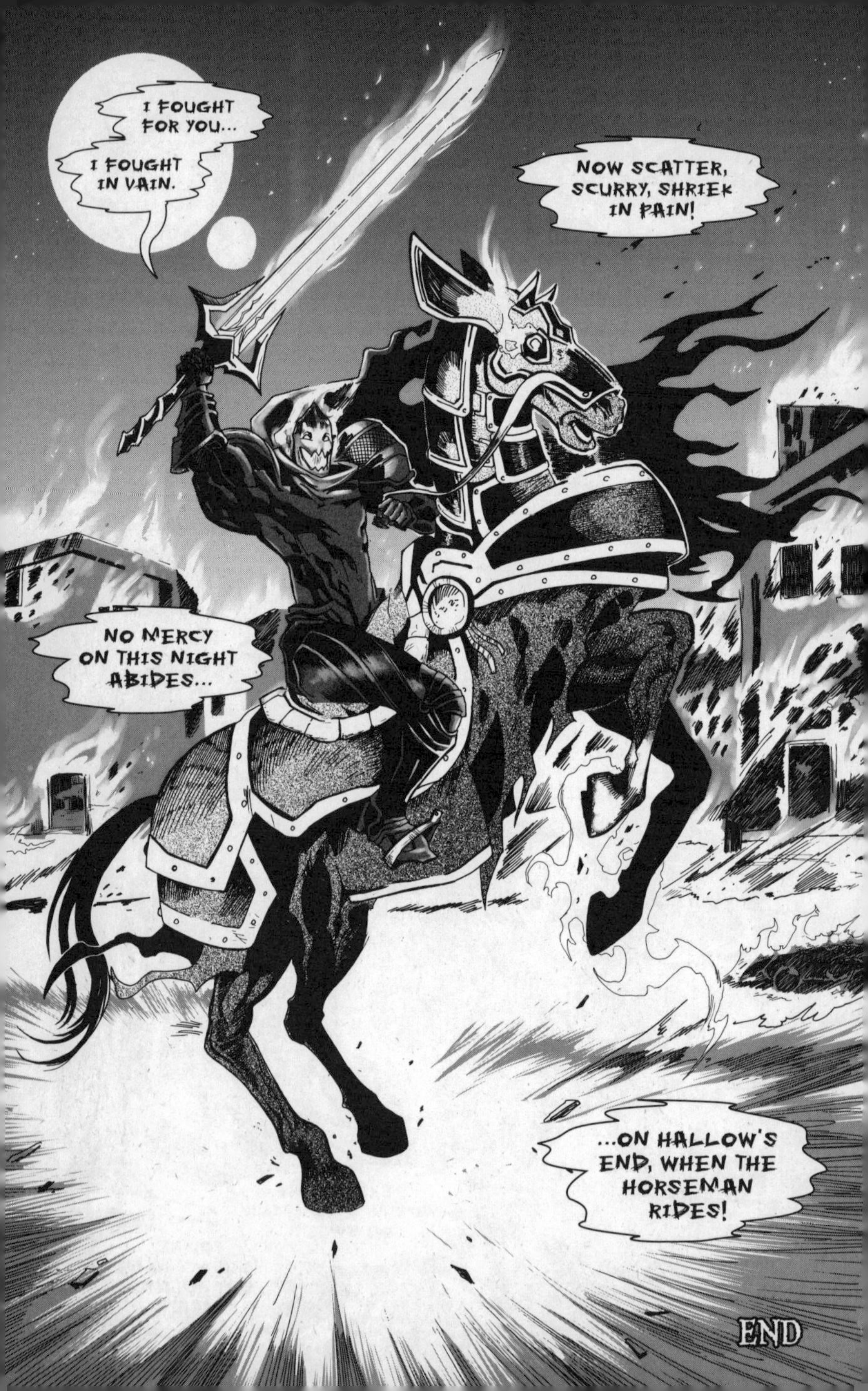
I FOUGHT FOR YOU...
I FOUGHT IN VAIN.
NOW SCATTER, SCURRY, SHRIEK IN PAIN!
NO MERCY ON THIS NIGHT ABIDES...
...ON HALLOW'S END, WHEN THE HORSEMAN RIDES!
END

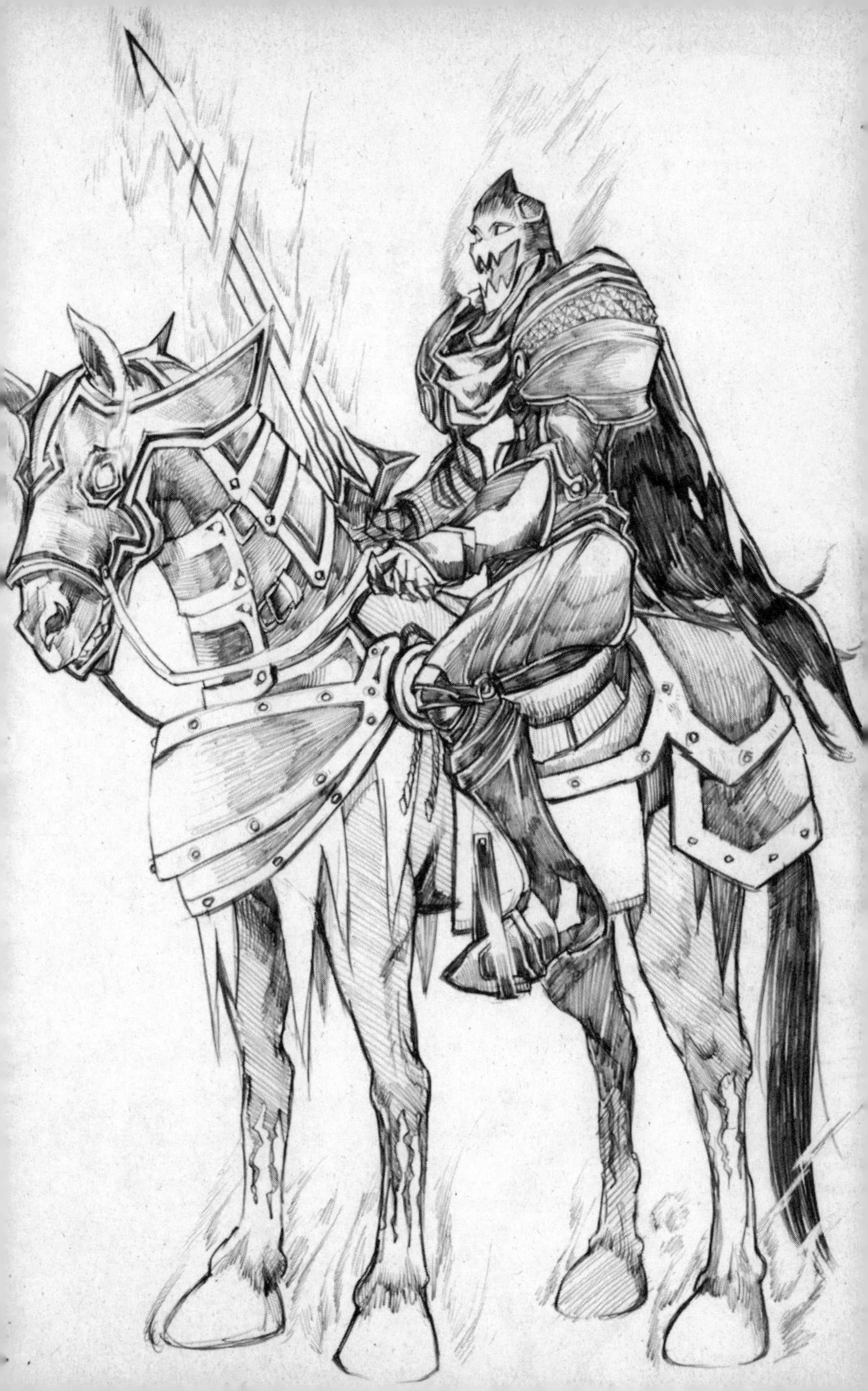

WARCRAFT

LEGENDS
VOLUME FIVE

NIGHTMARES

WRITTEN BY RICHARD A. KNAAK

PENCILS BY ROB TEN PAS
INKS BY WALTER GOMEZ, LEANDRO RIZZO
& ARIEL IACCI
TONES BY WALTER GOMEZ

LETTERER: MICHAEL PAOLILLI

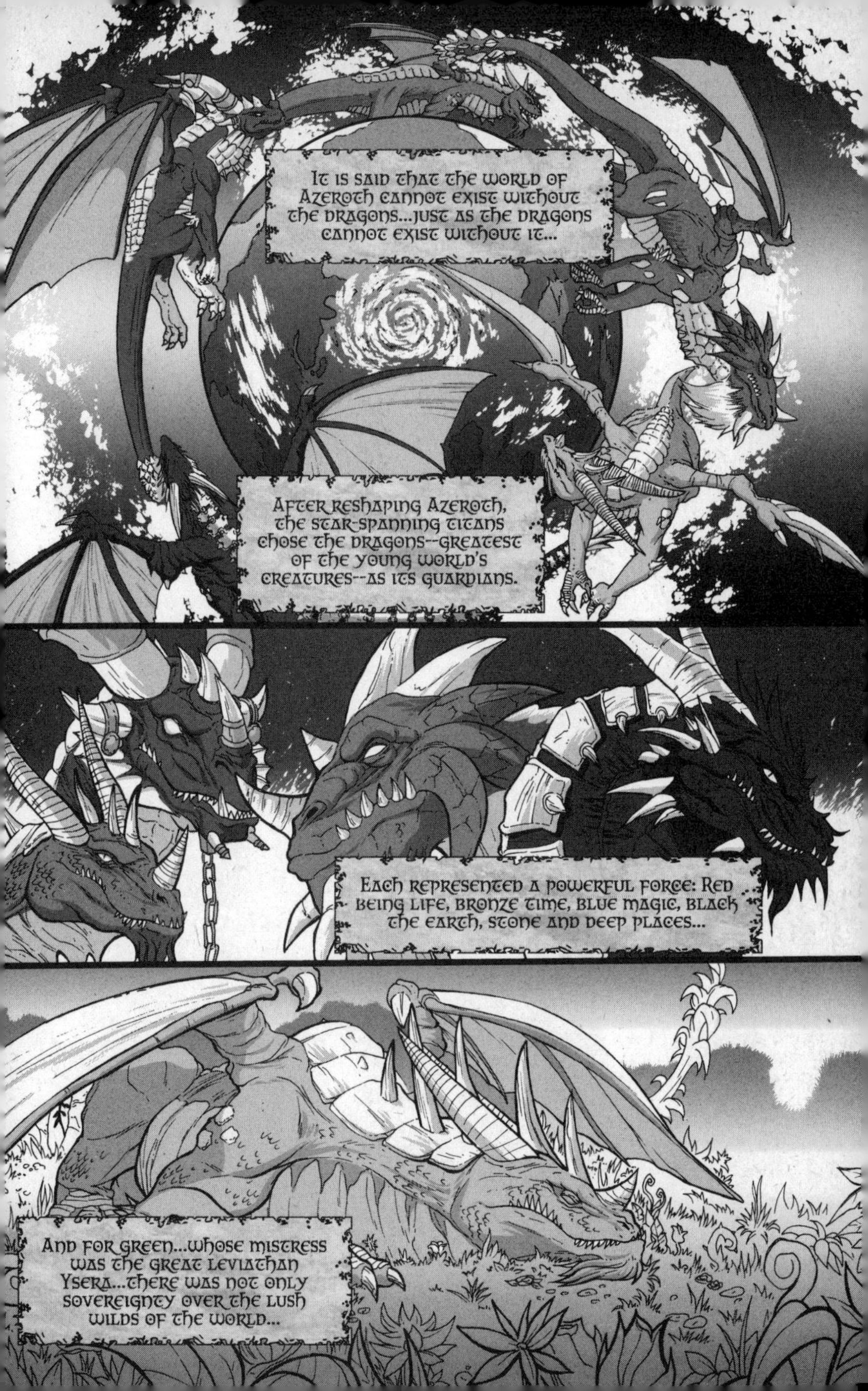
It is said that the world of Azeroth cannot exist without the dragons...just as the dragons cannot exist without it...
After reshaping Azeroth, the star-spanning titans chose the dragons--greatest of the young world's creatures--as its guardians.
Each represented a powerful force: Red being life, bronze time, blue magic, black the earth, stone and deep places...
And for green...whose mistress was the great leviathan Ysera...there was not only sovereignty over the lush wilds of the world...

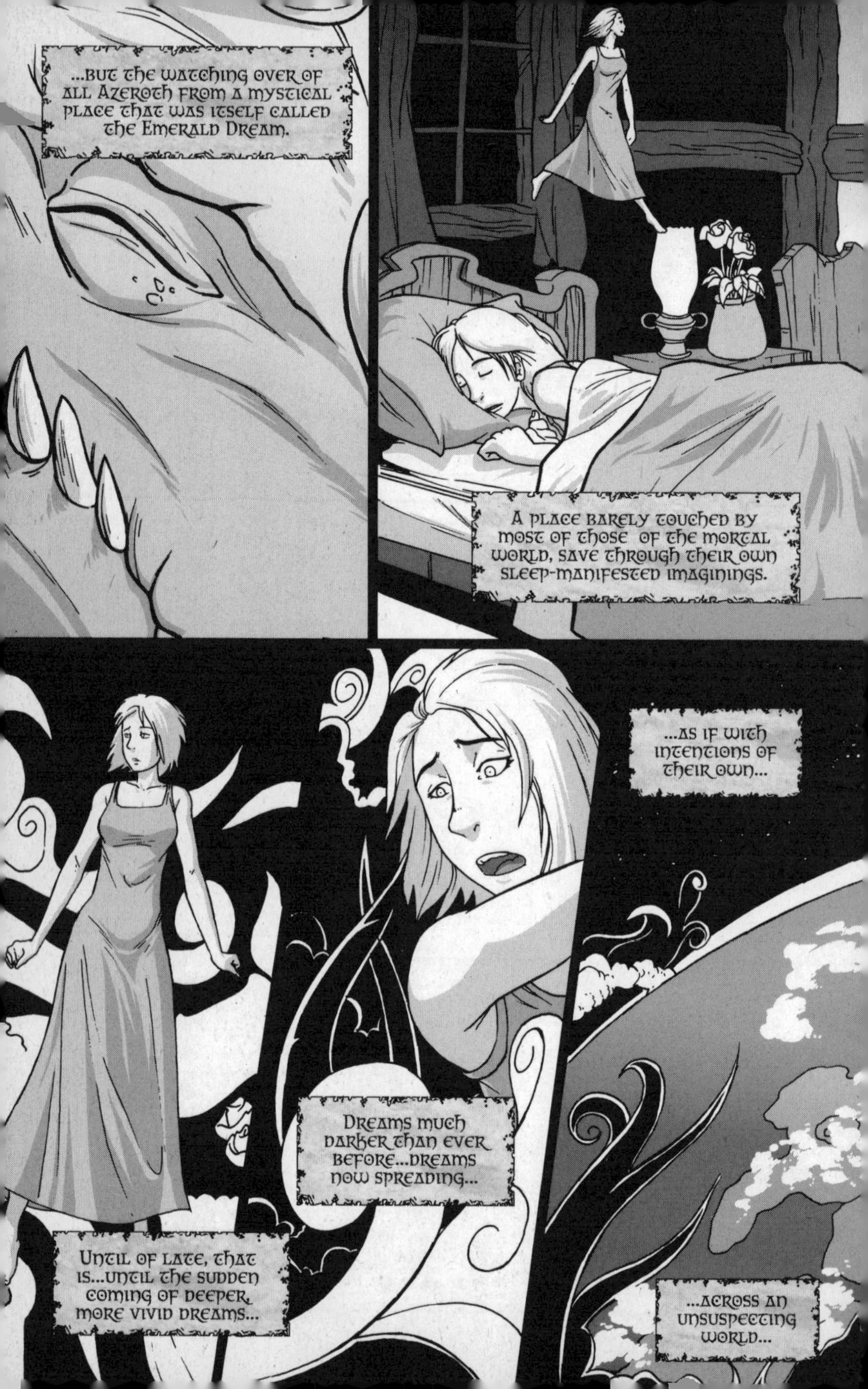
...But the watching over of all Azeroth from a mystical place that was itself called the Emerald Dream.
A place barely touched by most of those of the mortal world, save through their own sleep-manifested imaginings.
Until of late, that is...until the sudden coming of deeper, more vivid dreams...
Dreams much darker than ever before...dreams now spreading...
...as if with intentions of their own...
...across an unsuspecting world...

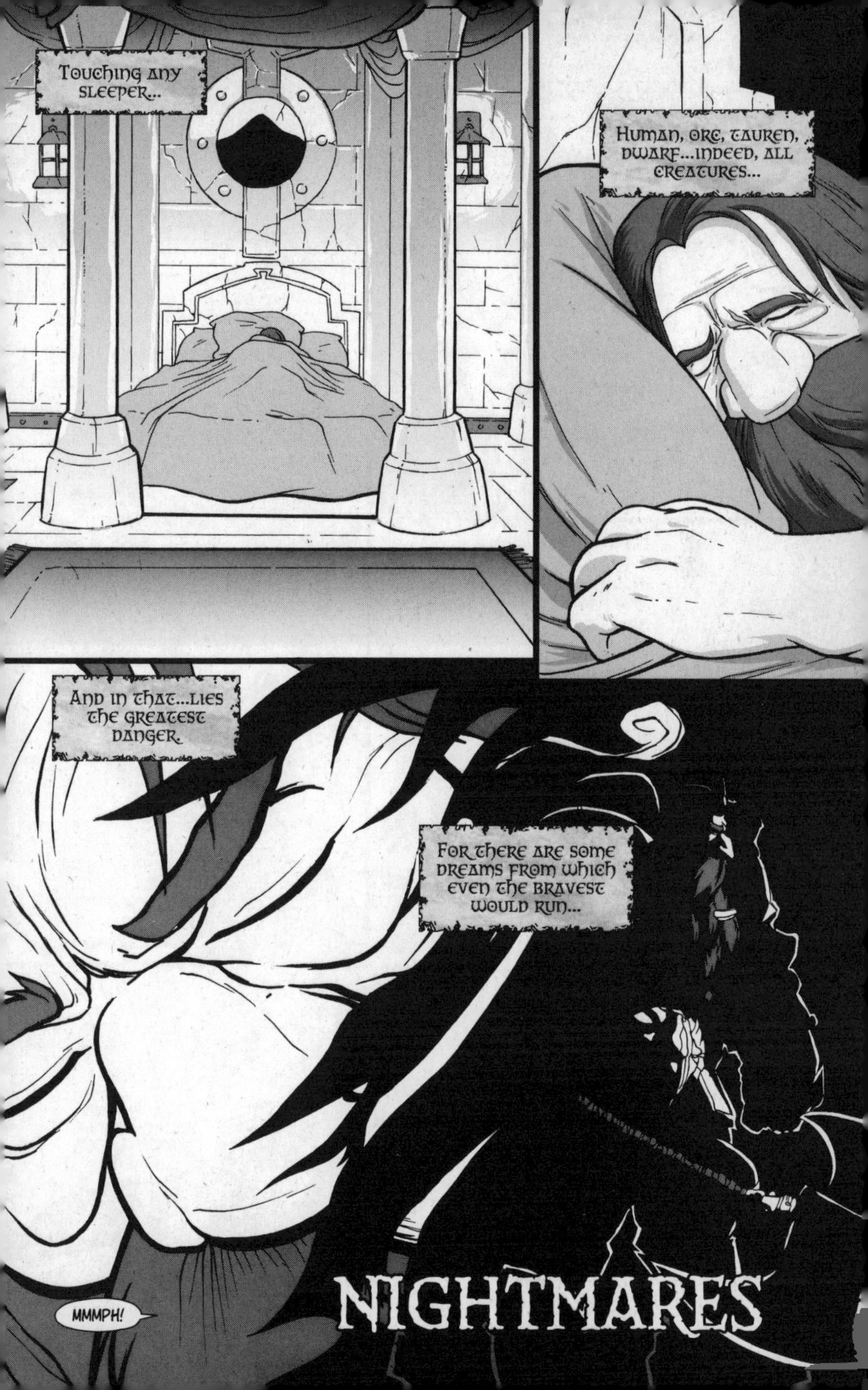
Touching any sleeper...
Human, orc, tauren, dwarf...indeed, all creatures...
And in that...lies the greatest danger.
For there are some dreams from which even the bravest would run...
MMMPH!
NIGHTMARES

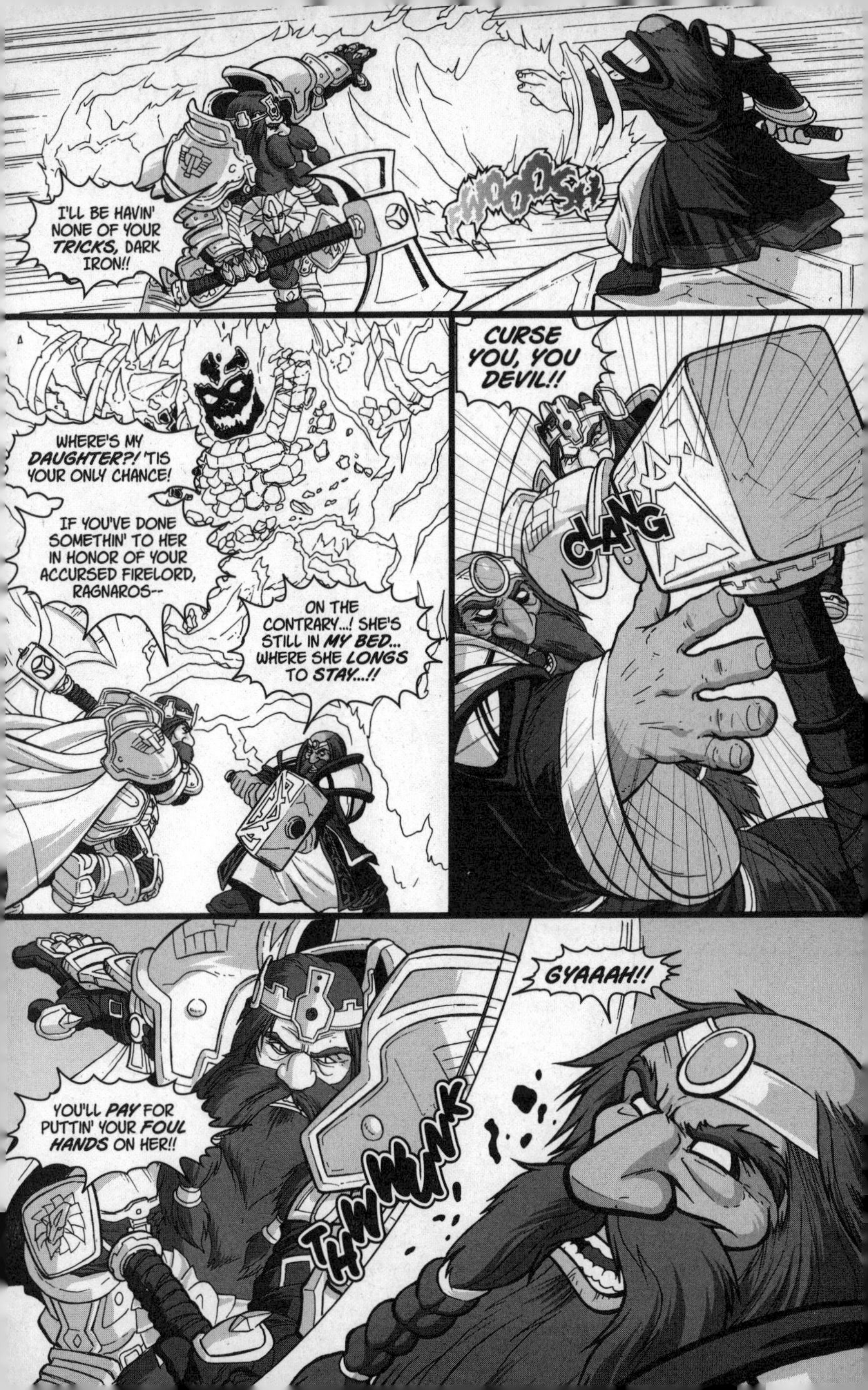

I'LL BE HAVIN' NONE OF YOUR *TRICKS*, DARK IRON!!
FWOOOSH
WHERE'S MY *DAUGHTER?!* 'TIS YOUR ONLY CHANCE!
IF YOU'VE DONE SOMETHIN' TO HER IN HONOR OF YOUR ACCURSED FIRELORD, RAGNAROS--
ON THE CONTRARY...! SHE'S STILL IN *MY BED*... WHERE SHE *LONGS* TO *STAY*...!!
CURSE YOU, YOU DEVIL!!
CLANG
YOU'LL *PAY* FOR PUTTIN' YOUR *FOUL HANDS* ON HER!!
THWAAK
GYAAAH!!

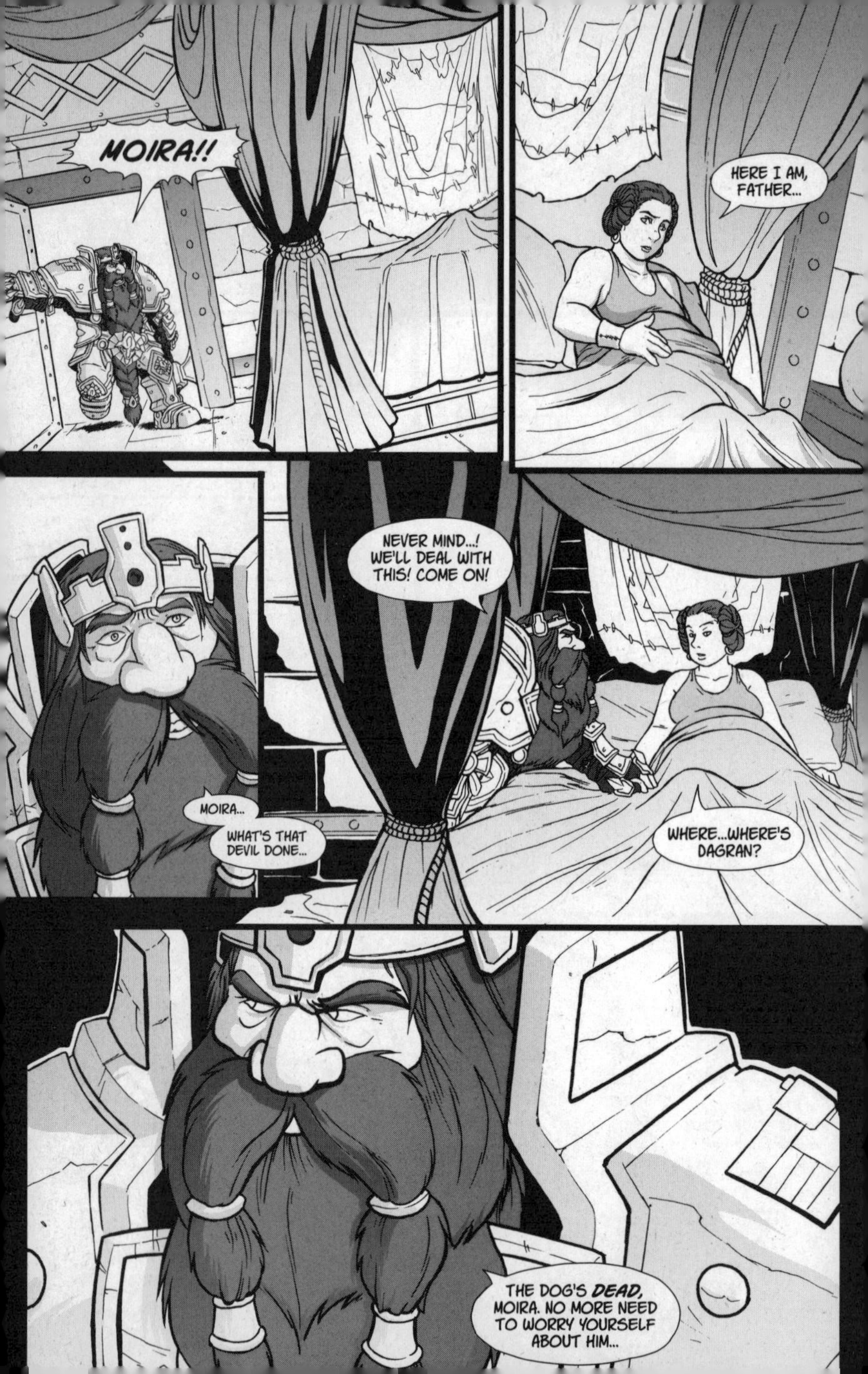
MOIRA!!
HERE I AM, FATHER...
MOIRA...
WHAT'S THAT DEVIL DONE...
NEVER MIND...! WE'LL DEAL WITH THIS! COME ON!
WHERE...WHERE'S DAGRAN?
THE DOG'S *DEAD,* MOIRA. NO MORE NEED TO WORRY YOURSELF ABOUT HIM...

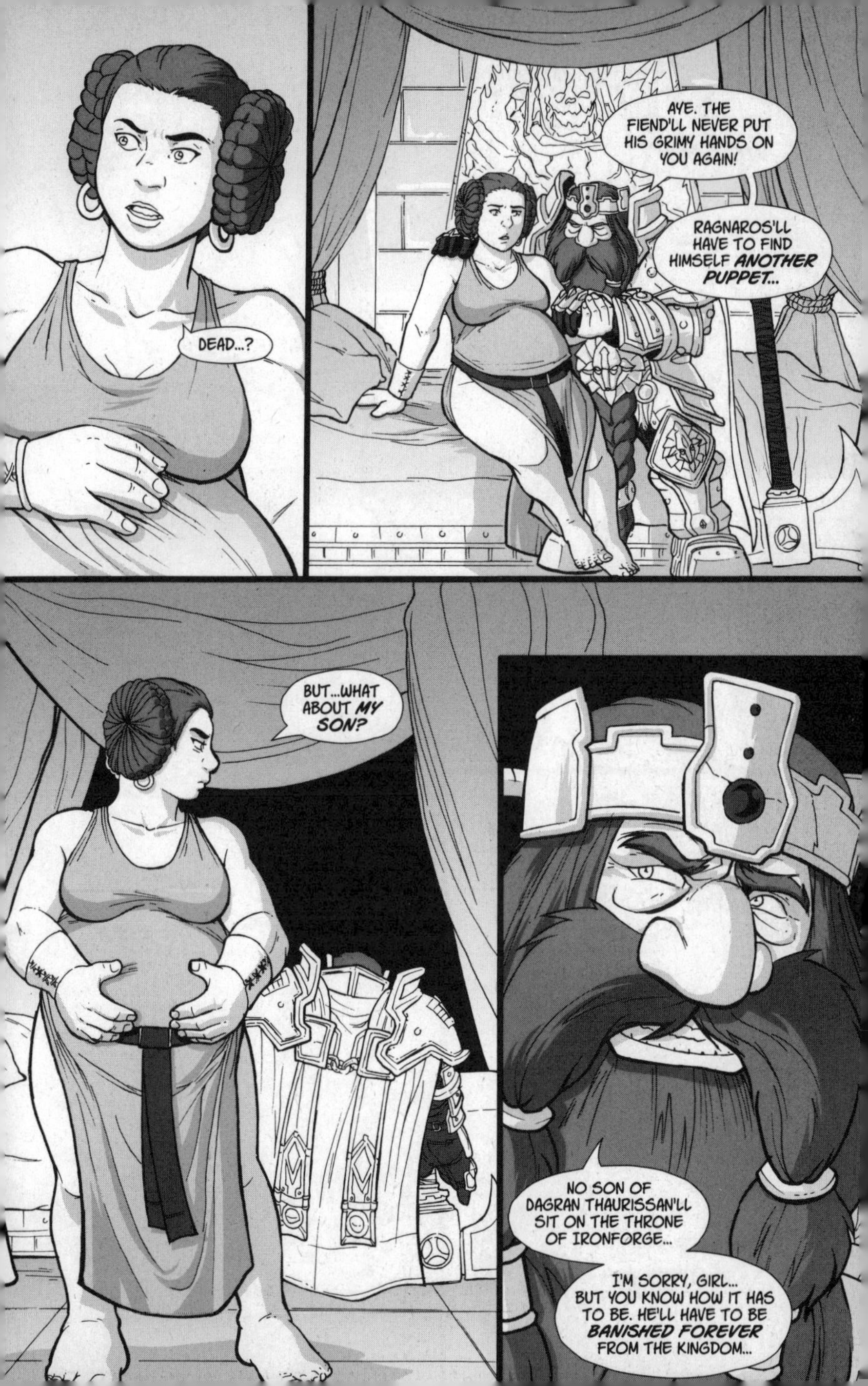
DEAD...?
AYE. THE FIEND'LL NEVER PUT HIS GRIMY HANDS ON YOU AGAIN!
RAGNAROS'LL HAVE TO FIND HIMSELF ***ANOTHER PUPPET...***
BUT...WHAT ABOUT ***MY SON?***
NO SON OF DAGRAN THAURISSAN'LL SIT ON THE THRONE OF IRONFORGE...
I'M SORRY, GIRL... BUT YOU KNOW HOW IT HAS TO BE. HE'LL HAVE TO BE ***BANISHED FOREVER*** FROM THE KINGDOM...

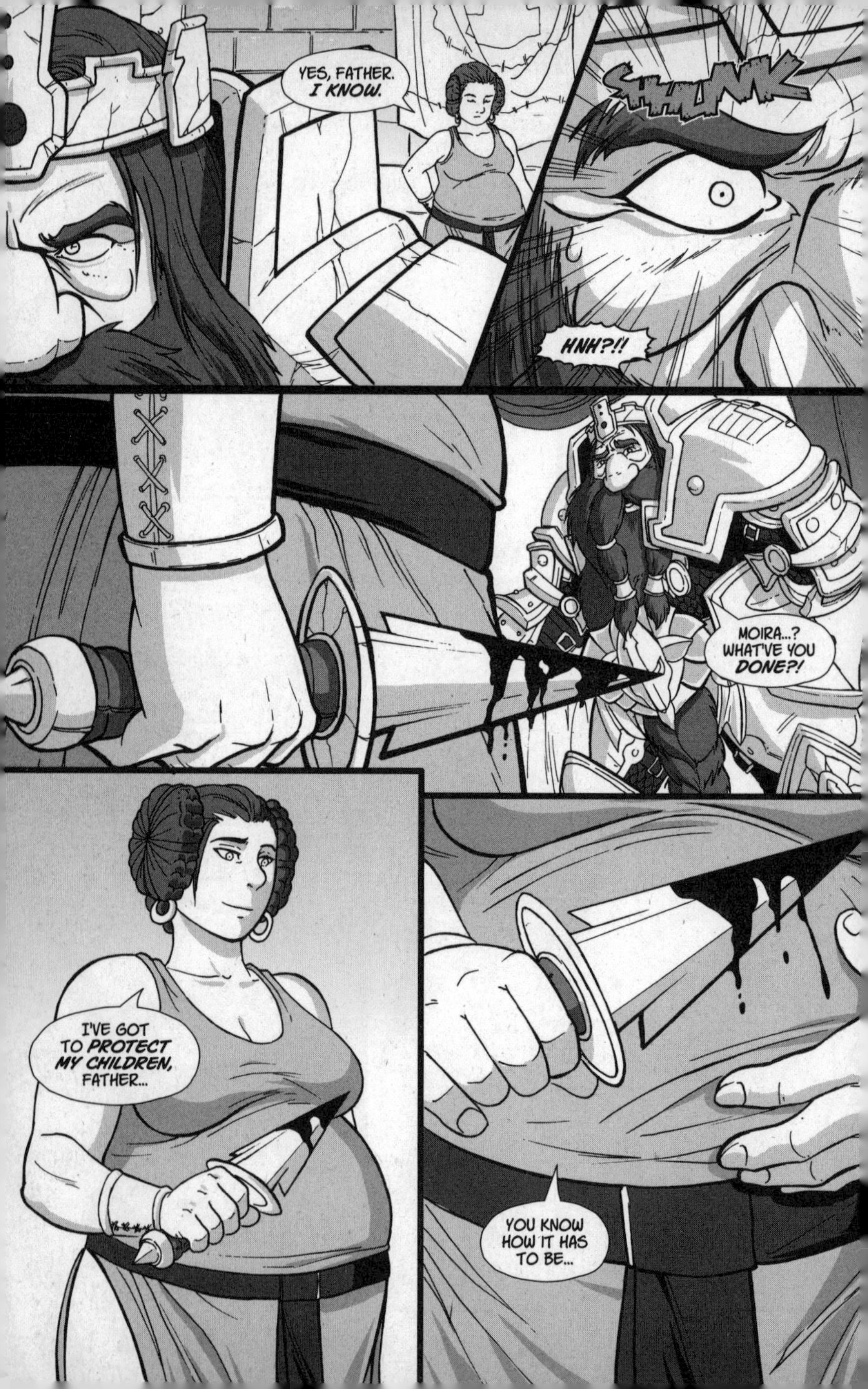
YES, FATHER. I KNOW.
SHUNK
HNH?!!
MOIRA...? WHAT'VE YOU DONE?!
I'VE GOT TO PROTECT MY CHILDREN, FATHER...
YOU KNOW HOW IT HAS TO BE...

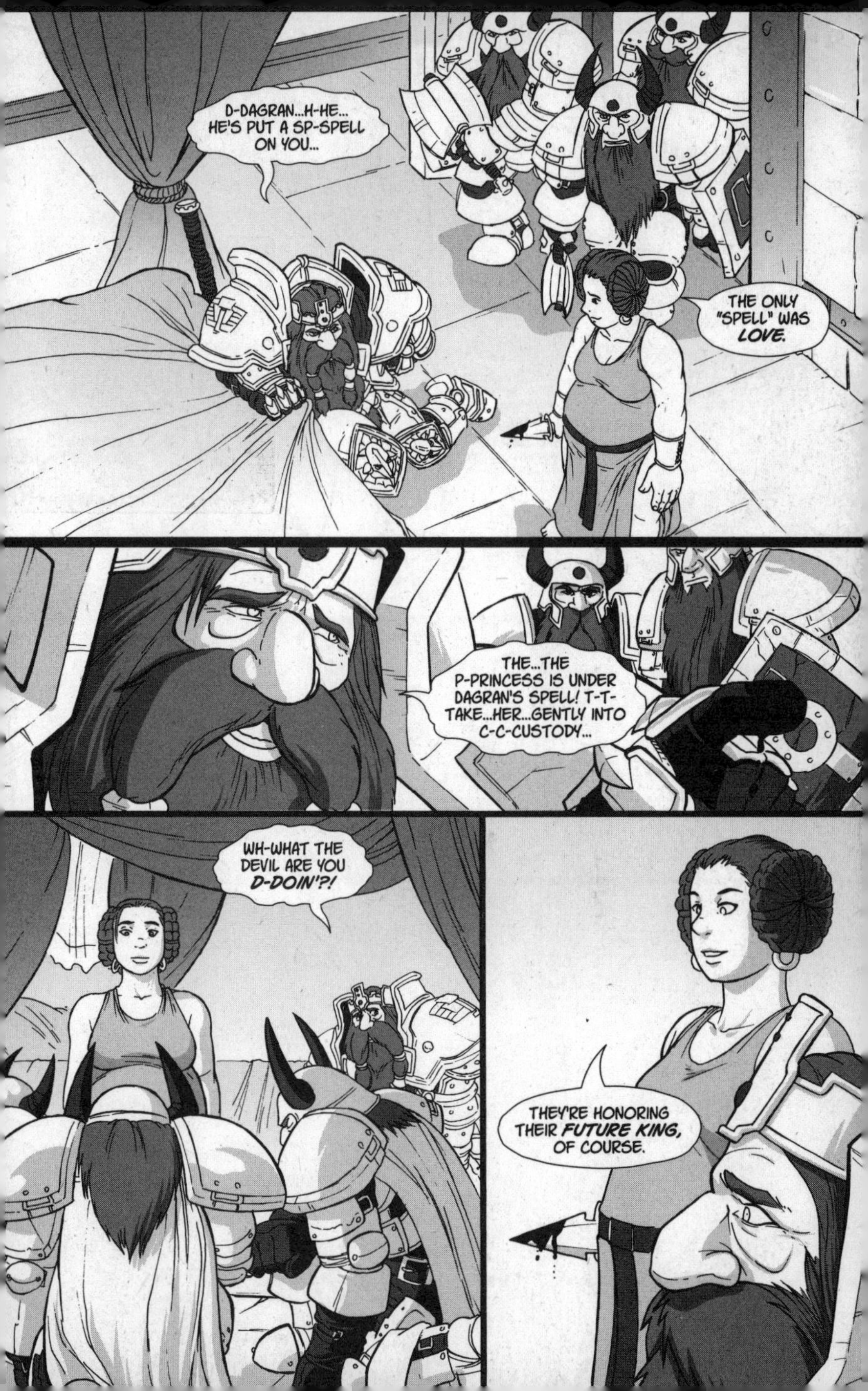
D-DAGRAN...H-HE... HE'S PUT A SP-SPELL ON YOU...
THE ONLY "SPELL" WAS ***LOVE.***
THE...THE P-PRINCESS IS UNDER DAGRAN'S SPELL! T-T-TAKE...HER...GENTLY INTO C-C-CUSTODY...
WH-WHAT THE DEVIL ARE YOU ***D-DOIN'?!***
THEY'RE HONORING THEIR ***FUTURE KING,*** OF COURSE.

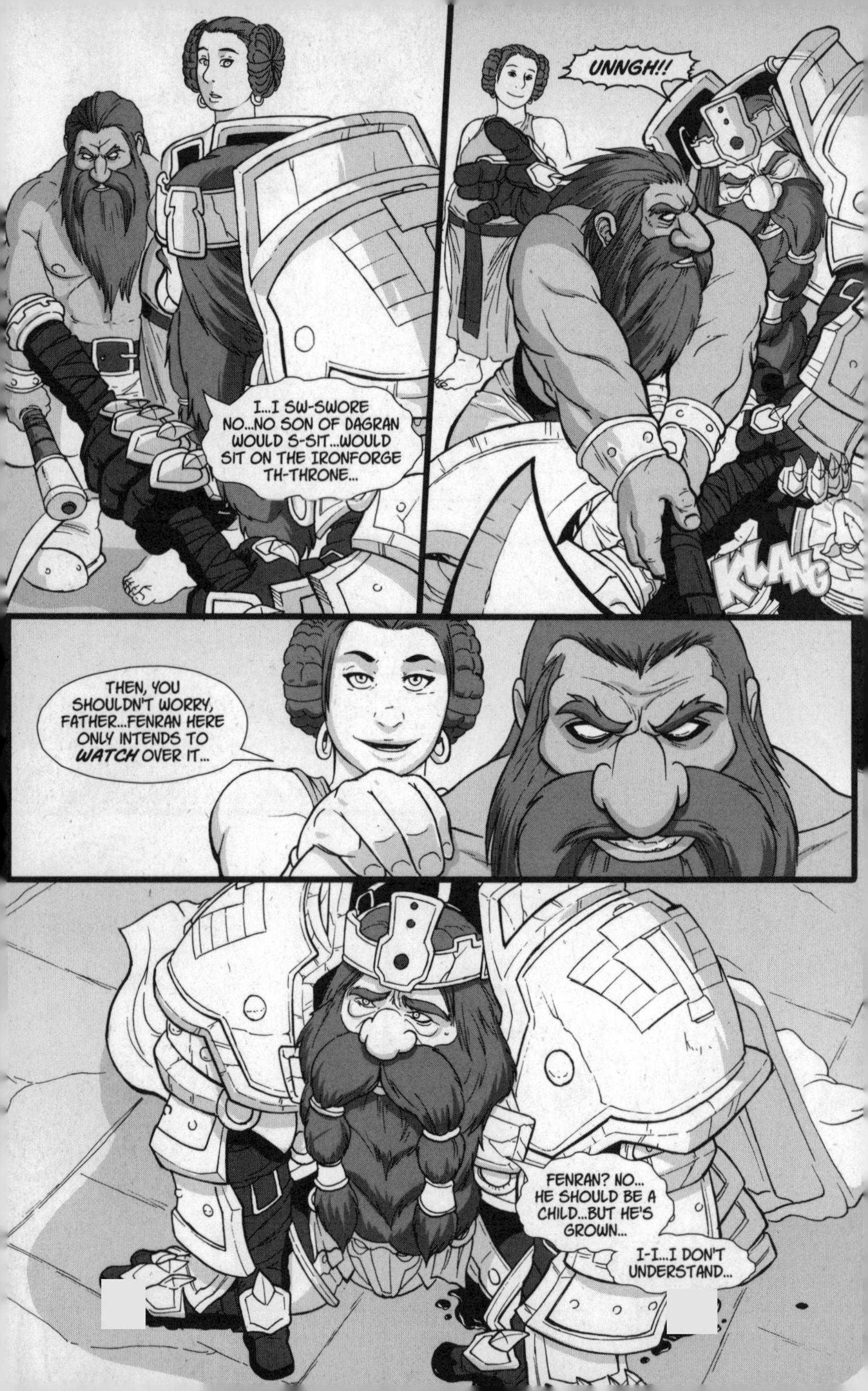
I...I SW-SWORE NO...NO SON OF DAGRAN WOULD S-SIT...WOULD SIT ON THE IRONFORGE TH-THRONE...
UNNGH!!
KLANG
THEN, YOU SHOULDN'T WORRY, FATHER...FENRAN HERE ONLY INTENDS TO *WATCH* OVER IT...
FENRAN? NO... HE SHOULD BE A CHILD...BUT HE'S GROWN...
I-I...I DON'T UNDERSTAND...

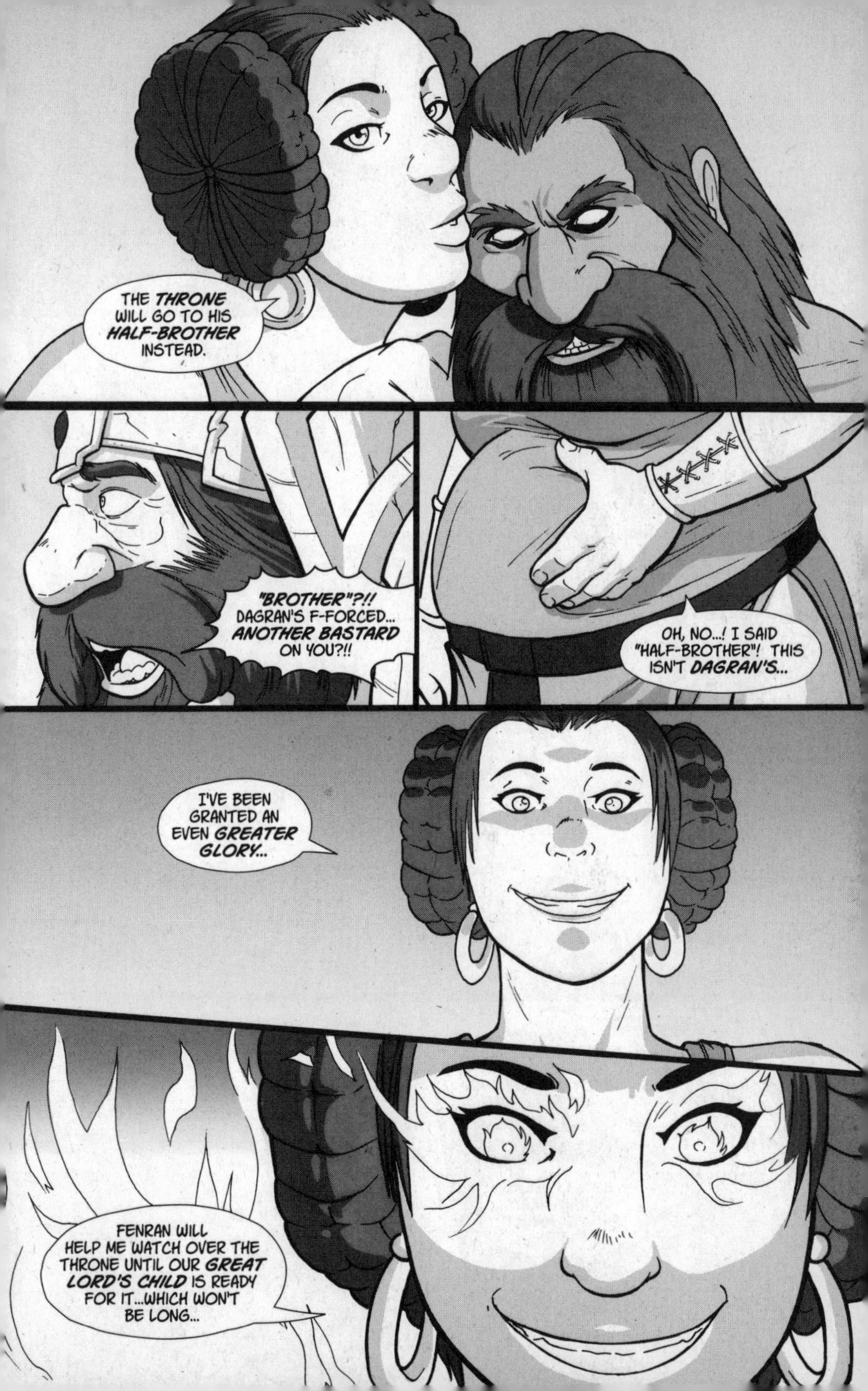
THE THRONE WILL GO TO HIS HALF-BROTHER INSTEAD.
"BROTHER"?!! DAGRAN'S F-FORCED... ANOTHER BASTARD ON YOU?!!
OH, NO...! I SAID "HALF-BROTHER"! THIS ISN'T DAGRAN'S...
I'VE BEEN GRANTED AN EVEN GREATER GLORY...
FENRAN WILL HELP ME WATCH OVER THE THRONE UNTIL OUR GREAT LORD'S CHILD IS READY FOR IT...WHICH WON'T BE LONG...

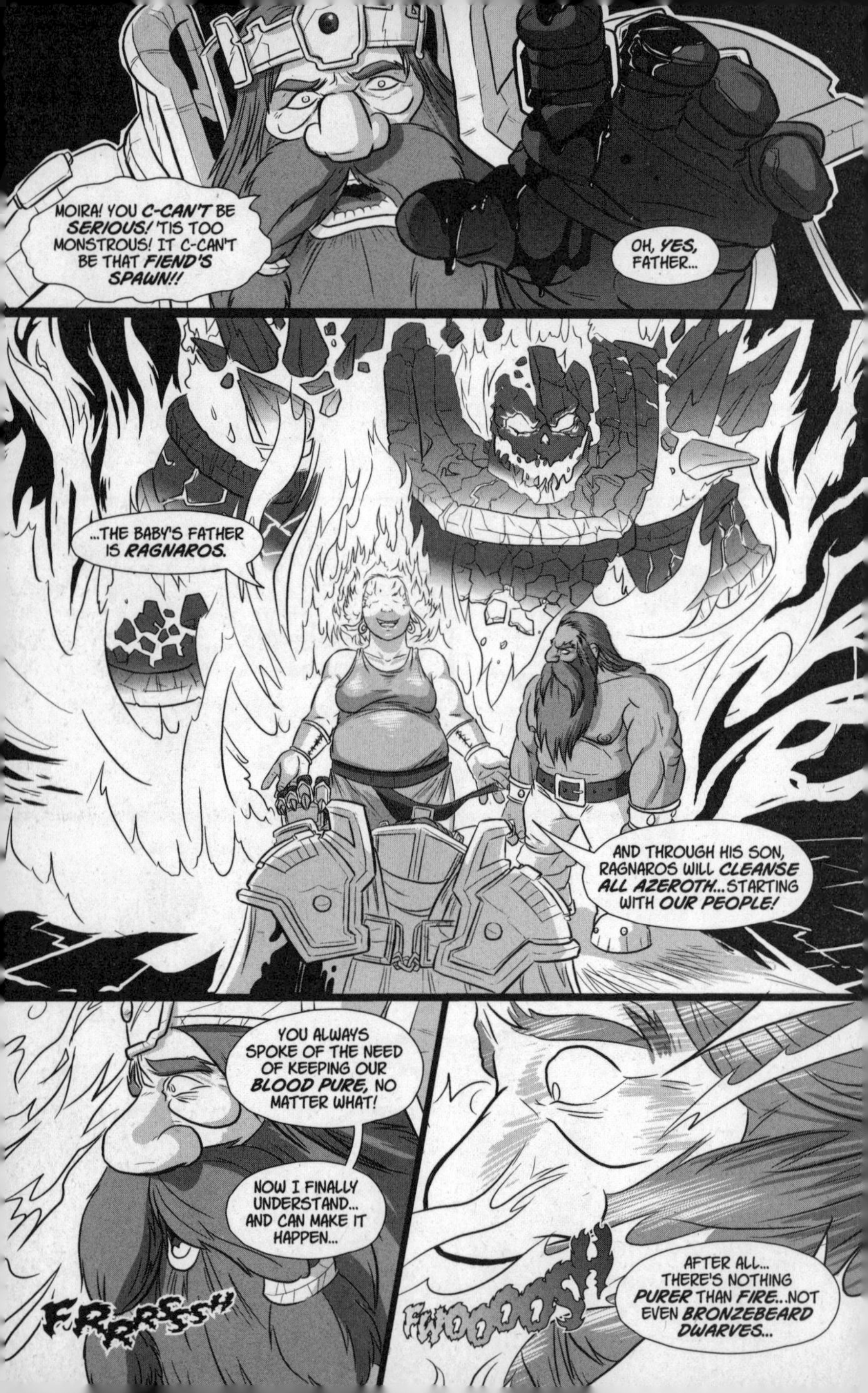
MOIRA! YOU C-CAN'T BE SERIOUS! 'TIS TOO MONSTROUS! IT C-CAN'T BE THAT FIEND'S SPAWN!!
OH, YES, FATHER...
...THE BABY'S FATHER IS RAGNAROS.
AND THROUGH HIS SON, RAGNAROS WILL CLEANSE ALL AZEROTH...STARTING WITH OUR PEOPLE!
YOU ALWAYS SPOKE OF THE NEED OF KEEPING OUR BLOOD PURE, NO MATTER WHAT!
NOW I FINALLY UNDERSTAND... AND CAN MAKE IT HAPPEN...
FRRRSSSH
FWOOOOOSH!
AFTER ALL... THERE'S NOTHING PURER THAN FIRE...NOT EVEN BRONZEBEARD DWARVES...

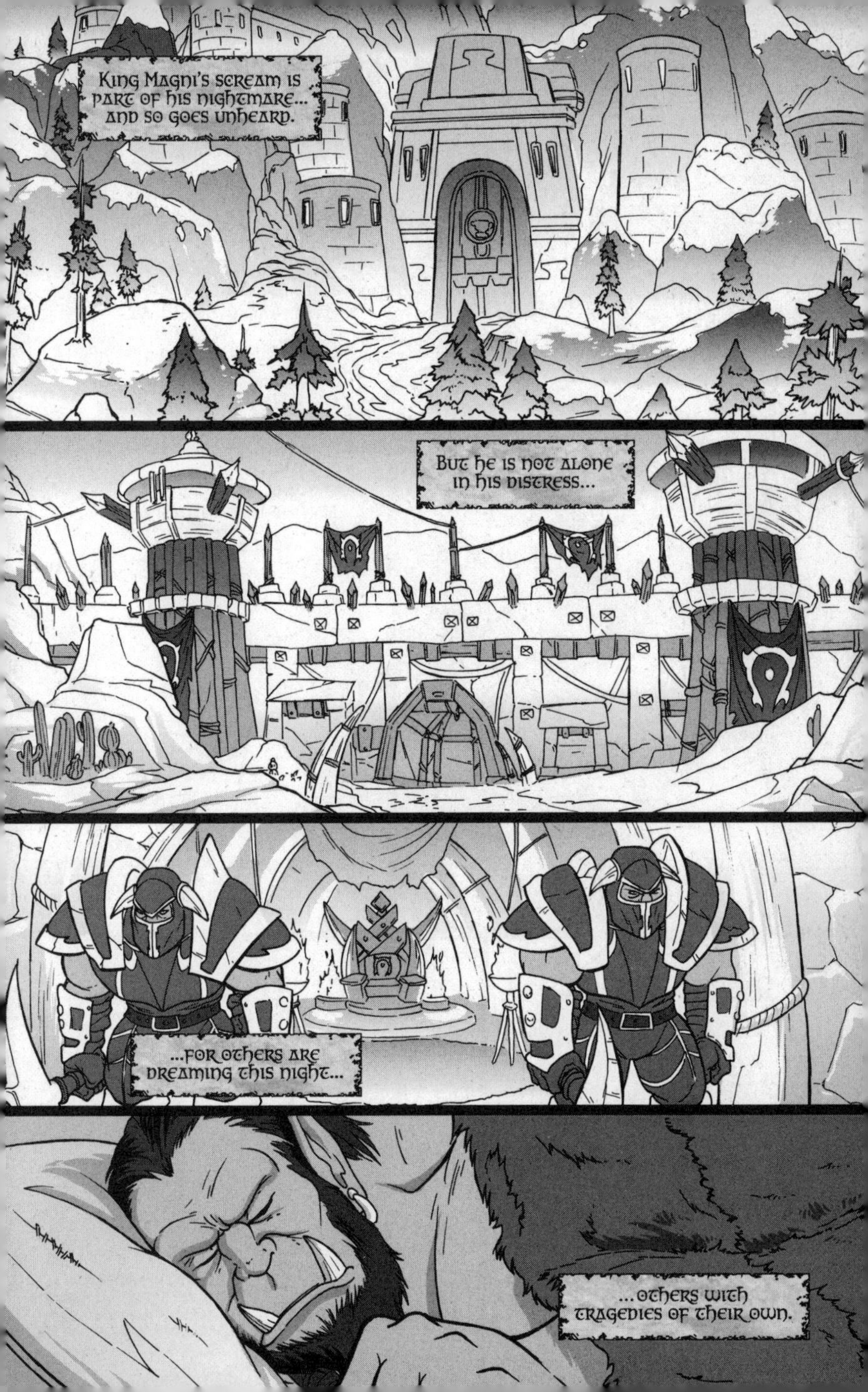
King Magni's scream is part of his nightmare... and so goes unheard.
But he is not alone in his distress...
...for others are dreaming this night...
...others with tragedies of their own.

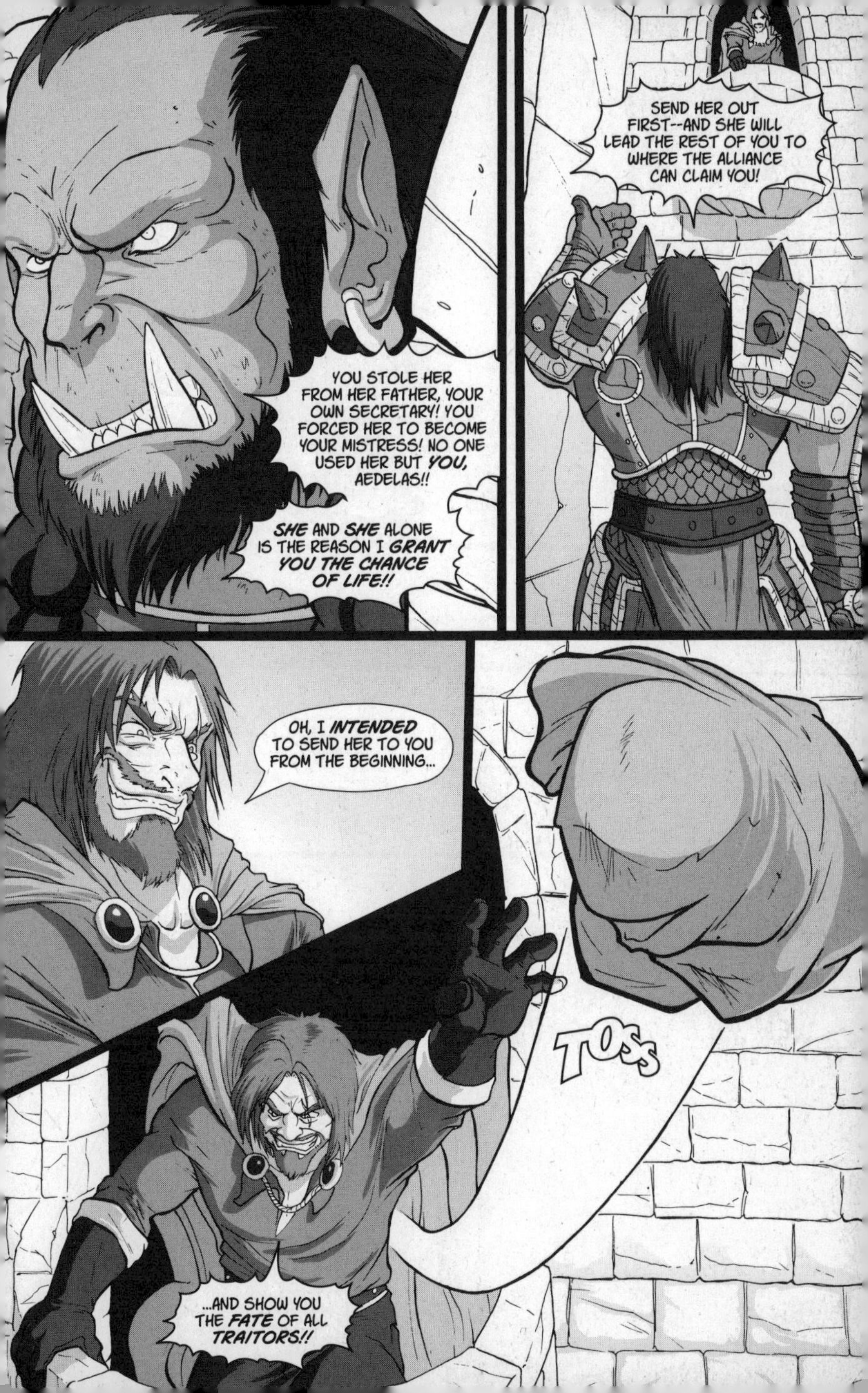
YOU STOLE HER FROM HER FATHER, YOUR OWN SECRETARY! YOU FORCED HER TO BECOME YOUR MISTRESS! NO ONE USED HER BUT *YOU*, AEDELAS!!
SHE AND *SHE* ALONE IS THE REASON I *GRANT YOU THE CHANCE OF LIFE!!*
SEND HER OUT FIRST--AND SHE WILL LEAD THE REST OF YOU TO WHERE THE ALLIANCE CAN CLAIM YOU!
OH, I *INTENDED* TO SEND HER TO YOU FROM THE BEGINNING...
...AND SHOW YOU THE *FATE* OF ALL *TRAITORS!!*
TOSS

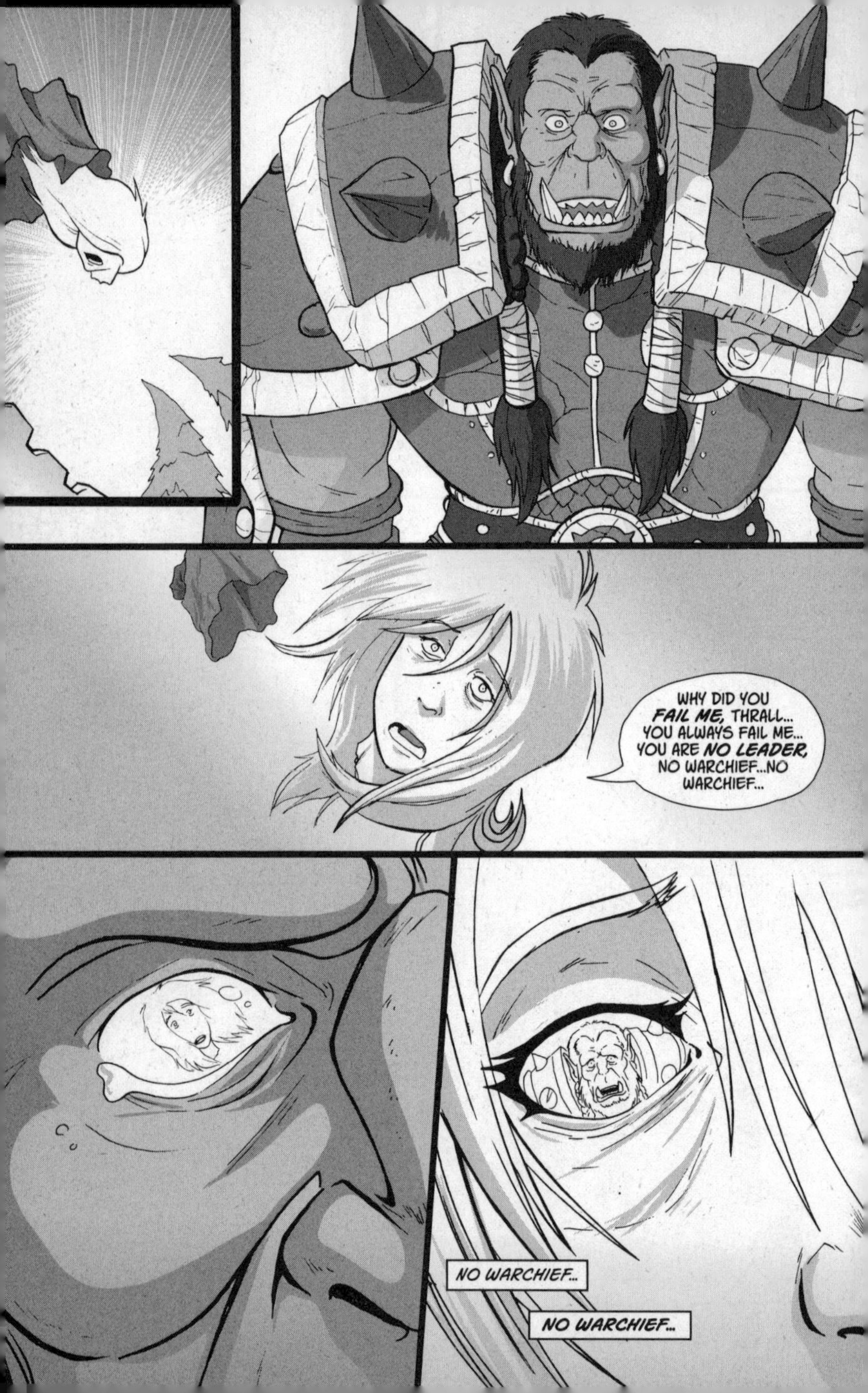
WHY DID YOU FAIL ME, THRALL... YOU ALWAYS FAIL ME... YOU ARE NO LEADER, NO WARCHIEF...NO WARCHIEF...
NO WARCHIEF...
NO WARCHIEF...

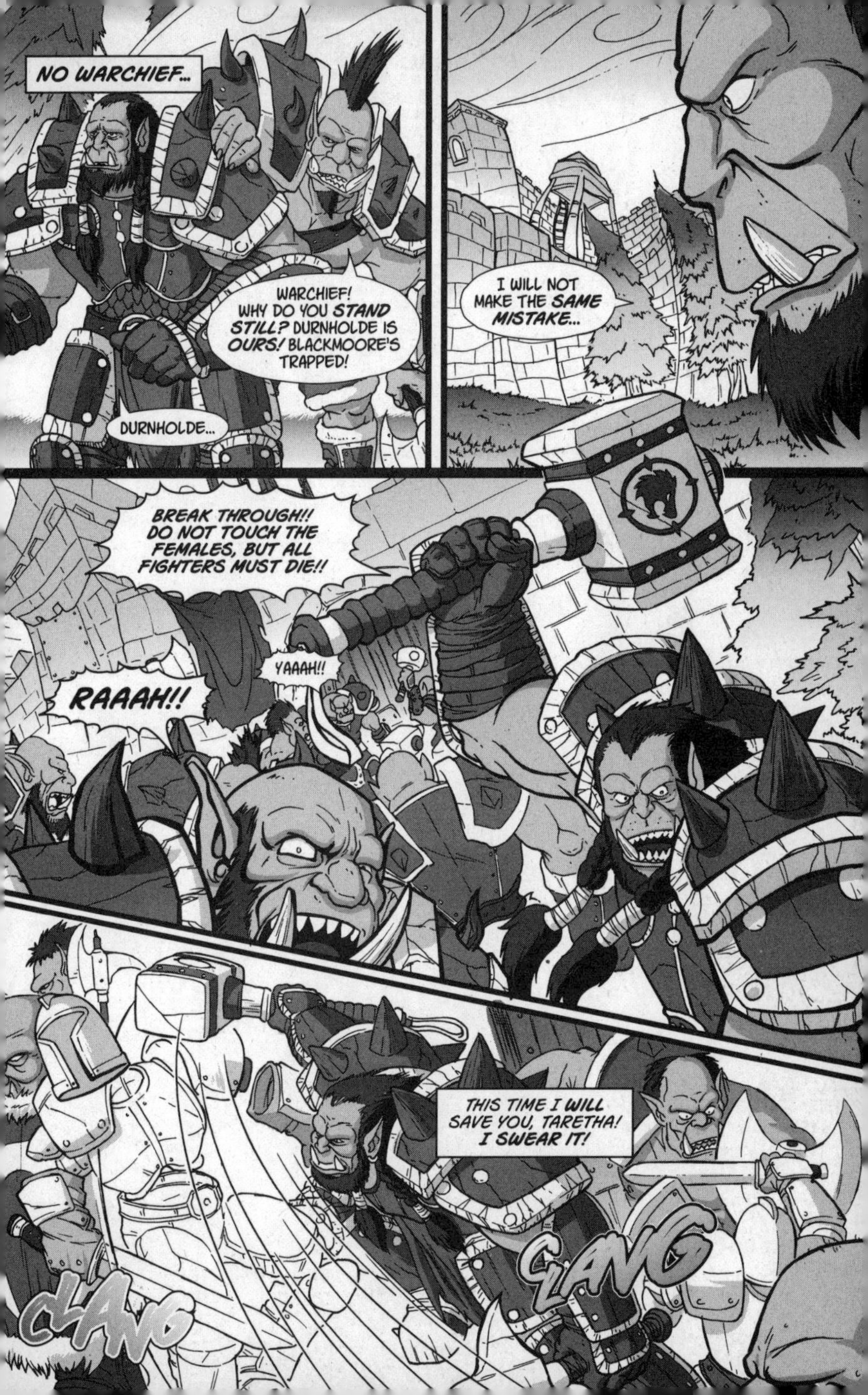
NO WARCHIEF...
WARCHIEF! WHY DO YOU STAND STILL? DURNHOLDE IS OURS! BLACKMOORE'S TRAPPED!
DURNHOLDE...
I WILL NOT MAKE THE SAME MISTAKE...
BREAK THROUGH!! DO NOT TOUCH THE FEMALES, BUT ALL FIGHTERS MUST DIE!!
YAAAH!!
RAAAH!!
THIS TIME I WILL SAVE YOU, TARETHA! I SWEAR IT!
CLANG
CLANG

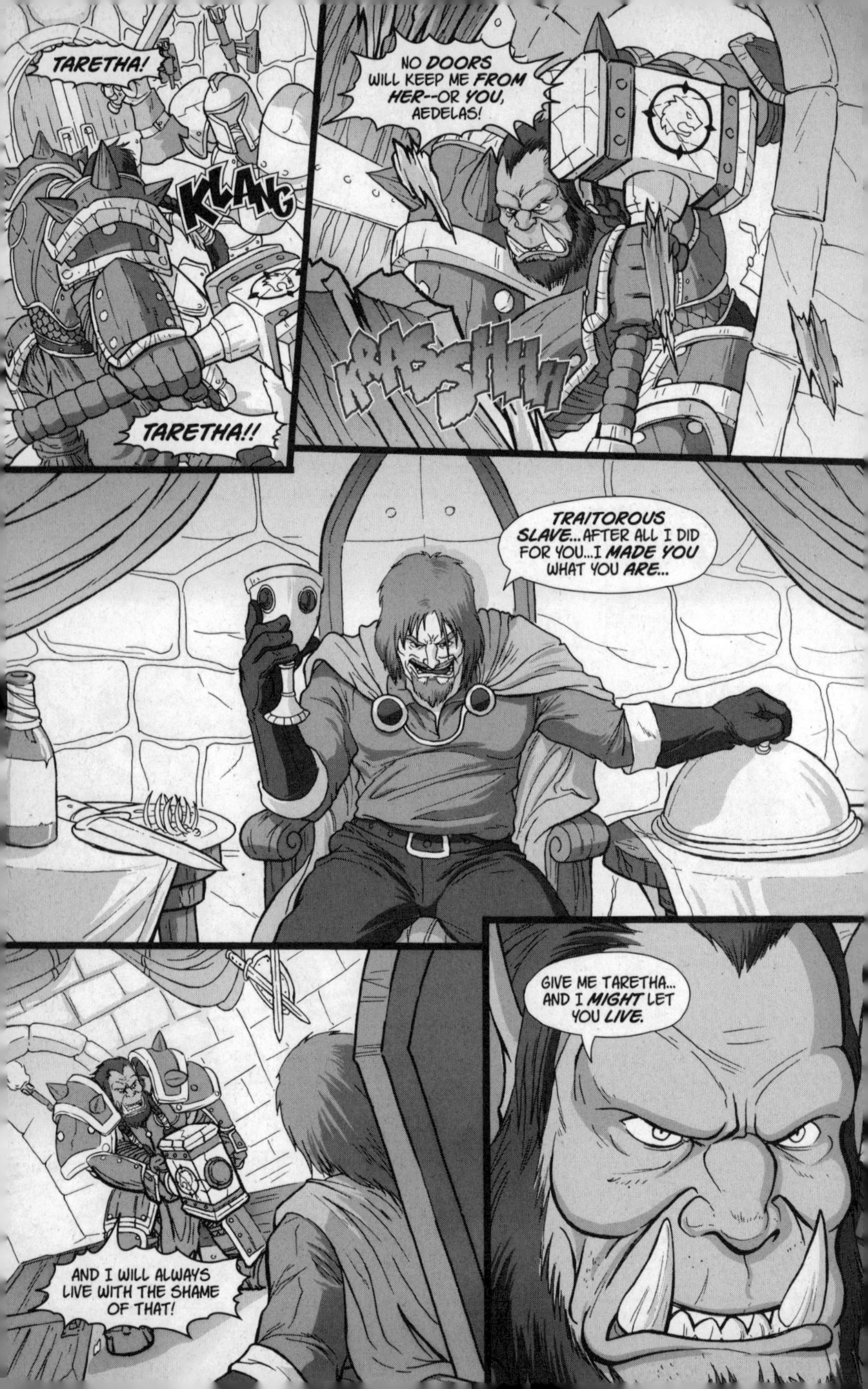
TARETHA!
KLANG
TARETHA!!
NO DOORS WILL KEEP ME FROM HER--OR YOU, AEDELAS!
KRASHHH
TRAITOROUS SLAVE...AFTER ALL I DID FOR YOU...I MADE YOU WHAT YOU ARE...
AND I WILL ALWAYS LIVE WITH THE SHAME OF THAT!
GIVE ME TARETHA... AND I MIGHT LET YOU LIVE.

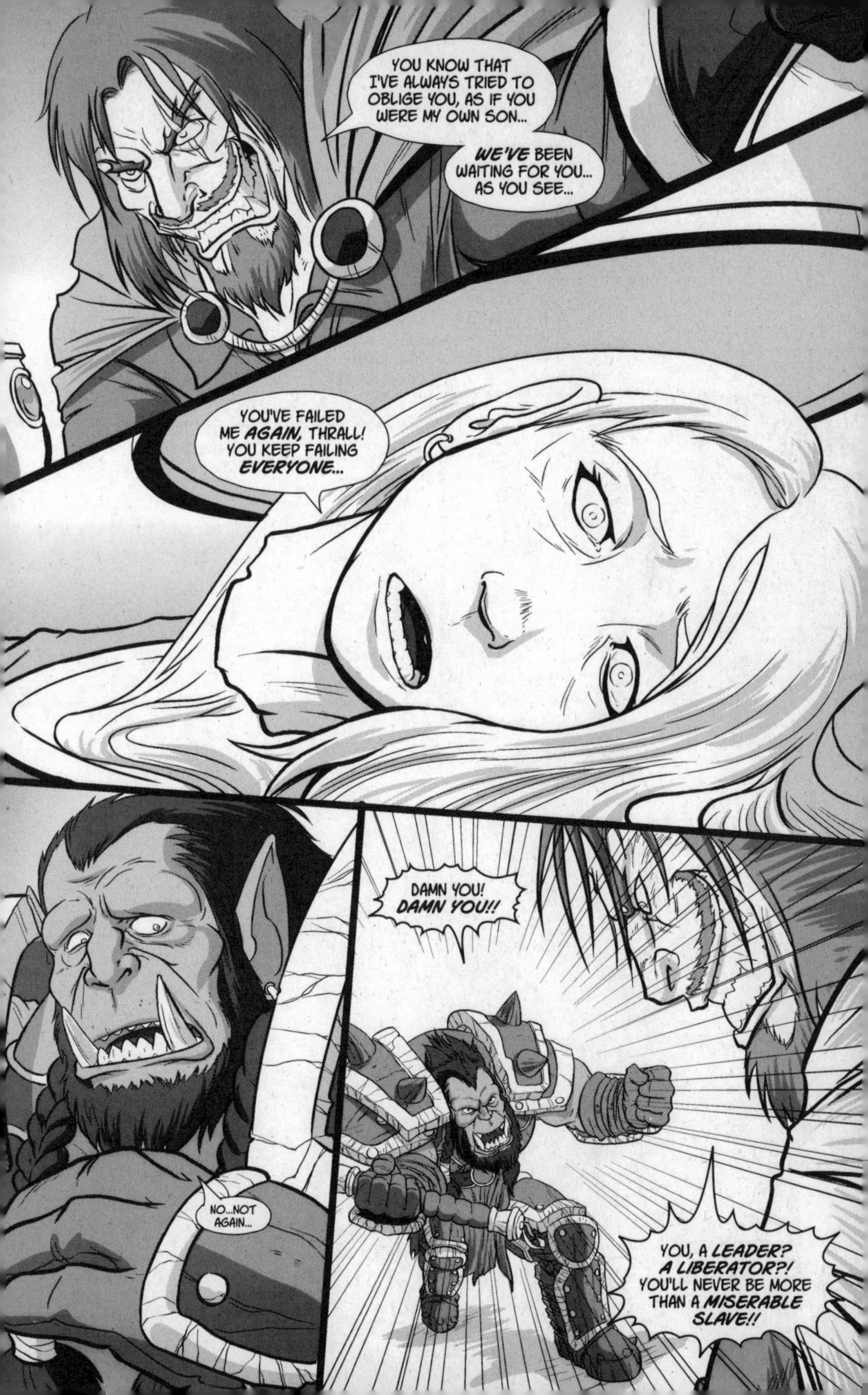
YOU KNOW THAT I'VE ALWAYS TRIED TO OBLIGE YOU, AS IF YOU WERE MY OWN SON...
WE'VE BEEN WAITING FOR YOU... AS YOU SEE...
YOU'VE FAILED ME AGAIN, THRALL! YOU KEEP FAILING EVERYONE...
NO...NOT AGAIN...
DAMN YOU! DAMN YOU!!
YOU, A LEADER? A LIBERATOR?! YOU'LL NEVER BE MORE THAN A MISERABLE SLAVE!!

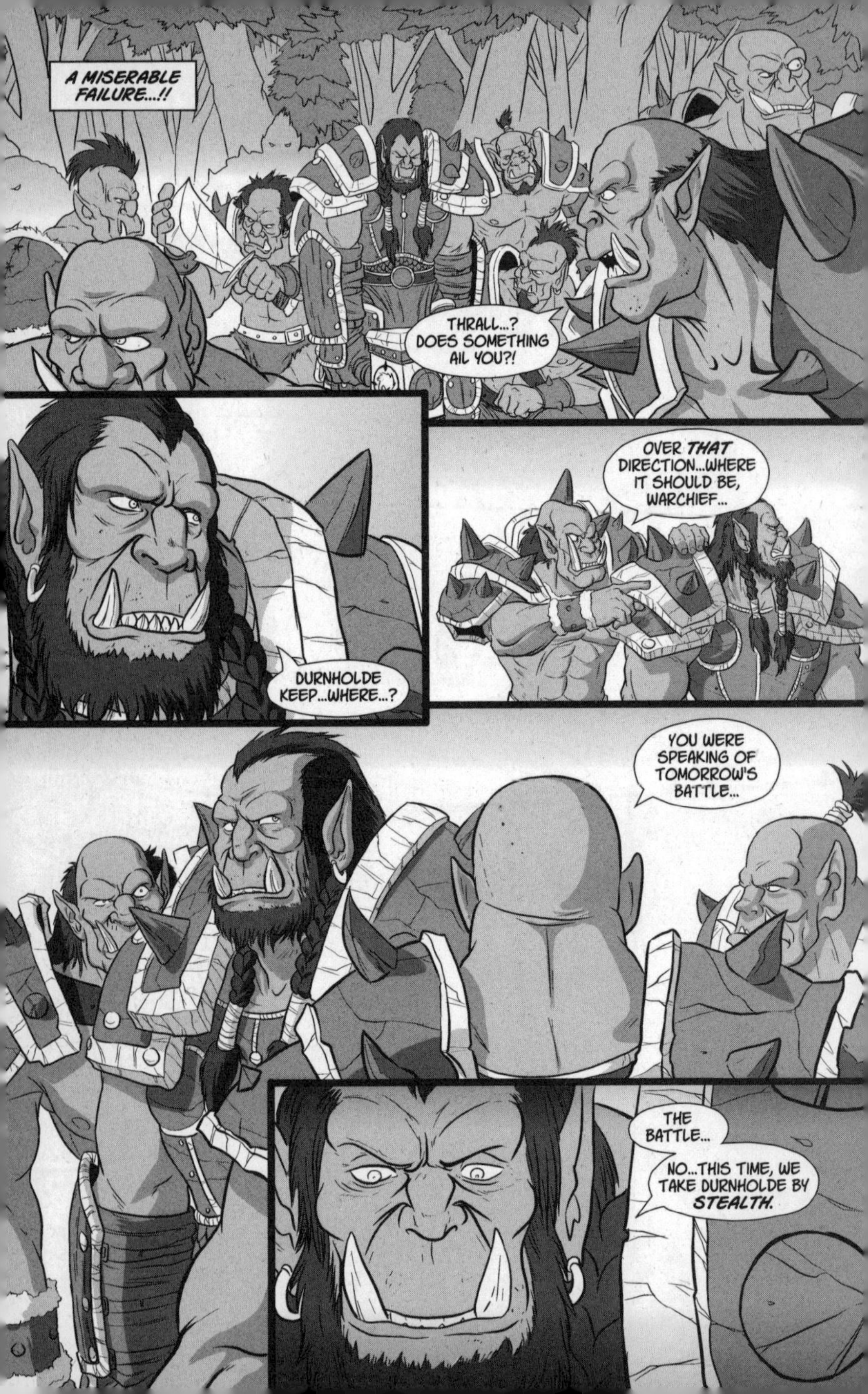
A MISERABLE FAILURE...!!
THRALL...? DOES SOMETHING AIL YOU?!
DURNHOLDE KEEP...WHERE...?
OVER THAT DIRECTION...WHERE IT SHOULD BE, WARCHIEF...
YOU WERE SPEAKING OF TOMORROW'S BATTLE...
THE BATTLE...
NO...THIS TIME, WE TAKE DURNHOLDE BY STEALTH.

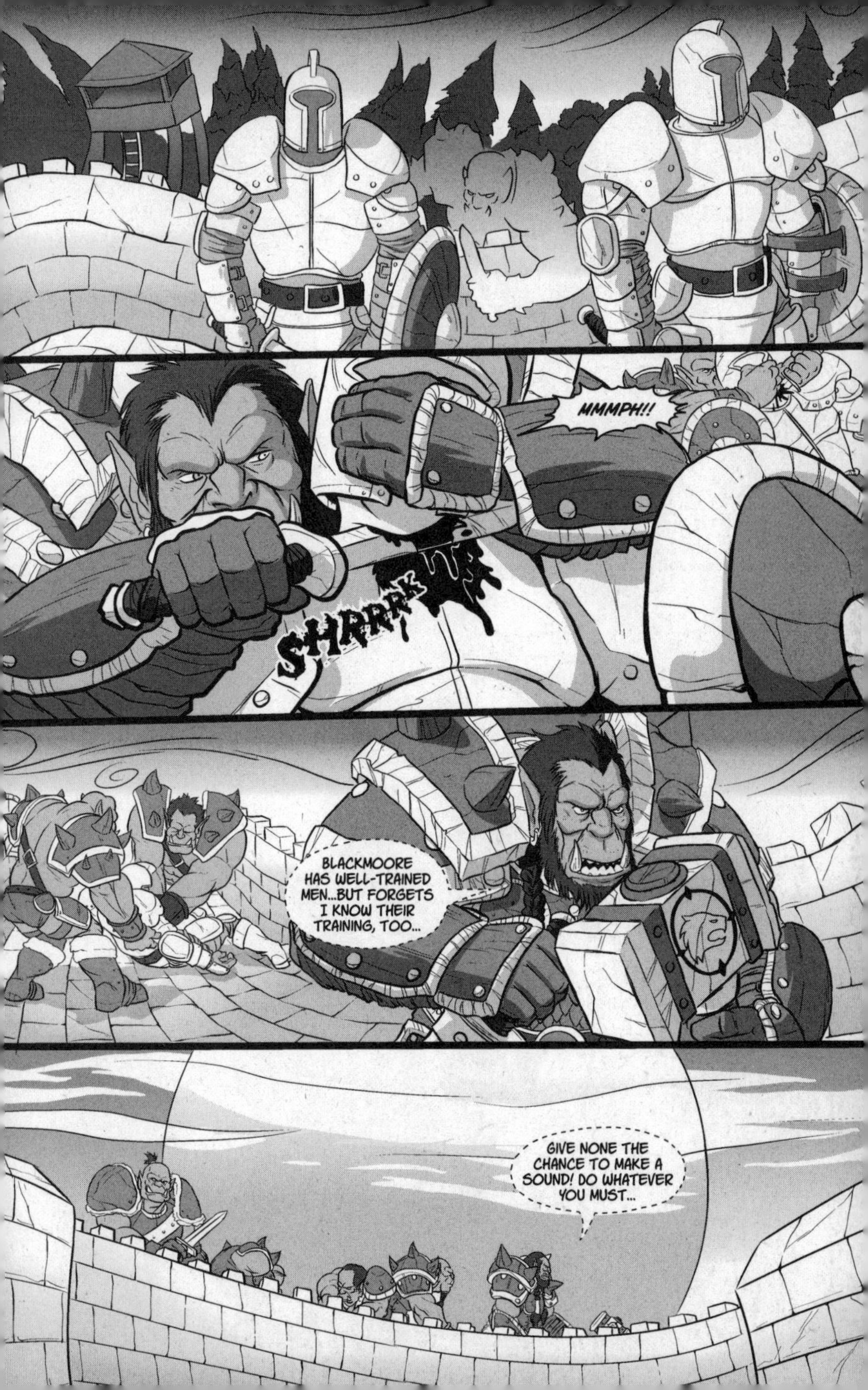
MMMPH!!
SHRRRK
BLACKMOORE HAS WELL-TRAINED MEN...BUT FORGETS I KNOW THEIR TRAINING, TOO...
GIVE NONE THE CHANCE TO MAKE A SOUND! DO WHATEVER YOU MUST...

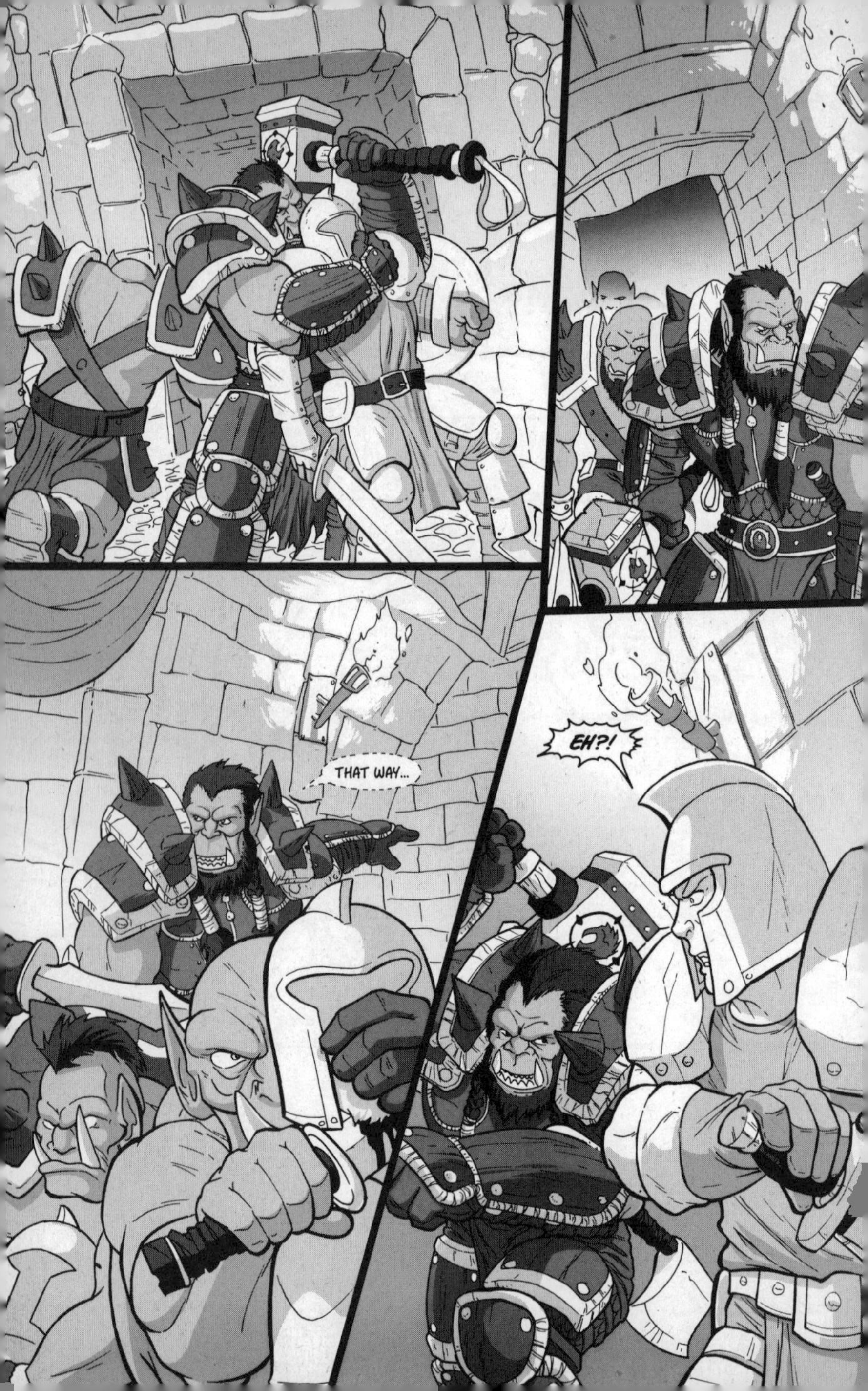
THAT WAY...
EH?!

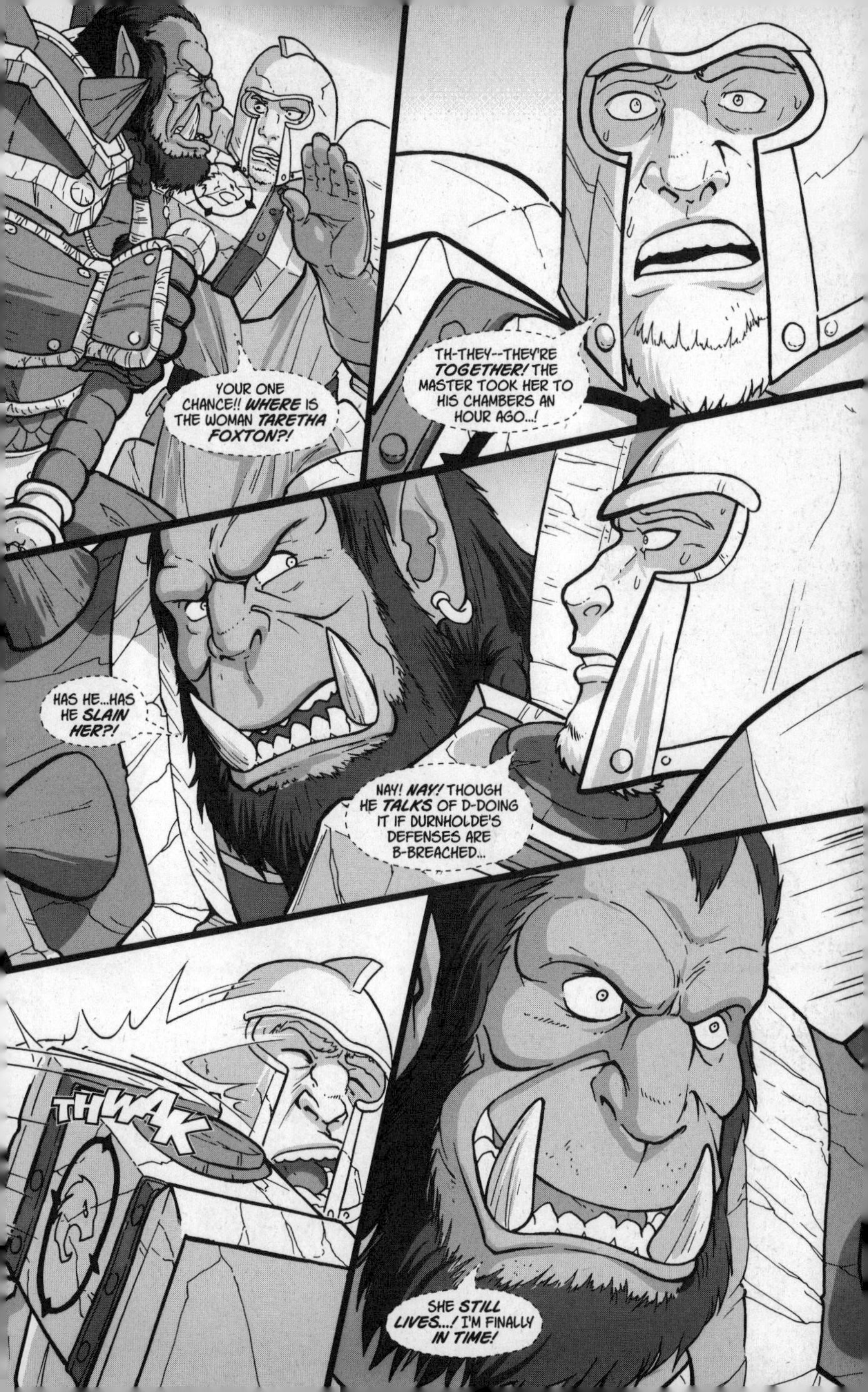
YOUR ONE CHANCE!! WHERE IS THE WOMAN TARETHA FOXTON?!
TH-THEY--THEY'RE TOGETHER! THE MASTER TOOK HER TO HIS CHAMBERS AN HOUR AGO...!
HAS HE...HAS HE SLAIN HER?!
NAY! NAY! THOUGH HE TALKS OF D-DOING IT IF DURNHOLDE'S DEFENSES ARE B-BREACHED...
THWAK
SHE STILL LIVES...! I'M FINALLY IN TIME!

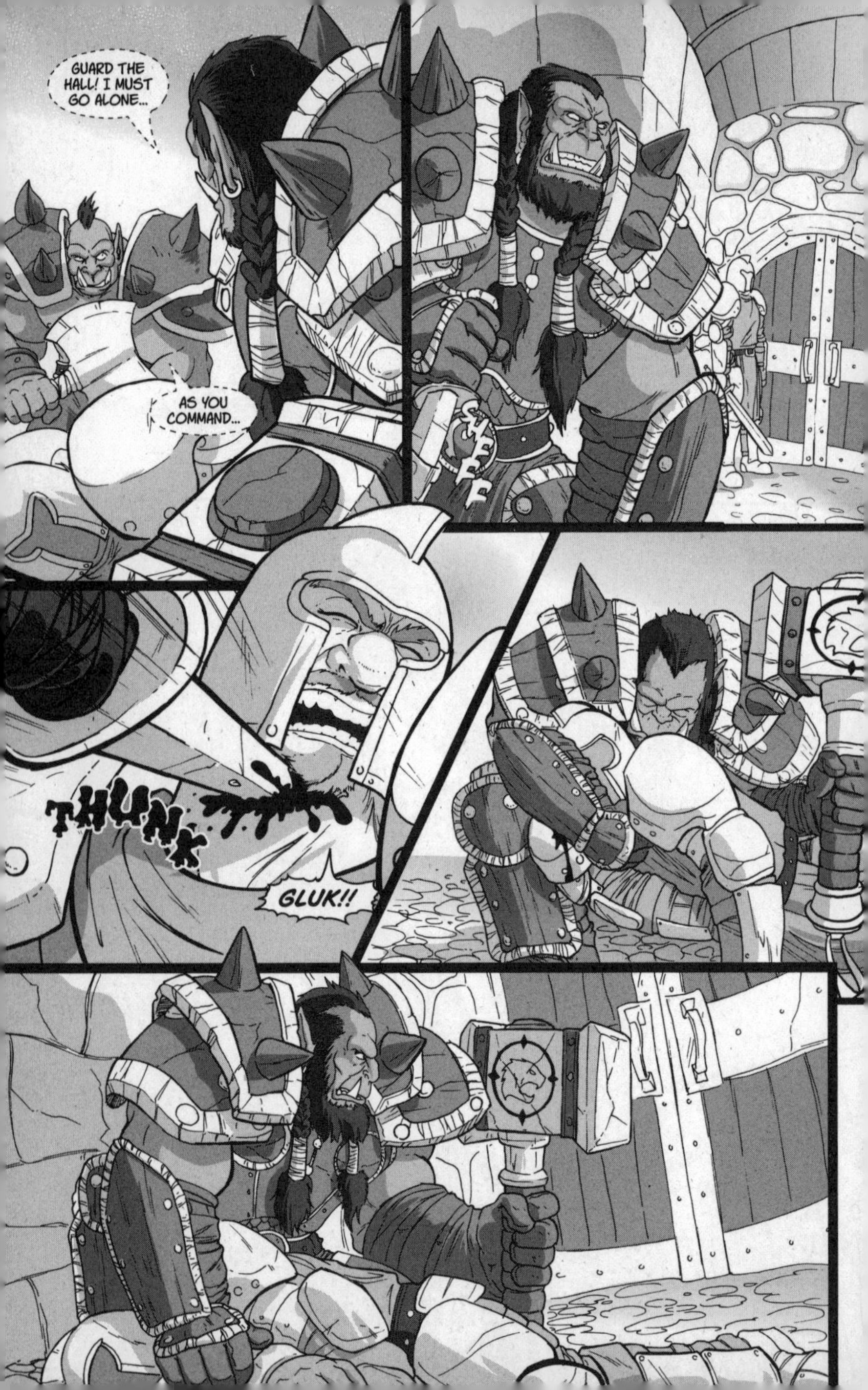
GUARD THE HALL! I MUST GO ALONE...
AS YOU COMMAND...
SHEFF
THUNK
GLUK!!

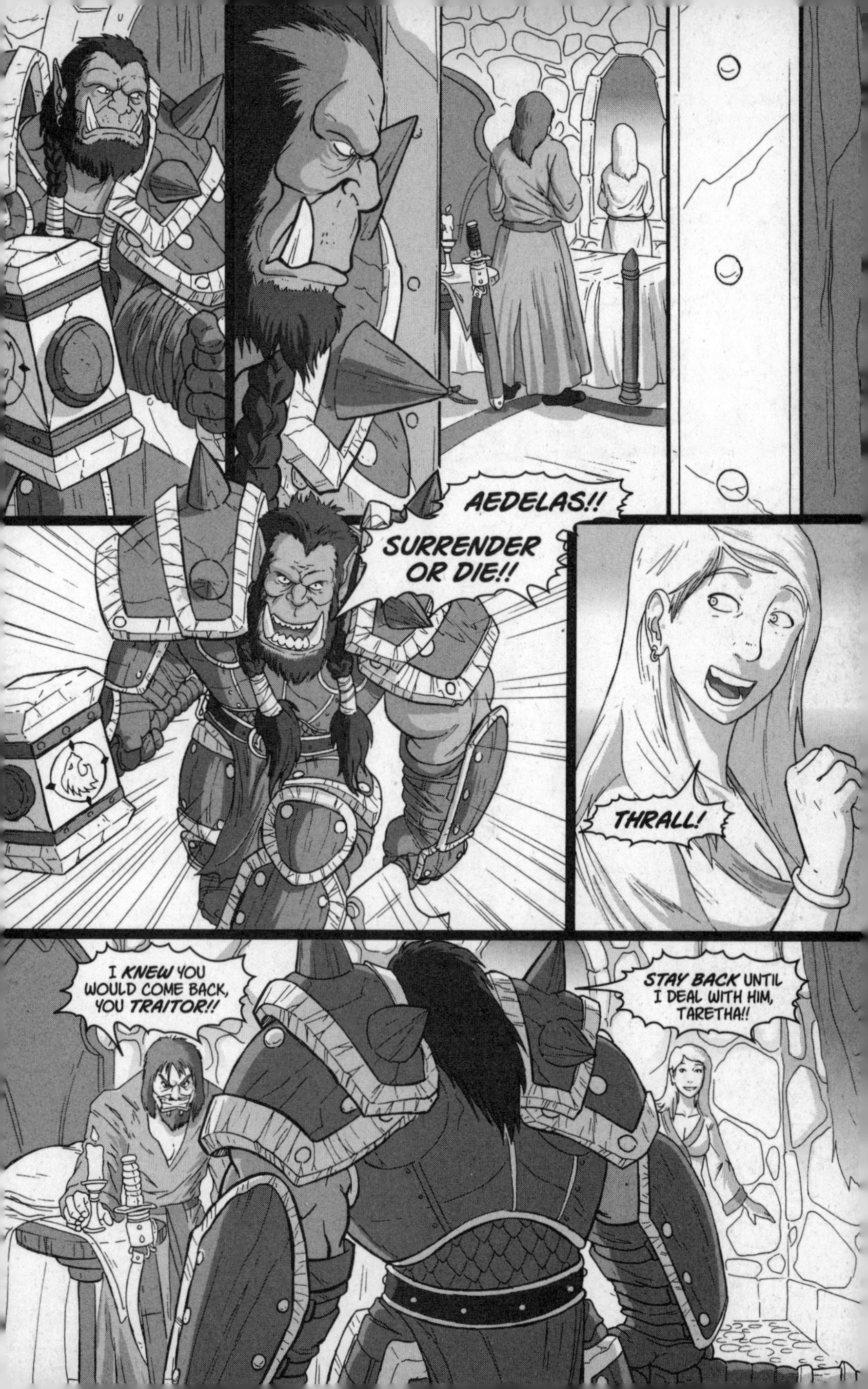
AEDELAS!!
SURRENDER OR DIE!!
THRALL!
I KNEW YOU WOULD COME BACK, YOU TRAITOR!!
STAY BACK UNTIL I DEAL WITH HIM, TARETHA!!

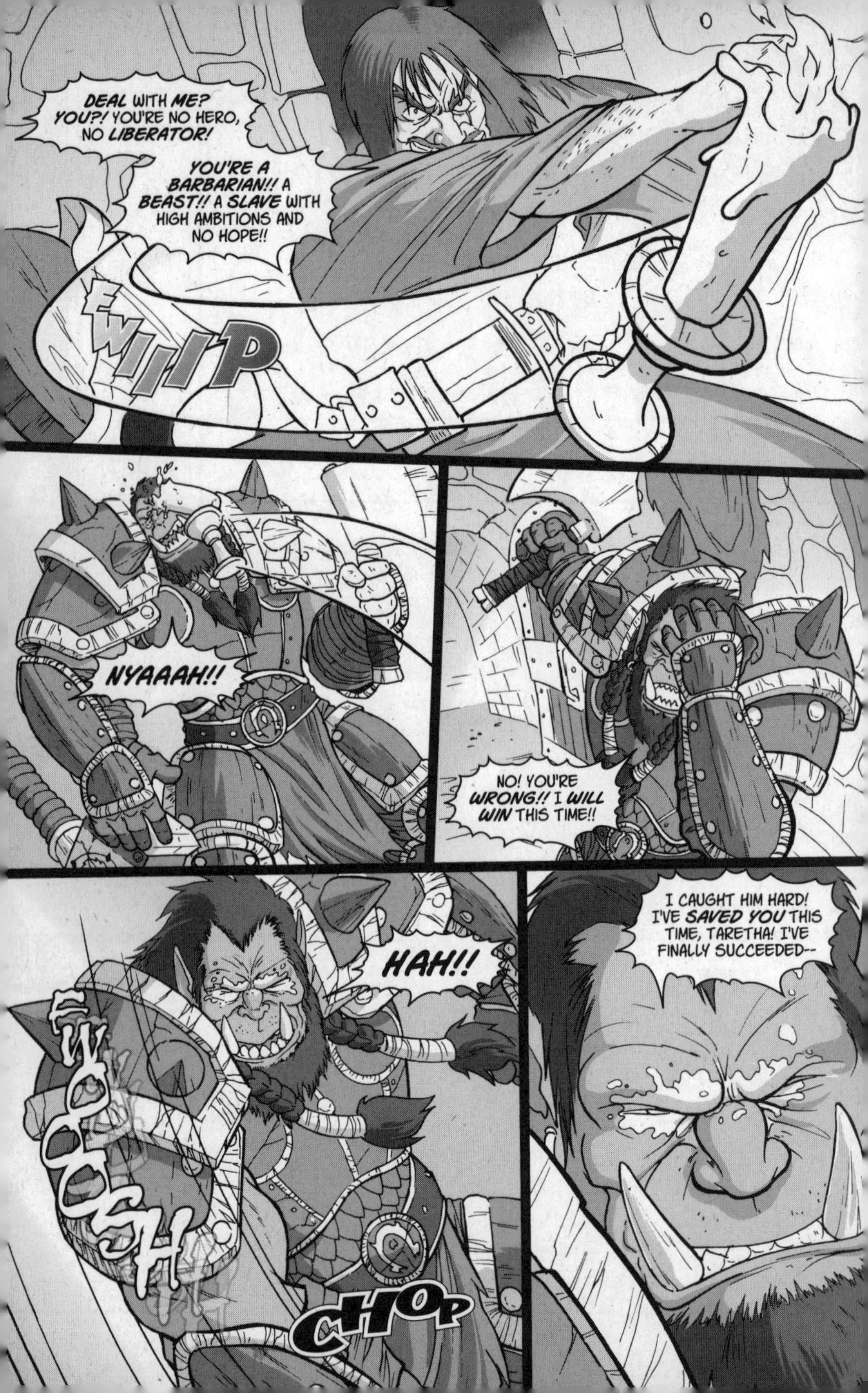
DEAL WITH ME? YOU?! YOU'RE NO HERO, NO LIBERATOR!
YOU'RE A BARBARIAN!! A BEAST!! A SLAVE WITH HIGH AMBITIONS AND NO HOPE!!
FWIIIP
NYAAAH!!
NO! YOU'RE WRONG!! I WILL WIN THIS TIME!!
HAH!!
FWOOSH!
CHOP
I CAUGHT HIM HARD! I'VE SAVED YOU THIS TIME, TARETHA! I'VE FINALLY SUCCEEDED--

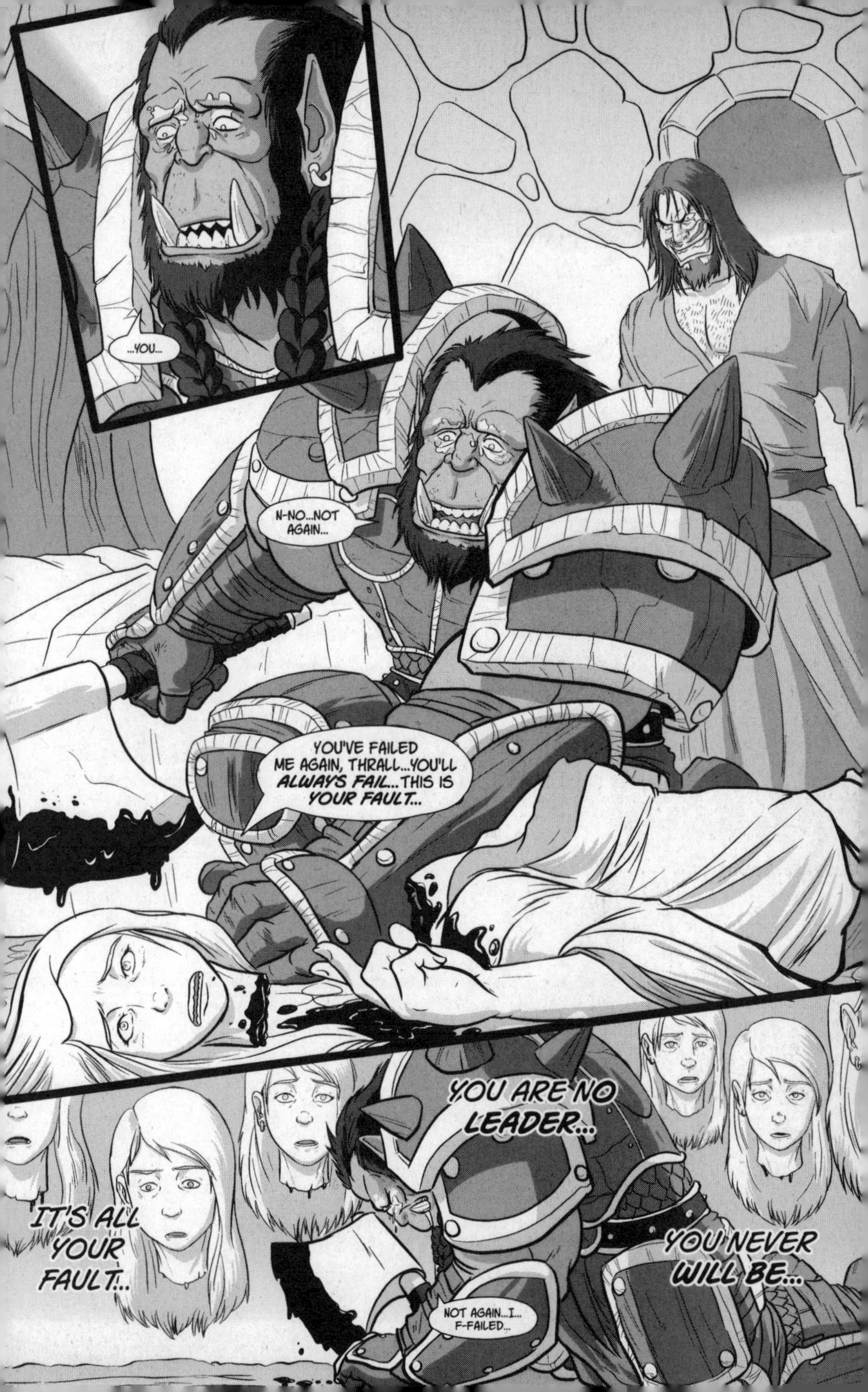
...YOU...
N-NO...NOT AGAIN...
YOU'VE FAILED ME AGAIN, THRALL...YOU'LL ALWAYS FAIL...THIS IS YOUR FAULT...
IT'S ALL YOUR FAULT...
YOU ARE NO LEADER...
YOU NEVER WILL BE...
NOT AGAIN...I... F-FAILED...

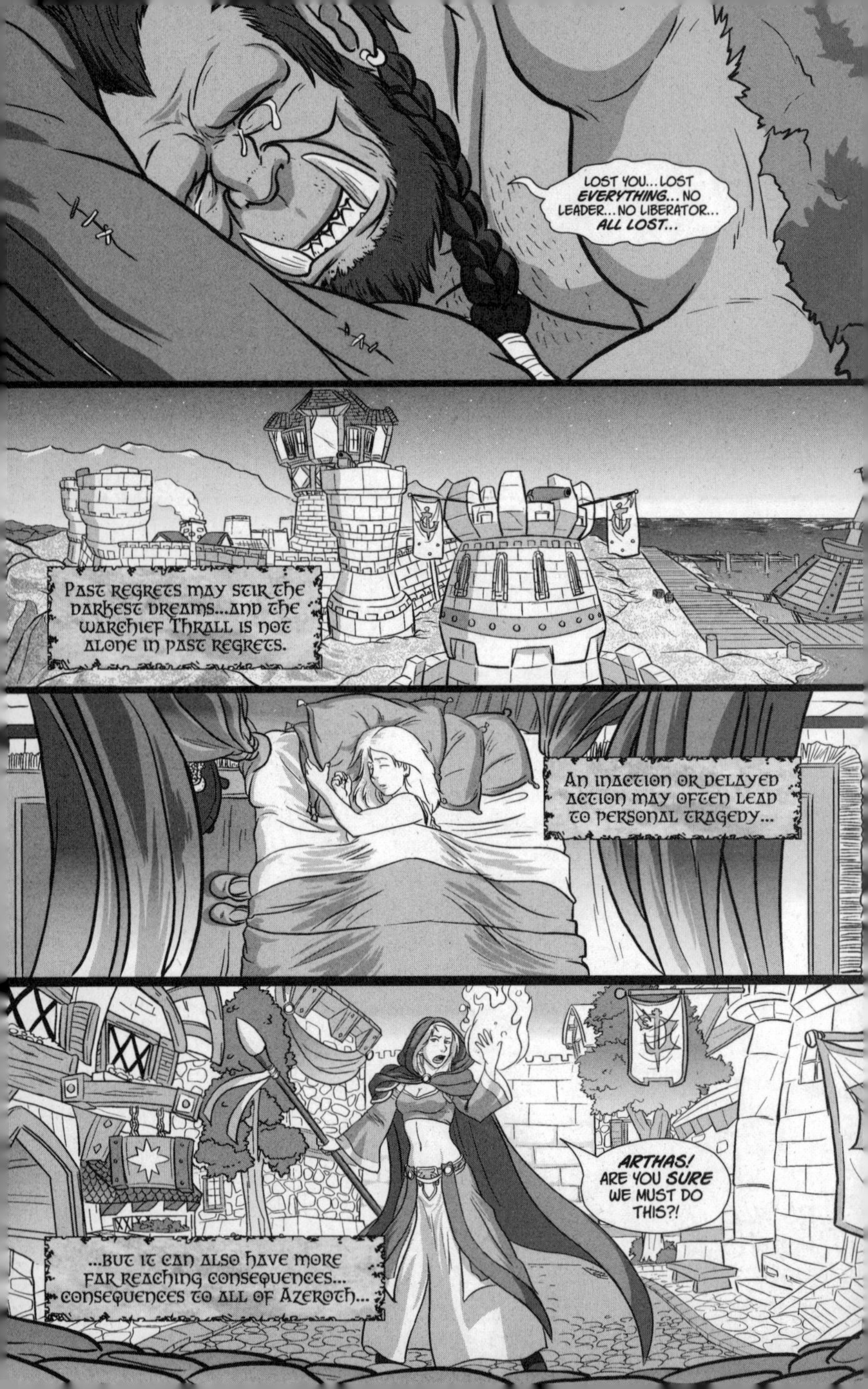
LOST YOU... LOST *EVERYTHING...* NO LEADER... NO LIBERATOR... *ALL LOST...*
PAST REGRETS MAY STIR THE DARKEST DREAMS...AND THE WARCHIEF THRALL IS NOT ALONE IN PAST REGRETS.
AN INACTION OR DELAYED ACTION MAY OFTEN LEAD TO PERSONAL TRAGEDY...
...BUT IT CAN ALSO HAVE MORE FAR REACHING CONSEQUENCES... CONSEQUENCES TO ALL OF AZEROTH...
ARTHAS! ARE YOU *SURE* WE MUST DO THIS?!

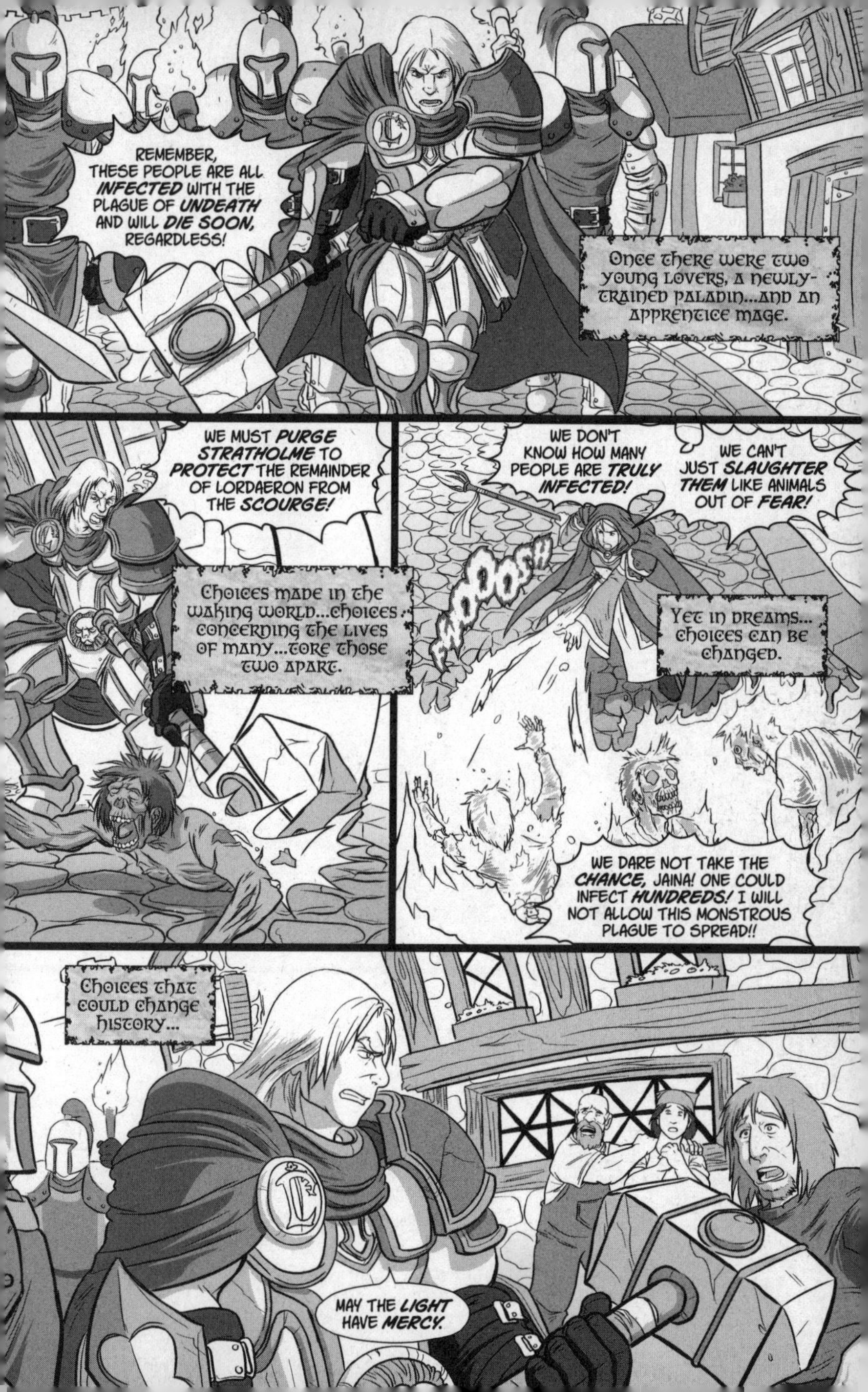
REMEMBER, THESE PEOPLE ARE ALL *INFECTED* WITH THE PLAGUE OF *UNDEATH* AND WILL *DIE SOON,* REGARDLESS!
Once there were two young lovers, a newly-trained paladin...and an apprentice mage.
WE MUST *PURGE STRATHOLME* TO *PROTECT* THE REMAINDER OF LORDAERON FROM THE *SCOURGE!*
Choices made in the waking world...choices concerning the lives of many...tore those two apart.
WE DON'T KNOW HOW MANY PEOPLE ARE *TRULY INFECTED!*
WE CAN'T JUST *SLAUGHTER THEM* LIKE ANIMALS OUT OF *FEAR!*
FWOOOSH!!
Yet in dreams... choices can be changed.
WE DARE NOT TAKE THE *CHANCE,* JAINA! ONE COULD INFECT *HUNDREDS!* I WILL NOT ALLOW THIS MONSTROUS PLAGUE TO SPREAD!!
Choices that could change history...
MAY THE *LIGHT* HAVE *MERCY.*

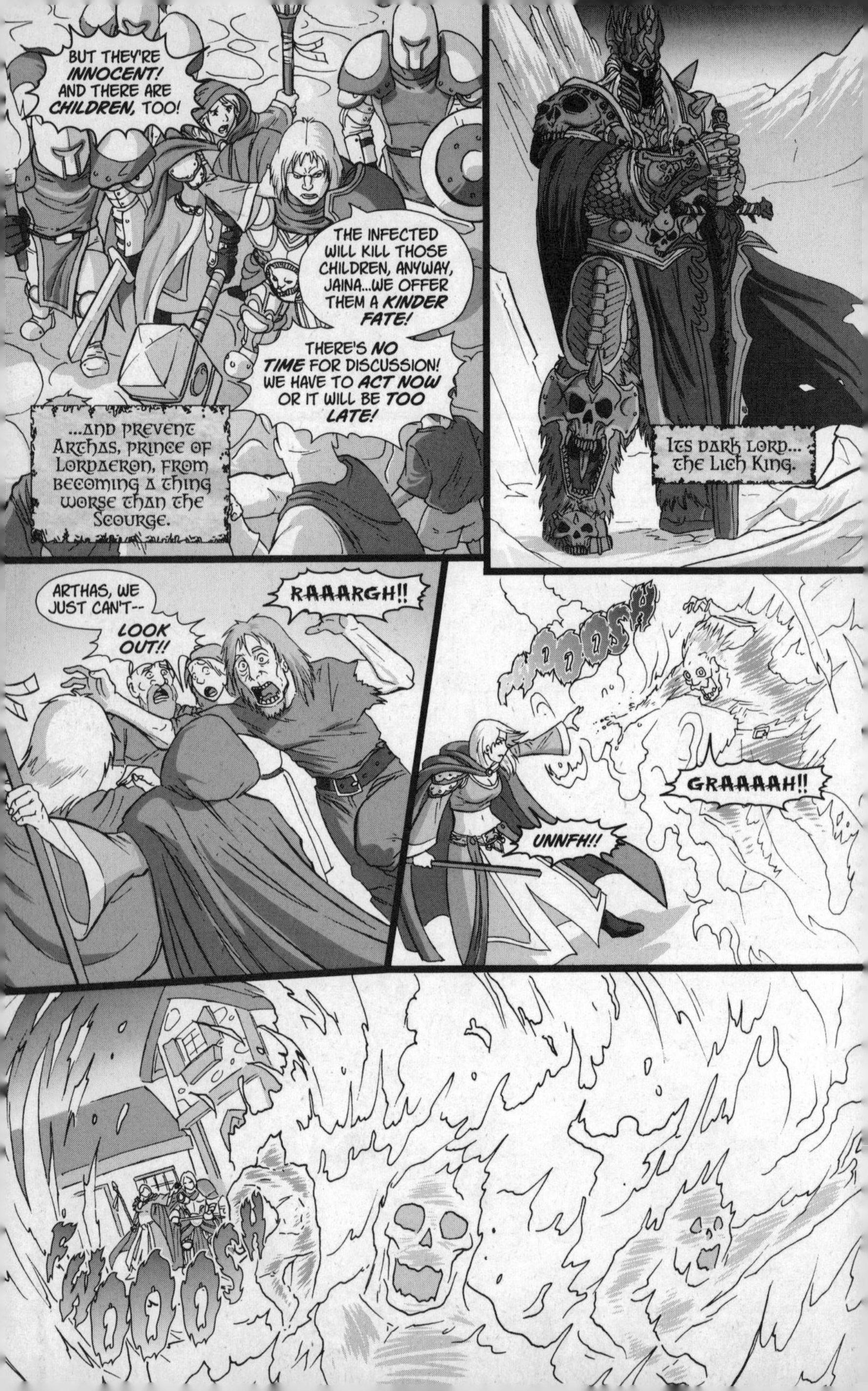
BUT THEY'RE *INNOCENT!* AND THERE ARE *CHILDREN,* TOO!
THE INFECTED WILL KILL THOSE CHILDREN, ANYWAY, JAINA...WE OFFER THEM A *KINDER FATE!*
THERE'S *NO TIME* FOR DISCUSSION! WE HAVE TO *ACT NOW* OR IT WILL BE *TOO LATE!*
...AND PREVENT ARTHAS, PRINCE OF LORDAERON, FROM BECOMING A THING WORSE THAN THE SCOURGE.
ITS DARK LORD... THE LICH KING.
ARTHAS, WE JUST CAN'T--
RAAAARGH!!
LOOK OUT!!
WOOOSH
GRAAAAH!!
UNNFH!!
WOOOSH

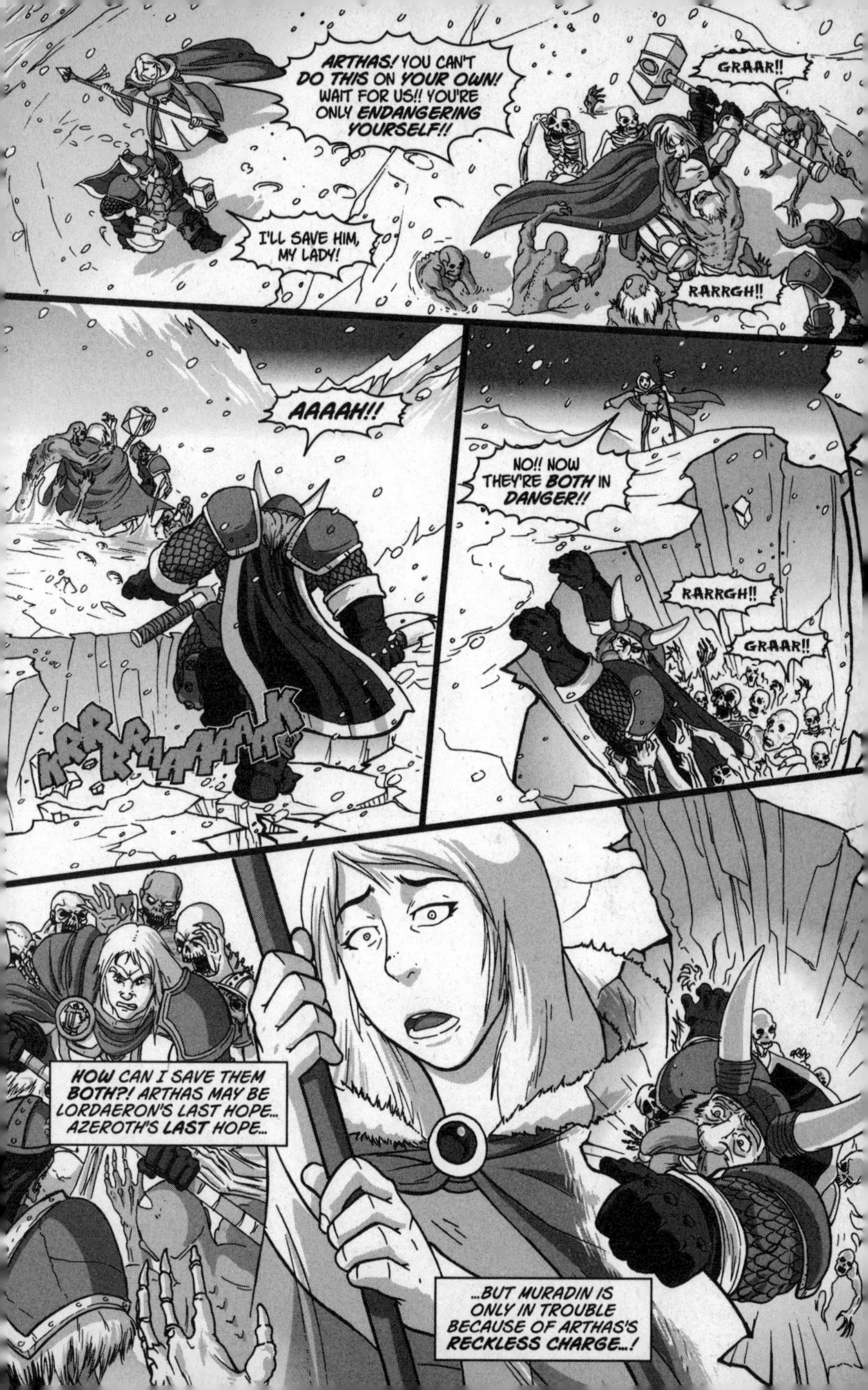
ARTHAS! YOU CAN'T DO THIS ON YOUR OWN! WAIT FOR US!! YOU'RE ONLY ENDANGERING YOURSELF!!
I'LL SAVE HIM, MY LADY!
GRAAR!!
RARRGH!!
AAAAH!!
KRRRRAAAAAK
NO!! NOW THEY'RE BOTH IN DANGER!!
RARRGH!!
GRAAR!!
HOW CAN I SAVE THEM BOTH?! ARTHAS MAY BE LORDAERON'S LAST HOPE... AZEROTH'S LAST HOPE...
...BUT MURADIN IS ONLY IN TROUBLE BECAUSE OF ARTHAS'S RECKLESS CHARGE...!

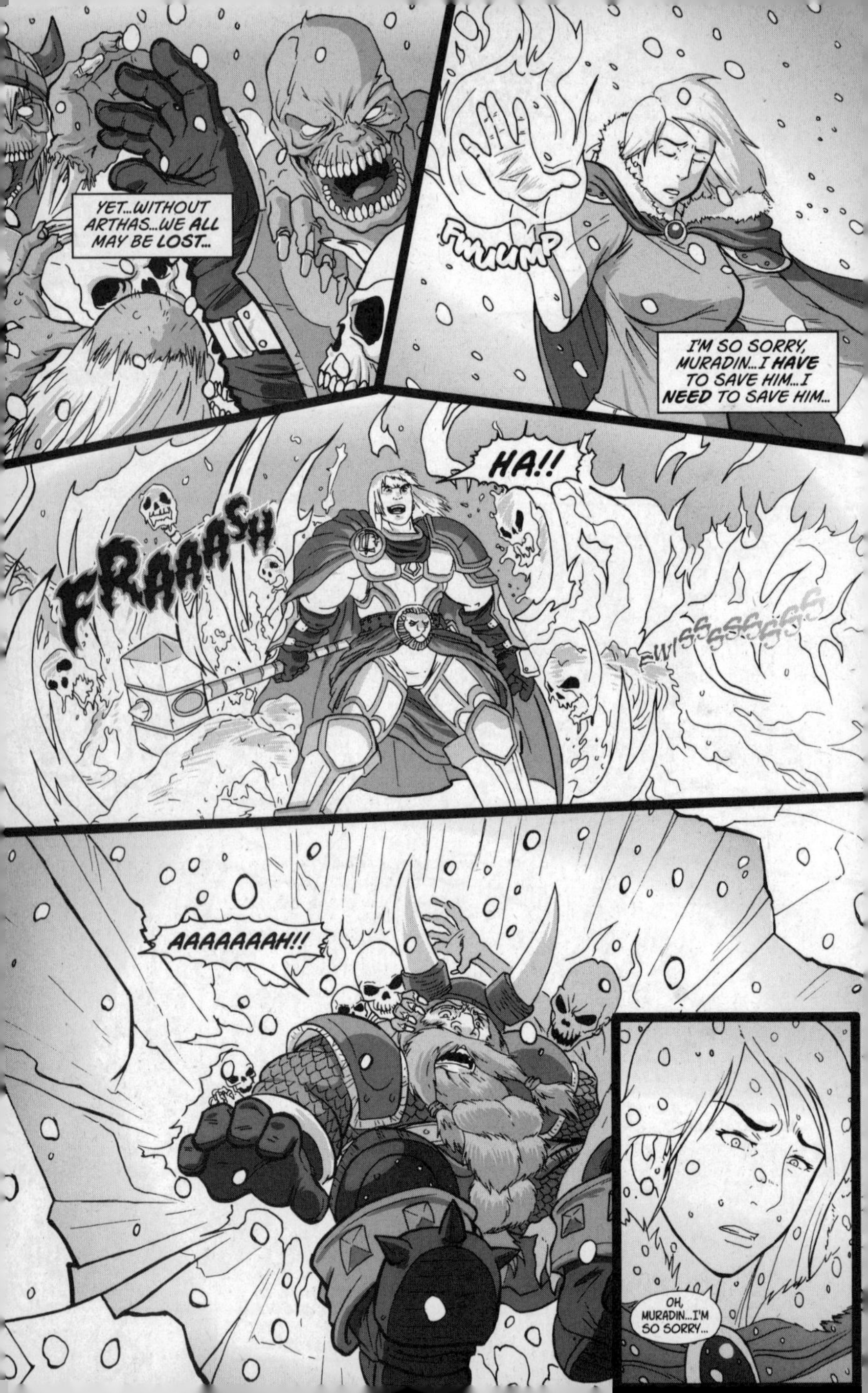
YET...WITHOUT ARTHAS...WE ALL MAY BE LOST...
FMUUMP
I'M SO SORRY, MURADIN...I HAVE TO SAVE HIM...I NEED TO SAVE HIM...
FRAASH
HA!!
FWISSSSSSSS
AAAAAAAH!!
OH, MURADIN...I'M SO SORRY...

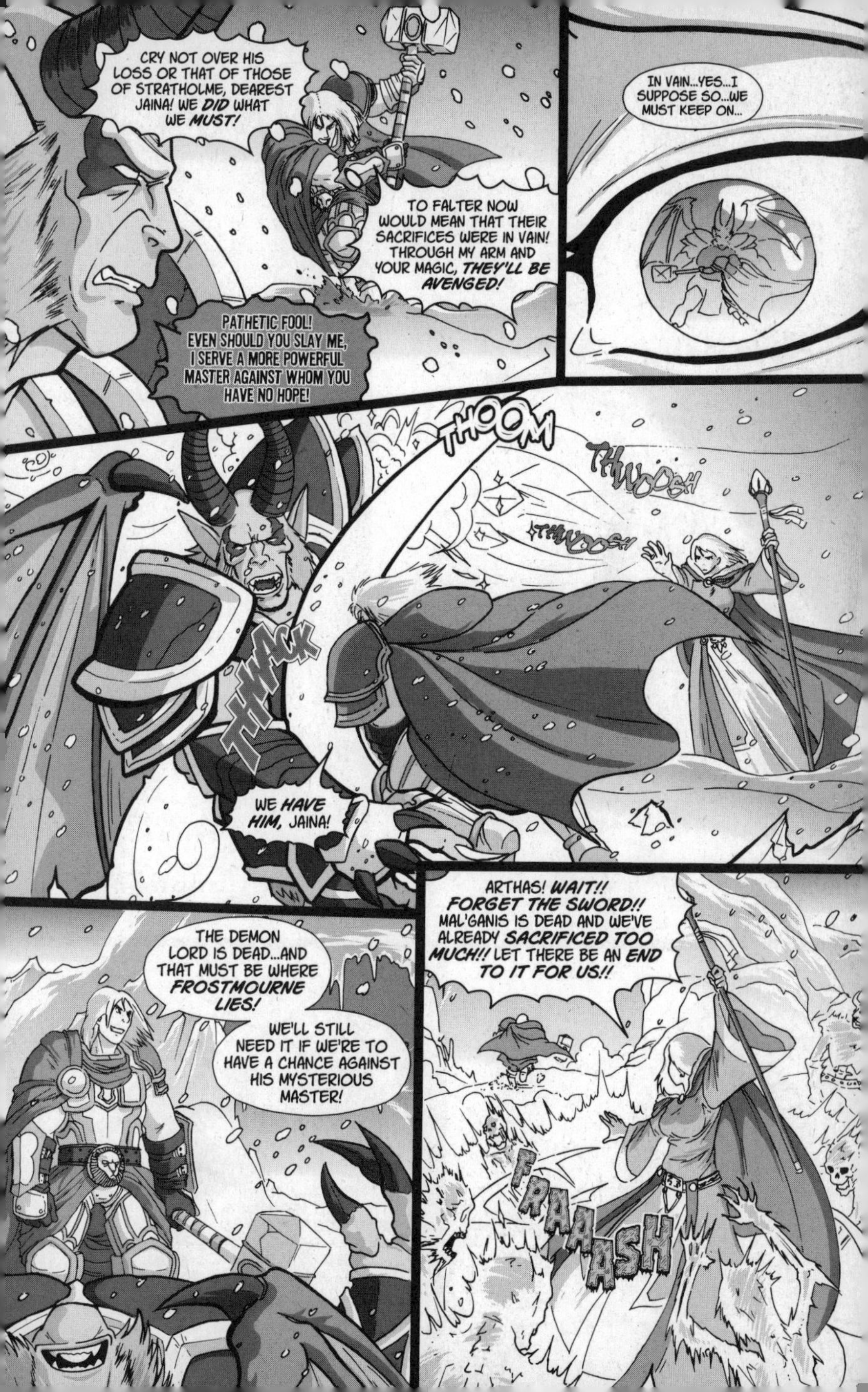
CRY NOT OVER HIS LOSS OR THAT OF THOSE OF STRATHOLME, DEAREST JAINA! WE *DID* WHAT WE *MUST!*
TO FALTER NOW WOULD MEAN THAT THEIR SACRIFICES WERE IN VAIN! THROUGH MY ARM AND YOUR MAGIC, *THEY'LL BE AVENGED!*
PATHETIC FOOL! EVEN SHOULD YOU SLAY ME, I SERVE A MORE POWERFUL MASTER AGAINST WHOM YOU HAVE NO HOPE!
IN VAIN...YES...I SUPPOSE SO...WE MUST KEEP ON...
THOOM
THWOOSH
THWOOSH
THWACK
WE *HAVE HIM,* JAINA!
THE DEMON LORD IS DEAD...AND THAT MUST BE WHERE *FROSTMOURNE LIES!*
WE'LL STILL NEED IT IF WE'RE TO HAVE A CHANCE AGAINST HIS MYSTERIOUS MASTER!
ARTHAS! *WAIT!! FORGET THE SWORD!!* MAL'GANIS IS DEAD AND WE'VE ALREADY *SACRIFICED TOO MUCH!!* LET THERE BE AN *END TO IT FOR US!!*
FRAAAASH

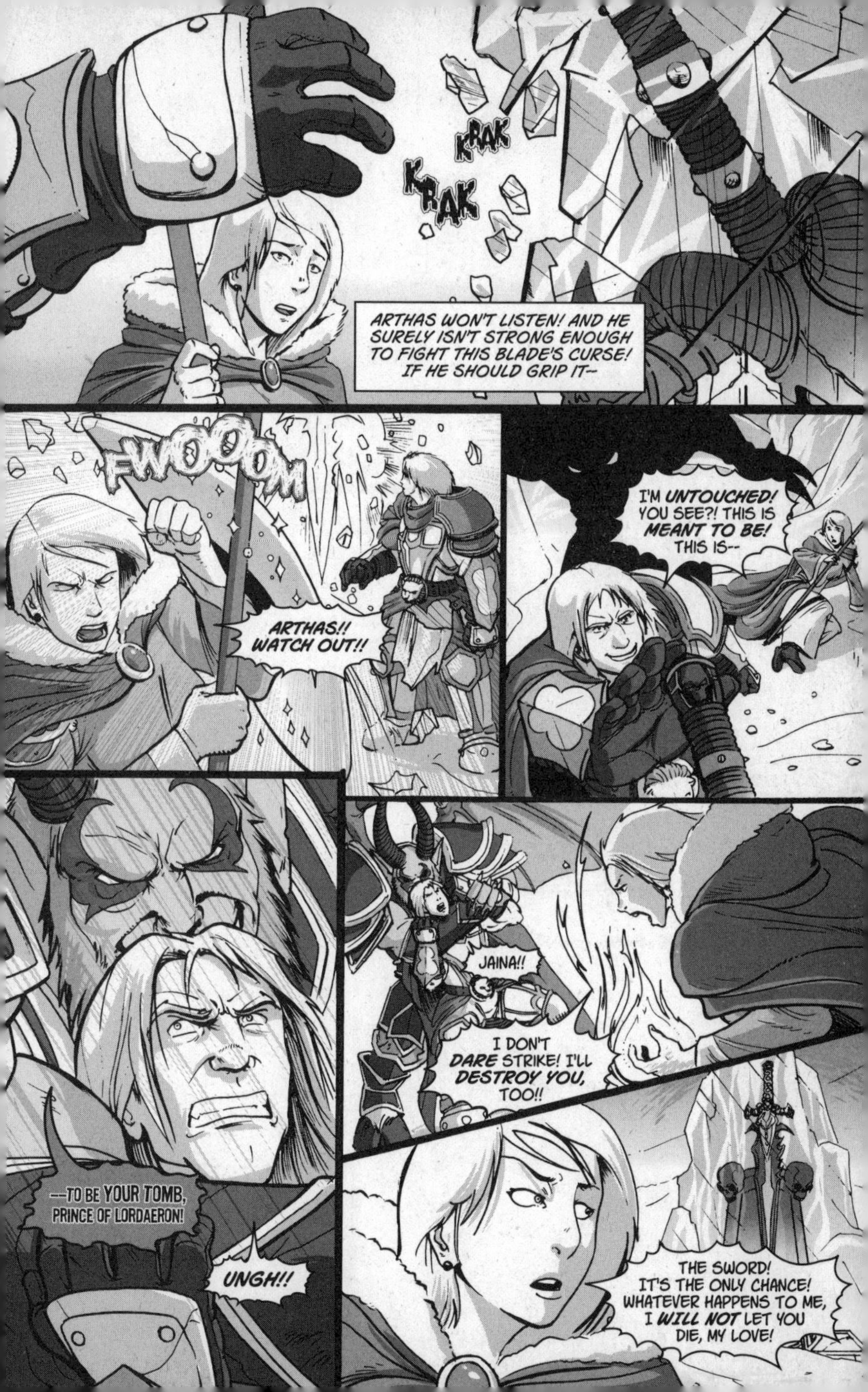
KRAK
KRAK
ARTHAS WON'T LISTEN! AND HE SURELY ISN'T STRONG ENOUGH TO FIGHT THIS BLADE'S CURSE! IF HE SHOULD GRIP IT--
FWOOOM
ARTHAS!! WATCH OUT!!
I'M UNTOUCHED! YOU SEE?! THIS IS MEANT TO BE! THIS IS--
--TO BE YOUR TOMB, PRINCE OF LORDAERON!
UNGH!!
JAINA!!
I DON'T DARE STRIKE! I'LL DESTROY YOU, TOO!!
THE SWORD! IT'S THE ONLY CHANCE! WHATEVER HAPPENS TO ME, I WILL NOT LET YOU DIE, MY LOVE!

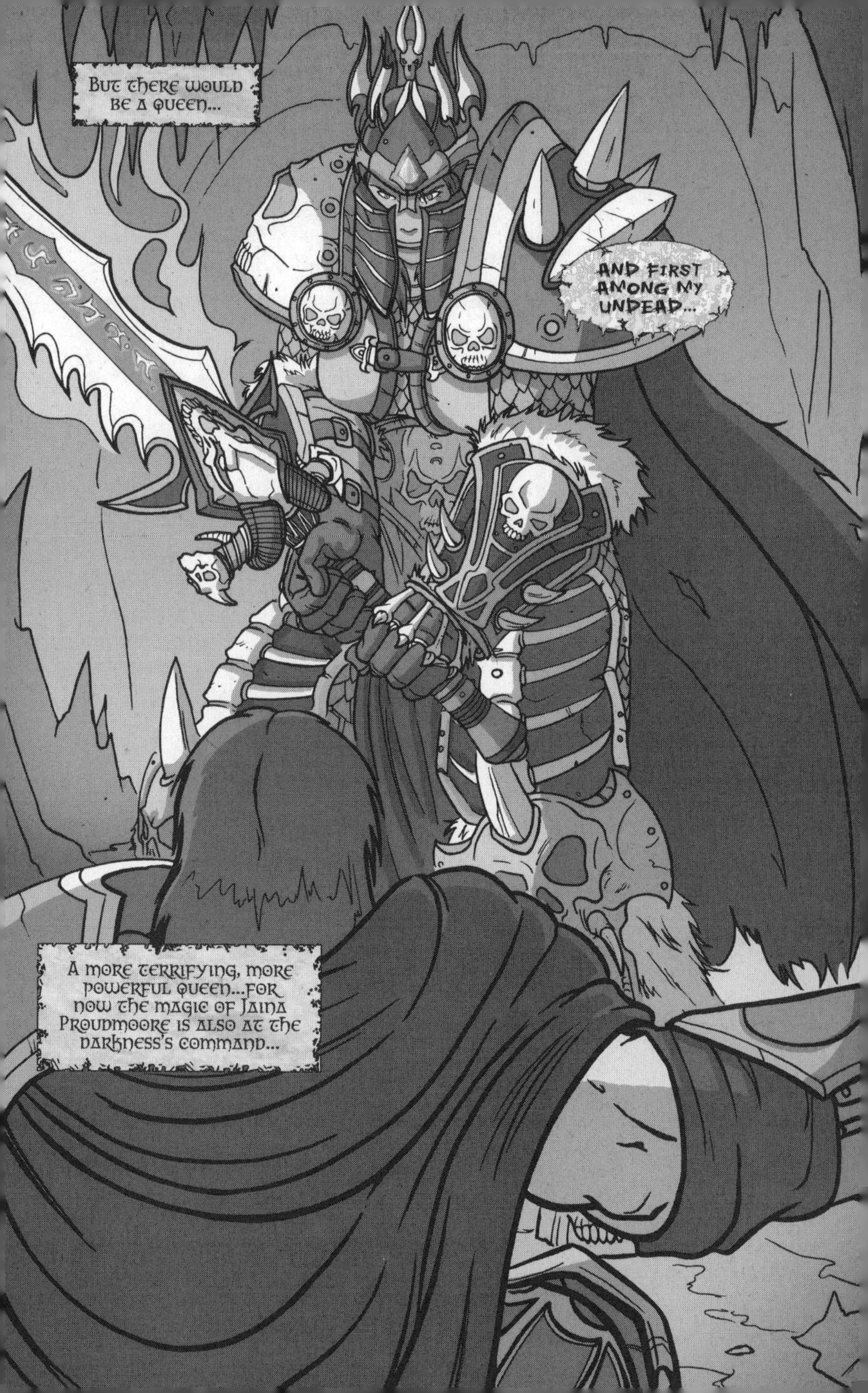
BUT THERE WOULD BE A QUEEN...
AND FIRST AMONG MY UNDEAD...
A MORE TERRIFYING, MORE POWERFUL QUEEN...FOR NOW THE MAGIC OF JAINA PROUDMOORE IS ALSO AT THE DARKNESS'S COMMAND...

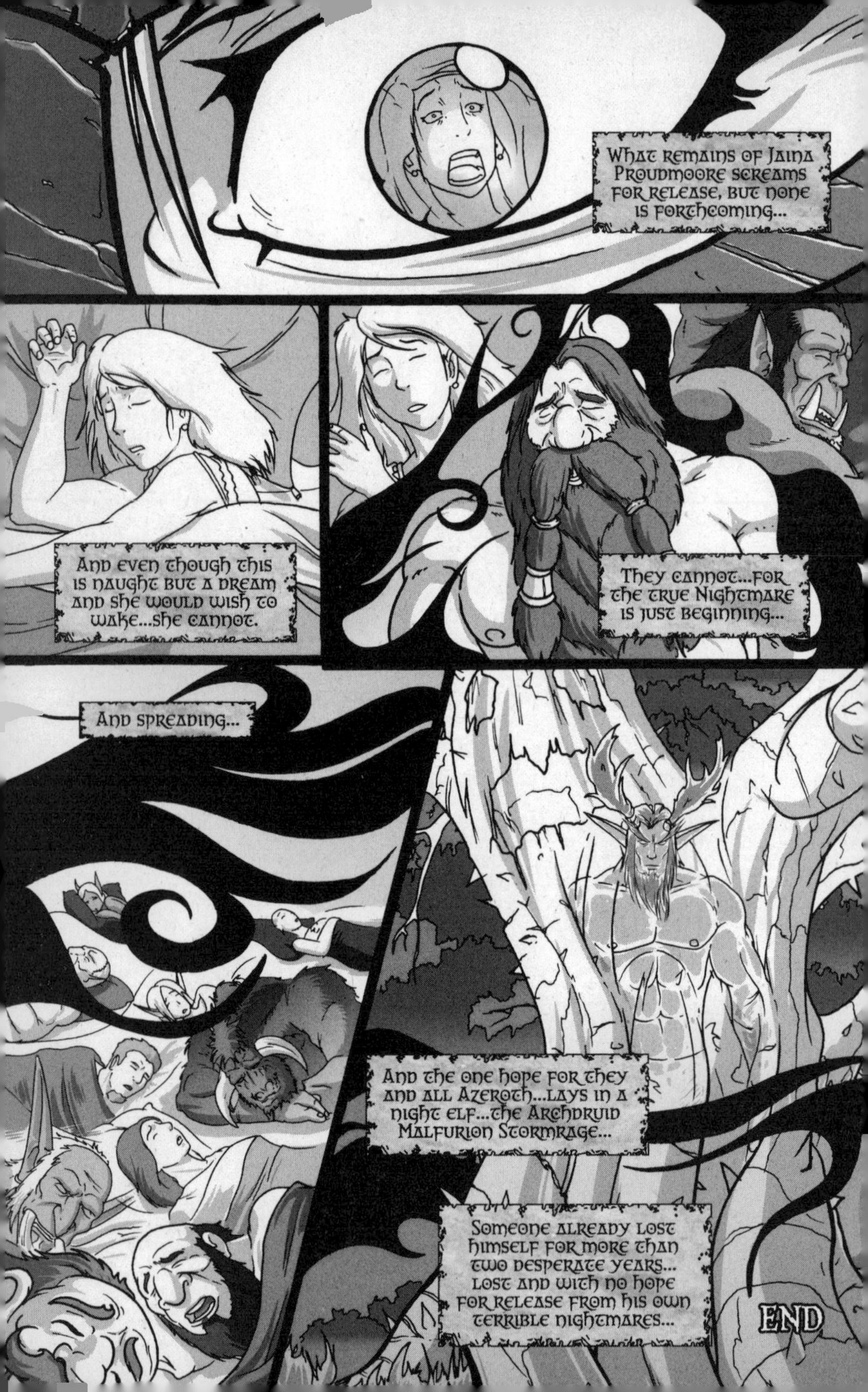
What remains of Jaina Proudmoore screams for release, but none is forthcoming...
And even though this is naught but a dream and she would wish to wake...she cannot.
They cannot...for the true Nightmare is just beginning...
And spreading...
And the one hope for they and all Azeroth...lays in a night elf...the Archdruid Malfurion Stormrage...
Someone already lost himself for more than two desperate years... lost and with no hope for release from his own terrible nightmares...
END

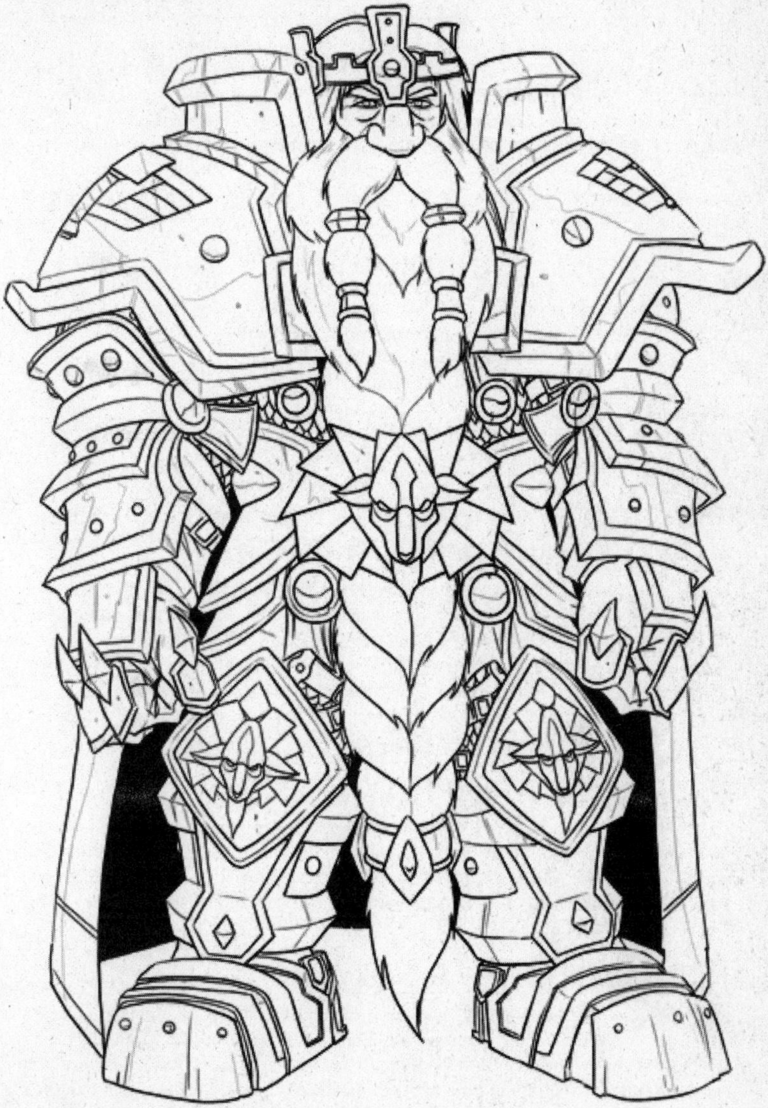

ABOUT THE WRITERS

CHRISTIE GOLDEN

New York Times bestselling author Christie Golden has written over thirty novels and several short stories in the fields of science fiction, fantasy and horror. She has written over a dozen *Star Trek* novels, several original novels, the *StarCraft: Dark Templar* trilogy and three *Warcraft* novels, *Lord of the Clans, Rise of the Horde*, as well as the New York Times bestseller *Arthas: Rise of the Lich King*, which was released in April 2009. Christie is currently hard at work writing on a yet to be titled *Warcraft novel*, as well as three of the nine *Star Wars: Fate of the Jedi* books (in collaboration with Aaron Allston and Troy Denning). *Omen*, her first book in the series, was released in June 2009. Christie has also written two short manga stories, "I Got What Yule Need" and "A Warrior Made," for the TOKYOPOP manga *Warcraft: Legends* Volumes 3, 4 & 5.

GRACE RANDOLPH

Grace Randolph is a comedic actor and writer born and raised in New York City. Her previous writing credits include *Justice League Unlimited #41* for DC Comics and *Nemesis: Who Me?* for TOKYOPOP's Pilot Program. She also has an upcoming manga adaptation of Meg Cabot's *Jinx*, as well as "Newsworthy" and "Last Call," short stories in TOKYOPOP's *StarCraft: Frontline* Volumes 2 & 3. Outside of comics, Grace is the host/writer/producer of the webshow *RevYOU*, which can be seen on YouTube and NBC/Bravo's *Television Without Pity* website. Grace also studies at the Upright Citizens Brigade Theatre (UCB) where she has written, performed and produced the shows "Situation: Awkward" and "Igor On Strike." Visit her informative--and awesome!--website at www.gracerandolph.com.

LOUISE SIMONSON

Louise Simonson has written and edited comic books for many years, including those in the superhero, science fiction, horror and fantasy genres. She wrote the award-winning *Power Pack* series, best-selling *X-Men*-related titles, *Web of Spider-Man* for Marvel Comics and *Superman: Man of Steel* and *Steel* for DC Comics. She has also written twenty books for children and adults, many about comic book characters. She is currently co-writing the *World of Warcraft* comic series for Wildstorm with her husband, artist/writer Walter Simonson. "First Guardian" is her first manga story.

EVELYN FREDERICKSEN

Blizzard historian Evelyn Fredericksen spends her time writing and talking about the stories from *Diablo, StarCraft* and *Warcraft* games and publications. This is her third foray into Blizzard fiction. Her previous two were short stories also set in the *Warcraft* universe: "Road to Damnation," the story of Kel'Thuzad's journey to Northrend, and "Glory," a retelling of the events at the Wrath Gate.

RICHARD A. KNAAK

Richard A. Knaak is the New York Times bestselling fantasy author of 40 novels and over a dozen short stories, including *The Legend of Huma & The Minotaur Wars* for Dragonlance and the *War of the Ancients* trilogy for *Warcraft*. In addition to the TOKYOPOP series *Warcraft: The Sunwell Trilogy*, he is the author of its forthcoming sequel trilogy, *Warcraft: Dragons of Outland*, as well a four-part short story featured in *Warcraft: Legends* Volumes 1-4, as well as the short story entitled "Nightmares" featured in *Warcraft: Legends* Volume 5. His latest Warcraft novel, *Night of the Dragon*, is a sequel to the best-selling *Day of the Dragon*. He also recently released *The Fire Rose*, the second in his *Ogre Titans* saga for Dragonlance. To find out more about Richard's projects, visit his website at www.richardaknaak.com.

ABOUT THE ARTISTS

IN-BAE KIM

In-Bae made his Korean manga debut in 1998 with *Tong-hwa-joong* (On the Phone). He followed that with several webzine short manga including "Film Ggengin Nar" (The Day I Blacked Out Drinking) and "Call Me." His serialized manga, "Bbuggoogi" (Cuckoo Bird), has been featured in several newspapers. In-Bae was also the artist for the short manga stories "Family Values" and "A Warrior Made" featured in *Warcraft: Legends* Volumes 2, 4 and 5.

ERICA AWANO

Born in São Paulo, Brazil, Erica grew up reading manga due to her Japanese hertitage. She attended the University of São Paulo (USP), where she graduated with a degree in Language and Literature. Soon after she turned her focus on her passion for comics and in 2001 drew several prize-winning series. In 2007 she was one of the finalists for a MOFA, a prize awarded by the Ministry of External Relations of Japan for manga artists that are active outside Japan. *Warrior: United* is her debut as the main penciller on a foreign publication.

SEUNG-HUI KYE

After publishing thirteen manwha and illustrating two light novels in South Korea, Seung-hui made her Japanese manga debut in 2008 with the one-shot story "Kuroi Ude" in *MiChao!* magazine, published by Kodansha. She made her English-language debut with the short manga story "Last Call" in *StarCraft: Frontline* Volume 3, which led to her drawing the art for "First Guardian" in *Warcraft: Legends* Volume 5.

RYO KAWAKAMI

Born in Miyako Island, Japan, Ryo lived in Okinawa Island until 1990, after which he and his family moved to the United States. Ryo currently resides in Greenville, N.C., where he studied Fine Art for two years at Coastal Community College. Ryo was runner-up artist in TOKYOPOP's *Rising Stars of Manga* Volume 6 for the short story "Little Miss Witch Hater," and his first full full-volume manga work, *Orange Crows*, was also published by TOKYOPOP (available in stores now). Ryo was the artist for the short manga stories "Blood Runs Thicker" and "A Cleansing Fire," two short manga stories featured in *Warcraft: Legends* Volumes 4 and 5.

ROB TEN PAS

Born and raised in Wisconsin (where he currently resides), Rob studied art at the Minneapolis College of Art and Design. His previous works include the short story "Bomango" in TOKYOPOP's *Rising Stars of Manga 6,* as well as the business manga *The Adventures of Johnny Bunko: The Last Career Guide You'll Ever Need* by author Daniel H. Pink. When not indulging in sketching and recreational comics, he works as a sign crafter and painter. Oh, and he's also an undercover narcotics agent, but that's a story for another bio...

SPECIAL THANKS

On behalf of TOKYOPOP and Blizzard, we really hope you enjoyed Volume 5 of *Warcraft: Legends,* as much as we enjoyed creating it! This of course includes the talented writers and artists, as well as the hardworking development teams at TOKYOPOP and Blizzard.

Without the assistance and guidance of Blizzard team members Jason Bischoff, Micky Neilson, Rob Tokar, James Waugh, Evelyn Fredericksen, Samwise Didier, Tommy Newcomer and Chris Metzen, none of these fantastic manga would have been possible.

On the TOKOYPOP side, there have been many people that played a pivotal role in the early stages of *Warcraft: Legends,* so I'd like to take this opportunity to thank Tim Beedle, Hyun Joo Kim, Shannon Waters, Louis Reyes and Rob Tokar. They are all former TOKYOPOP editors and good friends that started this long journey with me, but alas, fate placed them on different paths. And though some of you weren't here at the finish, you're definitely present in spirit! In fact, I still hear Rob's voice in my ear from time to time... mainly because he works at Blizzard now. Pow! Zing! Rimshot!

Big, BIG props go to Michael Paolilli for going above and beyond in ensuring I had the right reference shots for artists, for lettering the books, for retouching art, for being an invaluable consultant for all things *Warcraft* and *Star-Craft*...and most of all, for being a positive spirit throughout the chaos. You da cat's pajamas, my friend.

Thanks as well to James Lee for his wonderful interior page design and Louis Csontos for making these covers look so great. Special thanks goes to Hope Donovan, the *StarCraft: Frontline* editor. Hope took the full burden of *Frontline* upon her mighty shoulders, and I can say without any doubt I never could have pulled off *Legends* without her lightening the load for me by taking on those books. Hope was the editor for TOKYOPOP's *Rising Stars of Manga,* but I can't think of a star that has risen faster and blazed brighter than hers.

At this point I usually thank the writers and artists that poured tears and sweat (literally) into the volume you hold in your hands...but this time I'd like to thank not only them, but ALL the writers and artists that have contributed to all five volumes of *Warcraft: Legends* over the last 17 months (especially

Matias Timarchi and the entire *Altercomics* crew for bailing me out of tight spots time and time again). You guys are the real heroes for enduring *impossible* schedules to deliver fantastic stories to fans around the world. THANK YOU.

And while *Warcraft: Legends* may be over (for now, wink wink) there are still many more *Warcraft* manga to look forward to (including *Warcraft: Dragons of Outland,* the three volume sequel series to the critically acclaimed *Warcraft: The Sunwell Trilogy,* as well as *Warcraft: Death Knight*--pick up *Warcraft: Legends* 4 for an exclusive preview of that), so stay tuned for what TOKYOPOP and Blizzard has in store for the coming year. Also, don't forget to pick up Volumes 1, 2 and 3 of our other Blizzard anthology series, *StarCraft: Frontline,* all available in stores now!

Working on these anthologies has been not unlike stepping into the ring with a starving Mike Tyson (you're constantly on the move while checking your ears for bite marks). But just like going toe-to-toe with Iron Mike, *if* you can make it through in one piece...well, ladies and gents, you feel like you can take on anyone and anything. So as I oil up the ol' pythons and step through the ropes into the ring, I just have one question...

Who wants some of this?!

Troy Lewter
Editor

Level 80 Editors and Designers: Hope Donovan,
Michael Paolilli and Troy Lewter

A MESSAGE FROM RICHARD A. KNAAK, AUTHOR OF STORMRAGE

The nightmares of King Magni Bronzebeard, Warchief Thrall, and Lady Jaina Proudmoore have given some hint as to the dread dark now befalling Azeroth. The Alliance and the Horde are faced with an enemy that knows no boundaries. It invades where they are most defenseless: their very sleep.

From the Emerald Dream to the mortal plane, the Nightmare's touch is spreading. No one is immune, yet there is someone who may know not only the evil's secrets, but also how to defeat it. Unfortunately, that someone is the night elf Archdruid Malfurion Stormrage, who may have been the Nightmare's first victim.

But still there are those with hope, if only they can aid the great archdruid. Thus it is that two night elves -- Tyrande Whisperwind, high priestess of the moon goddess and the beloved of Malfurion, and Broll Bearmantle, druid and student of the legendary hero -- set out to discover the truth.

However, they are soon to discover that the Nightmare has many layers, many aspects... and they will need the aid of the extraordinary and the ordinary to survive long enough to rescue Malfurion.

The above is just a brief description of an exciting new tale I'm currently writing called *Stormrage*. I have penned many sagas for the *World of Warcraft*, but never one so unique, a story pitting the denizens of Azeroth against a foe whose weapons and strength are drawn from the defenders' very minds. It is my absolute pleasure to present a glimpse of the adventure to come when the novel hits shelves February 2010.

I hope that you will enjoy this first look at *Stormrage*...

Richard A. Knaak

COMING IN FEBRUARY 2010

WORLD OF WARCRAFT®

STORMRAGE

BY RICHARD A. KNAAK

The new novel from Pocket Books
Available wherever books are sold

Also available as an eBook
www.simonandschuster.com

TURN THE PAGE FOR A PREVIEW!

With her hippogryph, Jai, trailing her, Tyrande led Broll to the nearest of the dwellings. She then shocked the druid by entering the domicile without any hesitation, a sign that things were even worse than he had imagined. A sense of dread filled him over what they would find inside.

The interior had some of the trappings of a night elven home, but the plant life within looked sick, weak. The mist that covered Auberdine permeated even inside the dwelling, adding to the feeling of imminent disaster.

Jai, too large to fit through the entrance, peered uneasily inside. Broll watched as Tyrande glanced into the sleeping quarters. Withdrawing, she indicated that Broll should look as well.

With much wariness, the druid complied. His eyes widened at the scene within.

Two night elves—a male and a female—lay on woven mats.

The female's arm was draped over the male's chest. They were utterly motionless, which told Broll the worst.

"It is the same in the other places I have looked," his companion solemnly remarked.

The druid wanted to approach the pair, but held back out of respect. "Do you know how they perished?"

"They are not dead."

He looked back at her. When Tyrande added nothing more, the druid finally knelt by the two. His eyes widened.

Quiet but steady breathing escaped from both.

"They're . . . asleep?"

"Yes—and I could not awaken the ones I found earlier."

Despite what she said, Broll could not resist gently prodding the male's shoulder. When that failed to wake him, he did the same to the female. As a last attempt, Broll took hold of an arm from each and shook. Backing away, the druid growled, "We must find the source of the spell! There must be some warlock at work here!"

"It would take a powerful one indeed to do all this," said the high priestess. She indicated the door. "Come with me. I want to show you one more thing."

They left the home, and with Jai in tow, Tyrande led Broll over a bridge that connected to the more commercial areas of Auberdine. The mist kept many of the details of the village hidden, but Broll spotted a sign written in both Darnassian and Common that simply read TAVERN.

Broll knew that the tavern, of all places, should have been lit and alive. Along with the local inn, the tavern was one of the few public gathering places in the town.

Jai took up a position outside the entrance, the hippogryph peering into the mists in search of any potential foe. The high priestess strode inside without a word, her silence again warning Broll of what was to come.

The tavern was not like the home, which had been in order despite the bizarre scene inside. Chairs were scattered over the wooden floor, and some of the tables had been overturned. The bar at the end was stained not just from years of inebriated patrons but also from several smashed bottles and barrels.

And all over the tavern lay sprawled the bodies of night elves, a handful of gnomes and humans, and a single dwarf.

"I landed not far from this area and was disturbed when I saw no life or lights," the high priestess explained. "This was the most immediate public place, and so I entered."

"Are they also . . . asleep?"

Tyrande bent down by one human. He was slumped over a table and looked as if he had fallen there from sheer exhaustion. His hair and beard were disheveled, but his garments, despite some dust, were clearly of a person of some means. Next to him lay a night elf, a local. Although the night elf lay on his side on the floor, his hands were still stretched forth toward the human. Like the human, the night elf looked oddly unkempt. They were the worst in appearance, though all of the sleepers in the tavern looked as if they had been through some struggle.

"A fight broke out here," Broll decided.

Tyrande stood. "A very polite fight, if that was truly the case. The only bruises I found were caused by their falls. I think these two collapsed." She gestured at the dwarf and a few of the other patrons. "See how these others are positioned?"

After a moment's study, Broll scowled. "They look like they're taking a rest. All of them!"

"They are all asleep now, even this first desperate pair. Look around. The tavern looks as if it was set up for defense."

"I should've seen that myself." Indeed, the druid noted now that the tables and chairs created a wall of sorts that faced both the entrance and the windows. "But a defense from what?"

Tyrande had no answer for him.

Broll squinted. In fact, he had been compelled to squint more often for the past few minutes despite the fact that, with the sun down, his vision should have been sharper. "The mist is getting thicker . . . and darker."

Outside, Jai let out a low warning squawk.

Tyrande and Broll hurried to the entrance. Outside, the hippogryph anxiously moved about. However, there was no sign of anything in the vicinity, as more and more the deepening mist limited the distance that could be seen.

A moan came from inside, and Broll brushed past the high priestess to investigate its source among the slouched figures near the back end of the tavern. Then another moan arose from a different direction. Broll identified it as coming from the night elf near the human. He bent down next to the figure.

Tyrande joined him. "What is it? Is he awake?"

"No . . ." Broll turned the sleeper's head slightly. "I think he's dreaming. . . ."

A third moan joined the previous. Suddenly, all around them, the slumbering figures wailed. The hair on the back of Broll's neck stiffened as he detected the thing all the voices had in common: fear. "Not dreams," he corrected himself, rising and glancing back at the entrance. "They're having nightmares. All of them."

Jai again made a warning sound. Returning to the hippogryph, the pair saw nothing . . . but heard much.

There were moans arising from all over Auberdine.

"This is tied to Malfurion," Tyrande stated with utter confidence.

"But how?"

Jai stepped forward, the beast's head cocking to the side, listening.

A murky figure briefly passed into and out of sight. It was shorter than a night elf, more the height of a human. The hippogryph started after it, but Tyrande made a short sound that was clearly a command. The animal paused.

The high priestess took the lead again. Broll quickly moved to her side, ready to use his arts to aid her. Jai kept pace behind them.

"There!" she hissed, pointing to the left.

Broll scarcely had time to view the figure before it again vanished in the fog. "It looks as though it's stumbling. May be a survivor."

"The mist seems to thicken most around our quarry." Tyrande put her hands together. "Perhaps the Mother Moon can remedy that."

From the shrouded sky directly above the high priestess, a

silver glow descended in the direction of the mysterious figure. It burned through the fog, revealing everything in its path. Broll's brow rose as he watched the glow veer like a living thing stretching out to find the stranger.

And there he suddenly stood: a male human. His clothing bespoke of better times but he had clearly been put through a long decline of station. He stared back at them with eyes hollow from what seemed to be a lack of sleep. The human was more haggard looking than any of the group they had found in the tavern. Somehow, though, he kept moving.

"By Nordrassil!" blurted Broll.

The human had not only kept moving, but before the eyes of both night elves, he had also just *vanished*.

"A mage," Tyrande snarled. "He is the cause, then, not a victim. . . ."

"I don't know, my lady." Broll could explain no further, but there had been something in the manner of the man's disappearance that had felt . . . familiar.

The druid focused on what he had seen. The human had looked at them, then he had started to take a step. . . .

"He walked *through* something . . . walked *into* something," Broll muttered to himself. And when it had happened, the druid had sensed . . . what?

"Vanished, walked into or through some portal—what does it matter?" argued Tyrande, her aspect even grimmer. She quickly stepped back to the hippogryph and seized from the saddle something Broll had not paid attention to previously. Buckling the sheath around her waist, Tyrande drew her glaive. "He may be the key to Malfurion. . . ."

Before Broll could stop her, the high priestess darted toward the spot where the human had stood. Broll could not deny that perhaps the stranger was the culprit, as Tyrande had said, but even he knew that more caution was needed, especially if their quarry was indeed a spellcaster.

Arriving at the human's last location, Tyrande held the glaive ready while murmuring a prayer. The light of Elune surrounded her, then spread for several yards in every direction.

But of the human, there was no sign.

Broll joined her. "Great lady, I—"

She whirled on him. "Never call me that—it sounds too much like a title of nobility. You know that I want no reminders of Azshara's cruel past—" No sooner had she begun reprimanding him than Tyrande looked aghast at herself. She shook her head in apology and opened her mouth to speak.

But just then, more moans—the fright in them so very distinct—pierced the thick mist as sharply as the light of Elune had.

"We must wake them somehow!" Broll growled. "There must be some way . . ."

Jai let out a warning. Suspecting that the human had reappeared, both night elves turned at the sound—

And there, obscured by the mysterious fog, several figures lurched toward them as the mist carried forth a haunting, collective moan.

Broll experienced a rising anxiety. He suddenly felt the need to run or cower. He wanted to roll into a ball and pray that the shadowy figures would not hurt him. A nervous sweat covered the druid.

What's happening to me? he managed to ask himself. Broll was not prone to fear, but the urge to surrender was powerful. He looked to Tyrande and saw that the hand in which she held the glaive was shaking, and not due to the weapon's great weight. The high priestess's mouth was set tight. Even Jai revealed hints of stress, the powerful hippogryph's breathing growing more and more rapid.

Tyrande looked to the left. "They are over there too!"

"And to our right," Broll added. "If we look behind us, I'll wager they'll be there as well."

"I will not be sent to my knees crying like some frightened child!" Tyrande abruptly declared to the half-seen shapes. Her hands shook harder despite her words and served to fuel Broll's own swelling anxiety.

From above the high priestess emanated a silver light that wrapped over both night elves and the hippogryph. It spread toward the shadows, illuminating the first staggering shape.

And in the moonlit glow, they beheld a thing that was rotted and decayed. It stared with blank, unseeing eyes and a face twisted in pain even in undeath—a face that Broll suddenly registered as identical to the night elf lying on the tavern floor.

But if the face was that of the sleeper, the form was not. Rather, it was the shadowy outline of a thing Broll hoped never to see again. The night elf wore in body the semblance of a demon of the Burning Legion.

As the mob closed in, a second being was revealed, bearing the half-skeletal face of the human, but the guise of a ruined demon.

"They've—" Broll muttered. "They've returned. . . ."

"No . . . it cannot be them!" Tyrande murmured to the druid. "No satyrs . . . please . . . no satyrs. . . ."

The two night elves remained frozen. They wanted to defend themselves, but the monstrous figures converging on them had left the pair with minds in such turmoil that their bodies were paralyzed.

At that moment, a new figure stepped out right in front of the druid and his companions—the ragged human they had been chasing. He stumbled toward them, his eyes looking past.

Broll blinked his eyes, trying to adjust them, but it seemed the mist had thickened—or had his eyes gone out of focus? The fiendish forms with the faces of Auberdine's unfortunate inhabitants were once again murky shapes. Suddenly, the druid had the sensation of being near to the ground . . . and, feeling around with his hands, discovered he was on his knees.

"By the Mother Moon!" he heard Tyrande growl, but only as a faint echo. "What—?"

The hollow-eyed human who had stepped out of nothing finally spoke through the unnatural darkness. "Don't sleep. . . . Don't sleep. . . ." he whispered. Broll felt an arm drape over his shoulder and then he and Tyrande, kneeling alongside one another, were held together weakly by the haggard human who crouched behind them.

The world faded. It did not vanish. It *faded*, as if it were more memory than substance.

And in addition, it took on a deep green hue.

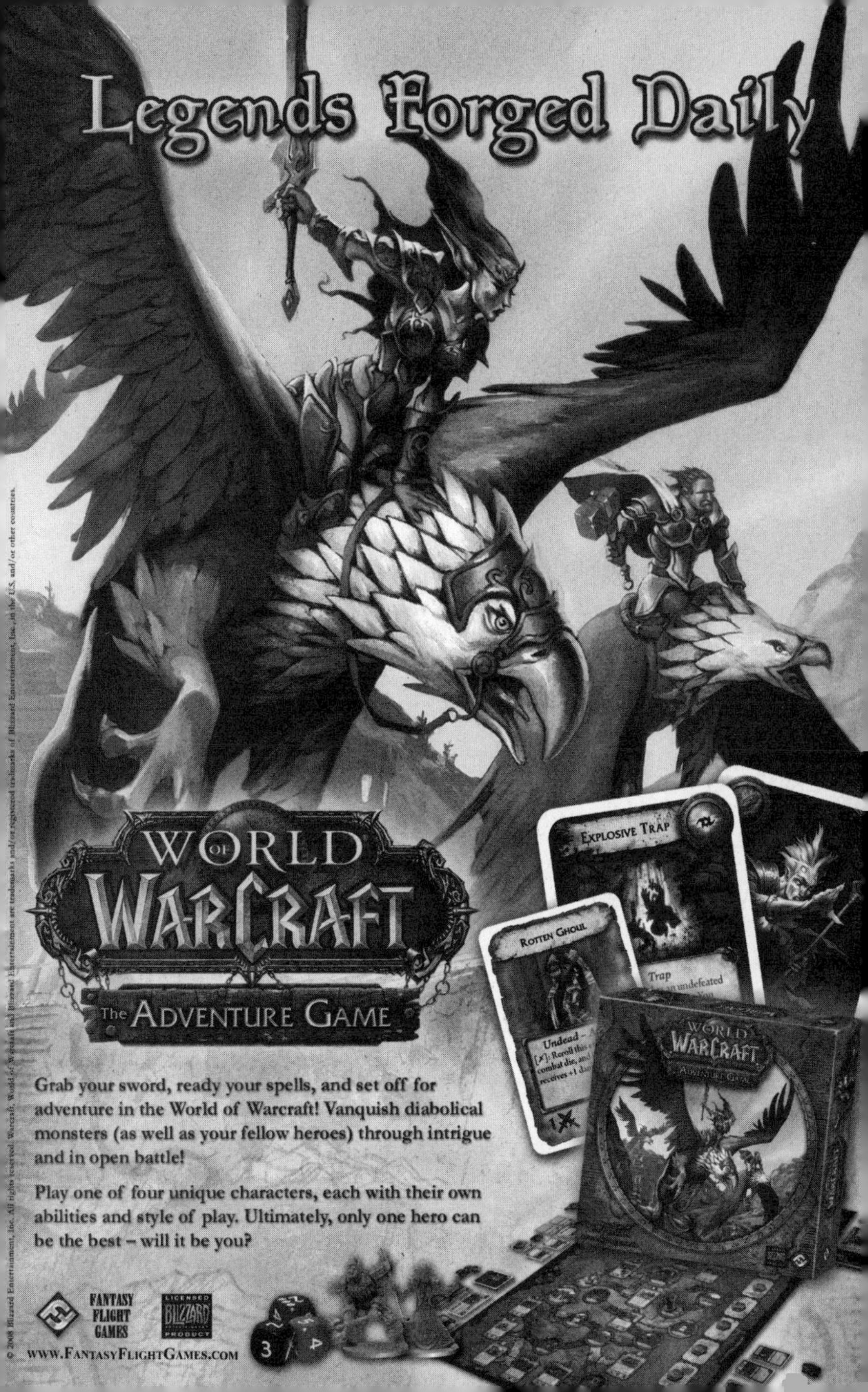
Legends Forged Daily
WORLD OF WARCRAFT
The ADVENTURE GAME
EXPLOSIVE TRAP
ROTTEN GHOUL
Trap
Undead
Grab your sword, ready your spells, and set off for adventure in the World of Warcraft! Vanquish diabolical monsters (as well as your fellow heroes) through intrigue and in open battle!
Play one of four unique characters, each with their own abilities and style of play. Ultimately, only one hero can be the best – will it be you?
FANTASY FLIGHT GAMES
LICENSED BLIZZARD PRODUCT
WWW.FANTASYFLIGHTGAMES.COM
© 2008 Blizzard Entertainment, Inc. All rights reserved. Warcraft, World of Warcraft and Blizzard Entertainment are trademarks and/or registered trademarks of Blizzard Entertainment, Inc., in the U.S. and/or other countries.

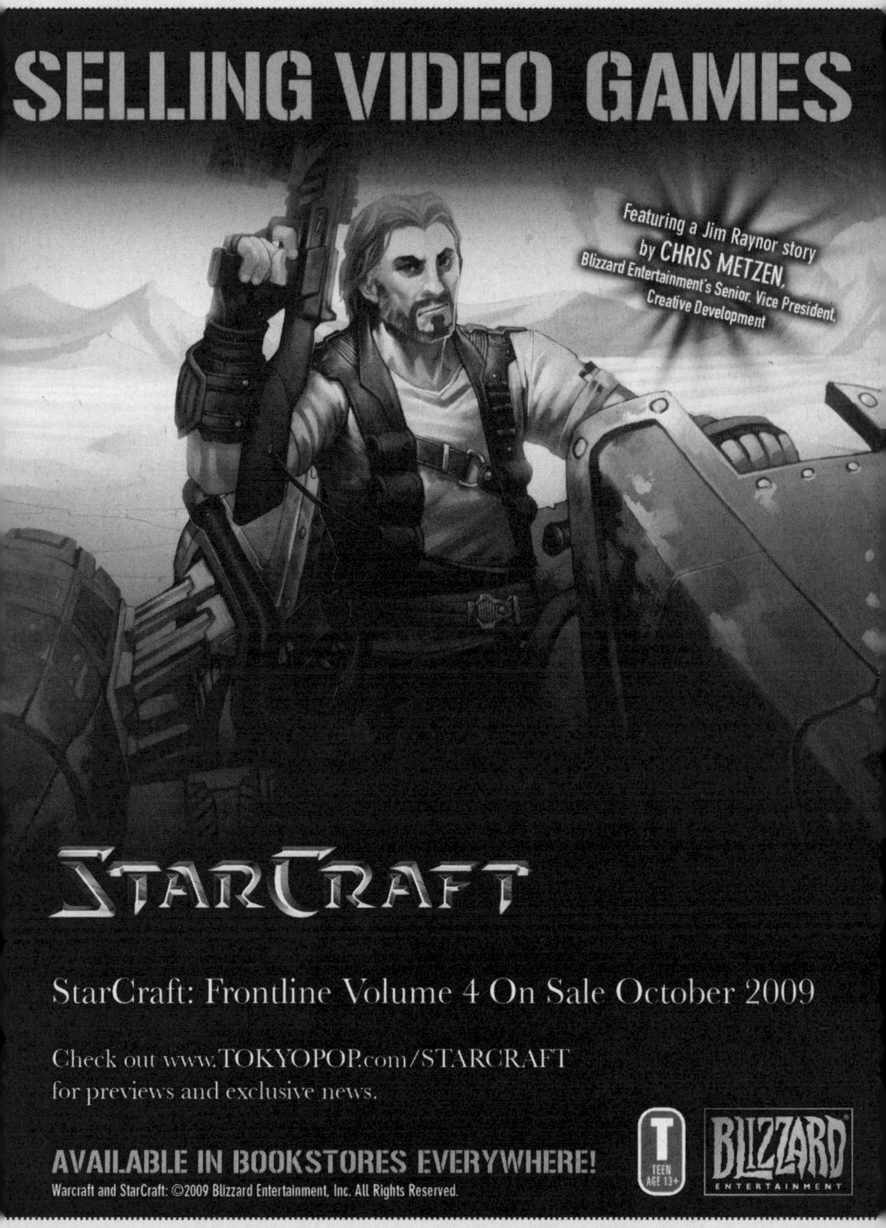
SELLING VIDEO GAMES
Featuring a Jim Raynor story by CHRIS METZEN, Blizzard Entertainment's Senior. Vice President, Creative Development
STARCRAFT
StarCraft: Frontline Volume 4 On Sale October 2009
Check out www.TOKYOPOP.com/STARCRAFT for previews and exclusive news.
AVAILABLE IN BOOKSTORES EVERYWHERE!
Warcraft and StarCraft: ©2009 Blizzard Entertainment, Inc. All Rights Reserved.
T TEEN AGE 13+
BLIZZARD ENTERTAINMENT

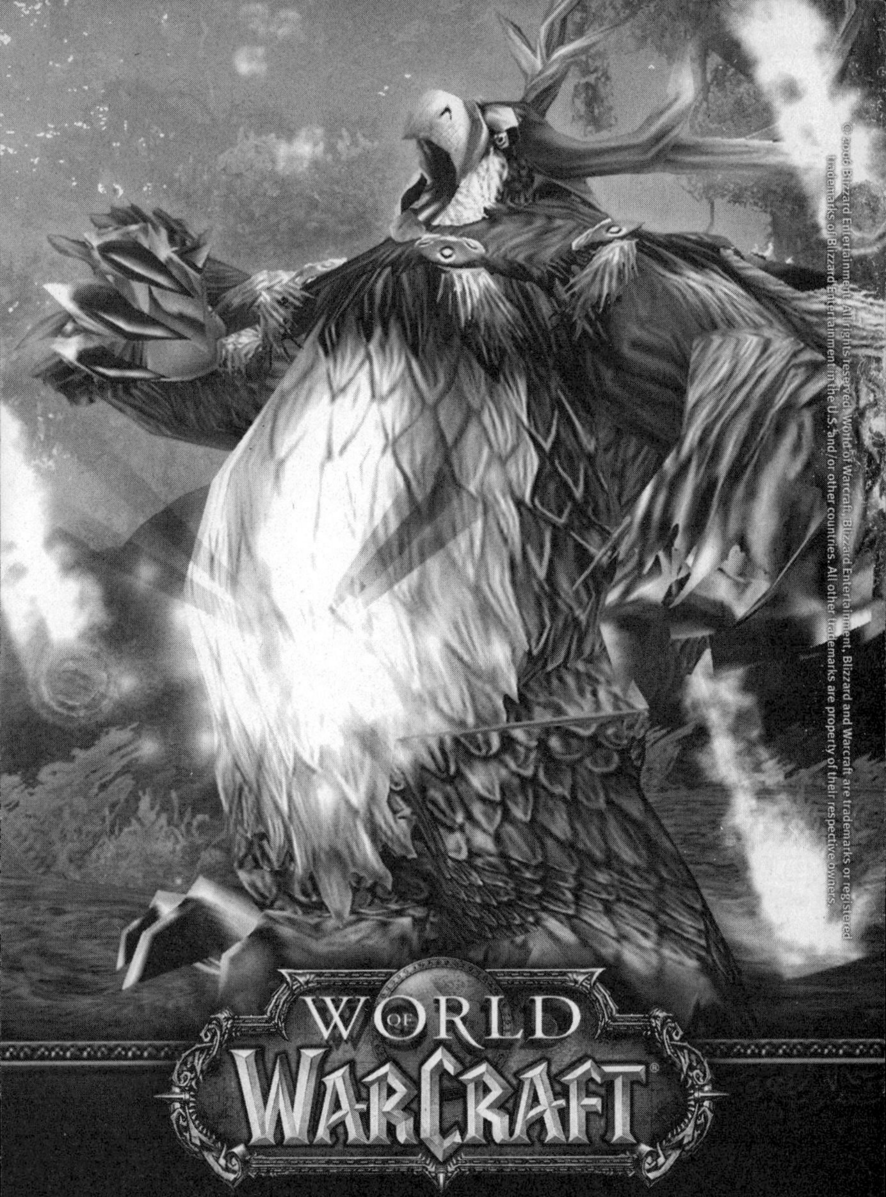
© 2006 Blizzard Entertainment. All rights reserved. World of Warcraft, Blizzard Entertainment, Blizzard and Warcraft are trademarks or registered trademarks of Blizzard Entertainment in the U.S. and/or other countries. All other trademarks are property of their respective owners.
WORLD OF WARCRAFT®

MMO GAMING MOUSE

World's first
gaming mouse
designed exclusively
for World of Warcraft®

Incredible customization options:
- 6 million illumination choices
- 15 programmable buttons
- Custom macro creation

Intuitive, ergonomic design and
premium components ensure superior
performance, comfort and control

Available Q4 2008

LICENSED
BLIZZARD
ENTERTAINMENT
PRODUCT

steelseries

EPIC BATTLES
IN THE PALM OF YOUR HAND

World of Warcraft® Collectible Miniatures Game
- Premium miniatures with detailed paints designed by Studio McVey
- Standard and deluxe starter sets plus three-figure boosters
- Innovative game play utilizing the unique detachable UBase

Coming Fall 2008!

For more information, visit

WOWMINIS.COM

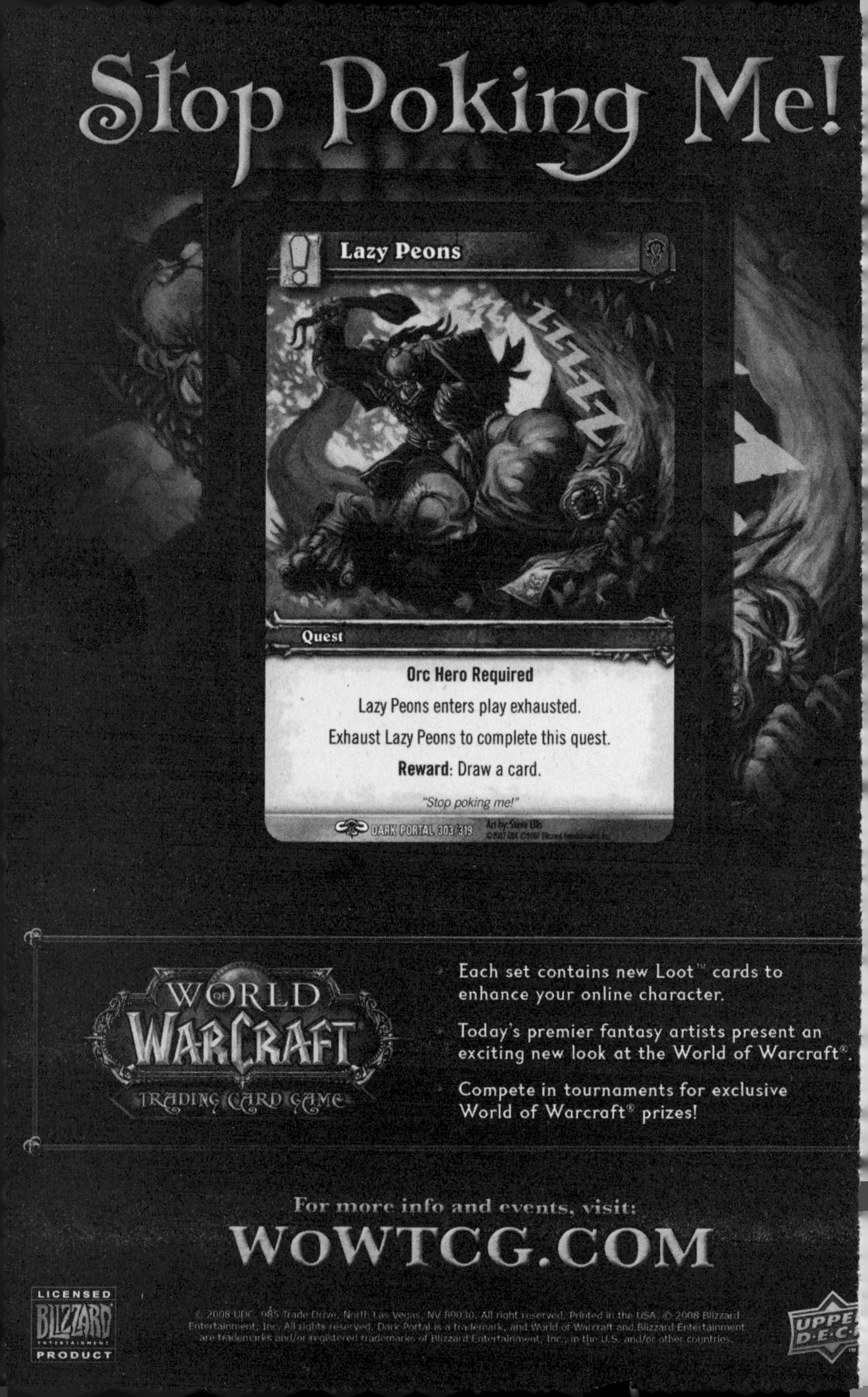
Stop Poking Me!
Lazy Peons
Quest
Orc Hero Required
Lazy Peons enters play exhausted.
Exhaust Lazy Peons to complete this quest.
Reward: Draw a card.
"Stop poking me!"
DARK PORTAL 303/319
Art by: Steve Ellis
WORLD OF WARCRAFT
TRADING CARD GAME
Each set contains new Loot™ cards to enhance your online character.
Today's premier fantasy artists present an exciting new look at the World of Warcraft®.
Compete in tournaments for exclusive World of Warcraft® prizes!
For more info and events, visit:
WOWTCG.COM
LICENSED
BLIZZARD
ENTERTAINMENT
PRODUCT
© 2008 UDC. 985 Trade Drive, North Las Vegas, NV 89030. All right reserved. Printed in the USA. © 2008 Blizzard Entertainment, Inc. All rights reserved. Dark Portal is a trademark, and World of Warcraft and Blizzard Entertainment are trademarks and/or registered trademarks of Blizzard Entertainment, Inc., in the U.S. and/or other countries.
UPPER DECK